The Failure *of* American Conservatism *and the* Road Not Taken

Claes G. Ryn

REPUBLIC
BOOK PUBLISHERS

The FAILURE *of* AMERICAN CONSERVATISM

FIRST EDITION

ISBN: 9781645720409 (Hardcover)
ISBN: 9781645720416 (ebook)

For inquiries about volume orders, please contact:
Republic Book Publishers
27 West 20th Street
Suite 1103
New York NY 10011
editor@republicbookpublishers.com

Published in the United States by Republic Book Publishers
Distributed by Independent Publishers Group
www.ipgbook.com

Book designed by Mark Karis
Printed in the United States of America

"You live by what you thrill to"

—D.H. LAWRENCE

CONTENTS

ACKNOWLEDGMENTS

This volume on American conservatism mixes previously published material and new writing. The help I received when completing it ranged from editorial suggestions to assistance with digitalization. I particularly want to thank three persons who commented on what I now wanted to say about the state of conservatism or had ideas about what articles or other writing to include. The three are former students of mine with whom I have often discussed issues in this book: Joseph Baldacchino, with whom I shared the leadership of the National Humanities Institute for many years, Emily Finley, who helped me select and digitalize previously published writing when she was a doctoral candidate at the Catholic University of America, and William S. Smith, who was Managing Director and Senior Research Fellow at the Center for the Study of Statesmanship (CSS) at the University when I was its Director. Andrew Sasser was a Research Assistant at CSS when he did additional digitalization and formatting. I also want to express my appreciation to the editors and the leadership team at Republic Book Publishers for their professionalism and sensitivity to the preferences and needs of the author.

INTRODUCTION

SUCCESS AND FAILURE—AND NOW WHAT?

This book consists mostly of previously published writings. They have been organized into five parts. This lengthy introduction was written exclusively for this volume. It binds together the diverse materials collected, discusses the birth and development of American intellectual conservatism since World War II, assesses intellectual conservatism's strengths and weaknesses, and comments on whether and in what form conservatism may recover its bearings.

WHY ANOTHER BOOK ON CONSERVATISM?

Something was wrong with post–World-War II American conservatism. That it did not achieve its stated goals is by itself not proof of this point. Conservatism was up against high odds in a deteriorating civilization. What revealed its shortcomings was the way in which it perceived and handled those odds. Even in more favorable historical circumstances, those weaknesses would have become apparent, if perhaps less conspicuous. The weaknesses in question help explain why putative conservatives have not learned much from their mistakes and why they have been unable to see that their accustomed approaches to problems were deficient or misguided.

Despite ambitious, extremely well-financed, and systematic conservative efforts over many years, America has suffered a broad range of disturbing developments. A brief review of how conservatives have related to those developments will indicate that a reexamination of basic attitudes and assumptions has long been needed. "Fiscal conservatism" or "fiscal discipline" has been close to the heart of American conservatism. Millions and millions of dollars have been spent for decades by the Heritage Foundation, the CATO Institute, and other organizations to advance this cause. Yet, even under supposedly conservative or at least Republican administrations, the United States' national debt has grown by leaps and bounds. It has become so enormous as to far exceed the gross national product. *Fiscal discipline* is about the last term that might be used to describe governmental spending habits. *New* deficit spending is routinely being contemplated. Sharply raising the debt ceiling has become routine. The staggering cost of wars has been put on the nation's credit card. President Dwight Eisenhower warned of the military-industrial complex, but it is today more bloated and influential than ever. Questioning defense spending is seen by many supposed conservatives as "unpatriotic." Vast sums of money have gone into advocacy groups that claim to want to "keep America safe." In practice, that has typically meant support for hawkish, even belligerent action in support of "American values" abroad. The American Enterprise Institute (AEI), for example, supported two misguided, hugely costly, and failed wars in which hundreds of thousands died or were maimed. It was while AEI-type scholars had great influence in or on government that 9/11 shattered Americans' sense of safety. Experts of the same kind urged American intervention in Middle East conflicts that dislocated millions of people. Although AEI scholars and their allies held senior positions at the Pentagon for many years, radical social experimentation was extended to the American military. Today the upper echelons of the military establishment are pleased to demonstrate their "woke" credentials, placing political correctness above military efficiency.

A staple of American conservatism has been advocacy of limited government. Most conservative organizations, including those mentioned, in theory stressed the importance of faithfulness to the US Constitution. But the federal government is today larger and more intrusive than ever, due in no small part to the willingness of conservatives to go along. American constitutionalism is crumbling. The states are forever yielding more authority to the central government. The old checks and balances are barely working. The executive branch has acquired powers and a reach that would have horrified the framers. Supposedly conservative defenses of the "unitary executive" have assisted some of these developments. Contrary to the explicit requirement of the Constitution, Congress has yielded its war powers to the president. A surveillance state has been created, and citizens are increasingly at the mercy of a politicized judicial system. Traditional liberties and free speech are under broad assault. The criminalization of political opponents is ubiquitous. Congress has yielded legislative authority to an enormous and expanding administrative state.

Outside of government, the mainstream electronic and print media are not vigilantly looking for power abuse on the part of the established order but are more disposed to help protect it against more than marginal challenges.

An important branch of an older American conservatism was concerned that the humanities and other high culture, including advanced scholarship, needed to be redirected and promoted, but organizations like the Philadelphia Society and the Intercollegiate Studies Institute have made almost no progress. Colleges and universities have become hotbeds for intellectually flimsy theorizing and idiosyncratic but tyrannical left-wing thought-control. Few if any of America's national institutions—political, military, educational, journalistic, or religious—can today be said to reliably represent traditional American civilization. Deepening division between what remains of the older America and the forces sympathetic to wokery and cancel culture is tearing at the social fabric.

These developments do by themselves raise questions about the ability of the American constitutional republic to survive, but to them must be added other equally alarming factors, notably America's deepening problem with ordinary criminality. That problem ranges from the staggering amount of drug abuse and deaths from overdoses in the general population to life-threatening violence. It is a disturbing commentary on the state of the country that each year about twenty thousand Americans are murdered, hundreds of thousands more are the victims of other violent crime, and millions live in fear because of lawlessness. Serious crime has also blended increasingly with general civic disorder, including violent protests, looting, arson, organized attacks on police, and destruction of property and monuments. Maintaining peace and security has always been regarded as government's most basic duty. The inability—in some cases the reluctance—of American civil authorities to contain even acute disorder shows that law and order and the very stability of society can no longer be taken for granted as central objectives of government. Together with the previously mentioned crumbling of constitutionalism, the abandonment of fiscal discipline and high standards and the spread of street-level lawlessness raise the subject of so-called failed states. Another sign of dysfunction and disintegration is the inability or unwillingness to enforce national borders.

But perhaps the most telling illustration of America's fraught condition is the wishful thinking of its dominant, trendsetting elites inside and outside of government: their inability or refusal to *recognize* and *act on* reality. There may be no more striking example than the trendsetters in America's foreign policy establishment, including many putative conservatives. Deeply ingrained in them is a certain strain of thought that has long dominated American foreign policy: that the United States must act as global umpire and guarantor of world order and must be sufficiently powerful to overwhelm any competitor. There are many reasons to question this view, but one does not have to be dismissive of it to think that, given the historical circumstances, dreams of American global hegemony are, especially in some versions, not merely unrealistic but dangerously fanciful. One might think that American foreign policy experts, especially ones calling themselves "realists," would be acutely aware that the country's pressing political, economic, intellectual, social, and cultural problems are sharply limiting its freedom of action in foreign affairs. Do these problems not mandate modesty and great restraint in strategic and tactical thinking? For the sake of American foreign policy alone, should these experts not be advocating emergency measures to stave off further domestic decline? Should they not recognize that in the concrete historical circumstances at hand their ambitious plans for American global leadership might lead to disaster? But no, with few exceptions, members of the foreign policy establishment continue to place all emphasis on America as the world's "indispensable nation." The cynical habit of leaders to deflect attention from domestic failures by stressing foreign threats is well-known to history, but when the American foreign-policy intellectuals assign a hegemonic role to the United States, it suggests a deliberate avoidance of reality—a form of escapism that in the nuclear age is terrifying.

How could all this have happened in the United States? This brief review of ominous developments, including conservative complicity in them, indicates that by any number of measures that should seem appropriate even to conservatives themselves, American conservatism has failed. It may defend itself by pointing to unfortunate historical circumstances and overwhelming opposition, but perhaps its most prominent and debilitating flaw is that it never fully understood those circumstances and the nature of the opposition. For that reason, it could not effectively address them. American conservatism has to a considerable extent *contributed* to the developments mentioned above, not just because of intellectual confusion but by advocating or accepting ideas and policies that a more mature intellectual conservative culture would have rejected.

The writings collected here all bear more or less directly on American intellectual conservatism from World War II to the present and on these two questions: Why, despite its many strengths, did American conservatism fail, and might the worst of the above-mentioned social disintegration have been averted? This book will take its readers into territory that will probably strike many as unfamiliar. It will introduce perspectives, including criteria of failure or success, that may initially confound some readers. The book will, among other things, show that the word *conservatism*, which has been used rather loosely above, has acquired many different meanings, some of which are incompatible and some of which would appear to have little claim to the term. The failure that this book examines and tries to remedy clearly does not pertain equally to all varieties of American conservatism. The failure has its main source in certain intellectual inclinations and currents. One of the reasons why sadness has to color the description of the failure is that the dubious influences undermined or drew attention away from major, very promising achievements.

What happened was in a way unexpected. The burst of intellectual energy and creativity in the early 1950s, which foreshadowed what would become a broad and manyfaceted conservative movement, was truly impressive. The leading thinkers were deeply rooted in earlier American and European thought, and their work revivified, extended, and creatively rearticulated old traditions. In decades to come, intellectual currents of a generally conservative cast produced an extraordinary number of books and other publications as well as organizations devoted to spreading such ideas. In anticipation of a subject that will be central to this book, it should be mentioned that in its early stages the movement was not merely or even primarily political in the narrower sense of that word. This would change. The movement's interest in politics would become more and more pronounced.

Over the last few decades, numerous studies have been devoted to recording and analyzing aspects of this large and complex historical phenomenon. This volume does not attempt to provide a history and comprehensive assessment of American intellectual conservatism. It is not even a systematic treatment of any particular dimension of it. It is a collection of articles and other writings that span a wide variety of subjects but which are all germane to deepening the understanding of American conservatism and weighing its strengths and weaknesses. The book pays particular attention to what made conservatism fail. These articles or excerpts were written at very different times but are held together by certain perspectives and themes. Although they were not written to become parts of a single whole one day, one can see in hindsight that they might have been. They express a certain view of human nature, society, and politics and address recurring central questions. The overlap that is inevitable in a book of this kind confirms an underlying philosophical unity.

The market for books on conservatism is in a sense flooded, but this volume is not typical of the genre. Its ideas are not new exactly because most of the material collected here has been available in some form for many years. But much of it was published in places not frequented by general readers interested in conservatism. Many of these writings appeared in predominantly scholarly outlets that have a limited readership. This book also raises issues different from those that have been emphasized by the people who have dominated public discussion of conservatism. I have spoken a partly aberrant and often rather philosophical language. In those of my writings that reached a fairly wide audience, I also criticized widely read, supposedly conservative public intellectuals, which, in the eyes of many, made me an exasperating dissenter, even a threat, one who should receive the silent treatment. Precisely because trendsetters within the conservative movement were disinclined to take up the concerns prominent in my writing, the contents of this volume may strike some as unusual.

It is today widely acknowledged that conservatism is in disarray or crisis. There is an obvious need for major rethinking of the meaning of conservatism and of what it means to be an American. This book suggests that the current disorientation springs in large measure from certain long-standing, seemingly chronic weaknesses. I have had much to say about them over the years. It can be argued that American intellectual conservatism is not well equipped to cope with the massive long-term challenges that it faces. A prerequisite for dealing with its problems, as with any serious problem, is adequate diagnosis. What went wrong and why? Those wishing to rethink conservatism and the meaning of America in the historical circumstances of today must try to understand the shortcomings that damaged and disoriented conservatism. While devoting much space to analyzing deficiencies, this book points to more promising varieties and potentialities of American conservatism, ones that might have yielded very different results in the past and that might help remedy pressing problems today.

THE LARGER SETTING OF POLITICS

It is common in America to think of "conservatism" as a term relating to politics and economics. It stands for limited government, a strong defense, and a free market. It is less common to include in the definition preferences that are not obviously connected to issues of government. In this book, whether the emphasis is on current practical politics or matters of political principle, it is assumed that issues of politics cannot be adequately understood without relating them to basic questions of human existence, some of which may appear "nonpolitical" or "noneconomic." All notions of government and politics imply assumptions about human nature and society, just as all notions of human nature and society have political implications. A thesis of this book is that politics is indistinguishable from and deeply influenced by society's general culture as expressed in churches, the arts, literature, music, movies, entertainment, education, and childrearing. Although readers of this volume will come across familiar names, ideas, and controversies, those unacquainted with my thinking may find the general perspective surprising, perhaps even far-fetched. Politics is here placed within a moral-cultural context, including its origins in history. There are frequent references to the history of Western thought. Each article or section represents a more or less explicit rebuke of the tendency, not least among self-described American conservatives, to treat political ideas or practices as if they did not assume and express views of human nature and society.

If asked to discuss the meaning of American conservatism and the direction in which it ought to move today, the typical conservative commentator will want to get as quickly as possible to questions of public policy. Should America advance the cause of freedom and democracy in the world, or should it limit its international commitments and pursue the national interest? Should America treat Russia and China as enemies or as competitors with which to seek peaceful, respectful relations? Should tariffs protect domestic businesses and workers, or should international competition be spurring Americans to greater productivity? Should markets be tempered with reference to a common good or be unfettered except for some ground rules enforced by a minimal state? Should immigration into the United States be easy or permitted only under selective and strictly enforced laws? When one seeks to define conservatism, a broad range of public policy issues are relevant, some of which will come up in this book, but nothing is more important than the frame of mind in which public policy questions are approached. Not even the most detailed and extensive familiarity with the pros and cons of policy choices will ensure that a wise course is adopted. The wisdom of policies selected will depend, in the end, on the quality of the view of life that guides judgment. To what extent does the decision maker have a realistic view of the world? To what extent do policy choices reflect a sound sense of priorities and proportion? What will stop a warped notion of how the world works from influencing decisions? This is to say that the frame of mind within which policy questions are addressed matters greatly. Anything more than a superficial definition or assessment of conservatism must place the basic view of reality at the center. When public policy preferences come up in this book, it is in relation to the general perspective on life that produced them or is implied in them. Much attention will be devoted to basic presuppositions regarding human nature and society in this introduction and elsewhere. It will be argued that certain influential assumptions undermined and diverted an otherwise impressive post–World War II American conservatism.

A recurring concern of this book is to broaden and deepen the meaning of the term *political.* Only when set within the larger whole of life can political thought or practice be properly understood and assessed. What political or intellectual activists or thinkers with narrow conceptions of power may think of as dwelling on "irrelevancies," "philosophical subtleties," or "fine points" is in actuality the only way to fully comprehend the meaning and entailments of policy preferences and to distinguish between tenable and untenable ideas.

Conservatism and politics are addressed here in a manner that ranges far beyond what most people think of as politics. Subjects like ethics, aesthetics, and epistemology may look distant from the world of political practice, but just the opposite is the case. Without exploring them in some depth, it is not possible to have a more than perfunctory view of the "real world." Properly conceived, these subjects do not take students of politics into a sphere of esoteric abstractions but make possible a more firmly grounded understanding of life in general and of politics in particular. Good philosophy weeds out distorting illusions, reveals important connections, and fosters an uncompromising realism. What is often *called* "realism" is prone to rather crude assumptions about politics. Many conservatives think themselves more realistic than others because they conceive of political power as being, at bottom, "coercion," a view held by so-called libertarians and by admirers of Thomas Hobbes (1588–1679), the latter famous for his view that the natural condition of human beings is a war of all against all. The key characteristic of government is thought to be that it has "a monopoly on violence." This reputed "realism" does in fact betray a cramped, even superficial understanding of power. Some sources of power have little to do with physical violence and coercion but nevertheless strongly influence political and other conduct. Any truly realistic definition of power must take these sources into account. That even highly intelligent American conservatives should find this view counterintuitive helps explain the disorientation of American conservatism today.

Although the writings collected in this volume are, for the most part, not philosophically "technical," they reflect a certain philosophical outlook that spans a great deal more than politics as ordinarily understood. This is not the place to explain that outlook in depth. It has been done in other books and articles.[1] Although I believe that what is offered to the reader in this book can stand on its own, it may be helpful to summarize at least some of the philosophical positions from which my analyses of conservatism and other subjects are derived. Because of the need for brevity, the philosophical terms used will have to be left rather vague, but they acquire further definition in the rest of this volume. It may soothe the reader to know that this brief philosophical excursus will be followed by a move into more familiar territory.

I have tried in my philosophical work to integrate the study of seemingly different but closely related aspects of life and to ascertain their roles and importance within the whole of human existence. The resulting philosophy has been called "value-centered historicism." It encompasses ethics, aesthetics, and epistemology and shows the intimate connections between goodness, beauty, and truth and their opposites. According to this philosophy, the higher values of human existence are apprehended and attained through a special interaction of will, imagination, and reason in which moral character is primary and indispensable. While defending universal values, value-centered historicism disputes the common view that these values are disembodied intellectual abstractions or vague emotive states. These values actually become known to human beings in experiential particulars—a notion that seems paradoxical to thinkers who are used to placing what is ultimately normative beyond what is near and concrete and used to regarding the universal as empty of concrete particulars. Value-centered historicism challenges moral rationalism—the belief that only abstract rationality can be morally normative—and challenges an equally ahistorical, merely dreamy notion of transcendence. The higher values of life become known to the well-integrated, morally grounded person in experiential particulars.

Contrary to an ancient tendency, which has been reinforced by some theorists associated with American conservatism, history need not be the enemy of higher values or philosophy. On the contrary, these values enter human experience and become available for philosophical scrutiny to the extent that human beings embody them in their lives. Historical-experiential patterns thus created guide new generations to the ultimate source of these values. Sound philosophy, I argue, incorporates the kind of historical consciousness that entered Western thought in earnest in the late eighteenth and early nineteenth centuries. That consciousness sharpened the awareness of what a good current state of affairs owes to the past, and it helped foster a generally conservative view of life, as exemplified by the British statesman-thinker Edmund Burke. The analyses of conservatism in this book flow from these larger philosophical interests. The particular writings are, in effect, case studies in the light of value-centered historicism and typically emphasize the moral-spiritual and cultural aspects of problems.

A topic that is central to my philosophical outlook and that receives much attention in this volume is the important role of the imagination in shaping human thought and conduct. How we behave and see the world is affected less by strictly rational considerations than by deep-seated *intuitions*—by a basic nonconceptual sense of the nature of existence, of what can be expected in life, and of what is desirable. Intuitions already formed direct the attention of the mind and are the material for its theoretical elaborations. Human beings are guided most fundamentally by an overarching sense of the nature of reality and by ingrained hopes and fears. These are derived from a broad range of cultural influences and personal experiences. This sense of what the world is like is intuitive-imaginative rather than rational-conceptual. Because of the influence of the prevalent surrounding culture, some of these intuitive suppositions are widely shared, but the sensibilities and outlooks of individuals are at the same time always unique to them by virtue of their special experiences and circumstances. Creative people—for example, novelists, filmmakers, composers, poets, and artists—who are able to capture the imaginations of others can enter the innermost selves of those others and affect their notion of what is desirable and undesirable, thereby influencing their conduct. Over the years, all the people who are able to color the inner life of others have a cumulative influence that ordinarily far exceeds that of particular political leaders. This is not to deny that political leaders can stir the imagination. They can derive power from an ability to enlist existing popular dreams and hopes in their support. A central theme in this book is the power of "the culture" to shape the predispositions of individuals and hence the evolution of society.

MOVEMENT CONSERVATISM

The term *movement* was used loosely above to refer to the expanding conservative intellectual current in America after World War II. This current reaffirmed and creatively applied and extended older traditions. But the phrase "the conservative movement" would in time acquire a more specific meaning among people interested in the subject. It became the label for particular patterns of thought, for a movement that had its own distinctive emphases and goals. The origins of what became known as "movement conservatism" can be traced back to William F. Buckley Jr. and his *National Review,* which was founded in 1955. A gifted writer and polemicist in his own right, Buckley connected to his magazine a number of prominent authors, notably James Burnham, Whittaker Chambers, Willmoore Kendall, and Russell Kirk. The magazine exhibited great intellectual vitality. Animated by Buckley's tastes and intuitions, the magazine became in effect the architect and umpire of movement conservatism. It could make reputations but also steer attention away from thinkers of whom it did not approve. It is important to understand that the inclinations of this conservatism were more political than they were cultural or philosophical. For Buckley, most of the *National Review* circle of writers, and most of the magazine's expanding number of readers, the chief and ultimate goal was to promote a certain political objective, specifically that of capturing the presidency for conservatism—as Buckley and his followers defined it.

The intellectual conservatism that surged in the decade just after the war had great strengths and considerable variety. It seemed poised to challenge "progressive" intellectual trends in America for dominance, but it had to develop in unfavorable intellectual circumstances, which will be discussed in more depth later. One impediment was that it had to evolve without the support of an accompanying mature philosophical culture. It was not assisted and boosted by high-level efforts to explicate, refine, and extend its contributions and to weed out weak ideas. The new conservatism also did not generate any deep desire to remedy that deficiency. One of the consequences was that the strains of early postwar American conservatism that showed the most promise as the foundation for a broad intellectual and cultural renaissance were never fully digested, appreciated, and absorbed. They were not the dominant influence in what became known as "the conservative movement." One can study this weakness in the otherwise highly successful intellectual enterprise that was *National Review*.

Buckley's chiefly political purposes made him prone to a rather dubious type of intellectual ecumenism. Ideas advanced in the magazine were sometimes philosophically incompatible—as when Catholic traditionalism was paired with socially atomistic libertarianism—but they appeared to Buckley sufficiently coherent in *political* terms to become parts of the political coalition that he envisioned. *National Review* senior editor Frank S. Meyer tried to make this alliance intellectually consistent in his theory of "fusionism," which was an attempt to blend classical individualistic liberalism and moral traditionalism. Only a lack of philosophical depth and discipline made it possible for this earnest but ultimately unstable amalgamation to became virtually synonymous with "movement conservatism."

The problem with Buckley's magazine and with the ferment that it triggered was not intellectual variety. Even in the most stringently philosophical and discriminating movement, diversity and tension are inevitable. They can be signs of intellectual vitality. The problem was variety stemming from a lack of philosophical discernment and depth.

In their basic interests and tastes, the typical movement conservatives gravitated toward politics and economics, which were perceived as having the most impact on the evolution of society. As directed especially by Buckley, Meyer, and *National Review* publisher William Rusher, the conservative movement formed the intellectual backbone of the effort to get Barry Goldwater elected president of the United States. Movement conservatives did not abjure advanced ideas and works of art—many of them cited the need for a revival of "Western civilization"—but most of them seemed to have thought of the churches as supplying what was needed by way of higher values. But what about "the culture"? How important were literature, symphonies, paintings, movies, and advanced education? Few movement conservatives stressed them as collectively indispensable to social well-being or evinced a deep personal desire for them. Were they not primarily a kind of adornment to real life? The idea that high culture might be the very lifeblood of civilization was far from their minds. Although tradition had long looked to works of high culture for profundity of vision and a deepening and softening of the spirit—needed not least to elevate politics—the typical movement conservative regarded books, for example, as worthwhile to the extent that they were directly related to politics: political biographies, exposés, documentaries, or policy tracts. Fiction was not positively disdained, but did it not have something insubstantial, vaguely unserious about it that suited it for rest and relaxation? Was a novel not something to bring to the beach for vacation and that should deliver thrilling "action," preferably having a political aspect? Only a minority in movement conservatism thought of drama, movies, music, and the best of literary fiction as essential to understanding and elevating human existence. Even fewer recognized that, at its worst, culture has the power to degrade society.

The way in which movement conservatives deployed their energy and financial and other resources showed that, for them, changing society for the better depended more on supposedly robust political efforts and intellectual activism directed to general audiences than on addressing seemingly intangible "subtle" issues of culture or "fine points" of philosophy. In the wake of the 1964 presidential election, which saw Barry Goldwater lose by a landslide to Lyndon Johnson, key supporters of Goldwater, including William Buckley, started the American Conservative Union (ACU). The ACU was to coordinate the work of existing organizations and provide intellectual leadership for continued political action. It attracted growing support and became the host of an annual Conservative Political Action Conference, which is attended by thousands. One might say that in its way of combining political ideas and political activism the ACU comes close to embodying the temperament and sense of priorities of the conservative movement. The point here is not that there is something wrong with wishing to organize politically and letting ideas guide politics. Any attempt to improve society will have to have a political dimension. What is at issue is what kind of change is most needed and what kind of political action can best assist that change. The problem has been that the conservative movement had a limited understanding of what forces ultimately move human beings and shape the future. It seemed to many conservatives far-fetched that there might be sources of influence more significant for the longer run than controlling government. The movement's activist political temperament betrayed a pseudo-pragmatism that will be discussed later. Another factor shaping the evolution of conservatism was that the currents within it that attracted the most public attention were those that most directly related to the issues of the day, as defined by the media and existing political and economic interests. Movement conservatism attracted media attention and gained a career advantage by adjusting to the concerns of the intellectual-journalistic establishment.

Despite the admirable efforts of a few leading thinkers, American conservatism never developed a sure and sophisticated sense of what was at the bottom of the problems of America and the Western world.

Movement conservatives placed the blame loosely on the growth of "the Leviathan state" and the retreat of religion, as if the expansion and centralization of government and falling church attendance were independent variables and not consequences of deep moral and cultural developments. Lacking a proper diagnosis of what was wrong, conservatives had difficulty identifying and applying remedies.

A recurring observation in the writings collected in this volume is that although American conservative intellectuals often considered the ideas of major thinkers, they were most comfortable with essayistic writing. Few of them felt a strong need for the kind of philosophical depth and rigor that might in time have yielded a more penetrating diagnosis and generated a broader intellectual renewal. A lack of philosophical ambition and a consequent flawed sense of priorities and direction made the movement liable to confusion and manipulation. Although many movement conservatives showed more than a nominal interest in formulating a basic view of the world and especially a notion of moral right, those who most influenced the direction of the larger movement were generally satisfied with middle-brow ideas, at best with a kind of near-philosophy. They might refer to European philosophers and use sophisticated-sounding terminology, but for the most part, they did not attempt systematic, thoroughgoing philosophical explorations. Too often, formulaic regurgitation took their place.

One illustration of the bias in favor of politics is that even when movement conservatives did show serious interest in the basic issues of human existence, they were chiefly attracted to thinkers in *political* philosophy, the Europeans Eric Voegelin and Leo Strauss prominent among them. Russell Kirk was a good deal more than a political thinker, and he was widely admired and cited, but many influential movement conservatives treated him with thinly veiled condescension because of his more "literary" emphasis. Kirk was not a philosopher in the stricter sense of the word, but he understood much better than his critics the importance to civilization and to politics itself of nonpolitical factors. He was never comfortable with *National Review's* fusionism and heavy stress on political-intellectual activism. He wrote a column for it on education from its founding until 1980, but he never allowed his name to appear among the editors on its masthead.

NEGLECT OF PHILOSOPHY AND "THE CULTURE"

Philosophy proper and culture of the most elevated kind will, of course, always be the province of relatively few, but at high points of civilization major figures at that level are respected and heeded by many others. Intellectuals or artists of lesser caliber are inspired by them and transmit their perspectives to the more discerning members of the general public. Sensibilities and insights that elites have in the most refined form spread to different parts and levels of society in simplified, diluted versions. The sense of reality and values that emanates from the most profound works of mind and imagination thus exert a magnetic pull. This pull moderates the tendency for popular tastes to be dragged down by indolence or polluted by intellectuals and artists pandering to humanity's lower desires.

In the postwar era, there was in American intellectual conservatism broadly understood no strong dynamic of the kind mentioned above that unified and elevated intellectual and cultural efforts. Many American scholars drawn to a conservative outlook made important contributions to particular fields such as political theory, sociology, American constitutionalism, literature, history, and economics, but few attempted the kind of overarching philosophical exploration of basic issues of human existence that might have anchored, informed, and connected particular fields of study. Original and important thinkers did not receive nearly the attention that they deserved. Perhaps the most significant example of this weakness was the failure to recognize the groundbreaking contribution that was made in the immediately preceding generation by Harvard professor Irving Babbitt (1865–1933). That Babbitt had been formally a professor of literature and a cultural critic was probably one reason why he did not attract broad interest among postwar conservatives, focused as they tended to be on politics and economics. Yet Babbitt's thought was interdisciplinary in the best sense and showed the intimate and crucial connection between culture and politics. Had it not been for Babbitt's strong influence on a few leading postwar American conservative thinkers, Russell Kirk and Peter Viereck prominent among them, American conservatism would have been without what was perhaps its most original and important ingredient. The case of Babbitt illustrates how major insights available to American conservatism were neglected or only partially appropriated. Important ideas were not philosophically digested and supplemented, were not widely applied to a range of subjects, and did not give rise to the kind of broad, penetrating intellectual and cultural renaissance that might have transformed the American mind and imagination.

The disinterest in more exacting philosophical explorations also made movement conservatism less than discriminating in its likes and dislikes. This book has much to say about movement conservatism's accommodation of ideas that are fundamentally inimical to conservatism in a traditional sense. Two prominent examples discussed at particular length in this book are its uncritical acceptance of key ideas associated with Leo Strauss and his numerous followers and of the ideology of so-called neoconservatism. This is not to assert that Straussianism and neoconservatism have been without merit, only that major ideas from those sources entered the mainstream of the conservative movement and undermined its ability to address the deeper problems of American and Western society. This was true of their prejudice against relying on history for guidance and their preference for purely abstract theorizing.

The conservative movement's failure to produce the kind of deep and enduring revitalization that could have transformed American society cannot be blamed solely on its own weaknesses. It should be stated without delay that when it made its first valiant efforts in the postwar period, general historical circumstances were not propitious for the emergence of an advanced conservative philosophical culture. Powerful moral, intellectual, and cultural trends had badly eroded core elements of Western civilization since the eighteenth century. In the universities, the arts, and the general culture, what Walter Lippmann called "the acids of modernity" had produced widespread indifference or hostility to the kind of older Western ideas and tastes that conservatives were trying to revive and develop. Progressive and radical sentiment in ever-new iterations were setting the tone, making conservative impulses a virtually alien influence. In the trendsetting reaches of academic and cultural institutions conservatives were like guerrillas living off the land trying to establish a foothold. That the political dimension of their ideas was often in the foreground intensified resistance.

There is another important reason why American intellectual conservatism did not develop a mature philosophical foundation. A significant feature of the American temperament is pragmatism. In its most admirable form that pragmatism is a salutary check on overly abstract or dreamy speculation. But there is a strong tendency for this pragmatism to become a general impatience with ideas or cultural-artistic phenomena that are not obviously and directly related to practical matters. This pseudo-pragmatism does not recognize that clear, penetrating thinking and a refined sensibility are indispensable to really understanding practical situations. It also overlooks that the culture of a society predisposes its members to practical conduct of a certain kind. In the minds of too many movement conservatives, pseudo-pragmatism combined with dislike of the dominant intellectual and cultural elites to produce a deep ambivalence regarding intellectual and cultural efforts of a more demanding kind. This unease helped keep attention on more obviously "practical" questions of politics and economics, and it served to conceal what is most needed for a society to change its direction—a partly subtle transformation of character, mind, and imagination.

Russell Kirk and Peter Viereck understood better than any of the other leading thinkers in the postwar period that the imagination and culture play a central role, for good or ill, in shaping the future. They had here been deeply influenced by Irving Babbitt. It was Babbitt who had explained the power and conflicting potentialities of imagination and who, using a phrase from Edmund Burke, had given substance to the term "moral imagination." But the writing of Kirk and Viereck was, though scholarly and often profoundly insightful, predominantly essayistic. They did not feel called to elaborate systematically and with conceptual precision just how the imagination shapes our picture of the world and governs human conduct. As this book discusses, Kirk would become much more influential than Viereck. The latter called himself a conservative but had, by the standards of the 1950s, "liberal" leanings in politics. These leanings seemed to *National Review* conservatives like Frank S. Meyer disqualifying. Some movement conservatives picked up on Kirk's stress on the imagination and often talked of the need for "the moral imagination," but rather than carefully examining the meaning and implications of that term and the deepest sources of human conduct, which would have helped the larger conservative movement to rearrange and focus its priorities, they remained at the level of essayistic expression or near-philosophy. With regard to the most important philosophical questions, members of the conservative intellectual movement as a whole were only loosely connected and headed in disparate directions.

One organization that played a significant role in the evolution of American intellectual conservatism and that would to a considerable extent buck the overall activist trend of movement conservatism was the Intercollegiate Studies Institute (ISI). Its mission was to bring the best of conservative thought to the attention of students and to assist bright young scholars interested in academic careers. Under the leadership of Victor Milione from the early 1950s to the late 1980s, ISI largely followed the sense of priorities defined by Russell Kirk. It gave much attention to basic political ideas and even economics but as integrated into a larger whole that included literature, philosophy, and religion. ISI, too, suffered from the philosophical deficiencies already discussed, but its broadly humanistic and serious intellectual ambitions were for a long time a counter to the movement's preoccupation with politics more narrowly conceived. ISI's emphasis on the nonpolitical sources of Western civilization and its intellectual integrity limited its fundraising potential. Milione's immediate successor, who had served in the Reagan White House, steered ISI closer to the neoconservative and Straussian networks that dominated a few rich foundations.

The most prestige-laden conservative intellectual organization was and remains the Philadelphia Society. It was founded in 1964 to advance the ideas of the free society, specifically, the heritage of the framers of the US Constitution. The Society elected to membership professors, educators, professionals, clergy, and journalists who were interested in discussion of basic issues of liberty and civilization. Among its many distinguished members there were even Nobel Prize winners. The Society's meetings often featured high-level speeches and panels. It was a truly national organization with a smattering of members from other countries. The Society reflected the variety of influences that had been prefigured in the intellectual coalition forged by William Buckley and the early *National Review*. The Society exhibited much of the paradox, tension, and confusion previously discussed, which will receive more attention here. The dissonances were, however, largely hidden behind a façade which declared that complementary or at least not incompatible ideas coexisted amicably in the Society. The Society abjured partisan politics, but the members liked to assume that a broad, rough agreement on policy issues reflected a deeper intellectual congeniality. The notion that shared political leanings should trump intellectual discord left a heavy mark on the American conservative movement.

I was able for many years to observe the Philadelphia Society from within, as a guest, a member, a member of its board of trustees, and its president 2001–2002. I appreciated the Society's commitment to discussion of central issues but was uneasy about its passing over what seemed to me major philosophical divisions. For example, there seemed to be little awareness of the radically anti-conservative implications of Straussian anti-historicism. But philosophical considerations like these attracted little interest or were expected to take a back seat for the sake of political comity. The problem was not diversity of opinion. Wherever serious thinkers gather, there will be differences of opinion. It can be a sign of intellectual vitality. What troubled me was a lack of awareness that ideas of an anti-historical and rather blatantly ideological cast were represented in the Society that, despite superficial appearances, were deeply at odds with traditional American culture and constitutionalism, hence also with the mission of the Society. I could see that these ideas, dubious in themselves, had disturbing practical implications that could discredit the Society. It was these questionable strains of thought that would in time make the Society receptive to, or at least tolerant of, the ideology of American exceptionalism and neoconservatism. In foreign policy these ideas helped feed a propensity for knee-jerk hawkishness, interventionism, and imperial ambition. This kind of thinking receives much attention in this book and will be discussed further in this introduction.

While these ideological currents and their more academic antecedents illustrated the deep but partly submerged philosophical fissures in the Philadelphia Society, it never fully succumbed to the most questionable of the ideas that it embraced. Some of its members, including me, worked to reduce their influence. I published pointed critiques of what I called the new Jacobinism or "democratism," which will be discussed further in this introduction. Despite these outspoken comments, including a feature article in *National Review* in 1989, I was elected president of the Society a decade later. I held that post when 9/11 occurred. This was a time when the justified anger of Americans created an opening for hawkish ideology. When, in a presidential address the week after the atrocity, I cautioned against rash, indiscriminate action and expressed the hope that America would heed its best traditions, I was up against just the kind of ideological, imperial thinking that had worried me. Democratist ideology was now showing its practical ramifications. Neoconservatives or people accepting of them now became more influential in the Society. In the years after my presidency I was invited to the Society a few times to speak on this controversial topic, and I continued my criticisms.

The conservative movement organization that comes the closest to embodying its preoccupation with politics and that has attracted the most money, by far, is the Heritage Foundation in Washington, DC. It put most of its munificent resources into Washington-centered policy activism, including systematic attempts to influence members of Congress. It paid lip-service from time to time to the conservatism of a Russell Kirk, but in practice it was mostly interested in directly affecting policy. Philosophical rigor mattered much less. Straussians and neoconservatives were influential. This was conducive to fund-raising and media approval but reflected and aggravated the intellectual confusion typical of movement conservatism. Heritage had great sway in other conservative organizations, including the Philadelphia Society. Because of its roots in Buckleyite conservatism, Heritage was not as close to neoconservatism as the American Enterprise Institute, which became known as "Neocon Central."

Heritage and its donors seemed not to notice that the enormous expenditures on policy activism did little to reverse "progressive" and radical trends in the country. In 2013 Heritage's long-time president, Ed Feulner, retired and was replaced by former US Senator James DeMint. He and his top lieutenants took Heritage in partly new directions. Interestingly, they seemed to recognize the limits of short-range policy activism. They evinced more interest in the power of ideas in academia and elsewhere to produce long-term change. This new departure was cut short in 2017 when the new regime was ousted by people committed to the old emphases. Ed Feulner was brought back to run Heritage and help find a new president.

The preoccupation of movement conservatism with politics and policy activism was reinforced by the willingness of corporate and other donors, including the military-industrial complex, to support much of this supposedly efficacious work. Policy shops and think tanks proliferated. The availability of money for this kind of writing and research generated more and more of it and also slanted the intellectual perspective of what was published. The sheer volume of books, articles, papers, and speeches of this type made the genre look more important than publications whose immediate significance for practical politics was not obvious. The preponderant flow of writing together with the aforementioned pseudo-pragmatism and the reluctance even among leading intellectuals to delve into the most demanding problems of philosophy helped make topics centered on politics and policy wholly dominant within American movement conservatism. That politics might be an off-shoot, consequence, or manifestation of other developments seemed utterly far-fetched.

There was of course nothing wrong with an interest in politics or with addressing general audiences on political issues. Politics matters, and writing for the general public must by definition be widely accessible. When it comes to conveying ideas or phenomena difficult for nonexperts to understand, essayistic or journalistic writing is positively indispensable. But what will stop popular writing from descending into a cacophony of superficial opinion, from being pulled down to the lowest common denominator? What will steer discussion to truly important topics? What will define a sense of direction, priorities, and proportion? One can imagine a state of public discussion in which emphases are decided by nothing more than the trends and fashions of the moment, by people with a gift for sniffing out and pandering to emerging tastes. Drift and confusion then become the order of the day. Or one can imagine an environment in which certain basic assumptions do structure debate but are so misguided that really bad consequences result. If no sophisticated, overarching, and unifying vantage point exerts a magnetic pull, intellectual and other standards will not only be low but subject to trendy opinion.

American movement conservatism in the last quarter of the twentieth century did exhibit a certain esteem for leading intellectuals, but this celebration of a few typically formed part of political-intellectual activism, serving the interests of the alliance or network with which the respected thinkers were associated. The task of deciding which writers were to be lionized and which ideas were to be viewed as brilliant fell too often to bright but intellectually limited people—magazine or newspaper editors, heads of foundations and think tanks, media figures, writers of snappy articles, or politicians. Intellectuals, books, and schools of thought acquired reputations out of all proportion to their intrinsic merit. A supposedly conservative book that fits that description is Allan Bloom's *The Closing of the American Mind,* published in 1987. The astounding amount of attention that this book received had little to do with its quality. But Bloom was a prominent figure in the large and growing Straussian network, and his message appealed to or intrigued members of the liberal establishment. Intellectuals with access to leading magazines and newspapers treated the book as if it were a profound work on education. It may have puzzled some conservatives that a putatively conservative book attracted so much favorable interest among people of whom they were ordinarily deeply suspicious, but conservatives were starved for favorable attention in America's trendsetting circles. Few conservatives actually read Bloom's bestseller, and even fewer detected that, contrary to its reputation, it had a barely concealed anti-conservative message. The anomaly that books and articles of poor or modest quality could turn their authors into intellectual authority figures is often compounded in America by the fact that audiences defined by ethnicity or religion routinely give exaggerated praise to writers who belong to their group.

The conservative movement tended to take its cues less from learned, incisive thinkers than from intellectuals who reached large audiences. But are not reputations and intellectual priorities always created by arbiters who influence many people although they have no particular intellectual stature of their own? They are. That is why intellectual gatekeepers, those who can steer discussion and make or break reputations, need to be as vitally connected as possible to thought of the highest caliber, thought that transcends special interests and the fashions of the movement.

The problem with the conservative movement was not that it had too few intellectuals or that they were insufficiently active. Their numbers grew quickly, and they addressed a wide range of subjects. Their debates were lively and often high-level. New conservative groups and venues often came into being. If anything, too many people were ready with an opinion. The trouble was that in the midst of all of this intellectual energy, movement conservatives were disinclined to look beyond general ideas to systematic, in-depth treatment of the most difficult issues of religion, ethics, aesthetics, and epistemology. It seemed to movement conservatives that the supposed distance of advanced philosophy from the world of practice excused them from paying close attention to it. What was missing was a link to a mature philosophical culture that might have guided, integrated, and sharpened intellectual efforts.

For the most part, conservative "schools of thought" in academia and elsewhere did not produce mutually complementary points of view. They tended to be self-absorbed and to take little genuine interest in each other. This insularity served in part to give members of the school a sense of self-importance and a belief that no widening of their intellectual scope was necessary. What was outside of the school was by definition inferior. A particularly good example of this kind of self-reinforcing intellectual isolation was the network of disciples of Leo Strauss. This network actively cultivated a sense of superiority and disdain for outsiders. Socially and intellectually insecure persons could here achieve self-respect by affirming the profundity of the Great Teacher, whose thinking they, but no others, really understood. Insularity of this kind became a prominent feature within American conservatism. A more ecumenical frame of mind and greater depth, discipline, and coherence at the philosophical center might have given rise instead to a multifaceted but more integrated and sophisticated intellectual movement. But this never happened. The kind of cohesion that movement conservatism did exhibit was more apparent than real, loose terminology concealing rather sharp intellectual tensions.

There is an example of weak conservative interest in advanced, "technical" philosophy that is all the more revealing in that it has characterized a supposedly intellectual conservative movement. I am thinking of the more or less veiled prejudice against, even condescension toward, German historical philosophy. The latter has been viewed as obscure, pretentious, and "abstract" as well as pernicious. It is worthy of note that the two modern European thinkers who most influenced the political theory of American movement conservatism, Leo Strauss and Eric Voegelin, were, despite their German background, unfriendly or hostile to the philosophy in question, Strauss especially so. There is much to criticize in this German philosophy as in all intellectual movements. The extravagances of Hegel are a case in point. But Strauss and Voegelin were strangely unreceptive also to the creative, groundbreaking features of the new historical consciousness and to related philosophical developments, including the contributions of Hegel. One major figure who was influenced by this philosophy was Max Weber (1864–1920). Voegelin and Strauss both wrote extensive and widely read criticisms of him that were deeply flawed but accepted as authoritative by their followers. The point here is not to attribute special significance to Weber, although he has had great influence, but to note that the criticisms Strauss and Voegelin directed against him betrayed obvious, even embarrassing misunderstandings and distortions. These disclosed a strange unfamiliarity with the modern historical consciousness, which had long stirred within philosophy and had been a major ingredient in the rise of modern Western conservatism. Edmund Burke was in important ways a forerunner of this German philosophy. It seems to have never occurred to Strauss and Voegelin that this new philosophical impulse had the potential for *strengthening* the ancient Greek philosophy they thought they were defending. They seem to have been psychologically resistant even to considering the possibility. It is no coincidence that in *Natural Right and History* (1953), based on his Walgreen Lectures at the University of Chicago, Strauss launched an elaborate attack on Burke. Strauss clearly wanted to make sure that Burke would not have an influence in America. Neither is it a coincidence that Voegelin showed no interest in exploring Burke's thought. Strauss and Voegelin had significant disagreements, but they advanced notions of moral universality that disconnected it from history. In large part because of the influence of the two thinkers, German ideas that should have been of great philosophical interest to conservatively inclined intellectuals were widely ignored or positively shunned. These ideas were also hard to understand, a difficulty that was blamed on German obfuscation, not on the interpreters' lack of philosophical preparation. The prejudices of Strauss and Voegelin, particularly Strauss's strictures against "historicism," became an excuse for philosophical dabbling and disinterest in tradition.

ANTI-HISTORICISM

Perhaps the best example of paradox and lack of philosophical acumen in the American conservative movement is that, partly through the mediation of William Buckley, the movement became widely associated with Straussian anti-historicism and a correspondingly abstract notion of higher values. When it comes to addressing questions of moral universality and right, Strauss asserted, history and tradition lack all authority. The paradox here is that students of modern conservatism in the Western world had long regarded Edmund Burke, the eighteenth-century British thinker-statesman, who was in some respects a forerunner of Hegel, as a key figure and as perhaps the most representative conservative thinker—even as the *father* of modern conservatism. And why had he been so regarded? Because Burke saw the close connection between attaining virtue, wisdom, and knowledge and learning from history. He believed in conserving the best of the human heritage, what he called "the bank and capital of nations and of ages," not as an *alternative* to pursuing higher values but, on the contrary, as an indispensable guide to those values. The individual is morally and intellectually weak, but the species is wise. Burke had an acute awareness that the past has shaped and moves in the present. Concrete instances of well-being now enjoyed owe greatly to the efforts of ancestors. Tradition at its best does not offer final answers but attunes human beings to goodness, truth, and beauty—to divine providence. The transcendent reveals itself as, guided by history, humanity struggles to articulate it afresh. For Strauss, by contrast, Burke's "historicism" represents a threat to moral universality, what Strauss calls "natural right." This historicism is, Strauss contends, a greater danger than the ideas of the French Jacobins, whose conception of universal human rights are at least appropriately ahistorical, abstract. According to Strauss, what is ultimately normative in human affairs can be discerned only by abstract rationality, while Burke's defense of the historical consciousness amounts to relativism or nihilism. This is historicism and must be flatly *rejected*. Strauss's view of Burke and historical consciousness betrays a pronounced reductionism. Strauss never contemplates that historical thinking might have a form entirely different from what he rejects. He seems psychologically resistant to consider the possibility. But, surely, the experience and achievements of the human race are a rich source of guidance for intellectually limited and otherwise flawed individuals. It is revealing that so many self-described American intellectual conservatives should have adopted moral rationalism and turned anti-historicism, previously associated in the Western world with radicals and revolutionaries, into an ideological staple.

Undermining respect for historical experience and advancing a purely abstract notion of universality was no marginal philosophical move. It was a stratagem with far-reaching ramifications. The implied view of human nature, society, and right was hard to reconcile, for example, with the old belief of mainstream Christianity that tradition is an essential support for religious life and thought and with its central idea that the Word was historically incarnated. The latter belief flatly contradicts the notion that moral right can have nothing to do with history. It has been a striking and curiously incongruous element of movement conservatism that numerous Christian movement conservatives, especially Roman Catholics, adopted Straussian anti-traditionalism and moral rationalism. That they could be so easily won over to a view sharply at odds with their supposed religious beliefs suggests a lack of elementary philosophical discernment. Strauss and his disciples may have intuited that in this quarter vague notions of natural law together with philosophical innocence would ease acceptance of his notion of natural right. A group that might otherwise have been the most likely to enroll in the defense of tradition would instead, unknowingly, set out to undermine it.

The anti-historicist prejudice against learning from history and the preference to be guided by purely abstract ideas also runs counter to the American constitutional temperament. The latter is reflected, for example, in Madison's view that the setting up of government is better informed by experience than by theorists "in their closets." One of the reasons why Edmund Burke was sympathetic to the American colonists in their resistance to the British government was that they were complaining of violations of long-standing traditions, including "the rights of Englishmen." Their thought, practice, and general sense of direction evinced continuity with classical, Christian, and British traditions. The framers built original features into the Constitution, but in essential respects it implied and extended the way of thinking about life and politics that the colonists had brought to America and adapted to their circumstances. The framers of the Constitution assumed and hoped that the culture and personality traits that had generated constitutionalism in the first place would continue to shape the American people and its leaders. Their constitutionalism grew out of and depended for its survival on the habits of moral virtue and responsibility that these traditions had fostered. These habits had to be carried forward. Followers of Strauss, by contrast, have argued, some with great intensity, that the founders deliberately *broke* with the past and constructed something new on the basis of abstract, ahistorical "principles." According to the late Harry Jaffa, to celebrate the American founding is to celebrate revolution. Jaffa's contrived, reductionistic view of the founding gained currency among young Americans who had little historical or philosophical education but who found in this ideology a language for expressing their patriotism. One has to wonder if Jaffa's reinterpretation of America and the Constitution as based solely on abstract principles rather than on an old heritage did not express a nonphilosophical desire: to be able to think of America and the Constitution as not being creatures of WASP culture. If understood as based on ahistorical principles, the Constitution would appeal more to Irish, Italian, and Polish Catholics and even to non-Christian recent arrivals in America. Jaffa's view of the American founding conflicts so much with the historical record that it is plausible to think that it serves a deep psychological need. It is as if Jaffa and theorists like him see America's actual past as a source of discomfort. Their anti-historicism might as well have been tailor-made to discourage Americans from studying and cherishing their historical origins.

The just-described abstractionist notion of "the founding" actually reinforced the old progressive view of the meaning of America, which was powerfully and persuasively challenged by Russell Kirk and other scholars before and after Jaffa and the Straussians. The ahistorical idea of the founding made it appear that the survival of the Constitution was a matter of Americans keeping certain ideas in their heads, which drew attention away from the more demanding task of nurturing the personal and cultural habits, most importantly the moral character, that had given rise to the spirit of constitutionalism in the first place. Looking back on the development of America since the adoption of the Constitution, it is possible to see that a failure to undertake this demanding work of transmission and revivification was bound to erode the accomplishments of the framers. The institutions they set up could not work as intended unless they were animated by people who embodied what I call the constitutional personality. Without people of that kind, the institutions would become mere plans on paper or would be put to nefarious purposes.

"A republic, if you can keep it," is how Benjamin Franklin is supposed to have described the new American form of government. To understand the actual origins of America's constitutional regime is the same as to recognize what is required for it to survive. Keeping it is not a matter of course. Repeating certain "founding principles" could never substitute for the arduously acquired traits of the constitutional personality, including the moral character on which everything else depends. To champion the US Constitution without emphasizing its moral and cultural prerequisites is in effect to undermine it.

It can be argued that, in the final analysis, it was precisely a failure to satisfy the demanding preconditions of American constitutionalism that produced the decline of the American constitutional temperament and the deep constitutional crisis of today. Some Straussians might argue that nothing could have been further from their intention than to weaken the Constitution, but their abstractionist notion of its nature helped produce just that effect. To be a good American did not require respect for, familiarity with, and cultivation of the cultural heritage that made American constitutionalism possible. All that was needed was adherence to America as an "idea."

Ahistoricist thinking regarding America helped prepare the way for the notion that, unlike other countries, America is not a historically evolved society with deep roots in a particular past. America is "exceptional." It is founded on principles that make it a model for other countries. One leading Straussian, the late Allan Bloom, referred to "the American Project." America's principles are everywhere applicable, he asserted. World War II was "an educational project" fought to force those who did not accept American principles to do so. This view of America's role, which receives much attention in this book, reinforced and ideologically garnished the already strong imperial impulse in the American foreign-policy establishment. Academic Straussianism here became indistinguishable from the more directly political ideological current known as "neoconservatism," which gained political prominence in the 1980s. Most of the leading neoconservatives had once been on the hard left. They had now had "second thoughts," but had a vision of the world transformed. They had global ambitions. What they desired for the world was a mixture of equality, democracy, and capitalism. Almost without anybody in the conservative movement noticing, neoconservatism became the dominant public voice of the conservative movement—another instance of philosophical incongruity.

Like Straussianism, neoconservatism was not uniform, but its representatives had foreign-policy views of a markedly hawkish and imperial cast. No advanced knowledge of intellectual history was required to see that its philosophically rather crude ideological universalism was closely akin to the radicalism of eighteenth century French Jacobinism, a resemblance that is discussed in depth in this volume. It is appropriate to mention that it was the fondness of the Jacobins for "abstract," ahistorical principles and their disdain for historically evolved beliefs and practices that scared Edmund Burke and inspired him to write his seminal *Reflections on the Revolution in France*, in which he accurately predicted many of the events that would become known to history as the "Reign of Terror."

The affinity of many self-described American conservatives for ahistorical theorizing, the virtual opposite of a historically informed and grounded view of life, exemplifies the sometimes glaring philosophical shortcomings and contradictions that will be taken up in these pages.

These preliminary observations regarding intellectual flaws are not meant to assert that Straussians and neoconservatives have made no salutary contributions to American conservatism. My emphasis has been on the basic assumptions that are most distinctive and characteristic of their thinking and that have been most detrimental to the intellectual development of the conservative movement. Straussians and neoconservatives have of course sometimes moved outside of those limiting assumptions and linked up with and contributed to more promising intellectual currents. In recent years, increasingly threatening social and political circumstances have also made ahistoricist ideology look more and more distant from historical reality. What is the relevance of formulaic notions of "the American founding" for facing the collapse of American institutions, the fragmenting of America, and precipitous cultural decline? These acute challenges have prompted many antihistoricists, especially of the so-called West Coast, Claremont variety, to frame responses. Straussians appear to be pushing their old formulas to the side as incidental to pressing needs. It remains to be seen whether the confrontation with the real world will trigger a more than superficial reassessment of old assumptions. Ideologues tend to hang on to their most cherished illusions even after reality has called them into question. It would not be surprising if the abstractionist mindset that created the notion of American exceptionalism lingered and reconstituted itself, for example, as an unsound form of nationalism. Another more cheering possibility is that worsening historical circumstances will help dispel abstractionism and generate a new intellectual seriousness.

THE NEED FOR INTELLECTUAL RENEWAL

Why give much attention to philosophically inferior and inauspicious ideas? One reason is that ideas of that kind can move entire societies and thus affect the course of history. I started to pay closer attention to Straussian anti-historicism and neoconservatism in the late 1970s because I expected their influence to grow, not because they had intellectual merit but because they appealed to and advanced powerful interests. What was curious, if not unexpected, was that, with very few exceptions, movement conservative intellectuals seemed oblivious to or unconcerned about what was happening. It seemed to me that to avert decline, stagnation, and worse, it would be necessary for conservatism to shake off the more dubious aspects of these intellectual currents. Yet something about the intellectual background of the movement conservatives made them strangely undiscerning—tolerant of, even receptive to, the mentioned ideas. It was this lack of awareness of danger that made me try to expose some obviously questionable ideological notions and to warn of their practical implications. A question that comes to the forefront in this book is why so many intellectual conservatives failed to notice or call out these ideas. One explanation is the previously mentioned bias in favor of politics narrowly conceived, which included the old Buckleyite practice of including in the movement whatever seemed to match certain roughly defined political criteria. Those criteria were themselves questionable, but to challenge the ideas of well-known "conservatives" was to risk censure as a troublemaker. With very few exceptions, those who did recognize or at least intuit the problem of misguided alliances were reluctant to offend people with the power to affect reputations and steer financial resources. A deeper, strictly intellectual explanation for the lack of opposition also helps explain the habit of giving primacy to politics, the less than mature philosophical culture that has already been discussed. It says much about the state of American intellectual conservatism that the criticisms of questionable ideas and alliances I started advancing a few decades ago are almost as relevant today.

I should elaborate on a qualification at which I have already hinted. It bears on whether conservatism might at this late hour begin to repair its flaws. It should be evident that there is need for a major critical assessment of basic assumptions, which will require considerable time. Given the weaknesses of some of the main currents of movement conservatism, might those currents be salvageable in some new form? Will people holding inauspicious views be able and willing to break out of ingrained intellectual habits and explore philosophically unfamiliar territory. It is relevant to mention what might not seem obvious to all: that intellectual currents or "schools" that are defined by general ideas are made up of human beings who are not all of a piece. They have a mixture of traits and thoughts, some of which are discordant. To take an example, some Straussians, who are pegged as such because of their intellectual leanings, mentors, and tell-tale terminological habits, may in important respects transcend the label. The anti-historicism of Strauss, for example, may for some Straussians be less a well-considered theoretical stance than a rhetorical signal that they reject moral nihilism or relativism. Ideological formulas that they are echoing—"the American founding," "the Declaration of Independence," "equality," "Lincoln," "natural right," etc.—may, in the end, mean less to them than very different views and leanings, such as Christian beliefs, a visceral love of America, or even a

Burke-like respect for the America of history. Because of their limited exposure to history and philosophy, it may surprise them to discover that the anti-historicism and abstract universalism to which they are at least nominally committed are actually incompatible with beliefs about which they care deeply, that they do, in fact, overlap with modern progressivism and radicalism. One can imagine the intellectually and psychologically liberating effects of recognizing philosophically and historically dilettantish beliefs for what they are and to be thus extricated from them. Young persons especially, who have been unknowingly at loggerheads with themselves, might discover a more appropriately named conservatism and an America quite different from that of their abstract, ideological formulas. An obstacle to this kind of intellectual broadening and deepening is that the Straussian network has for a long time relied heavily on psychological bonding and bolstering to induce self-confidence and loyalty.

Of the other more or less well-defined "schools" or strains of thought within movement conservatism whose weaknesses have similarly impeded intellectual development, so-called libertarianism presents a special intellectual challenge. The fact that the term "libertarian" has so many meanings, some of them incompatible, presents a basic problem of definition. Some libertarians defend limited government and liberty while recognizing what these goods owe to historical evolution, community, and moral responsibility, while others associate libertarianism with social atomism, abstract rationalism, hedonism, and moral nihilism. The fact that many libertarians are economists points to the need for distinguishing between different ways of understanding the free market. That some forms of libertarianism cannot be reconciled with conservatism in any meaningful sense should be obvious, but most movement conservatives have been uninterested in or incapable of making important basic distinctions. Deciding what is and is not tenable in libertarian and free-market thinking would be a large and worthy project, but this need receives only limited attention in this volume.

Another large subject that would deserve its own extensive treatment is how conservatives have dealt with religion. One might have thought that they would have been on high alert against deformed religious sentiment and that they would have quickly identified and opposed a hugely influential but spurious form of spirituality that receives much attention in this book. Conservatives reaffirmed traditional beliefs but have been only vaguely aware of, and not well-equipped to oppose, sentiments that were transforming the meaning of traditional terms. This failing has been closely connected to another major weakness that I am just about to discuss and that will take up much space in this book. Even belated efforts to remedy that particular problem could have wide-ranging salutary effects.

Many intellectuals who think of themselves as "realists" or hard-nosed pragmatists will of course resist my making a big to-do about conservatives having missed what the supposed realists consider fine and very subtle distinctions with minimal relevance for practical life. What matters in the real world, they think, is adapting to and winning a down-to-earth struggle for power. This way of minimizing the importance of ideas and other "nonpolitical" factors is but one example of what has greatly hampered the development of American intellectual conservatism. One can grant an element of truth in the putatively "hard-nosed" approach to politics, especially at a time when society and its culture are imploding, but even the harshest, roughest actions exhibited in the power struggle are bound to reflect "pre-political" sentiment so that no genuine realism can do without a more than superficial understanding of the deepest sources of human action. This book deals extensively with issues of national security and international relations. It shows that some highly dubious intellectual constructs and dreams would not stay in the mind and imagination but were rife with implications for practical action. Bombs would fall and many thousands would die. If there is to be an intellectual renewal of American conservatism worth the name, the greatest need to be addressed may be that of acquiring a better grasp of what makes human beings tick.

Much of what is here offered to the reader is an attempt to sort out what is what and to criticize thinking that would soon have been refuted or marginalized if American conservatism had evolved in an intellectual environment of greater philosophical maturity and stringency. As the previously mentioned anomalies illustrate, American conservatism has struggled to articulate its essential identity. It has had great difficulty defining key terms, including "virtue," "universal values," "nationalism," "freedom," and, of course, "history." Very loose definitions have often served as vehicles for very questionable ideas, as has the term "conservatism." The latter has become so flexible as to make room for opposites, putting it on par with the by now virtually useless term "liberalism." To a surprising extent, what presents itself as American conservatism often turns out to be on closer inspection quite different from the kind of conservatism that extended the thinking, temperament, and historically evolved culture of the framers of the US Constitution: a conservatism with deep roots in classical and Christian traditions, as transmitted through British culture. To point this out is to indicate that American conservatism faces a daunting intellectual challenge.

THE UNRECOGNIZED POWER AND THE ROAD NOT TAKEN

Postwar American conservatism produced a wide array of criticism of religious, moral, cultural, intellectual, political, and economic phenomena that it saw as threatening traditional Western civilization in general and American constitutionalism and liberty in particular. A recurring theme was the damage done by Enlightenment rationalism and positivism. A belief in allegedly scientific, strictly rational inquiry steered the Western mind away from the study of the moral-spiritual dimension of human existence, which had been given precedence in the previous millennia. For leading conservatives, the rationalistic fascination with science and neglect of transcendent higher values seemed the most important reason for the disorientation and decline of the West. Modern ideologies, most obviously Marxism with its admitted materialism, filled the vacuum left by a retreating Christianity. Conservatives properly warned of letting supposedly scientific methodology replace other ways of studying humanity. I call this inhumane epistemology "scientism." Conservatives sharply criticized the idea that the human condition could be transformed into something vastly better through scientific engineering. For many, C.S. Lewis's *The Abolition of Man* identified the greatest threat to a humane existence.

This book suggests that there was another, perhaps even more powerful source of what is by now the far-advanced deconstruction and replacement of the old Western civilization. Progressive modernity did celebrate reason, but it also had its own quasi-spiritual vision for humanity, and the latter as much as faith in science accounted for its appeal and profound influence. A few leading conservative thinkers in the postwar era who had read Irving Babbitt seriously knew of this other danger but were only partially aware of its scope and momentousness. They did not explore Babbitt's insights into this force in philosophical depth and did not fully incorporate it into their analyses of what was going wrong in Western society. Focused on other deleterious phenomena, movement conservatives never developed a more than limited grasp of the pervasiveness of this influence. What I have in mind is a new sensibility, a new way of viewing and reacting to the world—a new form of *imagination.* It changed the understanding of the basic terms of the human condition, most importantly of the nature of morality and goodness. It was not another brand of rationalism or scientism. It was a sentimental brand of caring and benevolence that was indistinguishable from a sense of moral superiority in the bearer. To explain further, I need to elaborate on an aspect of the subject of culture that was discussed above and to which movement conservatism gave wholly insufficient attention.

During the eighteenth century, the new way of imagining life started permeating Western elites. This development was roughly contemporaneous with Enlightenment rationalism and had in common with it a disdain for Western moral-spiritual traditions. Yet it had its own distinct dynamic and became a powerful strain of romanticism. A brand of "idealism" emerged that sought the remaking of the world. The inspiring sensibility can be summarized in the phrases "love of humanity" or "brotherhood of man." By the twentieth century it had probably become the dominant source of moral self-worth in the Western world, though still in competition with lingering older classical and Christian views of human existence. This new sensibility redefined justice and good and evil. One of the reasons it proved difficult for many even to detect the radical nature of this sensibility was that it bore a superficial terminological resemblance to classical or Christian moral-spiritual beliefs. It retained words like "virtue," "love," "justice," "responsibility," and "compassion" but gave them a wholly different meaning infused with "touchy-feely," teary-eyed sentiment. It could present itself as an improved, more deeply and broadly caring and liberating spirituality.

Another reason movement conservatives had difficulty pinpointing and understanding this force was that it did not fit the pattern of phenomena to which they normally affixed blame, such as "atheism," "rationalism," or "materialism." Eric Voegelin, who started influencing American intellectual conservatism in the 1950s, is a prominent example of a thinker who did not, except quite indirectly, explore the role of the imagination. The subject had long been extensively discussed by European philosophers, especially in the fields of epistemology, aesthetics, and literary studies, but Voegelin did not have a vocabulary for addressing this part of consciousness, as if he considered it of negligible or secondary importance. Voegelin did intuit some of the power of warped imagination, but he accounted for the pernicious effects of this unrecognized imagination by using his own accustomed analytical categories. For him, as for so many other intellectuals who defended a more traditional Western view of life, the key source of spiritual deformation and social decline was a corruption of *reason,* such as the one brought by Enlightenment rationalism. What I am pointing out is that the moral sensibility now under discussion was primarily a product of a transformation of the *imagination*—which is a preconceptual, primordial apprehension of the world. This new sensibility, felt by the possessor to be a form of high spirituality, had been drained of traditional moral-spiritual content, specifically of the view that man is morally divided against himself and capable of evil as well as good. It was suffused instead with dreaming and emotion. Hiding behind nonthreatening, familiar-sounding terms like "love," "compassion," and "service," this pseudo-spiritual imagination drastically changed the self-understanding of Western men and women.

The term "imagination" does not refer here primarily to the modality of the creative arts but includes it. It refers most fundamentally to the intuitive sense of reality and direction that accompanies and orients all of what human beings do and think. The "imagination" is a term for the comprehensive, prerational, and ever-present consciousness that accounts for life's most basic continuity. It is the general background that gives the person a sense of what is and is not real or possible, what is and is not desirable. While this intuitive sense of the whole gives an element of coherence and stability to existence, it is not static. It evolves with the life experiences of particular persons, including impulses streaming at the person from the prevailing cultural environment. How experience is interpreted and develops is strongly affected by people of powerful imagination. I indicated above that movement conservatism as a whole paid little attention to the power of "the culture" in shaping human conduct. It seemed barely aware of its importance. This was a major, even catastrophic neglect because creative figures in society's trend-setting elites, those who are able to capture the imagination of others, transmit to the general public some of their sense of the nature of reality and of good and evil. They convey what aspirations are plausible and desirable and what ones should be scorned or attacked as dangerous. Society tends to form around dominant general visions and sensibilities. These help constitute the intuitive-imaginative background against which most people live their lives. Great power lies in the hands of those whose visions penetrate the inner lives of others and affect their deepest hopes and fears. This power can be very dangerous because human beings are prone to believing what they want to believe. Visionaries who have vivid, compelling imaginations but dubious inspiration can pull others into appealing but illusory dreams that, in the real world, result in disaster and terrible suffering. No task is more important to civilization than discerning and protecting against illusory, reality-defying hopes and dreams.

Many factors contributed to how Western society changed in the last 250 years, but it can be argued that a root cause of the general direction of this change is what happened to the imagination. The sentimental, dreamy, "idealistic" imagination, for which Jean-Jacques Rousseau, the philosopher of the French Revolution, is paradigmatic, caught on and swept through the Western world. It remade an old sense of reality and priorities and gave human beings a new picture of themselves, most notably a new view of how to be virtuous in their own eyes and in the eyes of others. The great appeal of the new way of envisioning human nature and the world was that it gave the bearer a pleasant sense of moral superiority, a self-understanding sharply at odds with the ancient humbling notion that humanity is prone to self-indulgent, dangerous impulses. The crux of the older notion of morality was for human beings to learn to control their own lower natures, which required strength of character. In the struggle to develop their higher natures, people needed the help of family, community, and civilization in general. Christianity stressed the need for divine grace. The culture at its best, including drama and the other arts, helped human beings understand the human condition, strengthen their better selves, and resist escape from responsibility. For Rousseau, by sharp contrast, human beings were born good, and the institutions, habits, and general culture of traditional society had ruined and enslaved them. By casting off the old society with all of its traditional restraints, man's true humanity could be liberated and true freedom be realized. The new morality did not replace classical and Christian notions of virtue and goodness with materialism as ordinarily understood but with what it considered noble moral sentiment—a deep compassion for disadvantaged or suffering groups. This humanitarian emotional virtue, which soon suffused even Christianity itself, made people feel virtuous because they embraced ambitious, benevolent-looking plans for remaking society. To take an example of this idealism pushed to an extreme, what made people flock to the banners of communism was not primarily the intellectual power of a work like Marx's *Capital* or of dialectical materialism. Communism meant being a part of a great mission. It was a faith, a commitment to act for the sake of a better world for humanity. Whittaker Chambers stressed this characteristic of communism in *Witness* (1952), the autobiography that recounted his life as a communist and Soviet agent and his break with communism. That book became iconic for American conservatives, but rather than realizing that a kindred, if less extreme, idealism was inspiring the surge of progressive "liberal" reformism, they seem to have regarded communism as being in a category all its own.

For the new pseudo-moral idealism, evil was extraneous to the person. This meant that reform of self was no longer a central issue. According to Babbitt, this was a calamitous development. The way to counter this destructive sham spirituality, he argued, was to expose its real nature, importantly with the aid of the very different elevating and cathartic works of imagination that he called "the moral imagination." Unless the imagination could be reconnected to the real terms of human existence, especially the need for moral character, other efforts to reverse the decline of Western civilization would be unavailing.

The "idealism" and "caring" of the new virtue is inherently a form of self-praise that justifies ordering the lives of others for their benefit. Consciously or unconsciously, it serves the will to power. It has been the main warrant for the enormous expansion and centralization of government in the Western world. In the foreign policy field, this "virtue" has been for neoconservatives, humanitarian interventionists, and other globalist reformers the moral rationale for imperial ambitions. Still, most movement conservatives have yet to understand the moral-political dynamic and sway of this deeply ingrained idealistic imagination.

It was idealists of the aforementioned type, who claimed to be acting for the brotherhood and equality of man, who in the twentieth century showed themselves to be utterly ruthless and murderers on an almost unfathomable scale. Stalin and Mao, devoted to the vision of a better world, killed people by the millions. You might have thought that this record of boundless inhumanity would have permanently discredited this and similar leftist idealism, but such is the nature of this moralism that it always rejects blame for horror and destruction inflicted in its name. The *ideals* are not compromised by misguided methods used to enact them. The ideals remain as noble as ever. The results of serving them will be different next time. The idealism moves on to new projects.

Typical progressives during the postwar era have resented being criticized for being sympathetic to leftist extremism. A good number of them were resentful for good reason. Many people called "liberals" have been strong anti-communists. Yet many other "liberals" were very uncomfortable with efforts after the World War to expose communist infiltration of the US government. Peter Viereck called the anti-anti-communism of so many American intellectuals in the 1950s "the shame of the intellectuals." What, then, accounted for their unease? There was more than one explanation, but in the present context one stands out. Although they were not themselves communists, many of them felt that attacks on communists were also in some indirect way an attack on them. They did, after all, have a soft spot for the *ideals* of the communists. The communists were misguided, but did they not at least have good motives?

Exposing the pseudo-moralism of sentimental caring—of which communist theory and practice were extreme manifestations—should have been the primary objective of the conservative movement. In one form or another, this brand of "spirituality" has been the moral impetus behind virtually every progressive reform in the past several decades. This is the crusading, self-applauding virtue that always puts opponents on the defensive as being lacking in generosity and compassion. This putative moral nobility has exercised and continues to exercise an enormous, if subtle, influence. Yet American movement conservatives did not for the most part understand what would have been obvious to them had they understood the power of the imagination in general and of the sentimental imagination in particular. They were hence unable to demonstrate that the problem with the idealism at issue was not just the inhumane *means* employed by extremists; the problem was with the *dreams themselves*. Contrary to widespread belief, these dreams were not beautiful and admirable. Behind pretty words they hid the very opposite, as is discussed in this book. Because movement conservatives had an inadequate understanding of what most deeply inspires human conduct, they were not in a position to expose and deflate this sinister, destructive imagination. This may have been their greatest failing.

The sham empathy of idealism lives on. Its supposed caring for suffering collectives, its passion for liberation, and its opposition to oppression and intolerance are today eroding what remains of traditional Western civilization. It animates cancel culture. The great prophet of cancel culture was Rousseau.

The neglect of what gives people their basic outlook on life gave movement conservatives an often simplistic view of how to achieve their goals. Not surprisingly, they continued to be defeated by forces whose influence they did not recognize or understand. As a professor of politics, I do not need to be persuaded that politics matters, but politics is far more complex than most students of the subject assume. Political attitudes themselves have nonpolitical sources. A kind of power exists that can overpower politicians.

Rather than go into the most basic and subtle forms of this other power, let me point to an example of it of which movement conservatives have had at least a limited awareness. Strongly aligned with the Republican party, they have for decades bemoaned the tendency of newly elected Republicans to abandon earlier professions of conservatism after arriving in Washington, DC, and to "go native." More generally, conservatives have been frustrated by a lack of willingness on the part of self-declared conservative office-holders to stand their ground and give Democrats a taste of the kind of strong, sustained, and unified pressure that is attributed to the Democrats. Why is it so common for supposedly conservative elected officials to fall short of expectations? Out of several explanations, one is of special interest here: the role of the American mass media. Conservatives have long realized that these media—especially print and television journalism—have a pronounced "progressive," "liberal" bias, but they have never fully comprehended the nature of that influence. The power of the media comes from the ability to pull the public into a certain view of reality—day in and day out, year in and year out, decade in and decade out. They do this by conveying a sense of what is newsworthy and not, disturbing and not, moral and not, dangerous and not, admirable and not. This influence is all the more effective in that it reflects and reinforces kindred sentiments and ideas predominant in academia, book publishing, the arts, movies, and other entertainment. The media help create and maintain an entire cultural-intellectual milieu. Their way of affecting politics is less a matter of policy advocacy on specific issues than of imparting over time a general sense of what is desirable and undesirable. A key ingredient in the sensibility cultivated by the media in the postwar period has been the sentimental idealism and notion of social justice just discussed. When politicians or others contemplate taking action or voicing opinions that run afoul of the preferences dominant in the media, they know intuitively that if they were to go ahead they would violate unwritten rules and risk being discredited. They get used to trimming their sails in advance or to not even attempt initiatives that sharply challenge reigning assumptions. By contrast, politicians who accommodate media sensibilities are called "moderates" or "middle-of-the-road" and are able to avoid negative attention and censure. Those who are in accord with the media regime enjoy an enormous political advantage and freedom of movement. They are far less likely to be criticized for mistakes or wrongdoing. While aware of media bias against them, movement conservatives never wholly understood the ability of the media to get inside the public mind and imagination, create a sense of reality, and affect the hopes and fears of the general population. This ability gives the media an extraordinary influence over politics and others spheres of life. It is no exaggeration to say that the media and those whose interests they advance have been a crucial factor in shaping American postwar society—which is not to deny that they have had to compete with surviving older beliefs and attitudes or that "alternative media" have sprung up in opposition. Conservatives have in recent years become more alert to the power and increasingly leftist orientation of the media, but because they have had but a weak grasp of the role of the imagination and how it influences human conduct, they have greatly underestimated this power.

The general disinclination of conservatives to seriously explore an alternative or supplement to politics as the way to change society ran parallel to the general contraction and decline of the humanities in American education. Philanthropy continued to move in a utilitarian direction at the same time that it heavily and increasingly favored progressive or radical causes. The few large foundations and donors that had the reputation of giving a hearing to conservative-looking projects favored mainly grant requests proposed or endorsed by neoconservatives and Straussians, which were in line with certain political objectives. That the traditional humanities had their own nonpolitical reason for being and might in the long run shape society for the better seemed to most conservative donors far-fetched.

A concrete example of how insufficient interest in issues of culture retarded the intellectual development of American movement conservatism may be helpful. I tried in my teaching and writing to demonstrate how the culture orients and colors society, including politics. For decades I taught a graduate seminar on politics and the imagination. In 1984 a graduate student of mine, Joseph Baldacchino, and I started an institute whose purpose was to increase awareness of how the culture influences the sensibilities of persons and the imagination of society as a whole. We called the new entity the National Humanities Institute (NHI). Baldacchino served as president. He was an experienced political journalist who had observed at close range the drawbacks of not understanding the cultural context and background of politics. We had the support of Russell Kirk, who became a member of NHI's small board of directors. Kirk cautioned us that in all likelihood we would have to try to make do with modest grants from small foundations and private individuals. This is what he, the much celebrated author, had experienced when helping to raise funds for worthy projects. American philanthropy reflected the growing narrow-mindedness and superficiality of American life, and most conservative donors had little or no appreciation for what the arts, humanities, and letters at their best contribute to social well-being. Kirk's prediction turned out to be accurate. For thirty-five years NHI had to operate on a shoestring budget, which was boosted only occasionally by more generous donations. NHI was able to survive only through intellectual commitment, volunteer efforts, and personal sacrifice. Over the years Baldacchino and I coedited NHI's flagship scholarly interdisciplinary journal, *Humanitas.* Kirk had pointed out what we already knew—that most journals and magazines have a very short lifespan—but *Humanitas* beat the odds. It is a very widely read, internationally recognized journal. Its articles address fundamental questions of civilization, not the political issues of the day. A growing number of intellectuals gravitated in the direction of *Humanitas* and NHI as readers and writers. Historians know that journals or what Kirk called "little magazines" can have a large impact on their societies because of how they affect gifted people and seed significant future developments. Yet, in another example of the superficiality and shortsightedness that is spreading throughout society, foundations and donors do not like to support journals.

In 2017 NHI merged with the Center for the Study of Statesmanship (CSS) at the Catholic University of America, of which I was the founding director.

NHI's struggle is mentioned here to illustrate with concrete particulars the effects of the disabling lack of interest in cultural issues that is more and more common in American society and that appears to have been rather deeply ingrained in most movement conservatives. Occasionally NHI received from them a polite nod, but it appears to have occurred to very few that an institute stressing the high importance of arts, letters, philosophy, and the humanities—of *"the culture"*—might be far more significant, especially for the longer run, than the public policy shops and activist think tanks that attracted their interest.

One can speculate about how America's development since World War II might have been different if America's intellectual conservatism had been better equipped to comprehend what moves human beings and better able to address the most basic problems of America and the rest of the West. What if it had more fully discerned, absorbed, and acted on its own most fruitful potentialities? Suppose that it had directed a great deal more of its energy to refuting the moral smugness and self-deception of sentimental idealism, which has inspired such an enormous amount of social destruction. Could it have headed off the moral-spiritual, cultural, intellectual, and political decomposition that finally produced today's "wokeness" and "cancel culture"? It is thought-provoking to consider that, on the whole, the most important and promising elements of post–World War II American conservatism—especially the effort to understand the role of imagination in directing man's inner life—turned out to be the road *not* taken.

IDEOLOGY VS. PHILOSOPHY

Much of this volume criticizes ideas said to be conservative. Partly by implication, it also outlines an alternative way of thinking about conservatism. This different approach, which is more fully developed in other of my writings, involves basic assumptions and priorities that may puzzle many movement conservatives. Because of how the term "conservatism" has most often been used in postwar America, some of what is argued here may seem not even to have a strong claim to the term. But what is entitled to the term is less important than determining the quality of ideas. Although the meaning of conservatism is at issue in this book, that question is incidental to trying to make sense of the world.

Conservatism has often been called nonideological. My view of conservatism implies that, at its best, conservatism does answer to that description. It shuns the kind of putatively definitive intellectual systems or dogmas that put formulaic principles in the place of complex and ultimately mysterious reality. Because of the importance of this issue to assessing American conservatism, some time should be devoted to explaining it.

To say that conservatism is anti-ideological does not mean that it resists ideas, that it is unsystematic or incoherent, or that it rejects the possibility of truth. All serious thought recognizes that all particular subjects are interconnected and bear on each other, however remotely. They must, therefore, be studied systematically, as parts of the larger whole of human existence. Yet because of the scope and complexity of life, not even the most penetrating, comprehensive, and rigorous philosophy can ever be all-encompassing and exhaustive. Human thought must, to some considerable extent, always remain halting and tentative. Exploring the whole and the particular together can be done more or less consciously or adequately, but good philosophy tries to do it systematically and penetratingly without distorting living experience. The proper study of human life rejects premature classificatory schemes or theoretical abstractions. While philosophy advances truth by clearing away distortions, illusions, and general intellectual debris, it achieves no conclusive, final answers. Thought continues. That is to say that systematic philosophical inquiry into the nature and meaning of the whole is entirely compatible with—is, indeed, indistinguishable from—intellectual modesty. Omniscience is for human beings not even a distant possibility. It is ideologues who refuse to live with uncertainty and loose ends. Facing the daunting great questions, they produce the artificial and premature certitude of reductionistic, simplifying dogmas. One of the weaknesses of much of the conservatism criticized in this book is precisely an affinity for ideological formulas and rough general ideas. Philosophy shows no such impatience with subtlety and complexity.

The point here is not that broad "principles" and other simplifications have no place. They are in a sense inevitable and necessary, and they are often highly desirable. General discussion cannot do without intellectual shorthand, broad hints, and summaries. No debate could ever get off the ground if the larger context, the full implications, and different dimensions of ideas under discussion all had to be fully explained. The latter is the large, demanding, and inexhaustible work of the branches of philosophy. Practical politics cannot spare "platforms," statements of "principles," or slogans. Messages of this kind are understood by all to involve great simplification. Writers of op-eds or essays must obviously gloss over important distinctions and qualifications. Not even authors of rigorous philosophical treatises can deal in depth with all aspects of their topics. They must, if they are wise, select the topics that seem to them most important and penetrate them in depth. It is when impatience and willfulness overpower awareness of life's vastness, intricacy, and mystery that thought turns ideological.

It might be argued that in the decades after World War II American conservatism, though flawed and struggling to gain a foothold in the universities, came closer to answering the needs of the time than any substantial competing intellectual current. But the momentum produced by generations of culturally "progressive" and radical thought and imagination could have been overcome only by broad and exceptional intellectual creativity. The latter would have had to be supported by major corresponding artistic-cultural developments. In reality, the wholly dominant evolving "culture" of the West pointed in a different direction. Though American conservatism's highest achievements were impressive, they never received the recognition and influence they deserved in academia or the wider society. A largely hostile intellectual and cultural establishment, including media of all kinds, largely blocked transmission of its ideas. Even within the conservative movement, appreciation for its most important contributions was spotty. On balance, conservatism slowed and redirected rather than reversed dominant postwar trends

It did not help that, despite the advice of its wisest representatives, conservatism defined itself as primarily a political movement. It became closely connected with political figures and political generalizations, which contributed to the impression that it was first of all politically partisan. This intensified opposition not just among radicals but among people who thought of themselves vaguely as "liberals" because they resisted the putatively low-brow, philistine tastes of what they took to be conservatives and because they favored restraints on business interests and markets. The humane, historically rooted cultural conservatism of a Russell Kirk or a Peter Viereck appealed to many such people in academia and elsewhere and might have attracted more of them had

American conservatism not become so closely tied to certain supposedly conservative political ideas and politicians. Another source of unease was that, in the minds of many, conservatism was associated with hawkish interventionist foreign policy inclinations that seemed to go beyond what the Cold War required.

The complexity and changeability of the world speak against classifying ideas that relate to human life once for all as being either valid or invalid. Ideas commenting on human nature are not univocal and inert. It is the ideologue, not the philosopher, who categorically dismisses ideas with which he disagrees. "Communism," "liberalism," "conservatism," "anarchism," "fascism," "libertarianism," "socialism," and so on have distinctive traits that appeal to their supporters, but if they are approached in a philosophical manner, it can be seen that none of these idea systems is wholly clear-cut or in every respect dissonant or incompatible with other systems. Ideas are usually expressions of thought that has not stopped. Different meanings and aspects of ideas come to mind in different theoretical contexts or historical circumstances. There are no intellectual currents that do not contain an element of truth and that may not in particular situations acquire a new plausibility. Idea systems overlap or resemble each other in various ways. Is there a wise conservatism that does not contain within itself a prominent element of liberalism? It would be liberalism of the kind that rejects social atomism but regards individual liberty and personal creativity as indispensable means to higher ends. Only a dogmatic, ideological libertarian deliberately ignores the complexity and historicity of life and claims that individuals are self-contained units with rights and that the solution to problems is always less government and regulation. Similarly, only a dogmatic conservative will assert that "tradition" must always be followed. And would any thoughtful conservative anti-socialist deny that in some historical circumstances a "socialist" critique of the polarization of rich and poor may begin to sound more persuasive? Aristotle, an ancient pillar of conservative thought, warned against precisely this kind of polarization.

Life is in my view subject to permanent moral, intellectual, and aesthetical higher imperatives, but the complexity and variability of life defies attempts to capture these imperatives once and for all in formulas. Truth-seeking has more to do with weeding out obvious simplification and premature certainty. A deeper, richer understanding of life is always possible, but only dogmatic true believers—ideologues—assert the availability of comprehensive, definitive, incontrovertible Truth. Paradoxical though it may sound, the spirit of philosophy is indistinguishable from intellectual humility.

The reason why this may seem paradoxical is that in the past philosophy has often been associated with belief in preexisting, ahistorical, static Truth. It has been taken for granted that any truth-seeking worth its name must assume this kind of absolute, "objective" Truth. For such Truth not to exist would rule out the possibility of intellectual meaning. I dispute this claim and argue, to the contrary, that Absolute Truth is a merely abstract construct that does not accord with the epistemic conditions under which human beings labor. This notion actually simplifies and distorts what we know of human experience and of thought itself. The historical consciousness discloses the complexity and movement of life and the artificiality of turning truth and untruth into reified starkly separated binary opposites. As a practical matter, there is of course truth and untruth, but the ultimate mystery of life and the fact that life never stands still counsel against sweeping, unqualified assertions, just as they counsel against the arrogant idea of human beings attaining fixed, final Truth. Putting that notion aside does not create a confused blur but mandates greater care as well as modesty. Foregoing the crutch of preexisting Truth assists the truly open, truth-seeking mind. This mind is not bothered by the inevitably provisional element in thought or by ideas sometimes mixing in unexpected combinations.

Philosophy, then, does not retreat into abstractions and simplifications. At home in human history, that is, in human life, it tells us about what is and is not possible in the world in which we have our being—be it high or low. By elucidating the moral-spiritual and other terms of actual human existence, it offers guidance to practice. Indistinguishable from the historical consciousness, the philosophical spirit needs no encouragement to be alert to historical circumstances that create a need for new ways of thinking and for perhaps unexpected new combinations of ideas. There is often talk today of the possibility of a political-intellectual alliance between Left and Right. This idea bothers ideologues, for in their minds ideas are carved in stone or are—if another metaphor works better—separated into watertight compartments: "Left" and "right" are by definition incompatible. To this the philosopher says: think again—that depends on what is meant.

CAN POLITICAL ACTION SAVE AMERICA?

This book spends much time on the weaknesses of American intellectual conservatism that made it difficult for the movement to realize the objectives that it envisioned in the decade just after World War II. The insufficient understanding of the importance of "the culture," specifically the imagination, and the lack of interest in philosophy beyond the level of theoretical generalities go a long way toward explaining the undue stress on political practice and elections. Those who believe that politics is something like the nave around which society turns and want to refute my criticism might actually cite a point made in these pages—the point that changing a society's mind and imagination requires many years and may, indeed, take generations. In the meantime, all manner of large and pressing practical problems need to be handled. Even if it be granted that the culture is influential, these problems must be addressed here and now. Is that not to say that politics must always be given precedence? Critics of the importance-of-culture hypothesis might point to America's current historical circumstances as illustrating particularly well the primacy of politics. The country's institutions, including the Constitution itself, are crumbling, and there is social and political fragmentation, including large-scale, wide-spread civic unrest.

At a time when traditional American liberties are under intense and broad assault, what could be more obvious than that only determined political counteraction could make any difference?

Nothing in this book is meant to deny the importance of politics or to deny that in some circumstances a special mobilization of political forces may be necessary. The present seems to me to be such a time. A combination of alarming developments is threatening basic American rights and freedoms: the surveillance state; suppression of dissent in social media, on campuses, and elsewhere; the criminalization of political opposition; the politicization of the FBI, the courts, and the military; egregious violations by elected and nonelected officials of the Constitution and other laws; rioting, rising murder rates and general criminality; rampant violation of national borders; efforts to dismantle the police; and so on—all of this in tandem with a sharp radicalization of education at all levels and the general culture. These patterns call to mind periods in history when societies disintegrated or turned into tyrannies. Only a lack of historical knowledge could blind Americans to the great danger their country faces and to the spread of a totalitarian mentality.

In the larger context of this book, these signs of social dissolution could be offered as proof of the failure of conservatism and of the shallowness of the conservatives who celebrated the "triumph" of conservatism in the 1980s. But the issue at the moment is how much can be expected of politics. The point being made about the conservative movement is obviously not that it should have abandoned politics in favor of attending to "the culture." The problem has been that it held greatly *exaggerated* notions of the reach and power of politics and greatly underestimated the significance of other factors, whether as sources of decline or of potential revival. Nothing could be more appropriate today than to mobilize politically to try to avert disaster, but there is no reason to believe that the old strong bias in favor of politics will be any less debilitating if applied to a historical emergency. People who have what can be called the myopic view of politics will protest that at least in an emergency, surely the primacy of politics should be self-evident. No special insight is needed to realize that America is in danger, and hence what is obviously most urgently needed is political action. It must be pointed out in response that the first prerequisite of any effective political action is a well-founded sense of the actual circumstances to be handled. What created the acute problems in question? Differently put, what *are* the problems? Also, what forces can be expected to oppose or assist the contemplated action? Only people with a well-rounded understanding of what influences human conduct can answer such questions well. For there to be genuine political realism, the full range of human life needs to be known so that all significant obstacles and the deeper reasons for current difficulties can be considered and so that available sources of power, whether "political" or not, can be identified and tapped. Good leaders need an acute sense of both obstacles and possibilities. To regard the powers of politics as potentially salvific may be especially tempting if a society is descending into open conflict, but action taken in that spirit is likely to generate unrealistic, unimaginative, and self-defeating measures.

It is all-important to understand what *cannot* be achieved by political means. Movement conservatism misfired in large part because it expected too much of politics. Unless it has learned from its failures, it is likely to commit much the same error when dealing with a presumed emergency, that is, define poorly the situation at hand and what counteractions can be efficacious. It would be foolish to believe that politics and government can somehow repair the deeper damage caused by a deteriorated culture. Political emergency measures could never be much more than attempts to head off catastrophe, defensive actions taken to provide breathing room for more time-consuming reconstructive efforts. Only developments outside of politics as ordinarily understood can supply what the well-being of society most requires. There can be no civilization without law and order, but not even that minimal requirement can be satisfied by coercive methods alone. Peace and respect for law owe greatly to nonpolitical influences—which is another way of saying that good, truly realistic leadership must be not only strong-willed but broad-minded, discerning, and imaginative.

The old American constitutional order is crumbling because the moral-spiritual, intellectual, and other assumptions and practices that supported it have long been under attack along a broad front extending from the universities and schools to the media and entertainment. How well-equipped is American conservatism to address this historical predicament? There are signs that it is belatedly and slowly learning from its mistakes and revising its view of what went wrong and how to deal with it. Young intellectuals are making discoveries and putting forth analyses of what is amiss that have long been available but are now greeted as fresh and original. The importance of the culture has forced itself on them. Some long-influential and supposedly conservative ideological fashions are being more than superficially questioned or rejected. For example, although the neoconservatives have not disappeared—they continue to exert considerable influence in the more interventionist wing of the US foreign policy establishment—their intellectual credibility is much diminished. Libertarians of the more dogmatic type continue to advocate wholly free domestic and international markets and essentially open borders, but political and economic developments and new thinking have only widened the gap between their theories and what might be possible in practice. The anti-historicism and propensity for formulaic ideology that characterize the large Straussian network are losing momentum. Ridicule directed by critics against its shibboleths are mixing with shrugs of indifference. While these examples of intellectual movement and ferment may not be signs of the significant philosophical deepening that American conservatism needs, they show a growing ability to see through illusion and obvious error

Although cultural developments are today drastically impacting politics and alerting movement conservatives to their importance, most of them have only a limited understanding of just *how* they matter. They can see that cancel culture is ubiquitous among those setting the tone in national institutions and are particularly upset that schools are indoctrinating children in radical ideology, but they need to understand much better how, over time, representatives of the culture have influenced society's view of the world and exercised a subtle, not obviously political kind of power that has nevertheless transformed politics. The way in which, for good or ill, the imagination and the mind shape the direction of society is a central topic for any serious student of politics.

Let me expand in this context on the point previously made that the ultimate purpose of philosophy is to assist action—specifically, to help the moral actor understand the actual circumstances in which action is being contemplated. It is most generally essential to know the basic terms of human existence and the prerequisites for the deepest form of human well-being. More particularly, efficacious action assumes a realistic view of what is and is not possible in a given situation. The problem with theoretical abstractionism is that its simplifications and its lack of interest in historical experience undermine this kind of understanding. Even more than others, persons contemplating political action in deeply challenging, even ominous circumstances should have intellectual dispositions and temperaments equipping them to size up and handle concrete situations. They need to be "at home" in the real world known in history, not in the sense of *approving* of it with all its perversity and darkness, but in the sense of knowing what to expect and being suited to functioning amidst its imperfections, obstacles, and tribulations.

Many who consider themselves conservatives have convinced themselves that the way to really understand politics is to look away from life as it is and to contemplate ideal possibilities. This is thought to bring the person closer to reality. To dwell on human nature as it tends to be and on corresponding practical constraints, as did the American framers, is said to "lower the sights"—as if the first requirement of genuine moral responsibility were not to advance morality by recognizing and overcoming obstacles in the actual world. Too many self-described conservatives are used to thinking about politics in terms of deviance from or adherence to a preconceived, unchanging ideological conception of what *ought* to be. They have cultivated an anti-historical mindset that positively distracts them from considering what needs to be done in particular concrete circumstances. Machiavelli had a legitimate complaint against moral philosophy that was more concerned about supposedly desirable imaginary regimes unknown to history than about how to make headway in the actual world. That a moral actor needs the direction of some kind of vision of what ought to be is obvious, but for that vision to be something other than an abstract, dreamy distraction from the real world, it needs to be adjusted to what might actually be within reach.

It is not strange that when life threatens to overwhelm human beings with its darkness and pain, many of them will attempt some kind of escape. They will seek refuge in a contemplated comforting alternative reality and perhaps do so in company with others who can reassure them and validate their separating themselves from what is happening "out there." I have discussed above the very close connection between conservatism and the historical consciousness. The latter involves awareness that the present—not least that which makes life worth living—owes greatly to history and that human beings must adapt to this historical reality, however discouraging, not by acquiescing in its many elements of darkness, due prominently to human self-indulgence, but by learning how to make the best of available circumstances. Paradoxically, many self-described American conservatives have instead had a strong intellectual propensity to avoid addressing the actual threats, indignities, and complexities of the ordinary world. It often seems that the *distance* to what might be possible is what recommends a contemplated preferred state of affairs to its proponents—as when some libertarians advocate replacing the modern superstate with minimal government and a wholly free domestic and international market or some American Roman Catholics imagine a society in which the temporal power, including law, is wholly subordinated to the spiritual power. American pragmatism has here been turned into its opposite.

The odds are that if persons wedded to an abstract ideal turn their minds to dealing with highly fraught circumstances, they will have to improvise and will do so in amateurish, blundering ways. The same holds true of those who have an inflated view of the efficacy of politics.

A NOTE ABOUT THIS BOOK

The writings in this volume were selected because they bear on American conservatism. They approach the subject in different ways and deal with different aspects of it. This diversity presents a problem of organization. Should materials be arranged chronologically, by topic, genre, or some other method? My primary objective has been to communicate as well as I can the book's central themes and overarching point of view. I have, for the most part, let semipopular writing precede more philosophically challenging treatments of particular topics. I have also clustered materials that deal with similar subjects, although I am well aware that any such compartmentalization is ultimately arbitrary. Writings can be classified along many different lines. Some of what has been included in this volume was written long ago, but even though references to persons or events may be dated, the problems addressed have lost none of their relevance.

Much of this book may strike the general educated reader as scholarly and philosophical, but, whether it is obvious or not, all parts of the book are full of implications for practice. It is for me a basic epistemological assumption that the chief purpose of philosophy and ideas generally is to elucidate, inform, and guide practice. "Thought," "theory," or "philosophy" that becomes purely abstract and loses contact with the concrete life of experience may be useful in the natural sciences but has little relevance for studying the moral-spiritual, cultural, and political life of human beings.

The section of the book that follows this introduction broaches central ideas and themes of the volume as a whole. Consisting of relatively short pieces for general audiences, the section spans a wide range of subjects and reflects perspectives and emphases within the book as a whole. Though written at very different times, these pieces are held together by salient concerns and themes, and they reflect the element of unity and continuity among the diverse materials collected in the volume. Key terms and ideas used in this section receive further definition elsewhere.

With a few exceptions, the pieces of writing that have been collected in this book were intended to stand on their own. They all needed introductions and other cues to set them in a philosophical, historical, or other context and to indicate the author's general perspective and reason for writing. Since the book contains many such pieces and they are treatments of related topics or aspects of the same larger questions, some repetition and overlap is unavoidable.

A special challenge when preparing a volume of previously published material is what to do with occasional questionable statements or poor formulations or with writing that has been less than felicitously handled by an editor. The temptation to revise has in some cases been strong, but I have tried to resist. Outright errors, including mistakes of fact or grammar, have been corrected.

PART ONE

AMERICA'S DIVIDED SELF

9/11—A TIME FOR REFLECTION

On September 11, 2001, I was president of the Philadelphia Society. The regional meeting of the Society was to take place in New Orleans, Louisiana, on September 21. Members of the Society worried about new plane hijackings and wanted to cancel the meeting, but I thought it should take place as scheduled. This was my presidential address at the meeting. Concerned that neo-Jacobin ideology and reckless hawkishness would turn justifiable indignation into rash, foolhardy action, I counseled prudence and critical distance to what had just happened.

Allow me to offer some brief reflections on the purposes of the Philadelphia Society in relation to the atrocities of last week and in relation to the larger problems that those events brought into such terrible relief.

In a time of national crisis, it is proper and necessary that a country should recall its most cherished and enduring symbols and traditions. In the uncertainty, confusion and passion of the moment it needs to take its bearings, repair to the deepest sources of its national identity. It is natural in a situation like the present to ask, what are the country's defining and unifying allegiances and purposes? At its best, what does it really aspire to be? Without a historically rooted sense of self, a country and its leaders are adrift, potential victims of surges of emotion or the machinations of demagogues and opportunists. For a country truly to know itself and to find its way, it needs to remind itself of the convictions that have guided it and given it strength in the past and remind itself of the historical efforts that gave the country its life, its unity and distinguishing attributes.

The Philadelphia Society was founded to promote a deepened understanding of the origins and conditions of American liberty, as expressed and implied in the work of the Framers of the Constitution. The Society exists to articulate beliefs that are at the very core of the traditional American self-understanding. Among these is the belief that restraint, moral and constitutional, is indispensable to civilized freedom and is a necessary counter to the abuse of power.

Your officers in the Society started planning this year's programs about five months ago. We decided early on that the theme for the national meeting in April was going to be "Sources of American Renewal." The traditional American identity has long been under attack. Some have attacked it openly, making no attempt to hide their hostility to the view of human nature and society that shaped the thinking of the Framers. Some claim to defend "American principles" but give them a new, ahistorical definition that makes them look much like the principles of the French Jacobins. The effect has been to loosen the restraints on power, to invest government with an ideological mission to remake society and perhaps even the world.

The Philadelphia Society is about the business, here and now, of contributing to a renewed sense of national unity and purpose. This regional meeting on "The Taming of Leviathan" forms part of the intended inventory of sources of renewal. We are not here to bemoan yet again the expansion of the Central State and the erosion of federalism and local government, and to bemoan the continuing destruction of the old American understanding of life. We are here to reflect on how destructive trends might actually be reversed, to assist in charting a course for the revitalization of liberty.

The horrendous deeds of September 11 call for action. They call for a strong response. The specifics of that response are being considered at this moment. We all hope that the actions of the United States will be firm, but also that they be bounded by foresight, discernment and a well-founded sense of direction and limits. We in the Society are, for the most part, intellectuals. Indignant and grief-stricken though we are, we have the high responsibility of trying to maintain some critical distance from the emotions of the moment. We are in a position to provide a historically informed perspective on the events of the day. We can help steady the course. This is a time when rashness, superficiality, ignorance, and opportunism could do terrible and long-lasting damage, not only abroad but in the United States, where inherited liberties are already in danger.

We of the Philadelphia society have long pointed to and warned about the appetite for power and privilege in Washington. We have criticized the kind of voracious, grasping personality that tends to dominate the institutions of government. Not very many of the politicians and intellectuals who profess to want limited and decentralized government can be counted on to try to actually adhere to the Constitution and to turn down new power for themselves or for the government of which they are a part. A dynamic of empire building operates in Washington. Domestically, the Tenth Amendment is virtually a dead letter. How ironical that the Constitution almost was not adopted because of fears that the proposed new central power would swallow up State sovereignty and local independence. Only "iron guarantees" against such a possibility got the Constitution accepted. Still, today, there is no aspect of American life that is not touched by Federal power, not even the sphere called "private." In foreign policy, the most respected leaders in America's founding period warned not against trade and relations with other countries but against involvement in causes which are, in the words of George Washington's Farewell Address, "essentially foreign to our concerns." Today, many American politicians and intellectuals are prone to making almost anything "our concern." Some harbor a seemingly limitless ambition, a desire even for uncontested American global hegemony.

We all hope that extreme views will not prevail in the counsels of government. Unfortunately, times of crisis often give people of extremes an influence in inverse proportion to the quality of their judgment. Worrying about and trying to head off arrogant, immoderate power-seeking is nothing new for members of this Society, but now the stakes are very high.

The gradual transformation of the American people and their leaders since the days of the writing of the Constitution and the sometimes drastic consequences of that transformation bring up the question why and how the American national character has changed. More and more people in our circles are coming to realize that the disturbing economic and political developments in the United States and the rest of the Western world are not autonomous forces but are particular manifestation of deeper, more pervasive changes that have already taken place in the moral and cultural life of the nation. Before we got the politics of unlimited ambition, we got the unleashing of the spoilt, grasping, partisan, aggressive self.

Some might say that it is too late now to try to reawaken in America's leaders and opinion-molders some of America's old self and thereby to affect the shaping of America's reaction to September 11. Perhaps so, but many of our members can make a difference even in the present, partly because our kind of thinking is often a part, if only a part, of the inner makeup of many of those who are making the all-important decisions. That part can be articulated and boosted. We must not underestimate the danger that intense emotion and aggressive pressures will overpower restraint and balance and sweep everything before it. We of the Society can help temper determination with wisdom and humility.

For the longer run, our mission must be to proceed with the work of renewal. The defenders of liberty have expended a great deal of effort and a great deal of money in recent decades. They have had at their disposal many a think tank, but they have not been very successful in reversing the trends toward bigger government and growing government commitments abroad. The grasping personality has found ever new outlets for the desire to control others. Defenders of liberty have avoided too much the root causes of these destructive trends. They have been too preoccupied with politics and economics narrowly construed. Political and economic developments, good or bad, are not self-generating. They are outflows of the moral and cultural life of a people, are in a sense after-effects. If you want to change political and economic trends, you must first change the moral and cultural orientation of a people.

We are told again and again that various economic, political and military measures will create a better society and a better world. What is much more seldom discussed is that, in the final analysis, well-being at home and peace abroad have moral and cultural preconditions. These issues are more subtle and difficult, but they are, in the long run, even more important. They are issues that the Philadelphia Society is well-suited for addressing and bringing into the forefront.

Let me try to summarize the unmet need about which I am speaking. I hope you will not be too offended if I quote from something I just published. The passage in question connects the need for new thinking with the present crisis and its larger context. I will quote the very first paragraph of a brand new book. Paradoxically it was published not in the United States but in China, in Chinese translation. The book is based on a lecture series I gave at Beijing University. In a case of grim coincidence, the book appeared in print just a few days before the Horror of September 11. I quote:

> Probably the greatest challenge facing mankind in the twenty-first century is the danger of conflict between peoples and cultures. There is an urgent need to explore in depth possibilities for minimizing tensions and to undertake efforts to reduce them. Horrendous consequences can result from superficiality, carelessness and naivete in defining the dangers and from delay in trying to lessen them. Yet the all too human desire to avoid painful self-scrutiny and reorientation of action makes human beings indulge a seemingly unlimited capacity for wishful thinking. Many in the West and elsewhere trust in scientific progress and general enlightenment to reduce the danger

of conflict, but we need only look to the century preceding this one, the most murderous and inhumane in the history of mankind, to recognize that the spread of science and allegedly sophisticated modern ideas do not reduce the self-absorption or belligerence of human beings. It only provides them with new means of asserting their will. Others in the West trust in political and economic schemes to alleviate tensions, "democracy" and "free markets" being the two most popular at the moment. These prescriptions for how to promote good relations between peoples give short shrift to a subject that may in fact be far more important, one that requires greater depth and subtlety of mind and that is also not fashionable: the moral and cultural preconditions of peace. Whatever the importance of other factors, attempts to avoid conflict among peoples and individuals are not likely to be successful without a certain quality of human will and imagination. That this subject is receiving so much less attention than proposals for introducing technology and manipulating political and economic institutions is a sign that our societies are not now well-equipped to deal with the most pressing problem of the new century.

I am suggesting to you that the moral and cultural condition of a society is what ultimately shapes the political and economic direction of that society, for good or ill. For that reason we must not shy away from dealing with these matters in depth. If we do not confront the moral and cultural prerequisites of liberty, of constitutional government, and of peace, we will never get to the heart of the matter, and we shall never effect the deeper change in American society that is necessary for a new birth of freedom.

The Framers at Philadelphia understood human nature pretty well. They knew that we have every reason to fear ourselves. Original sin always threatens to infect human behavior. The impulse of the moment needs to be checked, for all too often it gives vent to the least admirable human traits: egotism, ignorance, recklessness, arbitrariness, etc. Just as, in the individual sphere, virtue should temper the inclination of the person, so, in the public arena, the Constitution should check the popular passions of the moment and the weaknesses of political leaders. Though constitutional checks-and-balances may restrain the worst excesses of partisan self-indulgence even in bad times, those checks cannot operate as intended without leaders and people of character. Where are such people to come from? The Framers of the Constitution thought they would be bred by the moral and cultural traditions that had nourished them. People like themselves would continue to sustain the Constitution and American liberty.

We all know that the traditions in which the Framers trusted have been terribly weakened. The checks on the lower potentialities of human nature have weakened correspondingly. The effects are everywhere to be seen, and we can only hope that those now making decisions for the American people and, indeed, for the rest of the world have in them still some of that older American personality.

In the international arena a civilized leader ultimately seeks peace. But genuine peace and mutual respect are not possible without there being leaders who are able to rise above narrow partisanship and the perspectives of the moment. Peace assumes peaceful individuals. It is forever threatened by individuals of voracious appetites, perpetually pushing their own advantage. In the end, the prerequisites of peace in the international arena are the same as the prerequisites of social harmony at home. Both require leaders who are peaceful at the center, even when they are forced to take drastic action.

The spirit of American liberty and constitutionalism is moderation rooted in humility regarding human nature. A purpose of the Constitution written in 1787 was to check ruthless ambition and give America's better self a chance to prevail. The Philadelphia Society can best serve the cause of liberty today by helping to revive and renew the moral and cultural heritage that made liberty and constitutional government possible in the first place.

AMERICANS NOW AND THEN

This is a speech given at the fortieth anniversary gala of the Philadelphia Society in Chicago, Illinois, on May 2, 2004. I had served as the Society's president in 2001–2002. I wanted to draw attention to the contrast between the Americans who had taken charge of US foreign policy after 9/11 and the Americans of old who had extricated the American colonies from the British empire. The old Americans had set up a Constitution that strictly limited power, including that of the president. Now a very different personality type had taken charge, and imperial ambitions, justified by ideology, were breaking through traditional inner and outer checks on power.

Quite often I have lunch at a McDonald's in one of the most affluent and pretentious suburbs in America just outside of Washington, DC. The residents are ambivalent about having a McDonald's in their community—it undermines their self-image—so the restaurant is tucked away inside a little mall and almost impossible for outsiders to find.

I like to arrive just after 10:30. I am up very early, and before 11:00 my McDonald's is still quiet. I eat and read in peace. Later, mothers drive up in their luxury SUVs with their preschool children and, if schools are closed, older children too. Some highschoolers show up. On Saturdays many fathers do McDonald's duty and older children come as well. My French café is transformed into bedlam. Near the playpen especially the noise rises dramatically. I have learnt when late to shut out the din, but sometimes I watch the scene in fascination. At the counter toddlers in strollers scream when parents do not give them french fries fast enough. Older children crawl on chairs and tables or rush about shouting and shoving while waiting for mom or dad to bring the food. Mothers and fathers scurry around, anxiously solicitous of their princes and princesses. They comfort the crying and apologize to little Ashley and Eliot for having taken so long. By now I know well the difference between the crying of a child in distress and the importunate crying of a child who won't wait or take no for an answer. At the playpen—the "hellhole"—it is obvious that playing without throwing yourself about and making lots of noise would not be real playing. Sometimes the playpen emits such piercing screams that the Asian-American children look at their parents in startled surprise. Deference to grown-ups seems unknown. I used to take offense, but the children have only taken their cue from their parents, who took their cue from *their* parents. The adults, for their part, talk in loud, penetrating voices, some on cell phones, as if no other conversations mattered. The scene exudes self-absorption and lack of self-discipline.

Yes, this picture has *everything* to do with US foreign policy. This is the emerging American ruling class, which is made up increasingly of persons used to having the world cater to them. If others challenge their will, they throw a temper tantrum. Call this the imperialistic personality—if "spoilt brat" sounds too crude.

But, surely, this rising elite has wonderful strengths. Are not its adults highly educated—about history, philosophy, geography, and world affairs—and masters of several languages? Do they not travel widely and have a keen understanding of other countries and regions of the world? Are they not sophisticated cosmopolitans suited to running an empire?

Pardon the sarcasm. I am well aware that a different type of American still exists. That American aspires to character traits virtually the opposite of those on display at my McDonald's. Americans used to admire self-restraint, modesty, humility, and good manners. They were acutely aware of original sin. They feared the self-indulgent ego, in themselves and others. Americans of an earlier era stressed the need to check the darker potentialities of human nature, the unleashing of which could wreak havoc on the individual and society. They hoped that in personal life moral character would restrain the desire for self-aggrandizement, just as in national political life the checks and balances of the US Constitution would contain the all-too-human desire for power. Personal self-control and constitutionalism were but different aspects of the effort to subdue the voracious ego. Human beings could not be trusted with unlimited power.

The old Americans were not so foolish as to try to extinguish the will to power. Nothing good could be accomplished without power in some form. But they recognized the great danger of the will to power being diverted from its legitimate ends and breaking free of checks.

The Framers assumed that for the Constitution to work, its institutions had to be manned by individuals who embodied its spirit. These individuals had to be predisposed to virtues like self-restraint, respect for law, and a willingness to compromise. They had to have what I call a constitutional personality. The spirit of the written Constitution stemmed from America's *unwritten* constitution, that is, the religious, moral, and cultural life that had inclined Americans to constitutionalism in the first place. The Constitution could not survive without character traits that the Framers hoped would be widespread. All know Benjamin Franklin's answer to the woman who asked what the Constitutional Convention had produced: "A republic, if you can keep it." The primary reason why today the US Constitution is a mere shadow of its former self is that it cannot be sustained without the constitutional personality.

The new imperialistic ego is shrugging free of the old American self and corresponding constitutional restraints. The desire for self-aggrandizement has transformed limited, decentralized American government into a national Superstate, which has given the will to power a scope far beyond the worst fears of the anti-Federalists. The Tenth Amendment, that ironclad guarantee against improper expansion of central power, is a dead letter, like so much else in the Constitution. Decision-makers in Washington reach into virtually every aspect of American life. But not even power on this scale can still a desire that is insatiable. Today it contemplates dominating the entire world.

Needless to say, the will to dominate does not present itself as such to the world. It wraps itself in phrases of benevolence and selflessness. There is always another reason for government to do good. The greater the caring, the greater the need to place power in the hands of those who care. It is, of course, sheer coincidence that this benevolence invariably empowers the benevolent. So well does the will to dominate dress itself up that it almost deceives the power-seekers themselves.

The ideas of the French Jacobins provided a sweeping justification for exercising unlimited power. As followers of Rousseau, the Jacobins were not content with *reforming* historically evolved ways of life. "Freedom, equality and brotherhood" required the radical remaking of society. Because of the scope and glory of the task, the Jacobins had to gather all power unto themselves and deal ruthlessly with opposition. Good stood against evil, all good on one side—their side. The Jacobins called themselves "the virtuous." In the twentieth century, their communist descendants offered an even more blanket justification for wielding unlimited power.

Although the classical and Christian view of human nature has eroded, big government still has a bad name in America. Challenging the Constitution outright remains risky. Americans attracted to the Jacobin spirit have therefore sought instead to redefine American principles so as to make them more serviceable to the will to power. They have propounded a new myth—the myth of America the Virtuous—according to which America is a unique and noble country called to remake the world in its own image. The myth provides another sweeping justification for dominating others.

An effort has been long underway to transfer American patriotism to a redefined, Jacobin-style America, seen as representing a radical break with the Western tradition. According to Harry Jaffa, "The American Revolution represented the most radical break with tradition . . . that the world had seen." "To celebrate the American Founding is . . . to celebrate revolution." In Jaffa's view, the American revolution was milder perhaps than the "subsequent revolutions in France, Russia, China, Cuba, or elsewhere," but it is "the most radical attempt to establish a regime of liberty that the world has yet seen." America thus reinvented is founded on ahistorical, allegedly universal principles summed up in such words as "freedom," "equality," and "democracy." These principles, the new Jacobins assert, are not just for Americans; they are, as Allan Bloom insisted, "everywhere applicable"—a theme echoed today by George W Bush.

The French Jacobins appointed France as the Savior Nation. The new Jacobins have appointed America. Its great, benevolent cause is to rid the world of evil. This cause gives the appetite for power the moral cover it likes to have. One kind of universalist ideology, communism, has been replaced by the ideology of American empire, and the stage is set for another cycle of crusading. With neo-Jacobins shaping US foreign policy, whether as Democrats or Republicans, America and the world can expect an era of chronic conflict.

Could any goal be more appealing to the will to power than ending evil? The task is not only enormous but endless. No conservative would need to be told that evil cannot be "ended"; Rousseau's notion of the fundamental goodness of man and his vision of society transformed are pernicious figments of a childish imagination. Evil can be tamed to some extent, as the Framers knew, but even Sunday schoolers used to understand that it cannot be ended. You wonder why, if America is called to end moral evil, it should not, while at it, also do away with poverty and illness.

Do the new Jacobins ever reflect on the remarkable coincidence that they should be alive at the precise moment in human history when the one valid political model was finally discovered and that, furthermore, they should happen to live in just the country that embodies that model and is called to bestow it on the rest of the world? But such questions do not bother ideologues who are arguing toward a preconceived conclusion: that they should preside over armed American world hegemony—for humanity's sake, of course.

The word "empire" does not yet have the right ring in American ears, so the new Jacobins try not to appear too grasping. But even when feigning modesty the will to dominate has difficulty keeping up appearances—as when Ben Wattenberg said, no, no, no, we Americans do not want to " *conquer* the world." We only wish to ensure that "the world is hospitable to our values."

The arguments for bold American assertiveness are familiar: We live in a dangerous world full of odious political regimes. Terrorism is a serious threat to America and its allies. America must, as the world's only superpower, play a leading role in the world.

But why keep repeating the obvious? Yes, the world is dangerous; it always was, more or less. Like other countries, America must be prepared to defend itself and its legitimate interests—of course—and as a superpower she will indeed have to carry a heavier burden than other countries. It does not follow that America must impose its will on the rest of the world.

But 9/11 changed everything, the neo-Jacobins cry. Well, not quite everything. The human condition has not changed. Terrible events do not cancel the need for those personal qualities and social and political structures without which the will to power becomes arbitrary and tyrannical. Unfortunately, 9/11 gave the imperialistic personality another pretext for throwing off restraint.

American unilateralism represents a reversal of the old spirit of constitutionalism and checks-and-balances. Just as, domestically, particular interests need to accommodate other interests, so, internationally, states need to check and balance each other. The notion that America knows better than all other nations and has a right to dictate terms to them betrays a monumental conceit. It also guarantees that other nations will see a need to arm themselves just to have some protection against American bullying. Already the Muslim world is seething with hostility. China, which has long found Western hegemony intolerable and is already strongly prone to nationalism, can be expected to respond to American assertiveness by greatly expanding its military power. If present trends continue, the time should soon be ripe—in 50 years perhaps?—for a horrendous Sino-American confrontation.

For Christians, the cardinal sin is pride. Before them, the Greeks warned similarly of the great dangers of conceit and arrogance. *Hubris*, they said, violates the order of the cosmos and inflicts great suffering on human beings. It invites *Nemesis*. On the Apollonian temple at Delphi two inscriptions summed up the proper attitude to life. One was "Everything in moderation," the other "Know Thyself." To know yourself meant most importantly to recognize that you are not one of the gods but a mere mortal. As for the old Hebrews, in Proverbs (16:18) we read: "Pride goeth before destruction, and a haughty spirit before a fall."

To the new Jacobins, such calls for humility have the quaint sound of something long outdated. Why should those who know how humanity should live question their own ideas or right to dominate? The world needs "moral clarity," not obfuscation. Many of those who shape the destiny of America and the world today are *just* such "terrible simplifiers" with absurdly swollen egos.

How very different the personality that defined the old America and conceived the Constitution! In 1789, George Washington proclaimed a day of thanksgiving for all the good bestowed by Almighty God on the American people. He asked his fellow Americans to unite "in most humbly offering our prayers and supplications to the Great Lord and Ruler of nations and beseech Him to pardon our national and other transgressions." This is the voice of the America that is passing. Today, increasingly, the imperialistic personality of Ashley and Eliot is being unleashed upon the world.

WHERE ARE WE GOING?

(This is a brief speech given at the annual meeting of the Philadelphia Society in 2006.) A few former presidents of the Society, including me, served on a panel addressing the question, "Where in the World Are We Going?" I had for many years been warning of what I called the new Jacobinism, which coincided largely with so-called neoconservatism. At the time of this speech neoconservatives were known to have played a key role in getting the United States to go to war against Iraq. It troubled me that a militant radical ideology, hubristic self-importance, and general imprudence could still be influential in supposedly conservative circles. My long-standing impatience with the lack of philosophical discernment within the conservative movement added to my exasperation. The speakers on the panel were allotted little time each. To be able to cover a range of issues, I made a short list, in bullet points almost, of how conservatism contrasts with Jacobinism, whether old or new.

Within the so-called American conservative movement, intellectual and political confusion are today rampant. Hence the following attempt to sort out what is what.

First of all, a conservative is acutely aware of the flawed nature of man. The capacity of human reason is limited. Our existence is ultimately a great mystery. Conservatives recognize that for these reasons we need the best of the human heritage to help guide us.

The Jacobin suffers from no such humility. Who needs history when there are universal principles that are also self-evident? It's all so clear. Traditions are but historical accidents, props for old elites that should be replaced by the enlightened and virtuous, people like him. Leo Strauss and his disciples have taught us to disdain "the ancestral" and heed only principles of reason.

Conservatives and Jacobins differ profoundly on what ultimately commands our loyalty. Conservatives stand in awe of a higher power. The ancient Greeks spoke of it as the good, the true and the beautiful. Others refer to it as the will of God. This higher reality is, in any case, not some ideological blueprint. To feel obligated to look for and to do the right thing is not the same as to know just what it is in particular circumstances. The complexity and unpredictability of life disincline the conservatives to sweeping, categorical assertions.

The Jacobin is a true believer. He has access to universal principles, you see, and they demand "moral clarity." You are either for his principles, which makes you virtuous, or you are against them, which makes you evil. It's all so clear.

To have unquestioning faith in one's own moral superiority is for Christians the cardinal sin. Only a profoundly conceited person could think that for another to oppose him is by definition morally perverse.

But the Jacobin assumes a right to have his way. Behind his moralism hides a desire to dominate. The hesitation or trepidation that may trouble men of conscience do not deter him. The will to power silences all doubt.

For the conservative, the universal imperative that binds human beings does not announce its purpose in simple, declaratory statements. How, then, does one discern its demands? Sometimes only with difficulty.

Only through effort can the good or true or beautiful be discovered, and they must be realized differently in different historical circumstances. The same universal values have diverse manifestations. Some of the concrete instantiations of universality take us by surprise.

Because there is no simple roadmap to good, human beings need freedom and imagination to find it. Universality has nothing to do with uniformity.

For the Jacobins, ahistorical, ideological precepts define universality, and these demand conformity. Comply with them, or else.

The conservative is attracted to both universality and diversity because the two do, in a sense, need each other. He does not cherish diversity for its own sake, for much of the diversity in the world offends all higher values, but diversity of another type is how universality comes alive in the infinite variety of individuals and circumstances.

Because universality manifests itself variously, the conservative is no narrow-minded nationalist. He is a cosmopolitan. This does not mean that he is a free floater, at home everywhere and nowhere. That describes the Jacobin ideologue.

The conservative is a patriot, deeply rooted in the best of his own heritage. It is because he is so attached to what is most admirable in his own culture that he can understand and appreciate corresponding achievements in other cultures. He is able to find in different places variations on a common human theme. The culturally distinctive contributions of other peoples deepen and enrich his awareness of goodness, truth and beauty.

The Jacobin is not interested in diversity, only in imposing his blueprint. What history happens to have thrown up is just an obstacle to what ought to be. Only what is "simply right" deserves respect. It's all so obvious.

Conservatives see in Jacobin principles a hair-raising obliviousness of life's complexity. To implement such principles may devastate a society. A society may be wholly unsuited or unprepared for changes demanded of it. So what, say America's neo-Jacobins. We need moral clarity. What was there before does not matter. "Democracy" must take its place. One model fits all. To ensure a democratic world, America must establish armed and uncontested world supremacy.

The will to power is here bursting at the seams. What argument could be better for placing enormous power in the hands of the neo-Jacobins than a grandiose scheme for remaking the world? At lunch yesterday we got to hear [from Max Boot] the pure, undiluted neo-Jacobin message.

All Jacobins warn of the Enemy with a capital "E." The Enemy is the embodiment of evil, a force with which no compromise is possible. For the American neo-Jacobins the Enemy is Terrorism with a capital "T." Though the only superpower, America must be in a permanent state of emergency, be armed to the teeth and relentlessly pursue the Enemy.

One current assumption about conservatives is nothing less than weird: that they are hawks, always looking for prey and always bullying. Conservatives are in reality normally doves, looking for ways to settle conflicts peacefully. They view war differently from neo-Jacobin desk-warriors. The suffering and destruction of war are frightful realities involving actual human beings. War is the very last resort.

Conservatives harbor no illusions about the international arena. Bad people behave badly. So conservatives want to be prepared to handle threats to their own society and civilization or to international peace. But their normal way of interacting with other peoples is to try to defuse conflict and to pursue a common human ground. This is the cosmopolitan way.

In domestic affairs, American conservatives have always feared unlimited power, partly because of their belief in original sin. Fallen creatures must be restrained by law. Government must be limited and decentralized, hence the separation of powers and federalism.

The spirit of constitutionalism forms the core of the American political tradition. Unchecked power is an invitation to tyranny. The framers even wanted the US Congress, which was to be the preeminent body of the national government, to have divided powers. Needless to say they disdained democracy.

Jacobins see no need for restraints on virtuous power. Today American neo-Jacobins are promoting presidential ascendancy and great leeway for the executive. Old restraints and liberties must yield to the needs of the virtuous national security state.

Neo-Jacobins undermine American constitutionalism by radically redefining its meaning. They have little loyalty toward the culturally distinctive, historically evolved America. This country, neo-Jacobins assert, represents a sharp break with the past. They love to speak of the "Founding" because that term suggests that America does not have historical origins but emerged afresh from enlightened minds. Harry Jaffa and others insist that to celebrate America is to celebrate radical innovation and revolution.

Conservatives cherish local autonomy and strong communities. As far as possible people should be able to shape their own lives, partly because the good life has to be lived differently in different circumstances. Jacobins resist anything that might interfere with ideological homogeneity. Individual and local autonomy could, they think, so easily get out of hand.

It should be obvious that, due in large part to barely masked neo-Jacobinism, American conservatism has in the last few decades been turned virtually inside out. In 1952 many conservatives regarded Dwight D. Eisenhower as too "liberal" because he was not willing to dismantle the New Deal. He would only prune it. Today, in all but rhetoric, people calling themselves conservatives accept a vastly larger and more intrusive central government. Under the current allegedly conservative president [George W. Bush] alone the federal government has expanded [as of 2006] by 25%. Yet representatives of the so-called conservative movement proceed as if nothing had happened and absurdly celebrate "triumphs of conservatism."

Only a major intellectual or moral flaw in American conservatism could have made so many susceptible to the neo-Jacobin bug. Many who caught it were myopically preoccupied with practical politics and Republican partisanship. They lacked historical perspective and philosophical discernment. Others dimly recognized what was happening but went along to reap financial rewards and advance careers. They concealed almost from themselves that they had become hired guns advocating the positions expected of them. Both groups made alliances that will prove compromising. Historians will wonder how so many could have been so easily swayed and manipulated.

Today the utopianism, recklessness, cynicism and sheer incompetence of the neo-Jacobins are becoming obvious. Many of their fellow-travelers are trying to save what remains of their reputations by jumping ship. Intellectually challenged supernationalists just raise their voices and call critics unpatriotic. As for the neo-Jacobins themselves, they are blameless. It is those who implemented their policies who should be blamed. They didn't do it right.

The neo-Jacobin virus should have been flushed out long ago.

THE PRESIDENCY UNCHAINED

("The Presidency Unchained," *Spectator USA*, July 17, 2019.) President Donald Trump announced a foreign policy that would put "America First" and end nation-building and interventionism. For this reason, neoconservatives were among the first to oppose strongly his presidential candidacy. Yet, in office, Trump appointed to his foreign policy and national security team persons who were known to oppose his preferences. In doing so he not only undermined his own stated goals but put himself in conflict with the Constitution.

When it comes to war, does the president have too much authority?

The Framers of the US Constitution had a rather dark view of human nature and went to great lengths to restrain, divide, and decentralize power. In particular, they believed that it was in the nature of executive power to be unduly prone to war. For this reason, they very deliberately placed the power to take the country to war in the Congress. At the Constitutional Convention James Wilson argued, "This system will not hurry us into war; it is calculated to guard against it."

Yet the presidency has over the years gathered more and more of the war powers unto itself, and at present intense political conflict is tearing at the fabric of the Constitution. As the momentous possibility of conflict with Iran is being considered you have to wonder whether the old checks and balances of the Constitution still have any efficacy.

Granted that the Executive's expanded role in foreign policy violates the *text* of the Constitution, could it be argued that the presidency, while adapting to changed historical circumstances, remains faithful to the *spirit* of the Constitution? The present moment affords an opportunity to test this proposition. The reason is that American conservatives have long viewed themselves as strong defenders of the Constitution and that putative conservatives are now in charge of US foreign policy. A comparison between them and the Framers will help assess the state of American constitutionalism.

The Framers' effort to tame power was not merely a matter of making ingenious institutional-procedural arrangements. Their notion of what structures would increase the likelihood of good government grew out of a view of human nature. They believed that humans have a potential for nobility and wisdom but that these are forever threatened by traits like ruthlessness, greed, ignorance, and, above all, an excessive desire for power. The Constitution was intended to bias decision-making in favor of man's better angels.

The institutional checks would ultimately fail without the restraint, integrity, and high-mindedness that could come only from within the political actors: from moral character, circumspection, knowledge, respect for the truth, modesty, and from a recognition that in politics no side has a monopoly on right. People of statesmanlike qualities concerned about the common good had to check partisan demagogues and bullies.

The Constitution thus had to be made efficacious by people capable of acting in its spirit. They would have to be temperamentally predisposed to self-control and long views—exhibit what we may call the constitutional personality. Without it, even the best-designed procedural checks would become hollow.

The Constitution assumes that decisions are best made in an atmosphere of calm deliberation. Popular representatives of broad views and critical detachment from the passions of the moment should set the tone. The American constitutional tradition disdains making important decisions when emotions run hot. It favors the more slowly emerging "deliberate sense" of the people. The task of popular representatives is, as Madison wrote in Federalist 10, to "refine and enlarge the public views." The Constitution puts a premium on defusing conflict, deliberating, compromising, and respecting the minority.

To contemplate the personality traits that the Framers hoped would animate the Constitution is to become aware how different they are from traits prominent among those now in charge of US foreign policy. In the latter group, you find a strong preference for assertive, hawkish, unilateral application of superior power. The preferred method of dealing with recalcitrant states is confrontation, saber-rattling, and other harsh, unrelenting pressure—not negotiation, compromise, and openness to the possibly legitimate interests of opponents, as if only the US had such interests.

Secretary of State Mike Pompeo and others on President Trump's foreign policy team have revived the "neoconservative" ideas that helped get the US into war with Iraq. We are again told that the US is morally and politically unique, based on universally applicable principles that make America the obvious and indispensable leader of the forces of freedom. Good stands against evil in the world. On July 8, in a speech to a convention of Christians United for Israel, Pompeo said that America "is given to defend the spiritual values—the moral code—against the vast forces of evil that seek to destroy them."

In a speech in June, at the Claremont Institute in California, Pompeo had reminded us that America is "exceptional . . . a place and history apart from normal human experience." By virtue of its noble global mission, America is entitled to dictate terms to a rogue power like Iran and confront countries like China and Russia that are "intent on eroding American power." Should this reasoning appear conceited and a recipe for conflict, understand that, according to Pompeo, "conflict is the normative experience for nations."

President Trump recently "joked" that if his national security adviser John Bolton had had his way "we'd be in four wars by now."

In a speech at the recent West Point graduation ceremony, Vice President Mike Pence made the military implications of the Pompeo-Bolton view of America's role in the world explicit. He told the cadets to put their "armor" on for conflict so that "*when*—not if—that day comes, you'll be able to stand your ground." They had to be ready to counter an "aggressive" country like Russia that is trying to "redraw international boundaries by force." Not to worry, Pence said, "you will fight and you will win."

In the Congress, the same confrontational attitude is represented by reputed conservatives like the always bellicose Sen. Lindsay Graham and his colleague Tom Cotton, who is challenging Graham for the role of uberhawk. The latter recently argued that the president or even "battalion commanders" should be able to decide whether to attack Iran.

These allegedly conservative sentiments indicate that at least when it comes to foreign policy and war the president should not be subjected to the kind of checks that, according to the Framers, needed to be placed on all power. Why, indeed, should a force for good in the world be restrained?

It should be evident that if devotion to the Constitution is a prominent feature of American conservatism, the appetite for unrestricted executive power in foreign policy represents something very different. Conservatism has somehow been turned on its head. Self-importance rather than modesty, confronting opponents rather than defusing conflict, dictating terms rather than compromising—these contrast sharply with the spirit of American constitutionalism. They also do not accord with Donald Trump's promises during his election campaign.

The constitutional personality is in short supply in today's America. Among those now setting the tone in foreign-policy it is often positively scorned.

A GREATER, MORE SUBTLE POWER

("Not By Politics Alone," *The American Conservative*, January 15, 2007.) A preoccupation with politics and a failure to understand the deep influence of "the culture" have given American movement conservatism a truncated notion of power and a correspondingly weak strategy for changing society's direction.

That leading politicians wield great power nobody will deny. What is not so well understood is how limited that power is. Over time especially, politicians are superseded by forces largely beyond their control. They must yield to those who mold the fundamental ideas and sensibilities of a people, those who affect their hopes and fears, direct their attention, and select and define the issues of the day.

Society's long-term evolution is profoundly affected by those who shape the mind and imagination of a people. They set the tone in the arts, the entertainment industry, the publishing houses, the electronic media, the press, and academia. When these are pulling in the same direction, not even a landslide political victor can overcome them. For real and lasting change to be possible, first the culture has to change.

In the following discussion, American and Western civilization will be described, for brevity's sake, as torn between traditionalists—those who stress humanity's dependence on the achievements of previous generations—and radicals—those who turn their backs on history and want to realize visions bearing no resemblance to actual human experience. That this is a simplified picture of our predicament hardly needs saying. Human beings do not fall into neat categories. Also, traditionalists, for example, could not hope to preserve the ancient heritage that they claim to cherish without restating and developing it in new circumstances. Indeed, at a time of profound dislocation, attempts to preserve and protect traditional insights and patterns of life may, to those who embrace dominant beliefs and practices, look like radical departures.

The power that may be ultimately decisive in setting society's direction is found in what will strike many as an unlikely place, in the arts and humanities broadly understood: in the arts—from dramatists, novelists, and movie-makers to composers and painters—and in academic disciplines—from philosophy, history, and English to politics and psychology. In these fields, trendsetters have long been chipping away at the moral and spiritual core of what can loosely be called traditional Western civilization. Hence the basic orientation of our society. Putatively conservative political victories here and there have made little difference to the fundamental trends of Western society.

To take up first the role of intellectuals, consider the late 1960s and early '70s when the New Left and the counterculture attacked not only the military-industrial complex but all traditional civilization. This rebellion could trace its roots at least as far back as Rousseau. These were the radical children of indulgent liberal parents who had already done their part to undermine traditional beliefs by rejecting moral universality and making abstract, "scientistic" rationality the arbiter of truth. The new campus radicalism soon spread into the larger society, partly through sympathetic coverage in the media.

Because the turbulence on the campuses and elsewhere subsided, many wanted to believe that radicalism was petering out. The opposite was true. The campus radicals and their less radical-looking sympathizers did not disappear. Many of them found permanent, congenial homes in the colleges and universities. They stayed—as faculty. Since their days on the ramparts they have, whether as unreconstructed or somewhat chastened radicals, taught millions of students. They or their students are now senior tenured professors, department chairmen, deans, provosts, and presidents. They sit on curriculum and personnel committees. They select new faculty. They influence the criteria for promotion and tenure. They pass judgment on which books will be published or rejected by university presses, which articles will be published or rejected by academic journals. They have profoundly affected standards of scholarship and truth and even define intelligence. By designing SAT, LSAT, GRE, and other tests, they bias admissions.

People do not inquire deeply into what their children or grandchildren will be taught in college. They are more concerned about the relative prestige of a school. And that ranking, too, is determined by the same trendsetters.

Perhaps the most telling sign of the state of academia is that even those most widely reputed to be the defenders of traditional beliefs are also helping to subvert them. The Straussians, for instance, have long sought to persuade unsuspecting traditionalists that philosophy is incompatible with convention and "the ancestral." To celebrate the American founding, says Harry Jaffa, is to "celebrate revolution." America, he asserts, is the "greatest attempt at innovation that human history had recorded."

The professoriate teach all future professors but also all future high-school, secondary, and elementary schoolteachers. Those entering academia are already acclimated because their high-school teachers tend to mimic the professoriate who taught them. In this way alone, professors in the humanities reach deeply into the popular consciousness. The biases of schoolteachers are all the more effectively inculcated because children are exposed to them outside of school as well. Television programs, movies, and music confirm and embellish the ideological and emotional slant that students absorb during the school day.

Of the old campus radicals who did not stay in academia, a large number gravitated toward communications and entertainment. As TV producers, directors, and editors, they decide what is news and how selected stories should be covered. As scriptwriters, they decide what behaviors to admire and detest, what to take seriously and what to dismiss, what to laugh and not to laugh at. As editors at publishing houses, they decide what subjects are of interest and which books deserve to see print. As critics, they decree what is art and what is not. As songwriters, they set society's musical beat.

Not all people in the communications, entertainment, and knowledge industries are drawn from the old campus radicalism, but each year for decades whole armies of new graduates, educated by a largely radical professoriate, have invaded these institutions and society in general. The business world and the professions are no exceptions.

Over time, the professoriate has evolved ideas even more radical than those of the 1960s and '70s. Yet many contend that in the 1980s conservative values finally triumphed in America when Ronald Reagan won two presidential elections in landslides. Now the ascendant neoconservatives tell Americans that their society is in good shape and getting better. They have assigned to the United States the ambitious task of bestowing its enlightened values on the entire world, starting with the Middle East.

To refute the triumph-of-conservatism thesis does not even require going outside of practical politics and economics. During this era of alleged triumph, the federal government expanded by leaps and bounds, while state and local autonomy contracted. The 10th Amendment is a dead letter. Laws that extend government's control over society continue to pour forth from Washington, and Americans are being asked to become the pliant wards of a national-security superstate. Traditional constitutional restraints are barely operating.

In the six years of the current administration alone, the national debt has doubled and the federal budget has grown by 25 percent.

The deficits in the federal budget and in the country's balance of payments are enormous.

And these are merely the political and economic symptoms of larger moral-spiritual, intellectual, and cultural developments. Have those who keep talking about triumph of conservatism no sense of the decline of education at every level, of private and public morality, of family, and of churches? In the movies, on television, in the press, in music, on videos, in novels, and elsewhere, attitudes and behaviors are portrayed as normal or admirable that would have dismayed virtually everyone just a generation or two ago. The institutions of America's national culture tolerate or welcome almost any denigration of traditional civilization. They teach those who resist to make their peace with inevitable change. The indefensible can always be defended with reference to freedom of expression or tolerance. Those who resent the radical bullying are afraid to speak out because they know the awesome power of the ruling forces to ridicule, intimidate, and retaliate.

Not even the most skillful politicians could reverse this sustained assault on what remains of traditional Western society, because politicians can only marginally change the imaginative and intellectual momentum that fostered the radicalism in the first place. Over time, Washington's power is dwarfed by the power of the elites in the arts, communications, entertainment, and publishing—the industry revolving around the Hollywood–New York axis—and the academic circles with which these elites are closely intertwined—what may be called the Boston-Berkeley axis.

Deep down, each society lives by a predominant vision of human existence: what life is like and what it should be. All of us have deeply rooted intuitions and ideas that together constitute our basic outlook on reality, our notion of its dangers and opportunities. We approach the world from within a particular sensibility that gives existence its pace and coloration. In our most private recesses, we form hopes for what life might one day become for us. We live on and for such more or less realistic visions. Though this inner self varies with the circumstances and personalities of individuals, societies evolve a predominant state of mind and imagination. Individuals are connected by an emotional and intellectual substratum that gives them similar aspirations. Whatever this predominant pattern of sensibility and belief, it sets the direction of social life in general and of public debate and practical politics in particular. Politicians who violate this mindset risk their political lives.

Enormous power lies with those who shape the mind and the imagination and make others see life through their eyes. Deep in our personalities are the marks left by the imaginative and intellectual masterminds who create the tenor of an age.

Granted, most people are not exposed to high culture and don't even want to be. But highbrow culture eventually reaches them in diluted, filtered-down, lowbrow form. The sensibility of seminal works of art and thought are transmitted into the general consciousness through popular movies and novels, soap operas, and the imagery of advertising.

When artists really capture our imagination, they make us see the world as they do. What they present as contemptible we, too, begin to despise. What they convey as admirable and intriguing we want to emulate. D. H. Lawrence wrote, "we live by what we thrill to." Those who enter deeply into our imaginations make us "thrill" to certain goals, make us want to realize them. They help shape our innermost values and our perception of reality.

Contemporary Western society exhibits deep tensions between what remains of traditional civilization and the spreading counter-culture, which by now has its own traditions. These are tensions not just among people but within particular persons who harbor incompatible dreams and have neurotically divided minds and imaginations. In a crunch, the anti-traditional elites can play upon and mobilize radical prejudices that have gained a foothold within many a self-described conservative.

Conservative intellectuals and activists often have an open or thinly veiled contempt for the arts and humanities. The disdain is only partly due to their thinking that this is where the Left hangs out. Many professed conservatives denigrate the humanities primarily because they believe that they have little practical importance, have little to do with "the real world." To turn society right, you need to win more elections. They have difficulty understanding why purported political victories are repeatedly nullified, though the values and beliefs of the American people continue to slide in a radical direction.

The greater the conservative neglect of the arts and humanities, the greater the grip of the anti-traditional forces. Conservatives have excused their inattention by telling themselves that the radical dominance of the humanities does not really matter in the long run. Who cares about flaky professors, writers, composers, poets, and artists? What matters is politics and economics. These "realists" do not understand that increasingly politicians and businessmen, as well as the general population, resonate with the sentiments of these "flakes." Inattention to and disinterest in the humanities reveal a failure to understand what really makes human beings tick. They are themselves signs of precipitous cultural decline.

Traditional civilization is threatened with extinction because pleasing but destructive illusions have become part of the way in which most people view the world and their own lives. The hold on society of those who created and fed these illusions cannot be broken mainly through practical politics.

What is most needed is a reorientation of mind and imagination. The great illusions of our age must be exposed for what they are so that they will start to lose their appeal. This can be done only through art and thought of a different quality.

While the so-called Right worried about so-called practical matters, the Left took control of activities that could help refashion society's imagination. The Left understood the power of directing the mind. Those who wished to dismantle traditional civilization thought and acted strategically and reaped extraordinary advantages. Having managed to dominate the artistic and intellectual life of Western society, they have had little difficulty keeping supposedly conservative political forces on the defensive, even when the latter ostensibly controlled the government. The countercultural forces have kept the Western world at war with itself.

Many conservatives seem to believe that artists and intellectuals are naturally and almost inevitably on the Left. If that were so, all efforts to renew traditional civilization would be condemned to failure. But there is nothing inevitable about the radical dominance of the mind and the imagination; these trends since the Enlightenment are in some respects a historical aberration. The radical mindset was created over many years by committed people. People of equal commitment and creativity could dismantle it over many years by unmasking and replacing it with a deeper, more realistic view of life. Radicalism advanced first and foremost by means of a march through the culture. A renewal of American and Western traditions, if one is still possible, could be effected only by another march through the culture. Such a development would require a surge of inspiration springing not from the political and economic periphery but from the moral-spiritual depths.

CANCEL CULTURE AND WOKE: NOT UNEXPECTED

("Conservatives Missed the Boat on the Power of the Culture," *Washington Examiner*, August 14, 2020.) During the summer of 2020, many American cities saw protracted civil unrest marked by confrontation with police, violence, vandalism, plunder, burnings, defilement or destruction of statues and public buildings, and even killing. For people alert to developments in the last half-century in the American mind and imagination—in "the culture"—these events and the rhetoric associated with them were not unanticipated, but were drastic manifestations of trends long discernible in the universities, the arts, and entertainment.

Who has the power to shape the future? American conservatives think they know. They have always been single-mindedly focused on politics. Nothing is more important than to elect presidents and members of Congress. That's where the real power lies.

William F. Buckley's *National Review* was an intellectual magazine, but its main concern was to capture the presidency. People in the *National Review* circle played a central role in getting Barry Goldwater nominated as the Republican presidential candidate in 1964. What became known as the conservative "movement" started out as the Goldwater movement.

When Ronald Reagan won the White House, the movement congratulated itself on having finally achieved its objective. Conservatism had "triumphed."

But the "triumph" was more imaginary than real. General developments within America's national culture (within academia, the arts, and entertainment) were pointing in a much different direction. These developments would have a greater impact in the long run than the Reagan presidency.

Preoccupied as they were with political victories and strategies, movement conservatives were not very attentive to how the deeper beliefs and sentiments of people were evolving in the United States. Yet political power is circumscribed by the culture of voters and what it will make them accept or reject.

People live according to deep-seated hopes and fears, which tend to reflect the moral, intellectual, and aesthetic sensibilities that predominate in their society. They will vote for politicians who seem to support their dreams and vote against others who rouse their anxieties—which raises the question of what gives human beings their notion of which is which?

There is no simple answer, but this much should be evident: If there are people who can strongly influence the basic worldview of others, they have the power to shape society's future. It should be a central task for students of society and politics to know who they are and what views they advocate and to offer criticisms of and alternatives to dubious ideas. But movement conservatives were largely uninterested in what informs the deeper beliefs of human beings. Their eyes were firmly on the need to win political victories.

The outlook and aspirations of human beings are affected from childhood onward by influences that color their views and tastes: the example and guidance of parents, children's tales, music, novels, movies, teachers, and preachers. We all have had experiences that we know to have affected our view of life permanently. In persons of refined sensibilities, great works of art may permanently color their outlook. Who really familiar with the impressionist painters can see blue skies, fluffy clouds, and water and trees without to some extent viewing them through their eyes? Who familiar with Shakespeare can be unaffected by his view of humanity?

Although we are never just passive recipients of such influences, our sense of what life is like is affected by how others have interpreted the world. We tend to absorb the sentiments and perspectives of creative people who capture our minds and imaginations. Those who are able to enter the innermost selves of millions of people and affect their idea of what will produce happiness and self-worth will have a power unmatched by politicians.

A particularly good example of this kind of power is the profound effect that Hollywood has had on the public. In the last few decades especially, this influence has, for the most part, been deeply subversive of the moral and cultural habits of traditional American civilization. Becoming attuned to the Hollywood view of the world and of the entertainment industry in general has rearranged the values and priorities of many people in the US In the media, the perspectives of news programs and talk shows have conveyed a new notion of what is newsworthy and not, admirable and despicable. Situation comedies and late-night shows have taught people what to laugh at and what to ridicule. Even the churches have absorbed a new type of moral sensibility. The overall result is a way of reacting to politicians and daily events.

In the intellectual life, universities and schools have "deconstructed" American and Western civilization. What might be called the Boston-Berkeley axis and the Hollywood–New York axis have interacted and mutually reinforced each other. Campus teaching and academic books in one axis and entertainment and news media in the other have, over time, produced a powerful new cultural substratum deeply at odds with traditional American moral-spiritual, intellectual, and artistic life. The now ubiquitous virtue signaling pays tribute to America's new cultural regime.

The counterculture and the New Left of the late 1960s and early 1970s grew out of cultural developments in the preceding decades. The demonstrations, burnings, and violence associated with them subsided, but the radicalism was carried forward and extended in the universities, the arts, music, Hollywood, book publishing, advertising, the corporations, and the churches. It soon permeated the mass media.

Reagan benefited from a grassroots resurgence of earlier American civilization, but the moral, intellectual, and artistic radicalism continued its long march through American institutions.

For students of the sources of human conduct who have also been attentive to the mentioned developments, nothing could be less surprising than the current woke rebellion and cancel culture. This is precisely what could have been expected from what has already happened in "the culture."

Some intellectuals did warn of the radicalization of the professors. Not as many have warned of corresponding developments in entertainment and the arts, which penetrate even more deeply into the heart of hearts of persons.

But movement conservatives never quite understood the centrality of what lies outside of politics narrowly understood. They assumed and stubbornly persisted in believing that what really matters is political power. They did not realize that once America's cultural trendsetters had transmitted their radicalism to the general public, it would overwhelm and transform politics.

Will it finally dawn on movement conservatives that, in the long run, the culture leads the way?

THE CRISIS OF RELIGION

("Catholics in Crisis," *The American Conservative*, March/April 2020). Many conservatives think that the crisis of the Western world is at bottom a conflict between religious believers and atheists. In reality, modern religion itself contains opposites. A new quasi-religious sensibility—a purported high morality—is a major source of the decline of America and the West. The emphasis below is on the Catholic Church, which many think of as the spiritual rock, the last bastion of Christianity, but the article is a case study of the effects of the teary-eyed "spirituality" of empathy that has deeply affected Christianity. Having replaced an older view of Christian love, this sentiment is the most influential morality in secular society as well.

Barely a day goes by without the news media covering some new instance of sexual debauchery, crime, or cover-up in the Catholic Church. Fingers are pointed at bishops, cardinals, and even the Pope. Coming on top of years of similar revelations, these stories confirm an impression of deep moral-spiritual crisis.

So abundant and disturbing has been the evidence of clerical wrong-doing, callousness, secrecy, and hypocrisy that leading laymen have issued calls for the laity to intercede. Considering that the Catholic Church has always emphasized clerical authority and hierarchical structure, this is an extraordinary development—yet, given the circumstances, a plausible one.

Because of the expectation that priests, bishops, and other religious should be models for the laity, it is not surprising that blame should focus on the hierarchy. And where to turn for remedies, if not to the laity? But to call on the laity to guide the Church is to raise the question of how well-prepared they are for the task. Thomas Jefferson famously believed that no country should go long without a revolution. Government had to be cleansed from time to time by the righteousness of the common people. But Jefferson had a romantic faith in the virtue of the common man that contrasts sharply with the traditional Christian view of human nature.

Bishops and clergy are not uniquely subject to the forces of corruption that have wreaked havoc in the Church. They have been affected by trends in the same society that the laity inhabit. In fact, the laity may well have been even more influenced by questionable views of life that have become increasingly prominent in Western society. Successful lay leadership would thus have to be acutely self-critical and discriminating.

The challenge to Christianity in the last few centuries has not been confined to denying the existence of God. The basic terms of human existence have been reconsidered. Not only Christianity but the classical Greek and Roman heritage stressed the importance of moral character for personal and social well-being. Human beings were morally cleft, and they had to learn self-control and responsibility. Any genuine social betterment had to begin in this manner. For Christianity, the main obstacle to improving human existence was the fallenness of man. The crux of the moral-spiritual life was to recognize evil in self, repent, and reform self. A central purpose of civilization was to support this effort.

But Western high-brow and popular culture alike have long portrayed such notions of self-restraint and character as vestiges of a perverse puritanism. We should not bottle up natural cravings but live out our dreams and longings. We are not to fret over little personal failings but show moral nobility by endorsing virtuous social and political schemes for transforming the human condition. Our goal should be not so much to love neighbor—the people just around us—with all of what it entails of *personal,* sometimes inconvenient up-close engagement. We should love *mankind,* whose advancement requires the mobilization of *government.* This shift from self-reform to socio-political reform proved very appealing in that it greatly relieved the moral burden placed on the person.

Christian love, which had been seen as inseparable from overcoming the sin of self-indulgence, was gradually replaced by the kind of "idealism" that Irving Babbitt called "sentimental humanitarianism." Moral virtue, previously understood as involving the self-restraint of character and personal responsibility, was redefined to mean feelings of empathy or pity, not for anybody in particular but for large suffering collectives somewhere in the distance, like the hungry or the downtrodden. Love of neighbor, which demands sometimes difficult action or sacrifice here and now, gave way to the sentiment of "brotherhood of man," which presupposes no difficult self-reform.

The pioneering and paradigmatic figure for this new moral posture was Jean-Jacques Rousseau, the philosopher of the French Revolution. A new form of spirituality started spreading in the Western world. Its ethos might be summed up in the phrase "daring to share that you care." The lover of humanity proves his moral bona fides by letting others know that he "feels their pain." A prominent and distinctive trait of sentimental humanitarianism is its element of self-approbation. Look at me! See how I love everybody! If I treat particular persons close to me badly, that is surely excused by my abundant love for humanity. Christianity had warned against pride and encouraged a humble view of self, but the new sentimental spirituality inflated the ego. Its emphasis was not on moral self-examination but on eradicating social injustice.

When Rousseau's famous work of pedagogy, *Emile,* was first published it was condemned by the Archbishop of Paris. Rousseau's central ideas, specifically his notion of the natural goodness of man, were obviously antithetical to traditional theological and moral assumptions. His notion of the common good—to be achieved through a soulful radical democracy that released unobstructed popular will—was as sharply anti-traditional. Still, Rousseauistic "idealism" began to transform Christianity. The "freedom, equality and brotherhood" of the French radicals acquired a "Christian" form, as did the corresponding faith in the People. The new idealism linked up with enlightenment-style social engineering to implement its vision of justice.

In Protestantism an eventual consequence was the so-called Social Gospel, according to which God wants a radical remaking of society. The old belief that sin is chiefly a personal matter and that personal character must contain it—which makes a better society possible—gave way to stressing the need for getting rid of existing socio-political structures. Soon many Catholics, too, came to view the sentimental brotherhood of man as more elevated and generous than the self-control and love of neighbor that had formed the core of Christian responsibility. This radical redefinition of morality and the corresponding change in priorities were somewhat masked because advocates of the new idealism retained the Christian *terminology*.

As this humanitarian spirituality was adapted to the moral-intellectual habits of the Catholic mind, it often assumed a quasi-Thomistic form. One sees this development particularly well in a mid-20th-century figure who would acquire iconic status: Jacques Maritain. His thought was not univocal, but especially his later work echoed 18th and 19th century liberationist themes. Breaking with the Aristotelian tradition, Maritain became a proponent of democratism, the belief that democracy is divinely ordained. He extolled "prophets of the people" like the fathers of the French Revolution and, in America, Thomas Paine, Thomas Jefferson, and John Brown. In ways that called to mind Auguste Comte's religion of humanity, he envisioned "a new age of civilization." In this new world order all human beings would enjoy basic material and spiritual benefits "free of charge." A "world council" of wise men would guide the world, overseeing the implementation of "human rights" and the common good.

From the beginning, these intellectual impulses were akin to those of progressive "liberalism" and social democracy. There was soon a Catholic version of the Social Gospel. An extreme form of this gospel was liberation theology, whose call for redemption through socio-economic transformation ran parallel to Marxism. This theology was highly influential in Latin America, especially among the Jesuits. It was in reaction to heavy clerical involvement in politics that John Paul II issued the call to his priests to "return home," that is, to the things of God.

Catholic attunement to mainstream progressive opinion in the universities and the media was assisted in the United States by status anxiety among the "ethnics." Catholics, too, could be intellectually sophisticated! A more or less conscious desire to impress secular, established elites or at least reduce their condescension reinforced an inclination to adopt "liberal" sentiments. These could be recast as being deep down not just compatible with but expressive of Christianity. The lines blurred between Catholic thinkers and secular "liberals" like the philosopher John Rawls. Rawls's highly ahistorical way of thinking about justice, which combined elements of Rousseau, John Locke, and Immanuel Kant, produced abstract principles, sub-principles, and casuistry reminiscent of the most rationalistic varieties of Thomism.

Many Catholic intellectuals continued to resist sentimental idealism. It did after all contradict a Christian view of human nature and traditional moral beliefs. But rationalistic bias made it difficult for Thomists to diagnose the root problem with the new moralism. They were used to giving primacy in moral philosophy to rational principles and rule adherence. Putting reason in charge—getting the mind to *think* right—was assumed to lead to proper willing. Moral character would somehow flow from or be the same as right reason. They did not see that the great appeal of sentimental humanitarianism was its capturing the *imagination*, stirring the entire personality with visions and images and benevolent-looking grand causes. The new spirituality also imparted a pleasant feeling of moral superiority. All that was required to be virtuous was to demand Social Justice and Human Rights.

The great socio-political causes made the difficult and often painful tasks of personal repentance, character, and responsibility look almost trivial. The plethora of moral principles produced by more traditional Catholic rationalists were easily swept away by dreams of liberation.

When considering how the laity might help restore the Church to health, it is essential to keep in mind that the *sine qua non* for curing illness is proper diagnosis. It is not far-fetched to suggest that the mentioned large trends, including the corruption of imagination and erosion of character, contributed to the crisis. The question is not whether these trends, by themselves, caused the crisis. The crisis has many partial explanations. But it seems evident that sentimental humanitarianism played a major role in morally and spiritually disarming and disorienting both laity and clergy.

All the media attention to problems in the Catholic Church has undoubtedly given old anti-Catholic prejudices a new lease on life. What do you expect from "the whore of Babylon"? But to believe that the Catholic Church is singularly susceptible to moral corruption shows great conceit. All of Western civilization has been profoundly impacted by the new idealism, the Protestant churches at least as much as the Catholic Church, though in different ways. Many volumes could be written about the effects outside of the churches. This writer has authored several books and many articles that touch on aspects of the broader problem.

The most nefarious element of the new spirituality may be that it takes little account of personal sinfulness as the central problem of the moral-spiritual life. It denies or downplays the importance of the moral struggle within the individual and the indispensability of character. Moral rationalism does not really understand how to arm the will against the lower desires. It employs such smarts as it has to formulate intricate rules and principles, but without character no amount of intellectual brilliance or teary-eyed sentiment can control the lower desires. Given the spread of sentimental humanitarianism, some such debauchery and evil as has come to light in the Catholic Church was well-nigh inevitable.

One might think that the *depth*, *scope*, and *nature* of the corruption will trigger a fundamental reexamination of common assumptions. Will, then, sentimental idealists start questioning their claim to moral superiority? Their self-applauding moralism is deeply rooted and very pleasing to the ego. The moral rationalists for their part are heavily invested in the belief that the crux of human conduct is for *reason* to guide us.

That there is imagination and idealism that are very different from what has been described here is not in dispute. Sound imagination and idealism are indispensable to elevating life. The problem is addiction to dubious and even impossible dreams. Terrible evil and suffering has resulted from benevolent-looking but perverse illusion. Neither is the indispensability of reason in dispute. Knowledge must inform conduct. But not even the most intricate ratiocination will rescue souls that are captive to alluring but shoddy spirituality. Rules and principles will not steer people right if will and imagination are pulling them in a different direction. Unless we be guided by what Edmund Burke calls "the moral imagination," which is sound will and imagination in one, some lower form of imagination will direct the person. Brilliant philosophers in the latter predicament will only argue themselves deeper and deeper into self-deluding illusion.

One prominent Catholic intellectual who did understand well what most shapes the life of human beings was Pope Benedict XVI. His emphasis on the role of culture and the arts demonstrated an awareness of the importance of imagination in shaping conduct, for good or ill.

The accumulating evidence of egregious moral-spiritual corruption in the Church might rattle Catholic intellectuals into a more than marginal reassessment of deep-seated propensities, but, because of the strength of the influences here discussed, there is a danger that instead they will double down on the same old same old, saying that this time we must really, *really* follow the rules, show that we *really* believe in them! Or they may say that now we must *really* commit to Social Justice.

Should the laity have these inclinations, they may be no more able than the hierarchy to steer the Church right. They would be falling back into a mindset and sensibility that not only failed to prevent the current crisis but must share the blame for it.

Fostering a more than superficial renewal of the moral-spiritual and intellectual life is a daunting task. It should be evident from what has been argued here that having the laity seize the initiative is not without danger. Yet the laity could, under wise leadership, play a redemptive role. The time may be ripe for creative, perhaps audacious, thought and action to revivify a faltering tradition.

CONSERVATISM AND NATIONALISM: DEFINITIONS NEEDED

("Definitions Please!," *The American Conservative*, July/August 2020.) Movement conservatism has long suffered from a lack of philosophical maturity. At a time of general disorientation, when many think that conservatism needs to be reassessed in the current historical circumstances, this deficiency continues to create confusion and generate dubious political alliances. Truly constructive efforts to rethink the meaning of conservatism must include major terminological cleanup.

Reactions to globalization, the Trump presidency, and the coronavirus pandemic have turned discussions of American conservatism increasingly into discussions of "nationalism." Regrettably, terminological confusion is rampant. Both "conservatism" and "nationalism" are words of many and even contradictory meanings.

The strengths of post–World War II American intellectual conservatism have been widely heralded. As for its weaknesses, one trait stands out that has greatly impeded intellectual stringency: a deep-seated impatience with the supposedly "finer points" of philosophy. Making do with loosely defined terms has made conservatism susceptible to intellectual flabbiness, contradiction, and manipulation.

This deficiency is connected to a virtual obsession with electoral politics. William F. Buckley's path-breaking *National Review* was an intellectual magazine, but its primary purpose was to prepare the ground for political victories, most of all for capturing the presidency. The desire to forge a political alliance among diverse groups pushed deep intellectual fissures into the background. Having a rather narrowly political understanding of what shapes the future, most conservatives thought that the election and presidency of Ronald Reagan signified the "triumph" of conservatism; but the triumph was hollow. The reason is that in the long run politicians have less power than those who shape our view of reality, our innermost hopes and fears, and our deeper sensibilities. A crucial role is here played by "the culture"—universities, schools, churches, the arts, media, book publishing, advertising, Hollywood, and the rest of the entertainment industry—which is why America kept moving leftward.

For post-war so-called "movement" conservatives, conservatism meant chiefly limited government, a free market, anti-communism, and a strong defense. These tenets were all focused on politics, and vastly different motives hid behind each of them. Why were these tenets called "conservatism"? Rather than point to a few policy preferences, should that term not refer to a general attitude to life, a wish to *conserve* something, the best of a heritage? One thinks of the moral and cultural sources of American liberty and constitutionalism. But, outside of ceremonial occasions, most movement conservatives placed their emphasis elsewhere.

A striking example of philosophical messiness and confusion is that the conservative movement even incorporated clearly anti-conservative ideas, specifically, the anti-historicism advanced by Leo Strauss and his followers. Strauss championed what he called "natural right," which he saw as sharply opposed to tradition. He called the latter "the ancestral" or "convention." To look to them for guidance was to be guilty of the great offense of "historicism," by which he meant moral relativism or nihilism. History, Strauss insisted, is irrelevant to understanding what is right. Only ahistorical, purely abstract reason is normative.

Hampered by a lack of philosophical education, many Straussians have been oblivious to the far-reaching and harmful ramifications of this anti-historicism. By blithely combining it with ideas of very different origin, they have concealed, even from themselves, its animosity to tradition.

One of Strauss's most influential disciples, Harry Jaffa, made the radical implications of Straussian anti-historicism explicit. In his view, America's Founders did not build on a heritage. They deliberately *turned their backs* on the past. Jaffa wrote: "To celebrate the American Founding is...to celebrate revolution." America's revolution belonged among the other modern revolutions. It is mild "as compared with subsequent revolutions in France, Russia, China, Cuba, or elsewhere," he wrote, but "it nonetheless embodied the greatest attempt at innovation that human history had recorded." The US Constitution did not grow out of the achievements of ancestors. On the contrary, radical innovators gave America a fresh start. What is distinctive and noble about America is that, in the name of ahistorical, abstract, universal principles, it *broke* with the past.

This view flies in the face of overwhelming historical evidence. The reason the Founders were upset with the British government is that *it* was acting in a radical, arbitrary manner that violated the old British constitution. John Adams spoke of "grievous innovation." John Dickinson protested "dreadful novelty." What the colonists wanted, Adams wrote, was "nothing new" but respect for traditional rights and the common law. The Constitution of the Framers reaffirmed and creatively developed an ancient heritage.

The Jaffaite notion that America *rejected* the past and was founded on revolutionary, abstract, universal ideas contributed to what this writer has termed "the new Jacobinism." According to this ideology, America is "exceptional" by virtue of its founding principles. Since these principles belong to all humanity, America must help remake societies around the world. "Moral clarity" demands uncompromising adherence to the principles. The forces of good must defeat the forces of evil. Inherently monopolistic and imperial, American principles justify foreign policy hawkishness and interventionism.

Compare this notion of America to what is implied in Benjamin Franklin's famous phrase about what the Constitutional Convention had produced—"a republic, if you can keep it." To sustain the Constitution, Americans would have to cultivate the moral and cultural traits that had given rise to it in the first place. To be an American is to defend a historically evolved inheritance, to live up to what may be called the "constitutional personality." Only such people are capable of the kind of conduct that the Constitution values and requires. Americans must, first of all, be able to control the will to power, beginning with self. They must respect the law, rise above the passions of the moment, take the long view, deliberate, compromise, and respect minorities. Whether applied to domestic or foreign affairs, the temperament of American constitutionalism is modesty and restraint. There is no place for unilateral dictates.

These contrasting views of America entail wholly different nationalisms. The moralistic universalism of American exceptionalism with its demand that all respect its dictates runs counter to the American constitutional spirit of compromise, deliberation, and respect for minorities. Exceptionalism does not defuse or restrain the will to power, but feeds it, justifying arrogance, assertiveness, and even belligerence.

During the presidency of Donald Trump many proponents of American exceptionalism who want preferment have recast their antihistorical universalism as "nationalism," showing that the term can mean almost anything. It is now "nationalist" to demand that American principles be everywhere respected. For example, Mike Pompeo, a person of strong appetites and great ambition, has put this belief behind his campaign of assertiveness and "maximum pressure."

In a speech in the spring of 2019, Pompeo declared that America is "exceptional." America is, he said, "a place and history apart from normal human experience." It has a mission to oppose evil in the world. America is entitled to "respect." It should dictate terms to "rogue" powers like Iran and confront countries like China and Russia that are "intent on eroding American power." This speech was given and loudly cheered at the 40th anniversary gala of the Claremont Institute in California, whose intellectual founder was—Harry Jaffa.

What may seem to political practitioners and political intellectuals to be hair-splitting philosophical distinctions can, on the contrary, have enormous practical significance. American exceptionalism is in important ways the opposite of a conservatism or a nationalism that defends the moral and cultural heritage that generated American constitutionalism. Exceptionalism fans imperial designs. The culture of constitutionalism opposes them.

CONFLICTING NOTIONS OF NATIONHOOD

(Excerpt from *America the Virtuous* [New Brunswick and London: Transaction Publishers, 2003.]) "Nationalism" is one of the most frequently used words in public discussion, but, like "liberalism," "conservatism," "democracy," and many other frequently used general terms, it is rarely defined with care. Those who give the term positive connotations often use it to describe the disposition that should govern US foreign policy, but what precisely is meant by the term? Here a distinction is made between two radically different notions of nationalism and nationality.

In preparation for later discussion of the neo-Jacobin view of international affairs and foreign policy it is appropriate to extend the dichotomy between two sharply opposed forms of popular government to two very different ideas of nationhood. A distinction is needed between what may be called patriotism and nationalism. Selecting terms for particular meanings is always to some extent arbitrary. "Patriotism" and "nationalism" have no universally accepted definitions. The proposed distinction may thus employ the terms in ways at variance with how they have been used by others.

The old morality of modesty and self-discipline, which has been seen here to be integral to constitutional democracy, does not preclude pride in personal strengths and accomplishments. Neither does it preclude local, regional, and national pride. Proper self-regard goes together with humility and appreciation for the attainments of others. Similarly, a proper patriotic celebration of national achievements does not signify a posture of superiority over all other societies or involve arrogance in the treatment of other peoples. Neither does it assume that there are no standards of goodness, truth, or beauty beyond national likes or dislikes. On the contrary, for the patriot, the standard for national self-regard is the same as the one that that may judge the flaws of his own people severely. The patriot is the first to feel shame and regret about unjust actions taken by his own country. Patriotism recognizes that right is not defined by national prejudice and passion. It maintains moral discrimination and self-control. The patriot, though always ready to defend his own country against threats, is less prone to impose his will on other nations than to try to set an example for them. Just as in domestic politics the constitutional democrat is not oblivious of the possibly legitimate claims of other groups, so in international politics the patriot is not insensitive to the interests of other countries. Indeed, as one looking to improve the quality of life in his own country, the patriot is receptive to the merits of other peoples and cultures and welcomes the variety of national customs as enriching the larger whole and adding spice to life.

Patriotism and cosmopolitanism, rightly understood, are compatible and complementary. The true cosmopolitan is not some culturally homeless free floater belonging nowhere in particular. He is just the opposite. It is because he has identified with and entered deeply into the finest achievements of his own people that he has learned to appreciate life at the highest level and become able to recognize corresponding strengths in other peoples. Like the patriot, the cosmopolitan is rooted in a particular cultural tradition but is to some extent at home in more than one country by virtue of the element of universality in his own particular background. Especially the more educated and cultured members of a civilized people are to some extent cosmopolitan to begin with. Russians are somewhat familiar with Italian music and painting, Americans with German philosophy, Englishmen with French cooking, Swedes with Anglo-Saxon political thinking, Chinese with Western technology and medicine, Pakistanis with Christianity, and so on. The cosmopolitan and the patriot both recognize that many peoples have contributed to civilization and that the highest values of human life can be realized in somewhat different ways depending on time and place. An awareness of a common humanity and destiny keeps the patriot considerate of competitors. Just as he does not demonize his opponents, so does he not regard his own side as above criticism. Even in the middle of a war with its practical imperatives, the patriot tries to hold on to his humility. Rarely in a conflict is all right on one side, and the present enemy is a possible future friend and ally. Civilization tries in various ways to keep warring parties in mind of the fact that they are fellow human beings. The Geneva Convention is but one example of the effort to keep that awareness alive even in the most unfavorable and difficult circumstances.

Nationalism, by contrast, is an eruption of overweening ambition, a throwing off of individual and national self-control. Nationalism is self-absorbed and conceited, oblivious of the weaknesses of the country it champions. It is provincialism without the leaven of cosmopolitan breadth, discretion, and critical detachment. Nationalism recognizes no authority higher than its own national passion. It imagines that it has a monopoly on right or has a mission superseding moral norms. The phrase "my country, right or wrong" sums up this attitude (though the person who originated it may have meant it differently). Nationalist politics is inherently intolerant, tyrannical, and expansionist. It bullies and creates ever-new enemies.

Especially when offered without appropriate definitions, the idea that democracies are inherently disinclined to aggression is conceited wishful thinking as well as historically questionable. All depends on whether a particular democracy has the self-restraint and wisdom that comes from character and civilized prejudices among its citizens and leaders. It makes a great deal of difference whether the democracy is of the constitutional or plebiscitary type. Plebiscitary rule aims to free the popular majority from checks on its prevailing will. In so doing it liberates also the desire for power and self-aggrandizement to which any people can sometimes be prone and to which nationalist demagogues can always appeal.

Rousseau can be seen as one of the founders of nationalism. His attack on traditional civilization was, among other things, an attack on the old cosmopolitanism of the West. With his idea of the general will as the ultimate standard of political good he simultaneously planted the notion that there is nothing above the will of a particular people to which other countries might appeal to try to restrain what they consider arbitrary and egotistical behavior. War becomes the only way to settle international disputes. In heeding Rousseau's general call for a new, virtuous society, the French Jacobins became pioneers for a special kind of nationalism, one that justified French expansionism by claiming that France, by virtue of its superior principles, was uniquely fitted to dominate and remake other countries. The Jacobins derived some pride and sense of superiority from their Frenchness, but the inner logic of Jacobin universalism is to shed specifically national characteristics and to become more abstractly ideological. The nation becomes an idea, the idea a nation. The nation becomes an instrument for universalist ambition. It is no longer something to cherish and defend for the sake of its unique culture. The American new Jacobins, though they do have some typically American traits, are attached to the United States less because they identify with the actual, historically evolved American nation with its ancient origins in the Western past than because they recognize the utility of the might of the United States and choose to regard this country as entitled to dominating and remaking the world because of its principles. Neo-Jacobin universalism has little relation to cosmopolitanism as previously defined. It does not have deep roots in a particular culturally distinctive nation. It arbitrarily invents a new moral and intellectual pedigree for America. In addition, it is neither humble nor prone to self-criticism. It is not inclined to respect the accomplishments and interests of other peoples. It wishes to impose upon other countries what it deems to be a virtuous order. In anticipation of a later argument, it might be added that many of the new Jacobins as well as many of their less ideological allies use high-sounding universalist language to dress up a strong will to power.

The world is wondering today whether in this century the most powerful nation on the globe will behave with humility and self-restraint or be an assertive, even bullying force. The influence of the new Jacobinism on American foreign policy, which will be discussed at length below, points in the latter direction. Indeed, the highly moralistic ideology and power seeking of the new Jacobinism indicate the likelihood of an era of international conflict and war. The neo-Jacobin quest for empire is bound to inflame international relations and generate opposition around the world—no matter that this push for control is undertaken for the sake of "democracy" and "virtue." Far from considering a subject of merely theoretical, academic interest, this book is examining an intellectual-political force that directly affects the future of the United States and the world. The nature and extent of the influence of the new Jacobins is an issue of great moment.

American discussion of the proper role of the United States in the world suffers from broad generalizations and false choices. Issues like trade, foreign aid, and military strategy are often said to pit proponents of a New World Order against persons who want to pull up the drawbridge around the United States. Those who have the greatest influence in the major media and in the two parties want the United States to be internationally active in promoting free markets, democracy and human rights. The only alternative to this stance is supposed to be the view that the United States ought to play an insignificant role in the world and single-mindedly stress the national interest. Opponents of the New World Order are portrayed as isolationists and protectionists.

But this classification of views, besides being a simplistic rendition of the positions represented in the debate, ignores the possibility of a very different kind of foreign policy, one that simultaneously rejects globalist ambitions, be they ideological or more frankly imperialistic, and national self-absorption. This third possibility may be called responsible nationhood. It is possible for a powerful country, and any other country, to be guided by a patriotism that is indistinguishable from respect and fondness for diversity. A country can take an interest in other countries without assuming that they have everything to learn. Responsible nationhood can be defined in contrast with two equally questionable and often overlapping orientations: one an ideological universalism that wishes to replace religious, cultural, and regional identities with an allegedly virtuous homogeneity; the other a less ideological nationalism that is so full of itself that it has difficulty tolerating anything but itself. In practice, the two orientations become difficult to tell apart. Both undermine the possibility of peace with other countries. Responsible nationhood, by contrast, stands for a policy of self-restraint and respect for others in the international arena. It is cosmopolitan but not globalistic and threatening. It is patriotic but not closed-in upon itself.

WHAT IS POPULISM?

("When 'Populist' Becomes a Slur," *The American Conservative*, September/October 2018.) Those who most often use the term "populism" mean to disparage what is so labeled. What then are the defining characteristics of populism that make it so distasteful, and how do they compare to the supposedly superior attitudes of anti-populists? Paradoxically, the attributes that critics ascribe to populism turn out closely to resemble practices that those critics defend. This analysis brings out what it is it about populism that so bothers its critics. Is also raises the question whether a form of populism might help shore up constitutional government.

In order to make sense of the term "populism" as ordinarily used today, we must first take into account that it has been defined almost exclusively by America's permanent ruling establishment.

This establishment is sometimes called the "deep state," but we should resist a narrow political conception of the power structure in question. To convey the nature and reach of it, we need something like the old Aristotelian term "regime," which refers not merely to government in the modern sense but also to an entire socio-cultural ethos that sets the tone in society and molds the way in which people view the world.

America's permanent regime consists most importantly of the elites in the media, the universities, Hollywood, Wall Street, Madison Avenue, Silicon Valley, and Washington. This multi-faceted ruling class, linked by similar sensibilities and perspectives on the world, has immense political influence, to be sure, but it has even greater power to shape the country's moral outlook, its mind, and its imagination through education, publishing, movies, music, and even advertising. It has the ability to define what is and what is not newsworthy, to lionize or demonize persons and phenomena. What the regime approves of is portrayed as "normal," "mainstream," or "moderate"—everything else it can dismiss as extreme, radical, or worse.

A great deal can be learned about this elaborate network of overlapping elites—a small minority of the population that nevertheless wields enormous influence—by examining how it uses the term "populism." The term is heavy with disapprobation, referring to popular movements that attract support through demagoguery, opportunism, and general irresponsibility. Populism recklessly questions the long-standing practices and assumptions of experienced, enlightened leaders. Populists are rash, unthinking, and vulgar. They make sweeping promises without regard to cost or practicality. They cynically fan and exploit the fears, resentments, bigotry, and hatreds of unsophisticated people. They focus anger on scapegoats. Populists do not much care about constitutional niceties and civil liberties. They are not moderates.

The regime's disdain for "populism" might seem to imply a principled concern about maintaining high standards of politics and rhetoric. But the increasingly common use of the term follows a revealing pattern. It is only those who challenge the regime who fall in this tainted category; no matter that representatives of the regime have long exhibited the despised traits of "populism" in sometimes egregious ways.

We are told that among the distinctive and disqualifying

characteristics of populism are short-sightedness and concealment of the true human and financial costs of policy. With regard to financial, political, and rhetorical matters, what is the standard for irresponsibility? Is it anything like the imprudence and negligence that gave America its staggering national debt—the unfathomable sum of $21 trillion dollars, to which might be added $100 trillion or so in federal, state, and local unfunded liabilities? For decades an allegedly responsible "mainstream" establishment has offered the American people benefits or promises of benefits, fully aware there was no money to pay for them, only more debt. If irresponsibility is the essence of populism, why has this brand of it never been discredited? Kicking the can down the road seems built into the very fabric of the regime. Yet the politicians, technocrats, and pundits creating, condoning, and aggravating this state of affairs are exempted from all charges. They can sit in judgment of others.

This ruling class took the United States to war in a number of distant places, demonizing those being attacked. None of these wars were declared, although the Constitution prohibits war without a congressional declaration. The regime spent enormous amounts of money on these military ventures, greatly adding to the national debt. It created a bloated national security state that undermined traditional American civil liberties, partly through electronic surveillance and the progressive militarization of society. With its Middle East wars, the regime has caused hundreds of thousands of deaths and other suffering and destruction, including rampant religious persecution. It has dislocated millions of people and caused a refugee crisis of monumental proportions that has overwhelmed Europe, which is already under great pressure from a migrant wave. The American power elite has destabilized almost the entire Middle East. You might think of this record as discrediting, but the only ones deemed guilty of recklessness, demagoguery, and short-sightedness are supposed "populists."

Consider this: for decades, the controlling establishment has tolerated or actively promoted porous or open borders. Permitting millions of undocumented immigrants to enter without a focus on assimilation or impact on American communities has undermined the cohesion of what many consider the American culture, with its classical, British, and Christian traditions and its distinctive Constitution. At a time when the waning of this heritage is already threatening our cohesion—politically, morally, and culturally—the regime has pressed the politically correct position that mass immigration of any sort, legal or illegal, is perfectly compatible with the United States remaining itself and staying unified and safe. It is "who we are." But this is a superficial myth and shows either deep ignorance or cynical disregard of history. Culturally disjointed societies are inherently unstable and prone to fragmentation. Contemporary Europeans—though not so much those in the transnational, Europeanist camp—can see even more clearly than Americans the actual effect of migrant waves on their countries. It has brought tension, disorder, and violence. Those who extol the benefits of large-scale immigration show irresponsibility on a grand scale. But who has the reputation for being superficial demagogues?

We are told that populists employ inflammatory slogans and crude appeals, but how exactly do they violate what has become the new normal within the establishment, whether it be politicians and pundits or the Big Media? Rank partisanship, rabble-rousing, incendiary language, and opportunism—it is all so ubiquitous today that serious, dispassionate public discussion has become virtually impossible. It is increasingly hard to tell so-called "reporting" apart from political activism. The mainstream media, acting like a palace guard for the regime, give favorable attention to regime favorites and ignore or attack people who violate the prescribed orthodoxy. Consider CNN and *The Washington Post*, which patrol and protect the left flank. As for the Republicrat duopoly, it shows, especially during political campaigns, that it thinks the electorate is made up of illiterates, distinguished only by geography and red or blue state impulses. The regime assumes that the voters are easily moved by appeals to their most primitive instincts and fears.

And so, one asks, what is it that makes populism so sinister? The ugliest and most typical feature of populism is, we are told, its paranoid style. It blames what is wrong on scapegoats. Yet we see in the establishment a zeal for blaming society's ills on dark forces. These include "sexists," "racists," "xenophobes," "homophobes," and, of course, "deplorables." After 9/11, the ubiquitous "terrorists" kept the national security state humming and justified interventions abroad. Now there is Russia. Though having a GNP about the same as Italy's, Russia is in contention for being the greatest threat to America. It even serves as the establishment's scapegoat for losing the 2016 election. The paranoid style could hardly be more integral to the regime.

It should be evident, then, that the American regime exhibits in abundance the characteristics it attributes to populists. It is financially irresponsible. It makes promises it cannot keep. It spreads deceptive myths. It has a shortsighted and reckless foreign policy agenda. It undermines civil liberties. It employs simplistic demagoguery and cheapens public debate. It plays upon popular fears and anxieties. It singles out groups and individuals for blame.

At least two conclusions can be drawn. The first is that the use of the term "populism" has nothing to do with principled opposition to the negative traits of so-called populism. The term has but one consistent meaning, more than marginal criticism of the regime that attracts widespread popular support. The purpose of the label is to smear all real opponents of the reigning elites as engaging in irresponsible rabble-rousing.

Secondly, most representatives of the regime seem oblivious of these ironies, which suggests a disturbing lack of self-awareness. They simply assume that they are moderate and enlightened and that all real criticism of their performance is extreme, dull-witted, and dangerous. They do not realize—or, in a few cases, they recognize but refuse to admit—that they have badly failed their society, and they are determined to hang on to power and privilege.

So what inspires the regime's charges of populism is a mixture of profound conceit and ruthless, cynical power-seeking.

To point out that these attacks on what the regime calls populism are hypocritical and self-serving is of course not the same as to approve of populism wholesale. Whether putative populists deserve condemnation depends entirely on what ideas, methods, and purposes they espouse. Populism, understood as reckless, unthinking assaults on authority, is, by definition, unacceptable. The ideological populism of Rousseau in France or Jefferson or Paine in America, for example, has been highly pernicious. This much is clear: we cannot turn to representatives of the American regime for standards of responsibility. Indeed, given its egregious mismanagement of American society, a responsible observer may have no choice but to issue his own call to drain the swamp.

PART TWO

THE CONSTITUTION AND ITS ENEMIES

AMERICAN CONSTITUTIONALISM VS. MAJORITARIAN DEMOCRACY

(Excerpt from *Democracy and the Ethical Life*, 2nd exp. ed. (Washington, DC: Catholic University of America Press, 1990; first published by Louisiana State University Press, 1978.) The framers of the US Constitution did not intend a democracy as they understood that term. They wanted government that would, as far as possible, limit the sway of special interests and serve the common good. They feared and tried to restrain the role of partisan, self-indulgent factions. They especially dreaded what they called "a majority faction." They set up a constitutional republic of limited, decentralized powers that would promote responsible representative government—rule by the people, but under self-imposed constitutional restraints. There has long been great confusion about how America's Constitution relates to democracy. Many liberals and all leftists have criticized the Constitution for not being sufficiently democratic, but that term can be understood in radically different ways. The framers understood themselves to be creating a regime that incorporated popular consent and elections, and, by the standards of the time, their Constitution had a heavy popular ingredient. Alexis de Tocqueville would write a big book called *Democracy in America*. But a distinction is necessary between constitutional and "plebiscitary" (or majoritarian) popular rule that pays attention to their respective assumptions about human nature and society. The one type of democracy is compatible with American constitutionalism; the other is not. Defending the Constitution was a central feature of American post–World War II conservatism, but that defense was complicated and undermined by often confused and confusing notions of how democracy relates to the American Constitution. For example, neoconservative democratism, the mantra that America is called to spread democracy in the world, can be connected to American constitutionalism only by means of the most willful ideological contortions.

The following excerpt from *Democracy and the Ethical Life* explains how a plebiscitary, "progressive" understanding of democracy clashes with the constitutionalism of the framers. The book was published over four decades ago and looked back on the thinking of the Framers with special reference to the decades just after World War II. A great deal has happened since the Constitution was adopted and since the book was written that has grievously undermined American constitutionalism. It would be anachronistic to equate the framers' suspicions of popular passions of the moment with denunciation today of "populism" or to equate their defense of responsible representative government with defenses today of the ruling political establishment. It can be argued that the latter has through oligarchic concentration of power, active violation of the Constitution, or lazy acceptance of unconstitutional practices brought American constitutional government to a point of crisis. It is hard to see how in our current historical circumstances anything like American constitutional government might be revived without widespread popular opposition to corrupt, irresponsible rule. Whether populist protests might serve the cause of constitutionalism depends in part on the extent to which the framers' notion of popular self-rule has survived in the public consciousness. While the passage of time has dated some of the references and illustrations in this excerpt, the distinction between the two notions of popular government has lost none of its relevance.

THE SPIRIT OF CONSTITUTIONALISM

Insofar as it is compatible with the needs of the ethical life, democracy seeks to promote a certain quality of popular will. This leads us to the role of the constitution. It may be viewed in analogy with the rules or principles which the individual person adopts for his "private" behavior. Aware of his own moral and other weaknesses, he gives sovereignty not to his impulse of the moment but to standards of conduct which he has pledged not to change or abrogate on whim or under the pressure of passion, but only after careful and sober deliberation. A constitution serves a similar function in the public realm. It is a standard of political behavior which is not supposed to be changed on the spur of the moment, but only through an elaborate procedure which enhances the likelihood that the decision be made when the emotions are calm and respectable motives uppermost. Needless to say, only people of high moral culture will subject their political wishes to constitutional restraints for the specific purpose of advancing the goal of community. Where citizens are lacking in this respect they will accept restraints, if at all, only as a way of advancing their own personal advantage. They may endorse the constitutional objective of leaving an appeal from the people drunk to the people sober, but that would be a means of promoting enlightened self-interest as distinguished from narrow-minded, short-sighted self-interest. There is a certain similarity between constitutionalism inspired by moral motives and constitutionalism inspired by mere sophisticated egotism. Both have the effect of curbing the expansiveness of the lower will of individuals and groups. I have argued previously that men's ability to discern what is in their own enlightened self-interest depends in the end on their having some notion, however vague, of what transcends the calculus of private advantage.[1]

But in order to establish the moral necessity of constitutionalism we need to state with more precision its relation to ethical conscience. A constitution, it may be said in general, is a recognition of the need to put checks on the tendency of individuals and groups to impose their own idea of what is politically desirable on others. It is an attempt to purge politics of blatant arbitrariness. Specific designations of power and various procedural requirements, whether prescribed by long-honored precedence or a written document, counteract the inclination to proceed with disregard for the rest of society. The requirement to follow a fundamental law gives a measure of impartiality to the formulation and implementation of public policy. It tends to promote a detachment of government from various competing special interests. The law, not any particular will, is sovereign. Short of destruction of the political order, the strong are not free to crush the weak. The latter are left an appeal against raw power. The very opposite of arbitrariness in politics would be correspondence between the political influence of individual citizens and groups and their contribution to community. No constitution can accomplish this goal. It can only be an attempt to limit the influence of selfish interests, not by eradicating them, which is impossible, but by taming them. In a democracy that means that the majority of the moment is not given total freedom to dictate policy. To do so would be to maximize the influence of the tendency, present to some degree in most expressions of political will, to disregard the good of the whole.

To become an effective regulating force a constitution must have the support of the citizens. Since the moral capacity of a people is limited, this support must also be found in a nonmoral source. For an elaboration of this point we may draw on one of the most original of American thinkers, John C. Calhoun. His constitutional reasoning is of interest here because it recognizes the existence of a common good in the higher sense while being adjusted to the preponderance of self-interest as a motivating force in politics. Calhoun is reconciled to the fact that the latter state of affairs cannot be drastically changed and that therefore self-interest somehow must be turned into the service of the common good, a need to which I have previously alluded.[2] It should be made clear that there is no necessary relationship between those of Calhoun's arguments that will be considered here and the specific, and to my mind rather awkward, institutional arrangements he proposes for the United States.

Concern for merely private advantage, Calhoun believes, must be restrained by constitutional checks. The only way that these checks can be made effective, however, is for the provisions of the constitution to give power to, and thereby become aligned with, various major interests which can help to enforce them in practice. The self-interest of each portion of the community which is recognized by the constitution can be counted upon to restrain the self-interest of other groups. "It is this negative power—the power of preventing or arresting the action of the government, be it called by what term it may, veto, interposition, nullification, check, or balance power—which in fact forms the constitution. Without this there can be no negative, and without a negative, no constitution."[3]

The American constitution with its elaborate system of checks and balances exhibits at least the likeness of the kind of "negative" on government which Calhoun is describing. It has a general effect of great ethical interest. The Constitution makes a consideration of the needs and wishes of numerous groups a requirement for a majority that wishes to achieve any part of its program. The approximation of a consensus is needed before government policy can be made. Competing groups, whether in the majority or the minority, are induced from the very start to adopt a politically inclusive perspective. To further their own cause, that same cause must be defined with a view to making it acceptable to other groups that might otherwise veto it.

This built-in inducement to consider the wishes of other groups will not necessarily, and indeed only in exceptional cases, lead to the adoption of a genuinely moral point of view, that is, to a subordination of private advantage to the needs of the common good. But it does tend to reduce the element of blatant self-seeking and thus to give some support to the moral aspirations also present in the people and its representatives. The self-restraints suggested by mere enlightened self-interest, it should be carefully noted, do not in themselves have any moral worth. But paradoxically they greatly facilitate the task of those who are striving to give politics a higher direction. These citizens can to some extent enlist the selfishly inspired restraint of others in support of the moral end. They may even be able to transform it by an appeal to ethical conscience. Since politics is not normally, if ever, a sphere of morally elevated activity, the ethical importance of this point can hardly be exaggerated. What might perhaps be called the Hobbesian intellectual tradition goes too far when it makes egotism the sole structuring principle of politics. There is as great a need, however, to guard against conceptions of politics which are based on unrealistic or even naive expectations about the degree to which morality can take the place of self-interest.

This reasoning ties in with Calhoun's argument in favor of government by "concurrent majority." We may cite his description of the contrast between that form of government and one of simple majority rule, by "numerical majority" in his terminology.

> The same cause which in governments of the numerical majority gives to party attachments and antipathies such force as to place party triumph and ascendancy above the safety and prosperity of the community will just as certainly give them sufficient force to overpower all regard for truth, justice, sincerity, and moral obligations of every description. . . . In the government of the concurrent majority, on the contrary, the same cause which prevents such strife as the means of obtaining power, and which makes it the interest of each portion to conciliate and promote the interests of the others, would exert a powerful influence toward purifying and elevating the character of the government and the people, morally as well as politically.[4]

What is of interest to our present argument is not whether the specific institutional suggestions offered by Calhoun will accomplish the stated goal, but the principle itself: in a government of concurrent majority self-interest is checked by self-interest in such a way that, willy-nilly, it becomes a potential support for moral aspirations. The extent to which a constitution will actually promote such aspirations, however, will depend entirely on the extent to which the perpetual conflict of interests is leavened by the motive of community among the political participants. To serve the higher goal the constitution must be sustained by considerable moral culture.

A constitution, then, is an attempt to purge politics of the kind of egotism which would crush everything in its way. Insofar as it is inspired by the moral motive, it aims even further, to the *substitution* of ethical conscience for enlightened self-interest as the ordering principle of politics. It then becomes the institutional embodiment of the rejection, not only of the kind of arbitrariness which threatens the peaceful balancing of group interests, but of every form of arbitrariness. Its provisions become a means of lifting politics in the direction of fulfillment of a higher law. As Walter Lippmann writes, "Constitutional restraints and bills of rights, the whole apparatus of responsible government and of an independent judiciary, the conception of due process of law in courts, in legislatures, among executives, are but the rough approximations by which men have sought to exorcise the devil of arbitrariness in human relations."[5] Although always imperfect and less than successful, constitutions serve their highest purpose by allowing the censuring of "caprice and willfulness" with a view to the *moral* end. Drawing on Plato, John Hallowell observes: "The absolute identification of moral and social restraints is possible only in an ideal state; and, while actual states always fall short of this ideal, the measure of their statehood is the degree to which that ideal is realized."[6]

But if it may thus be said that the principle of constitutionalism is disapproval of political power exercised for only particularistic ends, it is similar to the ultimate principle of morality itself. What is ethical conscience but the higher will in man which censures, and thereby defines, the arbitrary? Indeed, can it not be argued that to the extent that the principle of constitutionalism is not just the name for the flawed impartiality of enlightened self-interest, it is identical with ethical conscience? Clearly, whatever the apparent correspondence or proximity of self-interest and morality in some particular cases, man's ethical will is always in tension with the motive of selfishness. It cannot be said, therefore, that constitutionalism of every kind has moral worth. But as an activity by which men direct their common affairs, politics bears heavily on the achievement of the conditions of community. As such it is very much the concern of ethical conscience. What I am suggesting is that in one special sense constitutionalism is just another term for man's moral will applied to the organization of political activity. Constitutionalism is demanded by ethical conscience because it is necessary to the achievement of the moral goal. In its political aspect, the higher will may be called the spirit of constitutionalism. To develop this concept we need to remember that the words government and constitution are not names for something existing apart from the individual citizens. Those who participate in politics under the rules of a constitution accept it as a guide for their personal behavior, so that strictly speaking the constitution as a practical force is identical with the political activity of the individuals who assent to its provisions and supply or withhold the spirit of constitutionalism.

If the good life is to be approached, men's lower inclinations have to be disciplined in some way. According to Edmund Burke, "Society requires not only that the passions of individuals should be subjected but that even in the mass and body, as well as in the individuals, the inclinations of men should frequently be thwarted, their will controlled, and their passions brought into subjection. This can only be done *by a power out of themselves;* and not, in the exercise of its function, subject to that will and to those passions which it is its office to bridle and subdue."[7] In its moral dimension this restraining power is in a certain sense external to individual persons as Burke writes. It transcends man. It is not a part of his lower self of unprincipled impulse, but disciplines it from the outside. But in another sense, which Burke does not here recognize, it is also *in* man. It is man's own ethical conscience, the principle of true humanity he shares with others.

The "private" habits by which the individual tries to lift himself out of the ever-present inclination to yield to morally unexamined impulse cannot be sharply distinguished from those of his habits which he tries to follow for the same purpose in his "public" or "political" life. They are, in fact, only two aspects of one and the same attempt to achieve the moral end. Since the end itself is social but its attainment dependent on individual effort, the prerequisites are both "private" and "public." In the "public" sphere, ethical conscience demands a special type of cooperation with others, namely one which minimizes the influence of arbitrariness. It applies to a political context a question which describes all moral deliberation: "Is this contemplated action good?" As entertained by the individual in politics, the same question may be formulated thus: "Is this contemplated 'public' action of the kind that contributes to community?" Although concerned with "public" affairs, it puts a moral obligation on each citizen. The shared habit of asking this question is the moral dimension of constitutionalism. What should be carefully noted is that this concern is translated by practical necessity into a call for specific institutional restrictions binding on all. The higher will in man does not work in a vacuum but on the concrete material of political reality. Given men's selfish and otherwise flawed behavior and their unavoidable clashes of interest, the political advancement of community is not possible without common assent to some superior coordinating rule. The willingness to subject oneself to this kind of restraint out of concern for the moral end, therefore, is indistinguishable from ethical conscience itself. All actual constitutions are transcended by the ethical will, but the demand for them is directly rooted in it. Applied to the conduct of public affairs, thus, that will can indeed be described as the spirit of constitutionalism.

In a democracy, constitutional provisions are imposed by the people on itself. That does not mean that they will all meet with the full approval of every citizen. While a person may be critical of various parts of his country's constitution, he may still respect it, in the spirit of constitutionalism. He may recognize, in other words, that the continued curbing of political arbitrariness requires of him that he should abide by the provisions of which he disapproves as long as they are in effect, and try to change them, not by stretching or otherwise violating their meaning, but through the process of revision prescribed by the constitution. He may also be on his guard against the possibility that his own view of how the moral end can be promoted by government is mistaken. In its denial of all arbitrariness ethical conscience is a warning against premature certainty regarding the moral worthiness of concrete political proposals. There is a crucial distinction to be made between support for specific constitutional rules and the willingness itself to accept such rules, even when they may not seem wholly appropriate, in the interest of the higher goal.

Respect for the particular provisions of a constitution may be viewed as finally rooted in the intuition of a higher law, the approximation of which is understood to require the preservation of the dignity of man-made law. Thinking of constitutionalism as a "practical manifestation and reflection of the idea of natural law," Hallowell writes: "Constitutional government is a kind of self-restraint which the people in a democracy impose upon themselves; and, whether we have institutions of judicial review or not, its continued existence depends less upon the institutional checks provided than upon the commonly shared knowledge that there are restraints and upon willingness of individuals voluntarily to submit to those restraints."[8]

We may regard a constitution as forming a part of the varied cultural habits by which men direct their behavior towards the form of intrinsically valuable association which is community. These help to restrain the centrifugal, disruptive inclinations always present in society. They are tentative directives transcended by the directing principle itself. It is incompatible with the moral purpose of life to regard these habits as final, in need of no revision or improvement. The spirit of constitutionalism demands not only respect for the fundamental law, but the possibility to change that law on the basis of insight into how it could better serve the enduring goal. Particular constitutions are subject to a higher law. "To those who ask where this higher law is to be found," Walter Lippmann writes, "the answer is that it is a progressive discovery of men striving to civilize themselves, and that its scope and implications are a gradual revelation that is by no means completed."[9]

It has been one of my contentions that ethical conscience is better described as a principle of censure or self-examination than as a positive command to perform this or that act. Although moral conduct is attended by a sense of higher purpose, it never completely fulfills that purpose. The ultimate standard of good is always felt to have been betrayed to some extent. We may relate the idea of ethical conscience as a principle of censure to our discussion of constitutionalism by putting our own interpretation on the following compact statement by Calhoun: "It is, indeed, the *negative* power which makes the constitution, and the *positive* which makes the government. The one is the power of acting, and the other the power of preventing or arresting action. The two, combined, make constitutional governments."[10]

Against the background of the previous ethical analysis, these sentences may be read as a general description of man's moral life. The "negative power" would be the censuring, structuring activity of ethical conscience. The "positive power" we may understand as concrete human intentions. "The one is the power of acting," Calhoun writes, calling to mind our notion of impulse as the force which carries human action. The other is "the power of preventing or arresting action," he goes on, giving a description also of the role of ethical conscience in regard to impulse. "The two, combined, make constitutional governments." We may take that to mean that positive action, structured or disciplined by ethical conscience, is morality. This reading of the passage obviously strains Calhoun's meaning. He is referring in this statement not primarily to a moral "negative" on government. But since politics is largely the pursuit of partisan goals, the demands of ethical conscience in regard to the procedural rules tend to run parallel to those of enlightened self-interest. The moral goal can be advanced only through a pragmatic adjustment to the stubborn reality of political self-seeking. In relation to the latter, ethical conscience has to be a "negative." The spirit of constitutionalism, as distinguished from actual constitutions, written or unwritten, is identical to ethical conscience as applied to the organization of political life; it advances community by seeking to curb political inclinations incompatible with that goal.

We are probably well-advised to pause briefly at this juncture to recapitulate some of our previous reasoning. This rendering of the relationship between ethical conscience and constitutionalism might seem to put an undue emphasis on the negative aspect of morality. Surely, morality also has a positive side. While this is certainly true, words must not take the place of precise analysis of the underlying meaning. I have explained before in some detail in what sense ethical conscience should be regarded as an "inner check," but to avoid misunderstanding in the present context a few additional remarks may be called for.

It might be objected that quick and spontaneous decisions are often moral, and that decisions based on careful deliberation could well be immoral. The latter part of the objection need not detain us, since it is simply a restatement of the position here presented: an attempt to protect deliberation through constitutional provisions may have no other motive than a morally oblivious wish to facilitate bargaining between factional groups. Constitutional restrictions in themselves are no guarantee that morality will be promoted.

But what about the other assertion, that spontaneous acts may sometimes be moral? First of all, it is lacking in clarity. If what is meant is that impulse somehow defines morality, it is clearly false, for particular intentions are always transcended by the ultimate standard of good. If what is meant, however, is that impulse may come to participate in and thus advance the good, we are again entertaining a restatement of our original position: ethical conscience gives its sanction to certain impulses by withholding its censure and, as it were, aligning itself with them.

Most likely, the mentioned objection is the result of skipping over the essential question of just how impulses might acquire moral worth. It is a failure to subject this question to rigorous philosophical analysis which lends some credence to Rousseauistic ethics. Leaving aside the case of spontaneity which has moral consequences by mere chance, every moral act is by definition sanctioned by ethical conscience. But as I have argued at some length, that higher principle is itself never identical to the impulse calling for action. The finite reality of human acts is transcended by the good. In the strictest sense, therefore, moral virtue is always associated with a type of restraint. There is a never-ending tension between the imperfection of everything human and the standard of perfection. Man is under a permanent censure which loses some of its sharpness to the extent that he lives up to his higher self. Ethical conscience is indeed a sense of purpose, but in a world of flawed intentions and acts that purpose is revealed either through censure or a qualified withholding of censure. In the latter case, the specific act is attended by moral reassurance.

If we say that spontaneous acts are sometimes moral, we are describing in one highly ambiguous word what is in fact a dualistic experience, namely impulse and the structuring role of ethical conscience. The wording is acceptable only if it is understood that what is called a spontaneous moral act is one involving no *extended* ethical deliberation. Whether we take as an example a person whose character has already been morally structured, so that there is a certain moral momentum built into his impulsive life, or a situation in which the moral course is so clear that there might be said to be an "impulsive" inclination to follow that course, it is only after an impulse has been arrested for ethical scrutiny, however quick, that the individual can recognize it as good and thus become justified to act on it. Moral conduct presupposes the interference of the question, "Is this moral?"—which is the particularized embodiment of ethical conscience. Aristotelian good habits, to illustrate, are neither spontaneously automatic nor compelled. They are the willing ordering of impulse toward a permanent goal.

This analysis in no way contradicts the idea that ethical conscience reveals a positive purpose. It is only a reminder that in relation to human finitude in general and human evil in particular this purpose is necessarily felt as an "inner check." This point deserves special emphasis in a discussion of constitutionalism, for politics is predominantly the pursuit of selfish interests. Moreover, although it is true that individual persons sometimes act morally "on impulse," a theory of democracy must concern itself with the question of how a certain type of *collective* activity is to be organized if it is to respect and promote the moral end.

If the spirit of constitutionalism is a rejection of the arbitrary, it is also an affirmation of the good life as it is advanced by politics. It negates *because* it affirms. To say that it demands institutional restraints on partisanship is to say that it promotes the moral opposite, the substance of which is the discovery of men trying to achieve community. In a certain sense, the moral end of society can be said to be undetermined; it is a goal that has to be pursued in changing circumstances. However, as the *spirit* in which political decisions ought to be made, that end is always the same. While it is impossible to outline once and for all the particulars of the good society, it can be defined in its political aspect as the kind of society which is being realized when the people is acting in the spirit of constitutionalism. The belief that ethical conscience sanctions positive acts by government is faultless. But there is always a tendency among men of all political persuasions to exaggerate the moral purity of the cause they happen to advocate. And even when the motive is pure, as far as that is possible, the political wisdom of its translation into practical proposals may be questionable. The spirit of constitutionalism responds to human imperfection and depravity on the one hand, and the need for government action on the other. As a constant reminder of man's shortcomings, it casts a doubt on the moral worth of all political wishes. As an aspect of the principle of community, it is also what gives to politics its higher direction and final justification.

I have rejected Rousseau's idea of plebiscitary democracy because it ignores the need for moral restraints in the individual and the people. Could it not be objected that what is wrong with his democratic theory is not his rejection of constitutionalism but his failure to recognize the need for the moral self-discipline which could make his ideal of plebiscitary rule practicable? This is not really an objection to my argument, but actually a somewhat confused confirmation of it. Rousseau regards self-discipline in my sense of the term as the very root of evil.

Morality is served, he believes, by uninhibited spontaneity. What should be understood is that had he seen the moral necessity of self-restraint, he would have had to drop his ban on constitutionalism. The reason is that when men are engaging in political activity under the type of restraints which are necessary if it is to serve the common good, they are by that token also acting constitutionally. The goal requires that they order their behavior with reference to a common standard not subject to instantaneous repeal. The distinguishing mark of constitutionalism is not so much the laying down of written provisions, as is the belief of Thomas Paine.[11] It is rather the willingness for the sake of a higher goal to subject present political wishes to scrutiny according to a set of rules no itself resting on the preference of the moment.

Just how maximum room is to be made for moral considerations in the making of government policy is a matter of applying the acceptance of restraints to difficult practical problems. The formulation of specific constitutional provisions, including sanctions which increase the likelihood of adherence to them, has to be adjusted to the traditions and cultural characteristics of the particular people. In a democracy, this task is in the hands of the people and its representatives, the implication being that the common good is best served by the broadest possible participation in the process. Given the preponderance of selfish motives in politics, the goal of community cannot be advanced, except temporarily and by lucky coincidence, by simply implementing the most recent expression of majority will. There is need for an element of pause, of deliberation under the guidance of moral motives. Whatever the constitutional arrangements which are best designed to encourage such an examination of intentions before they can become government policy, those arrangements are demanded by ethical conscience.

CONSTITUTIONAL AND PLEBISCITARY DEMOCRACY INCOMPATIBLE

It is not my purpose here to develop a set of constitutional prescriptions. I have used the American constitution to illustrate a general principle and not to assert that in the American context its provisions offer *the* practical solution to the problem of making democracy compatible with the needs of the ethical life. The Constitution does tend to restrain temporary popular majorities in a way conducive to the emergence of government by "consensus." It does so without giving tyrannical veto power to a self-seeking, dedicated minority. A majority which is not merely transitory and partisan, but capable of putting sustained or even mounting pressure on the various bodies of government, can overcome the resistance of a merely partisan minority. With its builtin premium on deliberation the United States Constitution provides an opportunity for putting ethical checks both on the people's representatives and on momentary electoral majorities.

We may gain some perspective on the moral necessity of constitutionalism and at the same time give more attention to the institutional problems of democracy by putting the American constitution alongside an old and recurrent criticism of that document which has given a strong element of ambiguity to the American political tradition. I am referring to a general impatience with representative institutions as set up by the Constitution. This dissatisfaction, which has marked plebiscitary overtones, is exemplified in the thought of Thomas Jefferson. In this Enlightenment figure of eclectic and often poorly integrated views one finds an unresolved strain, reflected in American politics to this day, between the constitutional temperament as understood in this discussion and a rather different temperament, more akin to that of Jean-Jacques Rousseau. It should be made clear that in concentrating for my purposes on Jefferson's strong plebiscitary tendency, I am not claiming to be analyzing more than one side of his thought. Not only are some of his arguments to which I will refer contradicted or modified by other of his statements, but it is also possible to argue that his theory was often contradicted by his practice.

Although Jefferson finally came around to endorsing the American constitution, one need not study his political thought for long to discover reasons for regarding his approval of constitutionalism in general as qualified and ambiguous. It should be noted at the outset that when Jefferson comes down most clearly on the side of constitutional restraints, as in the case of his insistence on a bill of rights, he is usually more concerned about protecting the people against their governors than the other way around. Although by no means blind to the shortcomings of the common man, his admitted inclination is to entrust the public interest to the mass of the people or a majority thereof rather than to popular representatives. It is significant that his democratic sentiments are of a kind that tends to undermine the principle of constitutionalism. He speaks of the ideal, regarded by him as unfortunately unattainable in practice, that "every form of government were so perfectly contrived, that the will of the majority could always be obtained, fairly and without impediment." The best available type of government, which he terms "republican," is repeatedly described by him as one that allows for the most direct and faithful execution of the people's will. In its purest form, it would be "a government by its citizens in mass, acting directly and personally, according to rules established by the majority." Negatively, the principle is stated thus: "The further the departure from direct and constant control by the citizens, the less has the government of the ingredient of republicanism." Jefferson's majoritarianism is most clearly spelled out in his call for "absolute acquiescence in the decisions of the majority—the vital principle of republics."[1]

Jefferson's plebiscitary propensity brings him into collision with the idea of representation developed by Edmund Burke in his famous speech to his constituents in Bristol. Applying this Burkean idea to democracy, we may take it to mean that elected officials should not be mere executioners of shifting popular wishes. The people should have the ultimate political power, but the present majority should not have instant, unquestioned authority to dictate government policy. Popular representatives should have the opportunity to act independently to check and refine popular opinion. They should act as the people's higher self. Jefferson, however, in many places expresses deep suspicion of a conception of representation that might violate the principle of direct and immediate popular control. He applauds a treatise on the American constitution by fellow Virginian John Taylor, which, in Jefferson's view, "settles unanswerably the right of instructing representatives, and their duty to obey." Since direct popular participation or control is impossible at the national level, Jefferson settles for "the nearest approach to a pure republic, which is practicable," namely government through "representatives chosen either *pro hac vice,* or for such short terms as should render secure the duty of expressing the will of their constituents."[2]

Jefferson the plebiscitarian wants the removal of obstacles to the full and instant implementation of the people's will. Throughout he remains critical of important features in the Constitution which tend to thwart that goal. As might be expected, there is only one body in the national government of the United States that Jefferson is prepared to call "mainly republican"[3]—the House of Representatives. The reason is that, because the members of that body have a relatively short term of office, they can be expected to listen carefully to their constituents or else be rather promptly ousted. The Senate, the presidency, and the

Supreme Court are all criticized by Jefferson for being too far removed from the control of the people, by the length of their terms of office or by the fact that they are chosen or appointed only indirectly by the people. What arouses his dissatisfaction is the very real possibility of a government policy which does not always meet with the approval of the majority. The logical extension of Jefferson's line of argument are such devices as recall and referendum, which have played some role in the American political tradition.

But perhaps the most striking example of Jefferson's anti-constitutional temperament is his belief that no country should go long without a revolution. "I hold it, that a little rebellion, now and then, is a good thing, and as necessary in the political world as storms in the physical."[4] At the bottom of this lack of concern for the orderly process of government as a protection against arbitrariness lies a belief in the soundness or even goodness of the uninhibited popular will.

In view of the previous analysis of the relation between ethics and politics, it is not surprising that Jefferson's understanding of man should bear a strong resemblance in important respects to that of Rousseau. His view of human nature, like Rousseau's, is monistic. It comes in Jefferson's case steeped in an emphatic materialism and sensationalism.[5] Man's moral sense is not conceived by him as introducing a tension between immanent and transcendent in man's inner life. He describes it as a spontaneous force, an "instinct" which puts man on the moral course. Knowingly or unknowingly echoing Rousseau, he describes it as a pleasurable feeling of benevolence towards others which "prompts us irresistibly to feel and to succor their distresses."[6]

For Jefferson the plebiscitarian, we may state in conclusion, government does not have the purpose of restraining the momentary will of the people with a view to some higher moral standard. The wish of the majority at any moment is itself the most reliable expression of the public good. The best form of government is one which respects the principle that "the will of the majority is in all cases to prevail."[7]

The plebiscitary tendency in the American political tradition, contradicted in Jefferson's case by other elements, recurs in more recent expressions of impatience with constitutional restraints on the majority. A good example is the criticism directed against the so-called "deadlock of democracy" by James MacGregor Burns. The American constitutional system, Burns complains, is defective in that it "requires us to await a wide consensus before acting." It will not allow the speedy and effective implementation of the will of the majority, which should be the purpose of democracy. The basis of the presumption against simple majority rule in the Constitution, Burns observes, "has been a pervading distrust of the people when organized in a national block or party. The people, yes—but only in their separated, federalized, localized capacities. Popular government, yes—but not really popular rule by hungry majorities." The latter kind of government ought to be established, Burns argues, by revising the American form of government in accordance with what he calls "the Jeffersonian model." This model he draws from Jefferson the practical politician, whom he regards as wedded to the ideal of vigorous government action supported by a national majority coalition. Jeffersonian majority rule, Burns contends, has "a more popular, egalitarian impetus than the Madisonian."[8] Burns proposes several reforms designed to create a new form of government, such as abolition of the Electoral College, federal control over elections to the national government, making congressional districts more uniform, removal of procedures which discourage popular voting, centralization of the political parties, and removal of traditional congressional practices which undermine party discipline. What he wants is a system in which decisive power belongs to the numerical national majority and in which political candidates are members of national parties with distinct, well-defined platforms, so that elections can in effect become national plebiscites on alternative government policies.

What is of immediate concern to us here are not the specific reforms suggested by Burns, but the temperament that inspires them. According to Burns, the majority principle joined to a system of national party competition is not enough to make possible the sweeping governmental action that must be available to the majority in a more democratic America. It will take determined, central leadership. The decisive role must be played by the president. He must "assume full responsibility, in the priority areas, for the functions and effectiveness of the whole governmental system." When the power of the presidency "is exercised most responsibly it is not confined to mere tinkering."[9] The man holding that office must be able and willing to cut through the separation-ofpowers apparatus in order to get things done. For example, he has to "ignore the absurd 'rule' ... that the President does not interfere in the legislative department. He must interfere, and openly so." In his approving analysis of Jefferson's leadership in broadening executive power on the basis of a mobilized national majority, Burns observes: "The high point of Jefferson's majoritarianism ... came in the Louisiana Purchase. When the chips were down, when a great decision had to be made and pressed quickly, Jefferson violated congressional rights, by-passed accepted constitutional processes, refused to go through the long process of a constitutional amendment, and threw himself and his party on the mercy of the new popular majority that he was building up.'[10]

Whatever the accuracy of this interpretation of Jefferson's action, it is apparent that Burns sees a need for executive leadership that is willing to bend or even break the rules when it is necessary to serve the presumed interests of the majority. "The great political leader is not content to whittle down his goals to what he thinks he can achieve through the existing structure of political forces. Rather he seeks to enlarge and vivify the structure so that the goals can be realized as fully as possible. He knows that archaic governmental routines cannot always be broken up by adjustment and adaptation but ... by 'the application of overwhelming external force.'"[11]

Burns's impatience with constitutional obstacles to instant and sweeping change does not quite amount to a repudiation of the idea of constitutionalism. Whether for tactical or other reasons, he does not attack it head on. But he undermines it by advocating an exercise of power not overly sensitive to the intent or spirit of constitutional provisions. If he sees the danger of political arbitrariness, he is apparently less disturbed by it than by the risk that the popular majority might not get its way.

It has been suggested by critics that Burns's unwillingness to accept the restraints of the American constitution is rooted in frustration over the fact that at this time in American history those restraints happen to reduce the likelihood of public implementation of the particular policies that he believes to be mandatory.[12] Assuming, however, that his arguments for the empowering of numerical national majorities is not just a case of intellectual opportunism, we must take him to mean that there is something about the uninhibited will of the mass of the people which entitles it to a decisive influence over government policy. If Burns is to retain the idea that democracy can be defended on ethical grounds, the presumption must be that this type of popular will is somehow morally superior to other types. He would be leaning then in the direction of the Rousseauistic belief in the morality of spontaneous popular wishes as they emerge, not from citizens in their capacity as members of social groups, but in their capacity as members of the undifferentiated mass. Although Rousseau does not advocate strong executive leadership by one individual for normal circumstances, it is difficult not to see the affinity between his pervasive hostility to inner and outer restraints and Burns's belief that "the presidency at its best seeks to liberate American society as a whole from whatever binds it."[13] The premise at work would seem to be that only if the people is free to cast off all institutional shackles can true democracy be realized.

It would be possible to question the democratic claims of Burns's brand of plebiscitarianism by arguing that it enhances the danger of popularly supported despotism, or "Caesarism" in James Burnham's term.[14] The United States Constitution as it now stands implies a wide variety of sectional and local associations and attachments among the people. It might be said that the Constitution assumes the most significant meaning of "the people" to be the citizens organized in groups of various kinds. Contrary to the Rousseauistic ideal, it does not expect the citizens to disregard their membership in such associations when addressing public issues. The sense of the people is taken, not so much with reference to their mere numbers as their concrete, social natures. What is desired is that a concern for the welfare of one's own associations be joined to or at least tempered by a concern for the good of the people as a whole. A constitution that protects and also encourages sectional and local associations and a general decentralization and dispersion of power is among other things a potent obstacle against attempts to mobilize a people behind the man on horseback. Apart from the institutional hurdles sanctioned in law, citizens who have close ties to various social groups are not likely to give their undivided loyalty to a political leader or organization. One general effect of Burns's proposed institutional reforms, however, would seem to be to promote the transformation of the American people "in their separated, federalized, localized capacities" into something closer to the Rousseauistic ideal of an undifferentiated mass of individuals. Burns's wish is that the will of the people be determined with reference to the numerical national majority. One wonders if the institutional detachment or dissolution of the people which will make this possible does not also make easier the task of a tyrannical majority or a despotic popular leader who in the name of the people would like to establish complete political control. It is worthy of note that insistence on the unlimited authority of the popular will often tends to go together with a preference for highly centralized, or even totalitarian, forms of government.

Although not entirely clear-cut, Burns's theory of democracy exhibits a general tendency whose ultimate ethical and political implications are brought out in the thought of Jean-Jacques Rousseau. Burns and other theorists of democracy of the plebiscitary bent may not actually be self-admitted disciples of Rousseau and, needless to say, they are likely to differ with him in many particulars. They do share with him an impatience with constitutional restraints and a related presumption in favor of the spontaneous popular will. In the final analysis, their type of democratic theory must be defended on moral grounds. They may not all have recognized the full implications of their plebiscitary preferences, but the logical ethical basis for those preferences is supplied by Rousseau. And if my analysis of that archetypal plebiscitarian is generally correct, they do not withstand critical examination. We are justified, therefore, in approaching the institutional prescriptions of these theorists with considerable skepticism.

A theory of democracy which does not recognize the paramount need of constitutionalism evades the realities of man's moral predicament. An attempt to carry the plebiscitary ideal into practice will tend, in the long run at least, to defeat the ethical purpose of community and thereby also to undermine popular rule itself. Plebiscitary democracy, it may be suggested, is not really a political concept at all, but a quasi-concept. It is not based on a realistic assessment of the possibilities open to man, but on some highly dubious assumptions: *assuming* that political man is not predominantly or even partially motivated by selfishness; *assuming* that he is instead spontaneously propelled in the direction of morality; *assuming* that the popular majority of the moment is most likely to give expression to the common good—assuming all of this, plebiscitary democracy becomes a concept descriptive of human potentiality. But these things, I have tried to show, cannot be assumed. They actually run counter to concrete experience. Few modern democratic theorists embrace plebiscitarianism in the pure Rousseauistic form, but many lean in that direction. To that extent they give to democratic theory a utopian slant inimical to a realistic consideration of the institutional problems of popular rule.

That is not to say that each proposal for changing the American political system which is advanced by thinkers like Burns is necessarily destructive of the moral goal of politics. Precisely what constitutional arrangements will help to make democracy compatible with the needs of the ethical life under some particular historical circumstances is not just a matter of motive but of political prudence and imagination. Obviously, constitutional restraints are not an end in themselves. They are desirable insofar as they serve the higher goal. For many reasons even the most nobly and skillfully conceived constitution may at some time begin to defeat its original purpose. Profound social and political changes may necessitate constitutional amendment or even transformation. A sound constitution recognizes that fact and provides the means for its own revision. The point to be made about Burns's recommendations is that whatever merit may be found in them attaches to them not because of, but in spite of, his plebiscitary leanings.

This argument regarding the two available concepts of popular rule may perhaps be summed up by drawing a parallel between two types of citizens and two types of democracy. Rousseau asks us to picture an individual who always acts spontaneously. To this type of citizen corresponds a form of democracy which gives complete freedom to the spontaneous popular will. This plebiscitary notion of democracy is not founded in reality but in an utopian world. We may oppose to this another image, which pictures an individual who acts under self-imposed moral restraints. To that kind of citizen corresponds a popular government under constitutional limitations designed to promote a certain quality of popular will. Only this type of democracy recognizes man's real moral predicament. It allows an opportunity to temper the forces of political self-seeking by considerations of the common good. It can be joined to and sustained by man's sense of higher purpose. Constitutional democracy at its best, we may conclude, would be popular self-rule in the cause of community. To the extent that democracy approaches this high standard, it can be supported on moral grounds. Going a step further than is really warranted by my argument, it may perhaps even be said that in this concept of democracy we have the noblest idea of politics.

DECENTRALIZATION

Because I have sought to relate ethical conscience to institutions of government and used the American constitution as a practical illustration, it might perhaps be inferred that I am putting considerable faith in the potential of a large society like the United States to become a community as here defined. This implication is not intended. It should be understood that my theory of the reconciliation of popular rule with the ethical life is not restricted to any particular level of government. Indeed, the spirit of constitutionalism is the political aspect of a principle which applies to all forms of associated activity. The thesis is not so much that there can be a "national" community; it is rather that to the extent that community can be promoted by government at whatever level, the latter must be guided by the spirit of constitutionalism.

It has been persuasively argued by many theorists that the element of conflict in life tends to grow as you move from local to national relationships, and from national to international.[15] My theory of democracy is not intended to contradict this view, as long as it is understood that concepts like *local, national,* and *international* are not philosophically distinct categories but only pragmatically useful classifications. We cannot expect the cessation of the war of all against all. The motive of community is forever threatened by mere partisanship. National politics, even more than local politics, is likely to exhibit a weak impetus toward morality. Still, to the extent that a people is able to transcend selfish interests, it is making its government a partial manifestation of community.

One conclusion of my whole argument is that community could not exist in an undifferentiated mass of individuals. It consists in a special type of associated activity. The argument has not been designed to prove, but has nevertheless hinted, that the values of true community are most likely to be realized in groups which are much less than socially all encompassing. This theme has been developed with great care and perceptiveness by Robert Nisbet.[16] He argues convincingly that it is in the "autonomous groups" of society, such as the family, the local church, school, and club, that most men will be able to find a sense of meaningful belonging and personal worth. A feeling of community thrives in associations of small, manageable proportions. This line of argument raises a very important question which is intimately related to the one I have sought to answer in this study: must not democracy, if it is to be conducive to truly human values, keep the control over public decisions as close as possible to those who are affected by them? Here, it may be possible to find some considerable common ground with contemporary political theorists whose philosophical premises are quite different from my own. Looking for ways to counteract the powerlessness induced by big government (and big organizations generally) in today's Western democracies, Robert Dahl, for example, suggests the following as one "pragmatic principle": "If a matter is best dealt with by a democratic association, seek always to have that matter dealt with by the smallest association that can deal with it satisfactorily."[17]

One need not endorse Dahl's entire political theory or all of his institutional recommendations to accept this idea, which looks much like a rediscovery in modern circumstances of the classical idea of subsidiarity. The evidence about the conditions of community that has been presented, together with that supplied by scholars like Nisbet, indicates that Dahl's principle, which is of course not original with him among contemporary thinkers, is a necessary supplement to my own theory of democracy. If community does require decentralized government and vital autonomous groups, as seems indeed to be the case, it is obvious that the formulation of particular democratic constitutions must be adjusted to this need. My own contribution is the thesis that, whatever the level or scope of government, its activities must reflect the spirit of constitutionalism if community is to be promoted. This is not to assume that the "nation" is the primary sphere of community. Actually, my position coincides with Burke's view that the source of warm feelings for the state as a whole is in the affections that we develop for the smaller groups to which we belong in society.

"DEMOCRATIZATION"

According to some contemporary theorists, the time has come to extend democratic decision making to areas of social life which have long been regarded as belonging to the "private" sphere for example, the business corporation. In the United States, arguments of this kind have been advanced by Robert Dahl and Peter Bachrach. The issue is too large to be dealt with adequately here, but a few brief remarks may help to clarify my own main point. It should be obvious from the rejection of a sharp distinction between "public" and "private" that I am not inclined to accept the type of rigid, aprioristic notion of the proper role of government which is found in some socialists, laissez-faire liberals, and anarchists. By the same token, I could only be suspicious of the view that the salvation of modern democracy is in a broader application of a certain method of making decisions. With somewhat different emphases, Dahl and Bachrach contend that we are employing a too restrictive conception of what falls in the "political" category.[18] Significantly, the two men appear to be guilty of precisely the same mistake in that they treat democracy as primarily a set of formal rules. Theirs would seem to be a procedural view of popular government, only one with a majoritarian and egalitarian slant, strongest perhaps in Bachrach. It is symptomatic that Dahl is forced to speak of certain types of delegated political authority that he himself believes are necessary to effective popular rule as "nondemocratic."[19] Lacking in both theorists is a clear understanding of the difference between plebiscitary and constitutional democracy and of the fact that democracy, if it is to be a meaningful idea, must be viewed as implying a whole way of life.

Political institutions are indistinguishable from the cultural ethos of a people. Therefore, if a society is losing its commitment to what is above short-term economic efficiency and various kinds of narrow self-interest, the introduction of a certain decision-making device into new areas is not likely to lead to a restoration of genuine human values. The argument of Dahl and Bachrach is refreshing in that it challenges the conventional liberal and socialistic views of the role of the state. For the most part, however, the two men do not go beyond a new combination of these views under the guiding principle of "more democracy"—to which one may say with Irving Babbitt that what is needed is not more, but better democracy.[20] The problem of finding the institutional means through which the good society can be promoted in new circumstances is most certainly a very important one. It should be faced in a pragmatic frame of mind, and the magnitude of the difficulties confronting democracy today may well require some unorthodox solutions. The prerequisite of truly well-considered proposals, however, is an understanding of the nature of community. Much of the present concern about the undermining of democracy in modern Western society does spring from a sense that essential human values are increasingly threatened. Unfortunately, when it comes to showing what, ultimately, is a human value, most modern democratic theory is sadly lacking. In this area various doctrines of moral relativism or nihilism are a major obstacle to intellectual renewal. As long as this fundamental flaw persists, the institutional reforms that are suggested will all too often be desperate shots in the dark. It is not enough to insist, as is fashionable among social scientists today, that once again "values" have to be taken into account or promoted by scholars. What is needed in democratic theory is not some infusion of subjectively derived "value preferences" in the spirit of plebiscitarianism, but an effort to rethink the problems of popular government in the light of the transcendent standard of community.

THE WRITTEN AND UNWRITTEN CONSTITUTION

("Political Philosophy and the Unwritten Constitution," *Modern Age*, Vol. 34, No. 4, 1992.) It is common for conservatives to think that the meaning of the US Constitution is found in the text of the document. To respect the Constitution is to give intellectual assent to its words and principles. The remedy for violations of the Constitution is to educate as many as possible on what the document actually says. But American constitutional rule is only secondarily adherence to a text. An ahistorical, abstract notion of the meaning of the Constitution neglects the framers' assumptions regarding human nature and society and the historical practices and influences that pointed them in the direction of constitutionalism in the first place. Their Constitution is but a political manifestation of an entire view and way of life. It derives its purposes and practical authority from historically evolved habits and beliefs. The text of the Constitution is the tip of an iceberg. If the moral, cultural, and other supports of constitutionalism begin to erode, the Constitution loses its authority and practical efficacy—its meaning.

Discriminating observers recognize that political practice in the United States today bears only a faint resemblance to the Constitution written at Philadelphia. The old Constitution enjoys a formal, ceremonial existence still and possesses a limited practical efficacy, but American government and politics have been transformed in the direction of a centralized mass democracy greatly at odds with what the Framers envisioned.

To understand the distance between the intent of the Framers and current practice it is insufficient to compare the present state of affairs to the words of documents like the Constitution and the Federalist Papers. Their real meaning emerges only when the texts are put in their religious, moral, cultural, social, and political context. The Constitution and related documents all imply an entire view of human nature and society. The particular text assumes and forms an inextricable part of a more comprehensive and unwritten constitution, which includes the moral ethos of the Framers. The institutions and procedures prescribed by the written document imply a particular kind of civilization and a particular kind of human being. Without a certain personality type setting the tone in society, the government could not function as intended. The Constitution presupposes character traits in tune with its prescriptions, and those prescriptions are expected to foster that personality.

A consideration of what the Framers assumed and implied will demonstrate the inadequacy of interpretations that look for the meaning of "the Founding" in texts abstracted from historical settings and concrete substance. Neglect of the unwritten constitution may serve as an example of the debilitating effects of abstractionist, ahistorical modes of thought in contemporary political philosophy.

Of special importance in ascertaining the intent of the Framers is the moral ethos that permeates the unwritten constitution and informs their written work. Attending to this dimension of the Constitution helps reveal the extent of the decline of American constitutionalism. Studying the work of the Framers in this manner shows the futility of trying to restore crumbling constitutional structures by invoking the "principles" of the Constitution in the abstract. Returning to the intent of the Framers, if it were possible or even desirable today, would require nothing less than a revival of the constitutional personality and of the civilization from which it is indistinguishable. The disintegration of constitutionalism in America manifests the emergence of a different type of civilization and human being. To stress the need, in the face of that development, to recover the "principles" of the Framers neglects the presuppositions and concrete entailments of their ideas. Most of the assumptions behind their constitutional preferences are left unstated, because they are taken for granted. Abstractionist interpretations misunderstand both the intent of the Framers and the prospects for constitutionalism today.

Grasping the moral ethos of the Framers goes a long way toward explaining their preference for a decentralized, regionally differentiated, and group-oriented society. The Framers assume the preponderance of a particular type of moral responsibility with deep roots in classical and Christian civilization. The virtue they admire and hope will assist the realization of their plans is not some abstract precept or ethereal sentiment. It is a virtue of character and concrete obligations that generates social relationships and institutions of a certain type and quality. This moral ethos can be contrasted with a very different notion of virtue, one that has become increasingly influential in the Western world. While the older kind of virtue manifests itself in individual, personal responsibility and tends to foster private and local community and a decentralized society, the more recent kind of virtue manifests itself in abstract ideas and sentiments and tends to foster a collectivistic and centralized society. The two types of morality may resemble each other in terminology, but they represent incompatible views of human nature and society and have radically different social and political ramifications.

To bring out a crucially important aspect of the Framers' outlook it may be useful to present first a view that is very different from theirs. A distinctive feature of the political philosophy of Jean-Jacques Rousseau is the rejection of social subdivisions in the state. According to Rousseau, the citizens must not be distracted from the good of the whole by group loyalties and interests. The proper dedication to the common good requires that the people be dissolved into an undifferentiated mass of individuals. Traditional Western civilization is incompatible with Rousseau's vision and must be overturned. To accomplish that goal it is necessary to destroy the elaborate groupings and social patterns through which that civilization manifests itself. The Greeks argued that man is a social being who can realize his true humanity only through associations, starting with the household. Christianity continued that tradition, making its own additions and revisions. But Rousseau wants society swept clean of decentralized, group-oriented structures. He wants the state to have no "sectional associations" (*société partielle*).[1]

Rousseau's philosophy is thus in the sharpest possible conflict with American tradition. In America, groups and subdivisions have not only proliferated, but they have been encouraged and protected. Alexis de Tocqueville was struck by the habit of Americans to join together, privately and locally, to conduct their own affairs. He took special note of the influential role of the churches.

It is important to note that under the old Constitution the American people are recognized only as members of sub-divisions, of States and electoral districts. The Framers set up not a single institution through which the American people as an undifferentiated mass of individuals could express their will. The will of the people is plainly viewed as something very different from a numerical majority. The people, the Framers say or imply, are members of groups or subdivisions. The interests of persons are seen as more or less bound up with the interests of their most cherished associations. Beyond the Constitution itself, American tradition in general gives power, protection, and independence to countless social and political subdivisions. Without always making it explicit, the Framers view life in autonomous groups as fulfilling a basic human need.[2]

Federalism is just one of the more striking examples of the old American preference for local and regional autonomy and decentralization. The way in which the United States Senate is constituted illustrates the Framers' respect for sectional interests. According to the democratist standard of one-man-one-vote, all persons should carry the same political weight at the polls. The Constitution embodies a much different conception of popular rule. It gives all States, regardless of size and population, the same representation in the Senate. New York has the same number of Senators as Delaware, California as Wyoming. The votes cast by citizens of Delaware and Wyoming are, as it were, counted many times. This is done in deference to the States as semi-autonomous entities worthy of support and protection. The enormous expansion of American central government in the last century makes it difficult to remember that the Framers actually expected the States and the people to retain all powers not specifically delegated to the central government.

Even in the case of the allegedly most popular, or "democratic," institution of the United States Government, the House of Representatives, the Framers balanced regional against numerical considerations. A tiny State that purely quantitative standards would leave without representation in the House is guaranteed at least one representative. The Framers also assigned the task of selecting Presidents not to the mass of the people, but to the Electoral College, containing as many members from each State as that State had representation in the House and Senate. Again small States were deliberately given vast overrepresentation.

Traditional American society as a whole nurtured decentralized social and political structures and a multiplicity of subdivisions and associations. In asserting the one-man-one-vote formula as integral to the Constitution, the Warren Court introduced an atomistic and democratist notion alien to the Framers. The pervasiveness and proliferation of communal ties in the older American society are among the reasons why it is misguided to treat the political philosophy of John Locke as paradigmatic for the United States. Locke's social and political atomism, focused on the rights of discrete individuals, does not account for an American historical reality that is in some respects surprisingly reminiscent of medieval Western society.

It is crucial to understanding the written and unwritten constitutions to recognize the ethical import of the old American affinity for groups and associations. The Framers, their class, and the American people in general were steeped in a Western tradition whose conception of virtue gave precedence to the responsibility of the individual in personal relationships and associations. Aristotle had explained the centrality of the household in fostering sound habits. The Romans had also viewed family as preparing the individual for wider duties. Christianity gave succinct expression to what would become the heart of the moral ethos of the Western world when it stressed "love of neighbor." It is primarily in one's daily contacts with people that one should show goodness and charity. The person's chief obligation is to limit his own selfishness and generally to improve character so that he can do right by others.

By 'neighbor' is meant not people in the abstract and in the distance, but people of flesh and blood with names and faces. In his more intimate associations the individual gets practice in "loving neighbors." There virtue is concrete and personal. The individual is continually encouraged to consider the needs and wishes of others. In the family especially, the person learns both what it means to be loved and cared for and what it means to love and care for others. Taking others into account becomes a habit. It is not possible to get away with mere moral posturing. People who present themselves as better than they are are mercilessly exposed when their actions fall short of their words. Over time, life in groups and associations tempers the selfish ego. It fosters character traits conducive to a larger good. Having gotten its start in the family and other relationships at fairly chose range, moral responsibility can be applied to wider social and political concerns.

Note carefully that traditional Western moral virtue is not a sweet sentiment or a generalized concern for mankind in the abstract. Virtue is a matter of character. It means making the best of self and acting responsibly toward real people, which means that morality is hard. To make love of neighbor particularly difficult, real people are frequently less than pleasant, and they may be our competitors. Behaving charitably may require strength of will. Virtue shows itself, thus, not in high-sounding phrases or teary-eyed "compassion" but in responsible conduct.

Compare this older Western and American ethos to the common modern notion of virtue. The latter can be described as morality in the abstract. Unlike the older virtue, it does not presuppose improvement of self. It can be espoused by the worst of human beings, by people who are very difficult to live and work with. These same individuals can ooze benevolence for people in the abstract and talk incessantly about "justice," "human rights," and "the common good." They can advocate schemes for sweeping social and political change. In fact, the wider the scope of their virtuous project, the more compelling is supposed to be the evidence of a superior morality.

But this abstract and self-congratulatory virtue cares about nobody in particular. It is morality made easy. Anybody can do it. You can remain the same odious person as before while professing noble principles and feelings. From the point of view of the older Western ethic, the new virtue actually looks like a moral hoax. It is a more or less subtle escape from man's primary moral responsibility: to make the best of self and do right by neighbors. Abstract moralism is less interested in improving self than in improving others. And the need to take concrete action is somehow always transferred elsewhere, typically to government, which acquires ever new responsibilities and becomes ever more centralized.

The importance of this contrast between different notions of virtue cannot be exaggerated. The two kinds of virtue foster different human beings and build entirely different societies. From the old virtue of character springs a decentralized, group-oriented society. Those have the chief responsibility for acting on problems and opportunities who are most directly affected by them. Help is sought beyond the people most involved only to the extent that they cannot satisfactorily manage their own affairs. De Tocqueville found among Americans in the early decades of the 1800s a pronounced disinclination to hand over responsibilities to authorities further away.[3]

The traditional moral ethos of the West shows its own substantive meaning only in the kind of concrete social and political patterns that have been described. Man is thought to express his essential nature and find his greatest satisfaction in associations, starting with the family. Rousseau knew what he was doing when he turned against "sectional associations." Only by destroying the socio-political structures in which the older ethos manifested itself could you effectively destroy it.

Federalism and decentralization in the American tradition can be adequately understood only in the context of the old Western moral heritage. If regional, local, and private initiative and independence are eroding today, it is because a new ethos is replacing the older one. The new moralism is undermining the virtue of character and undermining the corresponding exercise of up-close responsibility. The new virtue generates a centralized and expansionist government which ceaselessly meddles in the life of the citizens.

No amount of abstract principle can restore decentralized constitutional government and a vital federalism. The political system envisioned by the Framers assumed the preponderance of a particular type of human being, what has here been called the constitutional personality. Without that personality of character a decentralized society is not possible. To revive American constitutionalism, if it can still be done, would require not more people who talk all the time about "justice," "the common good," and "the best regime" but people who are able to shoulder concrete responsibilities so that the reconstruction of society could begin where it matters most: in the personal lives of the citizens.

Trying to restore the intent and the work of the Framers by advocating abstract principle avoids the heart of the matter. It bypasses the central need of all civilized life. the shaping of moral character. Character, let it be underlined, is not the same as keeping nice-sounding "principles" in your head. In fact, talking about virtue in the abstract easily becomes an escape from what is much more difficult and needed, the actual improvement of self and the actual exercise of responsibility. To that extent, endless theorizing about "the good" aggravates the erosion of a free and decentralized society. One of the dangers of philosophical abstractionism is that it discourages attention to the concrete texture of responsibility and distracts the individual from obligations that are near and personal. It turns virtue into a matter of correct thinking.

Rather than attuning the individual to the actual moral opportunities of historical existence, abstractionism invites him to contemplate "ideal" propositions. "The good" of abstract theorizing does not belong to the world of particulars in which the person has to act and hence is not directly relevant to the needs of specific situations. Even if abstractionism encourages the individual to keep the idea of "the good" in his head, he becomes used to more or less ignoring it in practical conduct. The effect of centering morality in ahistorical contemplation is to undermine the virtue of character, including the self-restraint that can hold the individual's lower self in check.

This criticism of abstractionism is not directed against philosophy in general. There can be no question of rejecting or discounting reasoning that is truly philosophical. It should be said also that there is a special sense in which genuine philosophy can be said to be "abstract": it is contemplative and conceptual, not a form of practical action. The object of criticism here is poor philosophy, the kind that attempts to separate itself from the world of particulars in which human beings actually dwell. Good humanistic philosophy *embraces* historical particularity and *articulates it*: universality and particularity are at the same time inseparable and in tension.[4]

A most unfortunate weakness of postwar American intellectual conservatism has been its limited interest in philosophy beyond loosely held generalities and formulas. A lack of philosophical breadth, depth, and discipline made possible the paradoxical spread of ahistorical or anti-historical habits of mind. It is now widely believed that sound theorizing assesses ideas apart from considerations of historical substance and circumstance. The meaning of ideas and principles are looked for within textual formulations themselves, as if the concrete referents and larger experiential context of words and terms were not part of their meaning. According to this view, the principles of the good society can be discerned and pronounced by enlightened individuals who reflect in isolation from historical experience and circumstance. It is believed that doctrinal formulations can carry precise and definitive meaning. This philosophical and interpretive stance is the epistemological counterpart of religious fundamentalism.[5]

That anti-historical sentiment should be common among academics labeled "conservative" could not be more paradoxical, for if intellectually serious modern conservatism has any distinctive feature, it is surely the historical consciousness and the sense of the intimate connection between universality and historical particularity. Most persons of traditional views have a conviction, based in religion, ethical intuition, or philosophy, or all three, that there is a universal moral order and that right and wrong are not questions of subjective preference. But the term "conservatism" indicates that the position to which it refers is conservative of something, specifically, of the ethical awareness that emerges from the great classical and Judaeo-Christian heritage. As in the case of Edmund Burke, the sense of universality is indistinguishable from the historical sense. What is ethically universal transcends history and particular civilizations, but it becomes known to man only in concrete historical manifestations. Moral good cannot simply be a creature of convention, for history produces evil as well as good. But only a deep and wide-ranging historical sense can distinguish true universality from momentary and idiosyncratic preferences.

There has been much loose talk over the last few decades about the dangers of "historicism." A belief in moral universality and lasting truth is said to be incompatible with stressing the historical nature of human existence. That moral and epistemological relativism, as ordinarily understood, poses a danger to civilization hardly needs repeating, but it betrays ignorance to assert that the only real alternative to relativism is ahistorical ratiocination.

Although espoused by some individuals reputed to be "conservative," moral and epistemological abstractionism is profoundly anti-conservative. The notion that real universality must be sharply distinguished from historical particularity clashes, for example, with the belief that man is dependent for moral, intellectual, and cultural guidance on the human heritage of life and letters. Among those who have uncritically accepted a doctrine of abstract "principles" are many philosophically innocent Christians, perhaps especially Roman Catholics, who vaguely assume a connection between those "principles" and natural law. The latter is interpreted in a rationalistic and legalistic manner. Properly concerned to affirm universal morality, many Christians have, for lack of real exposure to philosophical alternatives, attached themselves to ahistorical assumptions that are not easily reconciled with what they presumably also believe: that the transcendent Word became flesh, that the Logos was *incarnated* in history. Drawing no philosophical lesson from this religious belief, they blithely accept the notion that universality could have no integral association with historical particularity. Many others with conservative instincts follow a similar suicidal course. The belief in "universal values" is transformed into an assertion of abstract principles that is sometimes hard to distinguish from the Jacobin advocacy of "rights" inspired by Jean-Jacques Rousseau.[6]

Abstractionism affords a limited and limiting perspective on the Framers and the state of the Constitution today. It lacks a sense of the concrete substance and implications of ideas. Abstractionism misses the central importance of the unwritten constitution. It diverts attention from the world of historical particularity. Appealing as ahistorical theorizing is to some academics today, such thinking was not the manner of the Framers. The Constitution is the result of deep and plentiful reflection, but it is not a blueprint based on ahistorical ratiocination.

Federalist No. 37 is here both explicit and emphatic: it is a strength of the Constitution, Madison writes, that it does not have "that artificial structure and regular symmetry which an abstract view of the subject might lead an ingenious theorist to bestow on a Constitution planned in his closet or in his imagination."[7] The work of the Framers was creative and distinctive, to be sure, but it was historically rooted and informed, and adjusted to concrete circumstances. If we are to understand their Constitution with all of its unstated assumptions, preconditions, and entailments, and if we are to understand the forces that are now destroying it, a philosophical outlook is needed that is attuned to historical realities, both past and present.

Many would like us to believe that the great intellectual struggle of today is between "historicists" of various kinds and defenders of universal truths and values. But this formulation of alternatives leaves out the one truly fruitful course of philosophical renewal. The intellectually significant choice is not between historical and anti-historical positions, but between historicism that does and historicism that does not acknowledge the universal. Abstractionism manages to misconstrue both universality and particularity. Rejecting the historical consciousness, it engenders rigidities and reifications that can only give universality a bad name. In its fondness for disembodied ideas and texts rather than historical realities abstractionism becomes an escape from the concrete and acute problems of our time.

THE UNSHACKLING OF POWER

("America's Coup D'État in the Making: Deception and Self-Deception," *Epistulae*, No. 4, 2008. A shorter version was published as "Power Play" in *The American Conservative*, October 6, 2008.) American conservatism has been closely associated with defending the Constitution of the United States, but in recent decades it has been surprisingly accepting of strains of thought that, superficial appearances to the contrary, justify and boost an already far-advanced centralization and expansion of power, not least in foreign affairs. This thinking runs counter to the framers' Constitution and is more generally incompatible with America's traditional culture.

Following Plato, many moralists have associated political virtue with a reluctance to pursue and exercise power. To want to rule others is to be morally disqualified from doing so. The strong tendency in traditional Western political thought to disparage a desire for power has been unfortunate. Without some people governing others, basic social order could not exist, to say nothing of effecting desirable change. The prejudice against power-seeking has left politics too much to people with the wrong kind of ambition, who want to rule as an end in itself.

The reason for observing that the pursuit of power need not be immoral but can be a means to good is that this article will challenge a particular manifestation of the will to power—one that finds expression in increasingly influential arguments for boosting the prerogatives of the American president and the federal government. The criticism that will be directed here against that hankering for domination must not be misunderstood as stemming from opposition to any and all efforts to acquire power. What will be rejected is an inordinate and blatantly partisan, and therefore perverse, craving to rule—a dream not just about taking over the US government but about dominating the world. The people who have this desire attempt to conceal its real nature by pretending that it comports well with the thinking of the framers of the US Constitution. It is in fact alien to that thinking. Would that power of a different quality could prevail against it!

A merely self-serving desire for power cannot present itself as such. It must portray itself as a wish to assist others. How best to argue for giving you or your group great power? If you are able to persuade others that the present world is grossly oppressive and destructive of human happiness but that you can make it much better, those others may support mobilizing massive power and placing it in your hands or the hands of people like you. The more ambitious your scheme for benevolent change, the greater the need for power.

Since the French Revolution, ideologies have been exceptionally conducive to power seeking. Jacobinism, Communism, and National Socialism are alike in promising glorious change and assuming the desirability of giving vast power to those who claim to know what needs to be done. A few years ago, David Frum and Richard Perle provided an all-purpose justification for unlimited power: putting "an end to evil"—the title of their co-authored book. Now there is a noble and ambitious goal! Power beyond the dreams of avarice would be needed to realize it. That rooting out evil might be an endless task only increases its appeal to a ravenous will to power. We are, of course, supposed to believe that the connection between advocating sweeping change and needing great power is purely coincidental.

Jacobinism and Marxism were openly revolutionary. They were the ideologies of out-groups challenging existing elites. What this writer has called neo-Jacobinism is the ideology of people on the inside, members of America's elites, who wish to make the military and other might of the United States a more pliant and powerful tool and who are attempting a creeping coup d'état from within. According to their ideology, America is called by history to create a better world based on universal principles. Virtuous American power must be unleashed. Their main excuse at present for exercising extra-constitutional power is to combat "Terrorism," but any threat to their great cause is a potential justification for setting the Constitution aside.

The rise of the huge, centralized Federal government and the corresponding decline of limited, decentralized government resulted from changes deep in the American mind and imagination. The new Jacobins take advantage of the fading of the old ethos and hasten its disappearance by advocating notions incompatible with it.

The old American idea of government was indistinguishable from the commandment to "love thy neighbor." That morality stressed the importance of the person trying to control his own evil and weakness. Strength of will—character—had to be built up so that the person would become capable of more loving familial and local relationships and more responsible citizenship. This morality made for strong communities and self-reliance and minimized the need for government. Alexis de Tocqueville pointed to the great reluctance among Americans in the early 19th century to give up power over their own lives to any distant authority.

The Constitution rested on an unwritten constitution, which was America's religious, moral, intellectual, cultural, and social habits and beliefs. Traditional America encouraged a strong attachment to life lived up-close. It fostered self-restraint, modesty, respect for law, and a willingness to compromise. It was this heritage that brought into being the constitutional personality. Just as people were in the habit of imposing internal checks on desire, so were they predisposed to accept and respect external constitutional and other legal constraints. Without such people, the Constitution could not work as intended.

But the self-understanding of Americans slowly changed. Throughout the Western world a very different moral ethos was spreading that shifted attention away from intimate associations and local community. It rejected the old notion of original sin and of personal responsibility for people up close. It found morality not in acts of character toward particular individuals—neighbors—but in "idealistic," sentimental caring for unfortunate collectives and mankind at large. The older personality, which the Constitution both assumed and required, began to wither. Americans started to abdicate authority to benevolent-sounding politicians far away.

Increasingly, doing good became perceived as the responsibility of government, which alone could take on the large projects now said to be demanded by morality. Governmental, collective action gradually replaced individual, private and communal responsibility. The moral momentum behind the old decentralized society weakened. Today strong, centralized Federal power seems to more and more Americans not merely acceptable but desirable. This is so because they are absorbing the anti-traditional moral sensibility now dominant not only in the universities, the arts, the news media, and the entertainment and publishing industries but in many churches. Hence Americans say increasingly to government: "Act for us!"

Much of the intellectual opposition to this trend has been confused and self-defeating. A prime example is the way many conservatives, thinking that they were shoring up traditional beliefs, attached themselves to the ideas of Leo Strauss (1899–1973), whose disciples became a major force in American academia and national politics. A refugee from Nazi Germany, Strauss taught for many years at the University of Chicago. Because he appeared to defend a classical, ancient notion of universal moral right, many did not notice that he was actually discrediting respect for tradition. Strauss and his disciples advocated an anti-historical, un-conservative notion of moral universality.

According to Strauss, no real philosopher gives any credence to "the conventional" or "the ancestral," to use his terms. To respect them represents the greatest of all intellectual sins, "historicism." Inherited ways are, he insisted, mere accidents of history. Respect is owed solely to "the simply right," which is ahistorical and rational. Strauss sharply criticized Edmund Burke, who saw the possibility of moral universality acquiring historical form. Strauss's abstract notion of natural right ruled out the idea that a particular tradition might, despite inevitable flaws, embody the quest for moral universality and be, for that reason, worthy of allegiance.

Strauss's ideas were blithely absorbed by many Christians, not least philosophically unsophisticated and naive Roman Catholics, who perceived him as a defender of moral right. They did not realize that his conception of universality was markedly different from that of Christianity and related philosophical currents. They did not understand or care that in rejecting tradition as a proper source of guidance Strauss was attacking one of the pillars of their faith. They did not comprehend that by sharply separating the universal from the particular Strauss ruled out universality becoming selectively incarnate in history and was striking at the very core of their professed beliefs. Specifically, he was denying the possibility of the Incarnation, of the Word becoming flesh.

Straussian political philosophy has sought to detach Americans from their historically existing tradition of constitutionalism with its deep and distinctive roots in history and to make them loyal instead to abstract principles of Straussian design that have been attributed to the founders. Straussians are not all alike—in a few, the anti-historical prejudice is diluted to some extent by respect for America's actual past—but prominent disciples of Strauss such as Allan Bloom, Harry Jaffa, and Walter Berns, who differ in some ways, all agree that what is admirable about America is not its concrete, historical self but the abstract principles of the founders. In the last few decades, Straussian conceptions of Americanism, patriotism and virtue have been widely advocated in academia, including America's military academies. That terms like these can be given a distinctly anti-traditional meaning has been little noticed.

By propagating a rationalistic, anti-historical notion of moral right Strauss and his disciples have created a deep prejudice against cherishing America's distinctive, historically evolved Christian and British past. But this was the cultural heritage that nurtured the inner and outer restraints of American constitutionalism. Because Straussian anti-traditionalism has confused and weakened so many who wanted to defend that heritage, it has been in some ways more destructive of it than standard liberal anti-traditionalism.

Despite plentiful ceremonial praise for the Constitution and virtual orgies of constitutional legalism, we are living through the progressive dismantling of America's proudest political achievement. One sign of the precarious condition of the Constitution is that many imagine that it could be restored by electing more politicians sympathetic to its tenets and by having more "strict constructionists" appointed to the US Supreme Court.

But the old American constitutionalism is inseparable from the moral-spiritual and other culture that gave it birth. Limited government and liberty were made possible by people who, because of who they were, put checks on their appetites, ran their own lives and communities, and behaved more generally in ways conducive to freedom under law. Restoring American constitutionalism would presuppose some kind of resurgence of that old culture. Americans would have to begin viewing life rather differently from how they are viewing it now. They would have to rearrange their priorities and start acting differently, placing more emphasis on family, private groups and local communities. They would have to want to take back much of the power ceded to politicians. Is that likely to happen? If not, the Constitution may not be salvageable.

The time has certainly come to consider what might take the place of American constitutionalism. That so many admirers of the old Constitution are prone to nostalgic dreaming and elaborate defenses of what is long gone is a sign of moral and intellectual paralysis.

But there are people who have thought for a rather long time about what should replace the Constitution of 1789. They include leading Straussians and neoconservatives who have masked their agenda by pretending to defend what is being lost. It is only fair to add that the strategic designs of secretive and obfuscating leaders are not always obvious to the rank and file.

Straussians and neoconservatives have warned against the consequences of abandoning America's "founding principles," but they are not referring to the ways and beliefs of the founders but to abstractions of their own devising that they falsely attribute to revered historical figures. Those principles are more reminiscent of the French Jacobins than of the founders.

Straussians and neoconservatives have also warned of the consequences of the "closing of the American mind"—the title of Allan Bloom's 1987 best-selling book—but the mind that they want kept open is not the old American mind but what they would have preferred it to be, their own version of the Enlightenment mind.

The same people have warned of American cultural decline, as measured some years back by William Bennett's "cultural indicators," but what they want is not the old American virtues of neighborliness, localism, self-control, compromise, and the rule of law, but the purported virtue of vigorously asserting universal principles in the world. The new Jacobins disdain moral hesitation and ambiguity, demanding what they call "moral clarity." You are either on the side of good, spreading "democracy" or "freedom" as they understand them, or you are siding with the enemy.

The new Jacobins have a double message. On one hand, they tell Americans that their society is in great danger: It is threatened domestically by fragmentation caused by lack of virtue and patriotism, by moral nihilism, historicism, and multiculturalism. It is threatened from abroad by Terrorism and "Islamofascism." But, on the other hand, the new Jacobins want to be reassuring: Be not afraid! We, the patriotic champions of American principles, are here to protect you! We promise you order and security and an America committed to right in the world.

Their notion of America reveals its alien origins even in strange-sounding language, as in the name "Department of *Homeland* Security." They are popularizing un-American ideas of governance, notably the so-called "unitary" executive—the notion of the preeminence of the president, who is to be as little constrained as possible by checks and balances and the rule of law. Their goal is wholly at odds with the constitutionalism of the framers.

Lest too many worry about the expansion and centralization of federal power, the neo-Jacobins do not let Americans forget even for a day the great and acute danger of Terrorism. A country that spends almost as much on its military and national security as the rest of the world put together has to tremble continuously before possible threats. People who resist the progressive erosion of American liberties are portrayed as unpatriotic and a threat to national security.

Those who would protect us are advancing the coup from within by teaching us to associate American security and virtue with the leadership of a strong man. Here, as in other ways, Straussian and neoconservative ideas have blended with and hardened standard liberal thinking. In the mid-20th century it was academics like James MacGregor Burns who inspired a cult of the presidency. Burns, who eventually became president of the American Political Science Association, was the quintessential modern American liberal. He advocated popular rule through strong presidential leadership in the Roosevelt-New Deal mode. He knew well that this notion flatly contradicted the framers. They opposed "democracy" and assumed that if any branch of the US government were preeminent, it would be the Congress. Now it is Straussians and neoconservatives who most extol strong executive leadership and more generally muscular federal government. They see the powers of the executive as trumping the powers of the other branches, especially at a time of national emergency. Then the president must embody and express the will of the nation as he sees fit.

Harvard's Harvey Mansfield is the intellectual figurehead of those attempting to justify the creeping coup from within. In *The Wall Street*

Journal (May 2, 2007) he has stressed that, now more than ever, America needs a "strong executive." Basing his argument on a strained and transparently unhistorical interpretation of the framers, he contends that the rule of law has drawbacks, "each of which suggests the need for one-man-rule." For one thing, the law can produce only what is mediocre, "an average solution even in the best case." For another, the law lacks "energy." In a crisis, government must put forth "energy," and "the best source of energy" is "one man." What America needs today, Mansfield declares, is "a wise man on the spot" with freedom to act for the whole. To "subordinate" the president to law and the legislature is "dangerous." Then "he could not do his job." Not only is a strong executive needed to deal with emergencies, Mansfield contends. It must also be able to overpower domestic opposition, "oppose a majority faction produced by temporary delusions in the people." Americans admire strong presidents not just in politics but also in corporations, he argues.

If it is suggested that there is a connection between a strong executive and imperialism, Mansfield regards it as better to err on the side of imperialism than isolationism. The difficulties of the war in Iraq arose, he writes, "from having wished to leave too much to the Iraqis, thus from a sense of inhibition rather than imperial ambition." It seems apposite that Mansfield, the advocate of muscular executive power capable of enforcing its will at home and abroad, should also be a champion of what he calls "manliness," the topic of his recent book.

The many proponents of the theory of the "unitary" executive include John Yoo, now a professor of law at the University of California, Berkeley. As a Justice Department lawyer in the Bush administration, Yoo, formerly at the American Enterprise Institute, famously defended broadly discretionary presidential power and the use of torture in the war against terrorism. Michael Goldfarb, previously at the *Weekly Standard* and now deputy communications director for the McCain for president campaign, has asserted that the framers "sought an energetic executive with near dictatorial power in pursuing foreign policy and war."

Voices calling for unleashing allegedly virtuous American power have long been heard in the electronic media, the major newspapers—*Washington Post* and *New York Times* prominent among them—the big news magazines, and the leading opinion periodicals. Long before 9/11 Charles Krauthammer wrote in the *Washington Post* that America must take advantage of being the only superpower to create a world to its liking. How should it accomplish this goal? "By unapologetic and implacable demonstrations of will" (March 5, 2001). Why should virtuous America not be "implacable"? Robert Kagan wrote in the same newspaper that "America . . . can sometimes seem like a bully on the world stage." "But really, the 1,200 pound gorilla is an underachiever in the bullying business" (November 3, 2002).

The handwriting is all over the wall. It is becoming clearer with each passing day that neo-Jacobinism and related currents, which may have seemed innocuous and "merely academic" to some, have provided ideological cover for an ever more grasping and ruthless pursuit of power. People of great ambition who want to exercise the power being abdicated by Americans are trying to make us accept and even welcome the final disappearance of American constitutionalism and its culture of modesty and self-restraint.

As already mentioned, some earlier assaults on traditional Western civilization were launched by openly radical agitators who saw themselves as on the outside of their societies. Their justifications for seizing power were revolutionary doctrines like those of Marx and Trotsky. Today's rolling, gradual coup is engineered by already powerful people who want to consolidate and expand their power. Wishing not to antagonize too much those who still identify with an older America and still wield some power, they try not to appear too radical and so often present themselves as "neoconservatives" or even "conservatives." As should be clear from their own words, that does not make them friends of traditional America.

Needless to say, neo-Jacobin ideology, though long a potent force, is not the only way of justifying the coup from within. Those working to centralize power are strongly entrenched in both major parties and in other influential American institutions, and they employ different ideas and symbols to woo and co-opt different constituencies.

Given the growing problems of the United States, why not welcome these efforts to rethink the ways of traditional America? Because they are inspired by highly dubious motives that color the proposals for change. Though those trying to impose a new power structure often speak in the name of America and their rhetoric is sometimes faintly conservative, they are not inspired by a desire to protect and reconstitute the best of the Western tradition. By changing the meaning of words, they are rather trying to reconcile us to the demise of that heritage and its replacement with their own enlightened and virtuous regime. Their response to the crisis is aggravating the crumbling of the American constitutional order. Their prescriptions contain the outlines of tyranny and must fill the friends of traditional American and Western civilization with trepidation.

What is ominous about these, our purported saviors, to repeat, is not that they want power. It is that they represent a conceited and self-absorbed special interest and have an obsessive desire to rule others—a desire that cannot be concealed by feigned benevolence toward Americans and all mankind. It is necessary to expose their false solutions to what are real problems and to explore by what measures the best of our civilization might, despite daunting odds, be given a new lease on life.

STATESMANSHIP FOR OUR TIME?

("Constitutional Leadership," *The American Conservative*, March/April, 2018.) The structures of government that the US Constitution sets up embody a constitutional temperament. The framers favored decisions made in a spirit of deliberation, compromise, and restraint. They assumed the desirability of statesmanship, an ability to rise above partisanship and the passions of the moment. The Constitution makes specific provisions for decision-making in domestic or foreign affairs, but what should receive more attention is that a certain temperament pervades the Constitution as a whole. If that temperament were applied to foreign policy, the result would be policies very different from those pursued today. More generally, what might statesmanship look like in the fraught historical circumstances of today? I suggest here that the first requirement of real statesmanship is uncompromising realism, an ability to adapt to and make use of actual conditions. I also raise a provocative, seemingly far-fetched and paradoxical question: whether the unorthodox presidency of Donald Trump might have been suited to the needs of the time.

The view that America is the indispensable leader in efforts to make a better world has long been so dominant in American foreign policy thinking as to seem axiomatic. Much of the current hostility to the Donald Trump presidency originated within the foreign policy networks that connect government, think tanks, media, and academia. Trump's assertions during the presidential campaign that America should play a more limited, non-interventionist role and put "America First" created profound discomfort. Though his real intentions as president are still unclear, his penchant for repeatedly violating conventions of speech and action has inflamed the passions of the national elites, particularly the foreign policy establishment.

So intense and confrontational is the hostility to Trump that it amounts to a constitutional crisis. It generates the potential for further political turbulence that might have devastating consequences. The danger is particularly acute in the area of foreign affairs, where decisions of far-reaching importance relating to Russia, North Korea, China, and other countries could fall prey to passion, short-sightedness, and recklessness. This is an alarming prospect, for sound leadership in international relations demands the very opposite—calm reflection, long views, and caution.

To recover their moral and intellectual bearings, Americans need to pull back from the demagoguery and turmoil of the moment. They would do well to remind themselves of an older model of debate and decision-making. That model, which should be for them a default setting, is today virtually ignored—the US Constitution. Here the primary source of wisdom is not constitutional prescriptions like the congressional prerogative to declare war or the Senate's treaty power, as important as they are. These institutional and procedural specifics are but the tip of an iceberg. What needs to be better understood and brought to bear on current problems is that the Constitution is the political expression of a general view of human nature and society. It embodies an entire American ethos, of which a certain view of how to make political decisions is but a part. The Framers' way of approaching political problems and life generally was not only realistic and far-sighted but morally astute.

Much more attention ought to be paid to the fact that prominent general assumptions and features of the Constitution, though not explicitly connected to international relations, carry important and wide-ranging implications for foreign as well as domestic affairs. Specifically, they assume a notion of statesmanship.

It used to be generally recognized that, especially in foreign affairs, inferior leadership can have disastrous consequences. There the need for circumspection and restraint is acute. Run-of-the-mill politicians may be prone to narrow-mindedness, demagoguery, and carelessness, but statesmen have the vision and the character to rise above the quarrels and opinions of the moment. They have a historical frame of reference and critical distance to their own time. They recognize dangers and opportunities not apparent to lesser men, and they have a capacity for audacious leadership. When necessary to advance the common good, they are willing to go against prevalent opinion and even to risk their political careers. Statesmen too will have human flaws, but they have as their models some of the most admirable members of the human race. A desire to move people with this kind of potential for leadership into influential positions was integral to the constitutional design of the American Framers.

Looking for modern Americans who exemplify statesmanlike qualities, one might turn to the end of the Second World War and the Cold War. Action taken by Senator Robert A. Taft after the defeat of Nazi Germany may illustrate the willingness to risk media censure or other unpopularity. It was John F. Kennedy who, in his book *Profiles in Courage*, pointed admiringly to Taft, who despite clamoring for vengeance opposed the plan to accuse the German leaders of war crimes before specially constituted courts and according to specially designed laws. The idea of applying *ex post facto* laws was, Taft insisted, repugnant to the American legal tradition with its deep roots in British and Western jurisprudence. Not even the vileness of the Nazi leadership could excuse legalistic posturing. At a time of growing anxiety about the Soviet Union and world communism

George Kennan exemplified another side of statesmanship by providing both a sense of direction and a calming, steadying influence, which were made possible by a rare combination of intellectual power, historical acumen, experience, and realism. Later in the Cold War when fear of the Soviet Union and communism still ran deep in America, one example of the boldness that statesmanship sometimes requires stands out. Only an American leader of unusual foresight, daring, and willpower could have conceived and acted on the possibility of an opening to China, which carried great political risks.

At the same time that the Framers sought to promote a leadership elite, nothing seemed to them more important than to limit, divide, and decentralize power. Even the best of men are prone to overreach. The Framers' deep distrust of human nature derived from biblical and classical sources and historical observation. Moral and prudential restraint on human depravity had to be imposed first of all by individuals on themselves, but constitutional and other external checks, individuals and institutions exercising checks on other individuals and institutions, were a necessary part of the effort to tame man's baser passions.

Realistic though they were about human weaknesses, the Framers sought to promote the common good. They looked in particular to the republics of Greece and Rome for models as well as warnings. Without republican virtue—self-discipline, modesty, and devotion to the public things—their constitutional system could not work. They wanted to increase the likelihood that people of wisdom, moral character, and the right experience—potential statesmen—would have a disproportionate influence over policy. For generations of Americans, George Washington stood out as the quintessential republican leader.

Though the Framers favored a system of popular consent, they dreaded demagoguery and short-sightedness. They feared a majority agitated by merely partisan interest, what they called a "majority faction." Such rule would endanger minority interests and threaten the general welfare. A representative system should, in the words of James Madison, "refine and enlarge the public views." The Senate, the Electoral College, and the Supreme Court illustrated particularly well the effort to promote "the deliberate sense" of the people. The Constitution was to protect the better self of the American people against bouts of ignorance, intoxication, or fear.

Directly relevant to foreign policy is the Framers' deep concern about the tendency of the powerful to want to lord it over others and to behave arbitrarily and ruthlessly. The inclination of the strong to consider themselves always right is at once prominent and dangerous. The weak need to be respected and protected. Though self-restraint and modesty are of the essence of republican leadership, all power has to be subject to sturdy institutional checks.

Genuinely to aspire to serving the common good is not the same as to know just what that good is in particular circumstances. Life is complex and the facts rarely clear. Statesmen will be predisposed to recognize the interests of different groups and to compromise. War may become unavoidable, but good leaders are predisposed to defuse conflict. Nothing could be more antithetical to America's constitutional ethos than to demand of opponents that they surrender unconditionally.

Statesmen must forever contend with people incapable of a balanced, many-faceted, and historically informed view of the world: conceited ideologues, nationalist yahoos, self-satisfied pseudo-moralists, ravenous investors, and other partisans. Their disparagement or demonization of opponents is inherently conducive to conflict. Only their side has legitimacy. When Vladimir Putin invaded Crimea mere partisans viewed it as an act of brutal aggression against a foreign country, no matter that since the fall of the Soviet Union the United States and NATO have pushed more and more deeply into the old Russian sphere of interest, in effect pursuing a policy of encirclement. A person of less partisan outlook will recognize that Russia has historical, cultural, and geopolitical reasons to think that it has legitimate interests in Ukraine, especially Crimea, and that it is pushing back against provocation. What seems unacceptable to one side may seem rightful or even imperative to the other.

Because of the propensity of the strong to run roughshod over others, the Framers of the US Constitution favored procedures and institutions that forced restraint and mitigated willfulness. They put a premium on settling disputes by give-and-take. They shunned unilateral actions, such as by simple majority vote. Their system would yield strong and enduring decisions only when a fairly broad working consensus could be achieved. Legislation passed narrowly and over intense opposition—the adoption of Obamacare comes to mind—would be unstable and a source of dissension.

To summarize the relevance of the American constitutional ethos for foreign policy, nothing could be more germane than that this ethos is, first and foremost, a strong disposition to self-control, deliberation, and compromise. It abhors autonomous, unrestrained power. Power is a possible source of ruthlessness and arrogance and must be limited and decentralized. Marked by modesty and humility, the spirit of American republicanism is inimical to arrogance and conceit. That the strong are often wrong and that the weak have legitimate interests are but two of the reasons for seeking compromise and common ground.

The post-9/11 decision to invade Iraq surely will stand out as a prime example in the 21st century of passions of the moment, shoddy thinking, and cynical manipulation robbing American power of restraint, deliberation, and caution. Decisions of great magnitude fell to a president who had little relevant education, experience, or familiarity with the world that could have protected him against being swept up in the agitation for attacking Iraq, which had nothing to do with the 9/11 attacks.

Some will object to these arguments that America is exceptional by virtue of its universal values and that the world needs and craves American leadership. In this view, since American power is a force for good, it does not need the strict limits that the Framers imposed. These limits are seen, in fact, as obstacles to the efficient use of virtuous American power. What is desirable today is not self-restraint, willingness to compromise, and checks on the ability to wage war. No, what is needed now is great "energy" in the executive.

People who oppose this attempt to subvert constitutional checks on power and would like to see these checks restored may at the same time plausibly argue that America has moved so far from character traits of self-control and modesty that the Framers' advocacy of deliberation and seeking common ground is anachronistic. What is desirable, to return to the Constitution, is not, at least not for the foreseeable future, practically possible. People strongly attracted to constitutionalism may also believe that in a political environment of increasingly blatant partisanship, crude and inflammatory ideology, and egregious demagoguery, the old-fashioned preference for debate and compromise will only play into the hands of the most pernicious and ruthless among the established elites. The only way to deal with such partisans and to give constitutionalism a chance to survive is to confront and defeat them.

The reasons for deemphasizing compromise and deliberation and for welcoming or accepting strong presidential leadership can thus have widely divergent motives, but they all illustrate the erosion of the moral and cultural supports for American constitutionalism. The old constitutional temperament is up against historical circumstances more conducive to rabble-rousing and authoritarian leadership—precisely the dangers that the Framers feared.

Hence we face a paradox. The US Constitution teaches urgent lessons about leadership, and the American constitutional temperament is highly relevant to foreign affairs. Yet today's historical circumstances seem to conspire against this temperament. What, then, of the prospects for statesmanship?

If the old-fashioned American ethos of leadership has dissipated because its civilizational supports have eroded, only a general revitalization of old moral and cultural traditions or the emergence of some new version of the same could generate a general resurgence of the spirit of statesmanship. Since there are few signs that this kind of renewal of civilization might emerge in the foreseeable future, the question becomes whether individual leaders with a potential for statesmanship might arise in the current deteriorated moral, cultural, and political climate. Could such persons create breathing room for even a partial recovery of constitutionalism?

In view of the sad state of American politics, some readers may believe that the kind of statesmanship described here must be a kind of political luxury, requiring fair-weather conditions. But true statesmanship is characterized by the kind of uncompromising realism that the Framers exemplified, and its sense of direction is applicable to any and all circumstances.

Thinking about specific practical measures that might constitute a statesmanlike agenda today would require an assessment not only of what is desirable but of what is possible, a very large subject. A central general point is that genuine statesmanship is animated by a distinctive ethos that tends to move societies towards respectful relations, domestically or internationally. To the extent that leaders share this ethos, they will tend to take each other's concerns into account. This is not to deny that they will often have competing objectives or that leaders of different countries must adjust their domestic and international agendas to their special circumstances. They have different and potentially conflicting interests. Leaders of countries must attend to military and economic imperatives. But statesmen realize that their counterparts in other countries must do the same, and they recognize the need for reasonable accommodation among contending parties. Thus does the spirit of statesmanship tend to moderate inevitable tensions and encourage negotiation.

At the very core of this ethos is an acute awareness of the baser inclinations of the human self and the need to control them. For genuine statesmen this need is not an abstract general observation about human nature but something deeply and personally felt. The moral realism in question is indistinguishable from a spirit of self-examination and self-limitation and a wish to act for the common good, an aspiration that was central to American republicanism. Integral to the same ethos of statesmanship are modesty, circumspection, and critical distance from the historical moment. Because the inspiring spirit is always the same, the diverse practical measures of statesmen tend to move their countries in the direction of peaceful coexistence.

If this is a summary of the moral and intellectual temper and practical import of statesmanship, what, more specifically, might comprise statesmanship in America today? It can be argued that the US Constitution has been so enfeebled as to be barely intact and that America is facing something like a moral-spiritual collapse. The forces that foster and benefit from this state of affairs are at the same time deeply entrenched. There is, however, in genuine statesmanship no inclination to retreat from difficult challenges. It has nothing to do with sanctimonious Platonic disdain for debased politics or with fruitless nostalgia for something lost, but neither does it resort to cynical expediency. Though marked by a strong sense of purpose, statesmanship is eminently pragmatic. Whatever the circumstances, it wants to make the best of them. Although it has no choice but to adjust to decadence, its purpose in doing so is not to yield to but to outmaneuver the destructive forces, for example, by using their methods against them. Statesmanship has to be at once creative and robust. To withstand the inevitably fierce counteractions of a threatened reigning establishment, it must be tough and skilled in the use of power. In an era in which public opinion and opinion polls are an important measure of political legitimacy it must somehow maintain popular support. Paradoxical as it may seem, one of the chief requirements of statesmanship in today's America must be to adapt to a media-centered and highly demagogic public discourse but to turn it to advantage by using similarly simplified but redirected rhetoric. As a readiness to act in any and all circumstances, statesmanship may today have to assume an unfamiliar form. Guardians of conventional respectability may find its audaciousness disturbingly unorthodox.

To look today to the US Congress for imaginative, courageous leadership seems fruitless. Its leaders appear incapable of thinking creatively about how to address deep-seated problems. Members of Congress collectively reflect a deteriorating and fragmenting society. Rather than transcending the usual posturing and demagoguery designed to avoid media censure and ensure reelection, the leaders of Congress appear content to shore up a crumbling status quo.

It is too early to assess the extent to which Donald Trump might represent statesmanship for our time. He certainly does not cling to the dilapidated status quo. That he sends defenders of the established order into paroxysms of outrage is not dispositive, although it does indicate that his opponents perceive him as posing a real threat. That is certainly how those who elected him viewed him. Only very deep resentment in the American people and Trump's special rapport with a large segment of voters could account for the rise to the presidency of this political neophyte with much dubious personal baggage. Many Americans, acting on gut-feeling rather than reflection, seem to have concluded that beggars cannot be choosers.

Not enough attention has been paid to how truly remarkable it is that Donald Trump was elected president. His winning the nomination of a reluctant party and then winning the presidential election was nothing short of miraculous. Political scientists and seasoned political journalists will tell you how utterly difficult it is for an aspiring politician to reach the presidency. Not only did Trump come from the outside, he had to run against experienced, well-organized, and well-funded competitors. He was also up against virtually monolithic media hostility. It says something about the viability, creativity, and timeliness of Donald Trump that this supposedly vulgar upstart was able to outmaneuver—everybody.

This blustering and almost roguish amateur politician who keeps violating conventional norms might appear the opposite of statesmanlike. Is it, then, out of the question that his high-wire act might be a form of statesmanship adjusted to a fraught moment in American history? Snobs and guardians of the status quo will of course scorn such an idea. Yet it is conceivable that the brashly self-confident style of Trump, so different from the formulaic conduct and speech of other politicians, might be a way of advancing a change agenda in an increasingly debauched and dully predictable political culture.

The upholders of conventional respectability should ponder the survivability of a leader who genuinely wants to challenge the established order but who also measures up to their refined standards of conduct.

Was their ideal candidate on offer in the latest presidential election? If so, how well did he or she do? Trump's braggadocio, hyperbole, and outsized ego offend traditional Christian sensibilities especially, but, given the magnitude of America's problems and the strength of the opposition to real change, would Americans have preferred a more unassuming, low-key leader? Trump's strong rapport with a core group of voters may have something to do with a subconscious identification with this caricature of a typically American personality, a larger-than-life embodiment of their own aspirations.

Establishment figures in politics and the media have been aghast at Donald Trump's rank demagoguery. Their criticisms have far from always been unjustified, but the conceit and nearsightedness of these arbiters of respectability has blinded them to how selective their indignation has been and to the fact that demagoguery, though of a different, approved kind, has long been an integral and expanding part of American political and media discourse. The established order with its main media outlets both fosters and takes advantage of a deteriorated political and journalistic culture. Trump infuriates those normally in charge of the view of the world and of public opinion by simply violating their prescribed rules and often beating them at their own game.

Many of Trump's supporters assume, mostly on good grounds, that much of his rhetorical bluster is merely conversational hyperbole or an act. His impetuous way of countering criticisms and his propensity for sweeping, off-the-cuff assertions seem to them a refreshing contrast to the scripted speech and conduct of other politicians.

Trump's stated general views do in important ways harken back to a more traditional ethos in American politics. He defends an old-fashioned sense of American national identity—"our country"—and opposes the kind of national self-effacement that results from open borders, politically correct multiculturalism, and other cultural radicalism. He wants to protect American workers against trade arrangements that he deems unfair. He has made the need for national sovereignty, that of the United States and of other countries, a central theme. His advocacy during the election campaign of limiting America's involvement in the world comported, if allowance is made for America's circumstances in the 21st century, with the disposition of George Washington and most of his American contemporaries. Trump's stated desire to make more room for negotiation and compromise with foreign competitors points in the same direction.

If there are thus elements in the Trump presidency that suggest at least the potential for a new kind of American statesmanship, other elements call that potential into question. Statesmanship includes an inclination to be self-critical, to check the impulse of the moment, and to have a sense of distance to the events of the day. By contrast, Trump often exhibits impulsiveness and a preoccupation with the concerns of the moment rather than calm reflection. Only an intuition of exceptional quickness and soundness might protect such a man from big mistakes.

In foreign affairs Trump ran on a preference for negotiation over confrontation, but in office he has been prone to bellicose rhetoric, assertive military action, and impatience with diplomacy. As president he has fallen back into and even reinforced the habits of the more hawkish members of the foreign policy establishment. He and his aides have brought into the administration many figures who represent just the kind of interventionism and push for global hegemony that he criticized during the presidential campaign. The president appears to lack the knowledge and intellectual independence to resist assertions of power from that quarter. The extent of the militarization of the upper echelons of his administration has contributed to an impression of foreign policy assertiveness and even militarism.

Similarly, in the economic field the president has given great influence to Wall Street, a power center that he attacked during the campaign. This suggests that here as in other areas he has only a vague idea of who are and who are not his allies in pursuing his stated larger objectives. A more worrisome explanation for seemingly paradoxical appointments is that he is more closely tied to the money power than he let on during the campaign.

It could be argued that Trump is simply looking for talent wherever he can find it. His fondness for generals may reflect a fundamental disdain for the creatures of the swamp and a preference for what he takes to be disciplined people who are used to serving their country and acting in tough circumstances. His alliance with Wall Street oligarchs and other big money people could conceivably exemplify a strategy of keeping his enemies closer than his friends. He may have decided that confronting a supremely powerful element in American society would not only be pointless but doom his presidency; only by reassuring at least parts of this element could he hope to gain some freedom of movement. There is another, perhaps more likely, explanation for his paradoxical appointments and his apparent pragmatism: that they are, for the most part, the result of poorly integrated, even contradictory beliefs, and of naiveté about the real nature of America's reigning elite.

Trump supporters disgusted with the established order may argue that there is no such thing as a flawless political leader. All leaders are mixtures of good and bad. One might add that debased, fragmenting societies tend to produce leaders who are prone to strong action but are also lacking in subtlety and caution. Whatever the case with Donald Trump, major shortcomings in a president of the United States can have disastrous consequences, especially in foreign affairs. That the US Congress has abdicated to the executive its authority to decide on war or peace is but the most striking example of an abandonment of constitutional restraint that could lead to catastrophe.

Real statesmanship is a crowning achievement of civilization. We recognize it precisely because it is out of the ordinary. America's current historical circumstances cry out for statesmanship adapted to the country's precarious moral-spiritual, cultural, and political condition. We had better not be too quick deciding what statesmanlike daring and vision might look like in today's America. Donald Trump has thrown a big monkey wrench into a flailing and yet intractable system dominated by confused, corrupt, and conceited leaders. He has created an opportunity for changing direction. Whether he has the moral compass, the understanding, the temperament, and the capacity for statesmanship and whether the American people are capable of the needed change remains to be seen. The alternative to major reform is further deterioration and, in foreign affairs, more wars and provocations that could at any time trigger a cataclysm.

PART THREE

CHALLENGES AND FISSURES

AFTER A QUARTER CENTURY: WHITHER AMERICAN INTELLECTUAL CONSERVATISM?

("American Intellectual Conservatism: Needs, Opportunities, Prospects," *Modern Age*, vol. 26, No. 3–4, 1982.) This article was written for the twenty-fifth anniversary issue of *Modern Age*, which was published about a quarter of a century after post–World-War-II American intellectual conservatism had acquired the contours of a distinct movement. *Modern Age* had itself played a significant role in the evolution of American conservatism, and the editor thought the time ripe for a retrospective on and assessment of what had taken place.

"The abyss of Hell itself seems to yawn before me," wrote Edmund Burke in 1793.[1] With the prescience of a sage he saw in the inhumanity of the Jacobins the horrors of a dawning age. If not checked, the pseudo-moralistic fanaticism exemplified by Rousseau and Robespierre would finally destroy Western civilization. In this century, the moral crimes committed in the name of a better world for mankind have confirmed some of Burke's worst fears: Lenin, Hitler, Mao, Stalin and the more recent rulers of the Gulag Archipelago have let us look into the yawning abyss of the diabolical.

The triumphs of the modem totalitarians would not have been possible but for the weak resistance to their ideologies or their secret attraction in the soul of Western man. The armed might reared today against the remnants of a great civilization is an outward manifestation of that inner power of destruction which Walter Lippmann called "the acids of modernity." The present struggle for the world is at bottom a struggle for the will, the mind and the imagination.

For those who entertain in relation to our time some of Burke's fears in relation to his own, intellectual developments in the United States in the last several decades have been a source of encouragement. The 1950s saw several mutually supportive intellectual impulses coalesce into a new ethical and cultural conservatism. The movement created by men like Russell Kirk, Peter Viereck, Eric Voegelin, Leo Strauss, Robert Nisbet and John Hallowell, to mention just a few of the most distinguished scholars, has enjoyed steadily growing influence in the universities and society at large.

The many strengths of American intellectual conservatism have been widely and justly celebrated. Yet, like other movements of ideas, it too is liable to succumb to repetitiveness and ideological petrification unless it addresses its own inevitable weaknesses and deepens the insights it has acquired. There follows an attempt by one observer to indicate, on the occasion of the 25th anniversary of *Modem Age*, a few of the areas which seem to present notable challenges or pose obstacles to further development.

THE NEED FOR INTELLECTUAL CONTINUITY

Truly to absorb the contribution of a major thinker means relating it to the enduring concerns of philosophy. It requires systematic interpretation over many years. On the whole, American intellectual conservatism has not subjected its leading minds and their precursors to this type of sustained examination. For that reason it has had some difficulty really incorporating and holding on to their central insights. The movement has been kept together more on the level of broad generalities than on the level of philosophic discourse. Partly because of this lack of deeper intellectual continuity, the movement is a rather loose conglomeration of groups which sometimes give the appearance of having only a vague understanding of their own respective origins, of having little knowledge of each other and of having no strong inclination to learn from each other.

There is of course considerable truth in the conventional view that modern American intellectual conservatism took its start in the years around 1950. But it is symptomatic of the mentioned weakness that little attention has been paid to the influence of earlier thinkers on the leading contributors of that period. One American source of inspiration which has been as important as it has been overlooked is the work of Irving Babbitt (1865–1933) and Paul Elmer More (1864–1937). The influence they have exerted, directly and indirectly, extends far beyond those who have openly and repeatedly acknowledged their indebtedness, Russell Kirk and Peter Viereck prominent among them. A fascinating topic for future intellectual historians will be the covert absorption of the ideas of Babbitt and More by numerous scholars who, for complicated reasons, have not publicly recorded their debt.

Modern American intellectual conservatism has benefited greatly from the strong influence of distinguished scholars of European background. Still, the significance of their contributions should not lead Americans to neglect the careful study of their own leading thinkers. If some Europeans tend to underestimate and even ignore American intellectual traditions (outside of the natural sciences), Americans have no reason to mimic their attitudes. To refer just to the area of social and political thought, one need only weigh the extraordinary historical fact of over two hundred years of constitutional popular government in the United States, the melting pot of the world, to infer that the American socio-political mind and the general culture that has harbored it must contain a very strong element of wisdom and realism worthy of the most serious reflection. Nothing could be more fitting than for Americans to cultivate extensive and sustained inquiry into the foundations of their regime and into the moral and intellectual requirements for its continuation and strengthening. Theoretical and historical writings of European inspiration which are ambivalent toward constitutionalism in general and popular self-government in particular can help alert Americans to the dangers of decadent democracy, but they may also create premature and exaggerated pessimism about the American form of constitutional government.

Much is written at present about so-called "neoconservatives" of "liberal" and radical background, as though their ideas represented something quite new in American intellectual life. While neoconservatism is not without elements of novelty, it has much in common with ideas that have long worked their influence in the United States. Neoconservatism is but one example of how this older movement is being slowly adjusted to particular intellectual needs and finding its way into the American consciousness. Intellectual origins are obscured by fading memory. In general, much energy is spent in the United States in the laborious rediscovery of ideas which have long been available in mature form.

A partial explanation for the lack of deeper, philosophical continuity is the tendency among American intellectuals to be drawn into the sphere of "public policy." For many, the pursuit of ideas retains its attraction only so long as the applicability of those ideas to current practical problems is clearly discernible. Insofar as this pragmatic attitude reflects a view of the proper role of thought and is not just a legitimate concern for the intellectual needs of politics, it betrays a limited grasp of what decides the future of a society. The latter is decided by those fundamental moral, intellectual and aesthetical dispositions which set the general tone and dispositions of civilization. These dispositions shape also the political inclinations that determine elections. Politicians are usually at the mercy of a cultural climate which was prepared long ago by poets, artists and thinkers caring little or not at all about the immediate practical effects of their work. Only the most tentative and limited conclusions regarding the essential direction of a society can be drawn from developments within that world of fickleness and myopia which centers on public policy and public opinion. Because of the role of fads and fashions, impressions can here be deceiving. A better indication of the future is the state of the arts and the universities. To the extent that American intellectual conservatism is diverted by shifting political issues of the day from a more truly reflective concern about the enduring issues of life, its long-term influence, including its influence on practical politics, is in doubt.

DEFINING THE ETHICAL LIFE

The failure or success of American intellectual conservatism will depend in the end on its ability to awaken a new spirit of ethical realism. The discovery of truth finds its ultimate justification and confirmation in the proper direction of the human will. A very promising dimension of the intellectual impulses challenging "liberalism" in the 1950s was the rejection of naturalism in various forms and the affirmation of a transcendent moral order. Yet, many learned discussions of this subject would probably have been made more effective by incorporating and stressing a certain truth about the moral life. This insight has deep implications for how we understand and deal with the predicament of modem Western civilization. According to Babbitt and More the gravest threat to Western civilization does not come from those who openly expound doctrines of naturalism and egotism; these individuals can be easily identified. More dangerous and insidious is the attack of those who perpetrate a radical perversion of the moral life behind a facade of concern about virtue and even religion. Vast confusion has been created by association of the ethical life (including religion) with sentimental sympathy. People in the Western world, and not least the intellectuals, have proved strongly susceptible to this confusion. Babbitt and More insist on an all-important distinction, one between genuine morality, which is an exercise of will based on moral character, and a pseudo-moralistic "virtue" of the emotions. Without this distinction sharply in focus, attempts to defend Western civilization will forever fail to address properly the fundamental problem it faces.[2]

Jean-Jacques Rousseau exemplifies a spirit of moral decadence which has tempted man in all ages but which acquired enormous new power in the eighteenth and nineteenth century. Rousseau is probably the most influential of those who have tried to redefine moral virtue in terms of emotion. More precisely, he lifts morality out of the sphere of action and places it in the sphere of morally conceited imagination. The subtle attraction of this new "morality" is that it liberates man from the painful effort of actual improvement of character. It does not require of him that he should ceaselessly criticize his own moral failings and undertake a continuous and difficult reform of self, as in the classical and Judaeo-Christian traditions in ethics. Man is essentially good and need only give free vent to a natural feeling of brotherhood. Unlike Christian love, which begins with love of neighbor and consists first of all of caring actions toward concrete living human beings close at hand, Rousseauistic sentimental "virtue" consists of a merely emotional benevolence toward nobody in particular. Its object is a distant and abstract "mankind." Sentimental "morality" places no burdensome obligations on the bearer; it conveniently transfers duties to some agency other than self, such as government. Far from being associated with a sense of sinfulness and need for self-improvement, Rousseauistic sympathy is inherently self-congratulatory: Only from a pure heart could issue forth such warm feelings of brotherhood. The more ambitious one's benevolent schemes for reform of society and the world, the more obvious one's superior moral sensibilities.

The grave danger of Rousseauistic "virtue" is that it encourages a profound conceit about the human self and invites neglect of the crucial training of the will. This perversion of the classical and Judaeo Christian understanding of morality has led in the West to the multiplication of a type of individual who takes great pride in his generalized "love" for the poor or downtrodden, or some other abstract category of humanity, but who exhibits actual personal behavior more suggestive of selfishness and hate. Some of the most passionate "lovers of humanity" are also among the leading tyrants of the modem world.

The substitution of a merely sentimental brotherhood for a morality of character continues to wreak havoc within Western society, including its Churches. Here lies the heart of that moral decadence and escapism which is eating away at the life nerve of Western civilization. The key to a restoration of ethical realism may be this deceptively simple and elusive truth: The only morality that counts is one which proves itself in actual personal conduct.

Social thought not strongly attentive to the mentioned problem of ethics and related questions is likely to give precedence to issues of secondary philosophical importance. A single example from the field of American political thought may illustrate the point. The conventional categories, "federalists" and "anti-federalists," are most useful for some purposes. Philosophically more important, however, are the sharply contrasting views of human nature and morality which can be found behind either of these positions. To consider the anti-federalist orientation, there is a world of difference between a belief in local community, closeness to nature, smallness and public-spiritedness which has a sentimental and utopian cast, as in the case of Jean-Jacques Rousseau, and one that is derived from the classical and Judaeo-Christian tradition. Granted that Thomas Jefferson is a complex figure exhibiting some conflicting strains of thought, his brand of anti-federalism is rooted to a large extent in a sentimental moralism and faith in "the people" which can be very easily transformed by circumstances into a nationalizing, centralizing social benevolence.[3] It is only superficially a paradox that Jefferson should be invoked by modem American believers in the centralized Welfare State. The differences between, for example, John Adams and Thomas Jefferson are poorly accounted for by such categories of interpretation as "federalists" and "anti-federalists." At issue between them is the nature of man and society, and it is Adams, the federalist, who provides the more reliable moral basis for a decentralized society. The old-age correspondence between Adams and Jefferson is just one source of evidence for regarding the latter, with some important qualifications, as an American Rousseau, and the former, also with qualifications, as an American Burke.[4]

THE PROBLEM OF INDIVIDUALITY AND "HISTORICISM"

American intellectual conservatism has given new life to the old truth that the central purpose of society and government is to aid man in the realization of his moral potential and of other goods as means to this highest end. One important example of this salutary development has been Russell Kirk's influential criticism of old-fashioned utilitarian liberalism.[5] Kirk has shown that "libertarianism" with its moral subjectivism and glorification of the autonomous individual is incompatible with a philosophy of universal values which also regards those values as finding realization in community and cooperation. There is a radical difference in fundamental assumptions between a doctrine of economic liberal atomism derived from Hobbes, Locke, Smith and Mill and a conservatism with deep roots in the classical and Christian notion of man as a social and political being. A prominent economist and social thinker who belongs to the latter tradition but who is also highly respectful of the economic insights of modem liberalism is Wilhelm Roepke (1899–1966), a writer whose reputation in the United States has deservedly only grown with time.[6] With Roepke, Kirk has insisted that any truly humane society seeks to implement civilized priorities. Economic production must ultimately serve the moral and cultural ends of society which lie "beyond the dreams of avarice."[7] The free market envisioned by Roepke is not an unleashing of isolated individuals who would be restrained only by minimal laws and their own more or less enlightened self-interest. A free economy compatible with the good society presupposes strong social groups and ties and a commitment among the citizens to moral-cultural norms which give rise to civilized demands in the market place and to intrinsic and extrinsic restraints on the forces of competition. Roepke's concerns are similar to those of Robert Nisbet, another major social thinker who was discovered early by Russell Kirk. Nisbet's argument that human well-being is dependent to a very large extent on the strength and vitality of society's "autonomous groups" has helped to demonstrate the futility of trying to reconcile radical individualism with genuine conservatism.[8]

Perhaps the most uncompromising critique of modern liberalism of different types has come from that distinguished historian of ideas, Leo Strauss. Condemnations of "modernity" of similar severity have been advanced in the name of Christianity. The rather sweeping nature of some contemporary criticisms which go much beyond those of thinkers like Kirk, Roepke and Nisbet brings up an ever-present danger: Reaction against the glaring weaknesses of a historical movement may lead to neglect of its possible strengths. Modem liberalism in the widest sense is a movement of extraordinary breadth and complexity and with strains and potentialities pointing in very different directions. Awareness of the enormous danger to civilization from an unleashing of the selfish ego should not stifle inquiry into higher elements in liberalism and "modernity" which may offer opportunities for strengthening the older traditions. Not to examine the possible justifications for assertions of individual freedom and uniqueness in the seventeenth and eighteenth century implies the desirability of simply returning to premodern ways of life and thought. The Greeks in particular did not stress—indeed, rather ignored—the value of human individuality to personhood and the common good. Their predominant tendency was to shun individual uniqueness and historical particularity in general for the sake of a universality conceived as ahistorical.

Many thinkers suspect or assume that emphasis on the inescapably historical nature of human existence and on the importance of respecting human individuality must lead to moral relativism or nihilism. Unrevised premodern philosophical instruments of interpretation do not allow for the possibility of a value-centered historicism, that is, for an historicism which stresses both the existence of a transcendent moral order and the historical nature of man's participation in that order. Left out of consideration is the synthesis of universal and particular. Needed in order faithfully to interpret human experience is the concept of transcendence and immanence in indistinguishable unity and tension. The transcendent is present to man in concrete manifestations, without ever being exhausted by or perfectly manifested in the material of immanence. Man is never aware of the universal in the abstract, that is, apart from all historical particularity. He always experiences, and has knowledge of, something; he is conscious of the universal through its concrete incarnations. For example, the transcendent moral order becomes historically immanent and is experienced by man in particular good actions.[9]

A fundamental distinction is called for between a type of individualism and liberalism that refuses obedience to any transcendent principle and one that conceives of man as properly the mediator between universal and particular. If we ought not to denigrate personal uniqueness and other historical particularity, it is because they may have value as unique and particular. When ordered with reference to the transcendent they are the material for the renewal and continuing manifestation of the universal in forever changing circumstances.

Edmund Burke's deep respect for tradition and his insistence on the need for adjusting to particular circumstances do not diminish or undermine universality; neither do they deify history. Although Burke does not himself systematically formulate the concept of synthesis, his emphasis on the historical represents a deepening understanding of the ancient idea of the participation of the One in the Many. He throws new light on the reality of methexis, a reality which has remained philosophically problematic in the Greek tradition because of the tendency in that tradition, especially in epistemology, to separate sharply the universal from the particular. Thinkers who are dedicated to the defense of the universal but do not draw on the notion of synthesis see in a thinker like Burke either a largely "modern" figure ushering in historical relativism and positivism or a thinker predominantly in the "ancient" mold who represents the tradition of Plato, Aristotle, Cicero and the doctrine of natural law.[10] The philosophical categories used do not allow for a third possibility, namely, that Burke is at the same time and indistinguishably "ancient" and "modern": a representative of the classical and Judaeo-Christian heritage in that he strongly affirms the existence of a universal moral order and the social and political nature of man, a conservative "modern" in that he sees history at its noblest as manifesting the transcendent, if only imperfectly, and thus as an invaluable guide in the realization of man's moral destiny. Burke's value-centered historicism is in sharp contrast both to value-relativistic or nihilistic positivism and to a monistic Hegelian metaphysic of history.

Definitions of "liberalism" and "modernity" which lump together a Hobbes and a Locke with a Burke or a Tocqueville play down or overlook so many important distinctions that they have only the most limited utility. For example, it is not possible to do justice to the American political regime without the distinction between the two different types of liberalism mentioned above, one boosting individuality and particularity for their own sake, the other more conservative and blending with the classical and Judaeo-Christian traditions.

Absorption of valid elements of historicism would counteract another, related weakness: the belief that political regimes can be the wholly deliberate intellectual constructions of particular individuals or generations. In reality, regimes are also the creations of a living past, of a historically evolving ethos of whose meaning and direction each individual and generation is only imperfectly aware.

If conservatism is in some sense an attempt to conserve something historically existing, it needs to be more clearly shown how this respect for history and concrete circumstances is compatible with respect for that universal moral order which is alone worthy of our allegiance. The alternative to the systematic development of a value-centered historicism is to attempt a return to a premodern static and ahistorical conception of the universal. Such an attempt, however, neglects the higher opportunities of modernity because of disaffection with modernity's obvious and more easily discernible dangers.

THE IMPORTANCE OF THE IMAGINATION

Among the American scholars who do have a deep sense of the possible inherence of universality in history and who are building on the insights of Burke and related thinkers are Russell Kirk and Peter Viereck. They view the historical heritage as offering indispensable material for our experiential and imaginative grasp of the universal moral order. A sense of transcendent reality permeates the history of civilized life. It lives most concretely and richly in the imagination, especially in the imagination of the great poets.[11] Explicating Burke, Irving Babbitt writes: "A man's imagination may realize in his ancestors a standard of virtue and wisdom beyond the vulgar practice of the hour; so that he may be enabled to rise with the example to whose imitation he has aspired." However, what Babbitt calls the moral imagination does not simply repeat or imitate the past. Burke "saw how much of the wisdom of life consists in an imaginative assumption of the experience of the past in such fashion as to bring it to bear as a living force upon the present."[12] The moral imagination creatively perceives life's transcendent purpose through the noble examples of civilization and creatively applies this sense of direction to the here and now.

In spite of the work of Babbitt, Kirk, Viereck and others, American intellectual conservatism seems not yet to appreciate fully the extent to which our understanding of life is shaped by the imagination. The poets provide in the most intense form a direct, experiential, intuitive sense of human existence. While they do in a sense invent their characters and events, these embody and transmit a vision of the nature of reality. This vision deeply affects the general outlook of a civilization. Even when the members of a society are not aware of it, they tend to see life, including everyday experience, through the eyes of the poet.

The visions of the great poets are not low-grade visions of intellectual ideas, i.e., preliminary or incidental to more profound philosophical insights. Instead, the philosophers are dependent on the poets and able to capture in their prose accounts of life only a part of what the latter have seen more immediately, more richly and more deeply, although not conceptually.[13] A pseudo-intellectual conceit lurks behind the view that the highest significance of poetic expression is the intellectual meaning which can be culled from it by the philosophic mind.

If the imagination has enormous influence over our view of reality, it is far from always faithful to life as it really is. An entire civilization may become captivated by intuitions which draw man deeply into illusion. Such a civilization invites horror and extinction. Only the truly great poets and sages of the human race convey a realistic sense of the enduring essence of human existence, its promises and dangers. The welfare of society depends on the quality of the imagination which inspires its actions. A central theme in the work of Babbitt with profound implications for how we view the crisis of Western civilization is his argument that dispositions of will and dispositions of the imagination are intimately connected. The quality of will dominant in an individual, whether moral or immoral, tends to produce a corresponding quality of the imagination. So also does the quality of the imagination dominant in a person tend to call forth a corresponding quality of action. We are prone to see life in such a manner as will allow us to indulge our strongest desire. Intuitions which question our present wishes we incline to ignore or overpower. Only men of strong and noble character permit themselves to view life without pleasing illusions and thus to face the truth about themselves and humanity in general. This is to recognize the need for difficult and painful self-improvement. Inspiring the imagination of a Jean-Jacques Rousseau is a wish to escape from the moral consequences of the human predicament.[14] Seeing man as inherently good and seeing evil as something to be blamed on historical society excuses the individual from that uncomfortable self-scrutiny and purification of action which the classical and Judaeo-Christian traditions see as necessary to real happiness.

The crisis of the modern Western world, Babbitt argues, is at heart a crisis of moral character in which a perversion of the imagination plays a central role. Flight from real moral effort has given rise to and been induced by visions of life which sanction a perversion of the will. A certain quality of will and a certain quality of imagination beget and reinforce each other. The interplay of will and imagination in the morally irresponsible soul tends to produce progressive self-delusion and moral decline. If Western society is to survive, Babbitt contends, there must appear an incisive and relentless critique of those dominant forms of the imagination which entice the will with pleasing but decadent illusions. There is a need for a joint training of the will and the imagination in which literary examples provide concrete illustrations of opposing modes of life. No amount of intellectual affirmation of sound ideas can change Western society unless there is also a reawakening of that highest form of the imagination whose nature it is to let man see life as it truly is and which makes his will stir with abhorrence of evil and love of good. To think that abstract intellectual doctrines in isolation can effect the needed reorientation is to attribute to reason a power it does not have.

Babbitt does not develop one very important implication of his insight into the relationship between will and imagination: the implication for how we understand the role of reason. Reason never works in an experiential vacuum. It has for its material what has first been constituted into a coherent whole by the imagination. The philosophical mind is rooted in a pre-logical intuition of reality. That intuition is truthful only in proportion as it does not repress elements of life, that is, in proportion as the will which underlies it wants to see life steadily and see it whole, to use Matthew Arnold's phrase. An imagination succumbing to illusion will offer to the mind for conceptual elaboration distorted views of reality. And no amount of intellectual brilliance can turn imaginative untruth into conceptual truth. Philosophers without a sensitive and open imagination will of necessity formulate misleading concepts of reality, even if it is done with intellectual brilliance. The weakness of a Karl Marx or a Bertrand Russell is not lack of intellectual power but a distorting intuition concealing from view what would have given genuine proportion to the perception of life. The modern world offers plentiful illustrations of the same point. For example, contemporary man has available to him overwhelming evidence of the inhumanity of the forces which would destroy Western civilization. Solzhenitsyn and countless others have spread the evidence before our eyes. But we cannot permit ourselves truly to face the truth, for really to do so would be to face all the uncomfortable and frightening consequences; indeed, to face the unpleasant truth about ourselves. And so we look, but do not see. The imagination creates for us convenient avenues of escape; and on the heels of imagination entire intellectual doctrines spring up which sanction our moral escapism. By subtle steps of self-deception the need to reorient action is evaded, postponed or transferred to others. In the United States, attempts are made to soothe the resulting nagging national conscience by piously berating President Nixon for Watergate crimes; but the truly enormous culpability of the forces which caused military-political disaster in Southeast Asia somehow escapes attention. As Russell Kirk has written in a different context, "Like a false religion, a false morality cannot tolerate a true."[15]

Philosophical thought, thus, is dependent on the imagination for the depth and comprehensiveness of its concepts; and the imagination is dependent for its depth and comprehensiveness on a will sufficiently selfless to permit the contemplation of uncomfortable truths. Hence, the training of the will and the imagination may be even more important than the training of the philosophical mind. Conservative intellectual victories not intimately tied to a genuine reorientation of imagination and character are likely to be precarious and easily reversible.

This is perhaps a good place to mention the danger of academic formalism. Also within conservative academic circles there seems to be a tendency to be impressed by books because they are rich in dry and involved scholarly prose, elaborate technical terminology, footnotes and other displays of learning and academic respectability and to be suspicious or even condescending toward books because they have a shortage of same. It is well to remember that a preoccupation with form rather than substance is usually evidence of a lack of scholarly identity and self-confidence. It goes without saying that academic scholarship has its special standards to maintain and that there is such a thing as a proper concern about the mode of discourse; for example, philosophy has its special and necessary demand for systematic conceptual elaboration. But it should not be forgotten that for men of the most genuine learning and profound insights, that is, for the sages of the human race, the expectations of academia may seem irrelevant to the expression of truth.

Works written in a "literary" or essayistic style can contain infinitely more wisdom than pretentious scholarly treatises. The former may be worthy of humble respect and the closest attention among academics who are attentive to the canons of scholarly communication.

A RESTORATION OF REASON

Those within American intellectual conservatism who have best understood the decisive importance of the imagination in the shaping of man's view of reality have not set themselves the task of examining in depth the role and meaning of reason. They have typically limited themselves to criticizing what is normally called reason today as being inadequate to understanding the essence of the human condition. This criticism has been amply justified. Rationalistic and positivistic reason sets reductionistic abstractions in the place of life as directly experienced; it knows nothing about the living and infinitely complex reality of human existence. Positivistic "data" are but reified fragments torn from a more fundamental and continuous whole. To grasp what is truly universal, it is necessary to have recourse to actual experience. Humane studies require sensitivity and openness to the full range of man's consciousness of the whole.

And yet, the tendency within some strains of American intellectual conservatism to assume a conflict between conceptual intellection and the needs of humane knowledge is based on a one-sided notion of reason. The abstract and reified thought-processes which are commonly called reason today have no monopoly on rationality. On the contrary, they have only limited utility and are wholly subordinate to philosophical reason. The kind of pragmatic thought which must dominate in the natural sciences has been mistakenly employed in the study of man as a social and creative being. To liberate the humanities and social sciences from the deadening influence of narrow empiricism and positivism it is not sufficient to insist on actual experience as a source of knowledge, essential though that insistence is. Experience as such is intellectually mute; it offers direct intuition of reality, not argument. A central idea which has yet to be widely considered within American intellectual conservatism is that truly philosophical reason is the close ally of experiential openness. Far from violating immediate awareness of the whole by forcing it into abstract formalistic or mechanistic schemes of explanation, philosophical reason is scrupulously faithful to this awareness. The office of philosophical thought is to raise intellectually mute intuition into conceptual, systematic self-awareness. Experience per se has no voice in intellectual debate, but conceptual accounts of experience can refute distorted views of life.

The reason which can speak faithfully and confidently about reality is not abstract or ahistorical: It grasps the universal in concrete experience. The whole of which it has knowledge is at once immanent and transcendent. The imposing work of Eric Voegelin has contributed greatly to our understanding of human life as the "in-between." His argument runs parallel to the ethical dualism of Babbitt and More. The needed epistemological supplement is the insight that philosophical thought is the conceptual perception and elaboration of the tension and unity of universal and particular. Affirming both history and what lies beyond it, American intellectual conservatism may here find the foundation for a sorely needed restoration of philosophical reason. In the often neglected field of epistemology, the now dominant assumptions seem to be either that conceptual thought is poorly equipped to deal with life's central questions or that a premodern, ahistorical notion of reason is still adequate.[16]

It is paradoxical that the term "historicism" should today be widely associated with the positivistic collection of "data." This methodological orientation is only tenuously related to the central themes of historicism and owes as much, or more, to the likes of Comte, Mill and Spencer. Indeed, it represents the denial of historical-philosophical reflection as we find it in a Benedetto Croce.[17] In epistemology and elsewhere historicism does present weaknesses and dangers. One of them is its strong monistic tendency which explains away the reality of evil. But systematic and discriminating analysis reveals other elements which can be reconciled with and used to strengthen the classical and Judaeo-Christian traditions. Philosophical efforts of that kind are still rare but offer perhaps the most promising opportunities for the continued development of intellectual conservatism.

DEMOCRATISM AND NEOCONSERVATISM

("The Democracy Boosters," *National Review*, March 24, 1989.) Having observed the advance of neoconservatism and Straussian anti-historicism during the 1980s, I feared the likely consequences. It was troubling that movement conservatives seemed unconcerned about an ahistorical ideology becoming prominent in public discussion and even in supposedly conservative publications and organizations. Neoconservatives were widely perceived as speaking for "conservatism." Movement conservatives were either unaware of the danger that this thinking posed or were afraid to offend people with access to the media and plentiful financial resources. Conservatives willing to voice more than marginal criticism of the neoconservatives did not have access to widely read magazines. I finally wrote this substantial article and submitted it to *National Review*. I did so although the magazine had been very friendly to neoconservatism. To my great surprise, the editor at that time, John O'Sullivan, accepted it, which showed courage. Neoconservatives would be upset, and they punish dissent. Publication of the article caused great but short-lived controversy. Several prominent intellectuals who did not like the article wrote letters to the editor. Sidney Hook wrote a lengthy, vituperative one. I responded to these reactions. The letters editor informed me that Michael Novak wanted to respond but that he would do so only if I would have no rejoinder. When I said that I would decide whether to respond once I had seen his letter, Novak dropped the idea. You might have expected that this intense controversy in a widely read magazine would have spilled over into other visible venues. Some large, serious questions had been raised. But why should neoconservative public intellectuals who had become used to speaking for "conservatism" draw any further attention to an annoying critic? The way to minimize attention to my arguments was the silent treatment. Those who agreed with me lacked access to widely read magazines or the big media or feared retribution. It was to try to break through this silence that, in 1991, I published my little book *The New Jacobinism.*

"Whom the gods would destroy they first make mad." One is reminded of this ancient saying by the flow of writing and rhetoric that today proclaims democracy as the salvation of the world. What brings the proverb to mind is the self-satisfied, utopian, and often quasi-religious manner in which a certain form of government is endorsed. A common theme is that a tide of democracy is sweeping the world and preparing the ground for remarkable progress. Everywhere humanity is demanding democracy, and in more and more countries their aspirations triumph. Rarely is democracy defined beyond a few generalities about human rights.

For some the term democracy has acquired religious connotations. Democracy is endorsed by, nay, demanded by God—a view that could hardly be more out of tune with traditional Western Christianity. The Christian tradition is reluctant to approve any one form of government as suited to all circumstances. It is acutely aware of the imperfect, sinful nature of man. It sees weaknesses in all human contrivances and warns against placing too much faith in political measures and institutions.

To those who today are extolling the wonders and triumphs of democracy, such traditional Christian caution must appear unacceptably gloomy, even perverse. In a recent column *(Washington Times,* December 23, 1988), Michael Novak abandons the old critical distance to particular political solutions in order to proclaim democracy (undefined, except as a vehicle of "human rights") as not only the way to human progress but the way ordained by God. Today people all over the world are "crying out against abuses of their God-given rights to self-determination." The spread of democracy is for Novak a great religious event, indeed an aspect of God's Incarnation. The "citizens of the world . . . demand the birth of democracy in history, in physical institutions: as physical as the birth at Bethlehem."

Does Novak consider the divinity of Democracy as his own discovery? No, this perspective, he asserts, is that of Jewish and Christian tradition. "This tradition instructs the human race to make constant progress. . . . It insists that societies must continually be reshaped, until each meets the measure the Creator has in mind for a just, truthful, free, and creative civilization." Yet St. Augustine is only one of the least sanguine of the many Christian thinkers who would have rejected out of hand, as utterly arrogant, and sacrilegious, a belief that mankind is destined for political perfection. Thinkers like Thomas Aquinas also counseled not perpetual change of inherited ways but social continuity and stability.

Pastor Richard John Neuhaus expresses similar, if somewhat less effusive, sentiments. He gives a very favorable account *(NR,* December 30, 1988) of a speech by Prime Minister Margaret Thatcher, who is reported to have stressed the connection between Christianity and democracy and to have declared herself "an enthusiast for democracy." She concedes that Christians should not primarily be interested in what the majority wants. They should try to "ascertain what is the mind of the Holy Spirit." But, Pastor Neuhaus writes, "in the civil realm . . . democracy is the thing." Championing democracy is to capture "the moral initiative." Democracy, Pastor Neuhaus explains, is an emanation of religious truth. "Only within the Biblical tradition" are democratic rights "self-evident."

George Will was once a political and cultural critic with considerable reserve toward democratist enthusiasms. Increasingly, he has given the impression of wishing to atone for previous sins against the spirit of the times. Today Will warmly praises what Larry Diamond at the Hoover Institution calls "a kind of global *Zeitgeist* for democracy." *(Washington Post,* December 18, 1988.) Countries around the world are being "cleansed" of dictatorships and authoritarianism. Will here applauds the work of the National Endowment for Democracy, the congressionally funded grant-making body. When first started the NED was viewed with suspicion by some because it would interfere in the internal affairs of other nations. But, according to Will, the NED is "one of this decade's good deeds." The people at the NED "know how to prepare the stony ground of authoritarian societies for the seeds of democratic skills—organization, mass persuasion."

That America should take the lead in reshaping the world is of course a familiar notion. Woodrow Wilson believed, in the words of Patrick Devlin, that "what America touched, she made holy." Thinking of this type, expressed with or without religious language, often unconsciously caricatures its own genre.

A writer who specializes in statistically documenting and celebrating the continual progress and beneficence of modern democratic America is Ben Wattenberg. "Never," he says, "has the culture of one nation been so far-flung and potent" *(Washington Times,* December 1, 1988). The prospects for spreading American values are enormous. "Consider: last year alone, forty million VCRs were sold; the cassettes that go in them show mostly American movies and music. Important newsstands around the world now sell three American daily newspapers. There is now a nearglobal television news station: Cable News Network."

Perhaps the best sign that the world has been exposed to and is ripe for more American evangelization is that "there is, at last, a global language: American."

Henry Luce thought of the twentieth century as the American century. According to Wattenberg, the task of President Bush is to "lead us to another century, different to be sure, but still American-inspired." Wattenberg does not wish to appear immodest. "Our goal in the global game is not to *conquer* the world, only to *influence* it so that it is hospitable to our values." (Emphasis added.) Probably to give his readers confidence in the authenticity of this democratic progress, he points out: "American political consultants peddle 30-second spots in the strangest places."

Max Lerner finds that American freedoms "are the freedoms for which the outside world yearns" *(Washington Times,* January 2, 1988). Perhaps before the end of this century, peoples around the world will finally have their wish. Lerner is hopeful that we can "look forward to a global social contract between nations and their leaders," to a worldwide "moral community of some sort."

One who applauds the passing of traditional societies is Professor Allan Bloom. Although in the universities Bloom would like to maintain some intellectual standards and professorial authority, for society at large he favors democratic majoritarianism. He endorses the authors of the American Constitution as "majoritarians." In a book that has been widely misinterpreted, Bloom bemoans the closing of the Enlightenment mind in American higher education. It was that mind, he believes, that founded America. He defends what he calls "the American project," a project of universal human rights. The latter conception was put forth by such thinkers as Locke and Rousseau.

For Bloom, the American Revolution represents the same basic outlook as the French Revolution of 1789. He castigates Europeans who tried to stem the revolutionary tide. Their fears that egalitarianism would threaten what is high and sacred and lead to a general narrowing of the human horizon are dismissed by Bloom as "the special pleading of the reactionaries." An appealing feature of social-contract theory is for him that its egalitarian assumptions put all human beings on a common level. "It pulls the magic carpet out from under the feet of kings and nobles." The American project is ideologically and politically expansionist. "When we Americans speak seriously about politics, we mean that our principles of freedom and equality and the rights based on them are rational and everywhere applicable." Bloom sees in the American involvement in the

Second World War not merely an effort to defeat a dangerous enemy. "World War II was really an educational project undertaken to force those who did not accept these principles to do so."

American political culture has long contained the notion that America should help change traditional societies, not least in old Europe, where conceited elites oppressed the common man. For Woodrow Wilson, it was not really until America's entry into the First World War that it became a war to make the world safe for democracy. Wilson remained suspicious of his European allies for not caring as deeply as he did for the right of popular self-government. In the Second World War, one of the reasons there could be a special relationship between Franklin Roosevelt and Josef Stalin was that the latter seemed to share the American wish to remake insufficiently democratic societies.

The men behind the American Constitution had a rather different outlook and temperament. They were steeped in the classical and Christian traditions generally and in specific English traditions, although their thought and practice also evolved in distinctively American directions. They entertained few illusions about the wisdom of the common man. They certainly did not wish to create a democracy in the sense of majoritarian rule according to the formula one man, one vote. Many of the key decision-makers were protected from popular pressures.

An individual like Thomas Paine with his egalitarian and majoritarian dreams bears a much closer resemblance to today's ardent advocates of democracy. So in some respects does Thomas Jefferson, who saw such representatives of the old European order as kings, nobles, and priests as a "confederacy against the happiness of the mass of the people." It was he who expressed his trust in the virtues of the common people. And it was he who repeatedly promoted the idea of popular rebellion as a way of cleansing governments of power abuse. Not even the cruelty and bloodshed of the French Revolution could shake his belief that it was ushering in a new and better era. An American who assessed the French Revolution very differently was John Adams. Seeing a bad omen already in the ideas behind that revolution, Adams reflected the dominant ethos of America's political founders and their English sympathizer Edmund Burke. It bears repeating that Thomas Jefferson was not one of the authors of the Constitution. At the time of its writing he was away in France, in more ways than one. It is also pertinent that he was and remained deeply dissatisfied with essential features of the Constitution, specifically the weak or non-existent popular control over many office-holders. Allan Bloom is mistaken in calling the American founders "majoritarians." His term may apply, with qualifications, to Thomas Jefferson.

A person who is not familiar with American history and observes today's celebrations of democratic progress might get the impression that such is the essence of American political and intellectual culture. But, as has been indicated, American tradition also contains a very different view of human nature, society, and the world with deep roots in the classical and Christian traditions. That ethos permeated the US Constitution, and it shaped America's leading classes, its most important social institutions, and its general culture, although frequently and increasingly it did so in competition with other currents.

For most of American history the originally prevalent ethos retained sufficient power to keep democratism in check. By supplying a critical element and stressing the hard facts of life it managed to chasten utopian visions and to head off or moderate their practical consequences. Has the original American ethos exhausted itself and finally capitulated? Or has it merely withdrawn from public debate, thinking itself above refuting intellectual enthusiasts? But such individuals, if left unchecked, can have practical influence out of all proportion with the quality of their ideas.

Who are those today who are so euphoric in their praise for democracy and in their belief that America should lead the way to remake the world in its image? Are they leftist ideologues promoting a utopian blueprint for global happiness? Curiously, most of them carry the label "neoconservative." Conservatives used to have a reputation for being spoil-sports, for exposing the naïve and superficial to the hard realities of existence, for warning of the flaws of human nature and the severe limits of politics, most particularly for reacting viscerally against political panaceas and cant. American conservatives might also be expected to conserve or at least maintain continuity with the wisdom of those who authored their popularly oriented but anti-democratist Constitution.

What is disturbing about the burst of democratism is not that it is favorable to democracy. The present author has written at length in defense of democratic government. (See, for example, my *Democracy and the Ethical Life*.) The trouble is the blatantly uncritical and utopian nature of the endorsements of democracy. Few who urge the democratic transformation of the world bother to consider, except in the flimsiest manner, the special circumstances of time and place. Although democracy can be understood in vastly different ways, so that careful definitions are urgently needed, most of the champions of democracy seem virtually oblivious to that need. They give the impression that in order to extend the blessings of democracy to countries previously deprived of them, all that is needed is to *proclaim* democracy in the particular country. It will automatically work wonders, perhaps after a little coaching of the population by the National Endowment for Democracy.

The present author has suggested elsewhere that a distinction is necessary between what may be called constitutional, representative democracy and plebiscitary, majoritarian democracy. These two types of popular government are institutionally far apart and assume radically different notions of human nature and society. So different are they that it may even be undesirable to use the same word in speaking about them. The American Constitution is compatible with the constitutional form of democracy. The latter is conducive to limited and decentralized government and a proliferation of autonomous social groups. Plebiscitary, majoritarian democracy exists nowhere in pure form but aspires to the Rousseauistic ideal of unrestricted majority rule by the undifferentiated mass of the people on the basis of one man, one vote. To the extent that majoritarian democracy is realized, it tends to promote demagoguery, expansion and centralization of government, and totalitarian mobilization and organization of society.

Constitutional democracy is not the least demanding form of

government, one easily implemented around the world. It is, on the contrary, perhaps the *most* demanding form of government imaginable, having extensive moral, intellectual, and cultural prerequisites. It is no mere coincidence that popular government of this type came into being here and there in Europe and America. A failure to understand the highly demanding preconditions of workable and lasting popular government and to take into account national and historical circumstances can produce disastrous practical consequences. But will anything deter democratists from pressing ever onward and upward?

The reservations here expressed about democrarist progressivism do not signify a wish to return to some earlier age, if that were possible. Modernity has brought genuine and indispensable advances, among them a deeper appreciation for human creativity. It has revised an overly static conception of the higher good for man in earlier Western thought. Modernity has a greater awareness of the dangers of stagnation in various spheres of human life. But all too frequently these insights have assumed dangerous utopian and sentimental forms. They have been perverted into fantastic beliefs that man can outgrow the limitation s of his existence. Millennialist dreams and ideologies cause terrible human suffering when attempts are made to impose them on intractable reality. This modern temptation needs to be identified and resisted in whatever form it may appear.

Perhaps the most striking and telling fact about the present enthusiasm for spreading democracy throughout the world is that it should flourish at a time when Western democracies would seem to have every reason to fear for their own future. But being self-critical is out of character for democratism. Indeed, writing of this type usually comes across as glaringly and ominously escapist.

A person not inclined to wishful thinking cannot shrug off the evidence of social disorder in the Western democracies. A few examples will indicate a serious deterioration of self-restraint, responsibility, and standards. In the world's leading democracy a sense of insecurity is chronic and generally accepted as inevitable. In its bigger cities especially there are large areas where citizens fear to tread. In many places criminals compete successfully with government for control. Most crimes go unpunished.

In society at large traditional mores and the corresponding social institutions are eroding. The disappearance of an older sexual morality is not only undermining the family and all of what it contributes to society but producing epidemics of venereal disease and AIDS. Abortions are performed routinely in staggering numbers. Drug use or abuse is rampant. Standards of personal behavior and deportment are low or declining. Honesty and integrity are fading away. Low academic standards are actually insisted upon by many teachers. Workmanship is poor. In the arts, the weird, the morbid, and the vulgar qualify for praise. The representatives of organized religion speak little or not at all about sin in the traditional sense or about the need for repentance but turn religion into a sentimental ritual of "compassion." Worship of news replaces a concern for lasting truth and wisdom. Some of what is demanded and tolerated in the marketplace today would have horrified earlier generations. Throughout society, an ever-tolerant permissiveness chips away at lingering norms.

In politics, standards of character are deteriorating. Persons of genuine insight and capacity for leadership are exceedingly rare and hesitate to participate because of the "rules of the game." Hypocrisy abounds. While democracy and the wisdom of the people are lauded, candidates for office show in their campaigns that they actually assume the electorate to consist of ignorant fools. The media compound a distressing situation by their own superficialities, irresponsibilities, and ideological agendas.

A decline of moral, intellectual, and cultural standards is thus much in evidence. Do then the democratists incessantly call for rejecting all illusions about the state of democracy to try to avert its self-destruction? Do they repeatedly warn that American constitutional democracy cannot survive without the kind of moral, intellectual, and cultural underpinnings that made it possible in the first place? If they did, they would not be democratist enthusiasts.

Democratists do take note of imperfections, including remaining obstacles to equality of democratic opportunity. But what is most compelling to them about contemporary democracy, especially in America, is not its flaws but its great progress and promise. The lasting impression left by them is one of self-satisfaction: democracy exudes a radiant health that should be shared as soon as possible with the rest of mankind. With champions like these, democracy does not need enemies.

THE IDEOLOGY OF AMERICAN EMPIRE

("The Ideology of American Empire," *Orbis*, vol. 47, no. 3 [Summer 2003].) Starting in the 1980s, I followed and wrote extensively about the growing influence of the new ideology that greatly and increasingly impacted American politics, especially foreign-policy-thinking. It became known as neoconservatism. It became ever clearer that it had little to do with conservatism. In fact, it closely resembled the thinking of the French Jacobins, who inspired the French Revolution. In 1991 I published a little book called *The New Jacobinism*, in which I analyzed its ideas and warned of their likely practical fallout. In the early 2000s it deeply bothered me that experts in international relations and foreign policy seemed virtually unaware of or unconcerned about this ideology. Especially in the aftermath of 9/11 neo-Jacobin rhetoric had become prominent among people shaping national policy. Neoconservatives and others were, consciously or unconsciously, embracing an ideology of imperialism, and it seemed to me urgent to explain its intellectual dynamic and practical implications, first of all to students of foreign policy and international relations.

The president of the United States has committed his country to goals that will require world hegemony, not to say supremacy. In numerous speeches and statements since September 2001, President Bush has vowed to wage an exhaustive, final war on terror and to advance the cause of a better world. "Our responsibility to history is clear: to answer these attacks and rid the world of evil."[1] In the president's opinion, the United States represents universal principles. He summarizes them in the word "freedom." As mankind's beacon of political right, the United States must, he believes, remove obstacles to freedom around the world. Accomplishing this task is associated in the president's mind with using American military might. In June 2002, he informed the Congress that the "Department of Defense has become the most powerful force for freedom the world has ever seen."[2] Since 9/11, the US government has relentlessly mobilized and deployed that force far and wide, with effects that remain to be seen.

What had happened? In his 2000 presidential campaign, President Bush had repeatedly called for a more "humble" US foreign policy and expressed strong reservations about America's undertaking nation building and following a generally interventionist foreign policy. A cynic might suggest that, having won the presidency partly by appealing to Americans' weariness of international over-extension, President Bush had now seized an opportunity greatly to extend his power. A less cynical observer would note that the 9/11 attacks outraged the president. They aroused nationalistic feelings in him and shifted his focus to world affairs. Since then he has also gained a new sense of the military and other power at his command.

Yet it is not likely that George W. Bush would have changed his stated approach to foreign policy so drastically had he not been affected by a way of thinking about America's role in the world that has acquired strong influence in recent decades, not least in the American foreign policy establishment inside and outside of government. A large number of American political intellectuals, including many writers on American foreign policy, have been promoting what may be called an ideology of empire. Many of them are in universities; some are leading media commentators. Today some of the most articulate and strong-willed have the president's ear.

When the 9/11 terrorists struck, the time had long been ripe for systematically implementing an ideology of empire, but in his election campaign George W. Bush had seemed an obstacle to such a course. He advocated a more restrictive use of American power. If he had done so out of genuine conviction, 9/11 brought a profound change of heart. The already available ideology of empire helped remove any inhibitions the president might have had about an activist foreign policy and helped shape his reaction to the attack. It can be debated to what extent his advisors and speechwriters, who were to varying degrees attracted to the ideology, along with numerous media commentators of the same orientation, were able to channel the president's anger. In any case, President Bush moved to embrace the idea of armed world hegemony. The attack on America could have elicited a much different reaction, such as a surgical and limited response; it became instead the occasion and justification for something grandiose.

In spite of its great influence, the ideology of empire is unfamiliar to most Americans, except in segments that appear disparate but are in fact closely connected. Drawing these connections is essential to assessing the import and ramifications of the evolving Bush Doctrine.

Though heavily slanted in the direction of international affairs, the ideology of American empire constitutes an entire worldview. It includes perspectives on human nature, society, and politics, and it sets forth distinctive conceptions of its central ideas, notably what it calls "democracy," "freedom," "equality," and "capitalism." It regards America as founded on universal principles and assigns to the United States the role of supervising the remaking of the world. Its adherents have the intense dogmatic commitment of true believers and are highly prone to moralistic rhetoric. They demand, among other things, "moral clarity" in dealing with regimes that stand in the way of America's universal purpose. They see themselves as champions of "virtue." In some form, this ideology has been present for a long time.

There are similarities between the advocates of the ideology of American empire and the ideologues who inspired and led the French Revolution of 1789. The Jacobins, too, claimed to represent universal principles, which they summed up in the slogan "*liberté, égalité, et fraternité.*" The dominant Jacobins also wanted greater economic freedom. They thought of themselves as fighting on the side of good against evil and called themselves "the virtuous." They wanted a world much different from the one they had inherited. The result was protracted war and turbulence in Europe and elsewhere. Those who embody the Jacobin spirit today in America have explicitly global ambitions. It is crucial to understand what they believe, for potentially they have the military might of the United States at their complete disposal.

The philosopher who most influenced the old Jacobins was Jean-Jacques Rousseau (1712–78), who asserted in *The Social Contract* (1762) that "man was born free, but he is everywhere in chains."[3] The Jacobins set out to liberate man. The notion that America's military might is the greatest force for freedom in human history recalls Rousseau's famous statement that those who are not on the side of political right may have to be " forced to be free."

The new Jacobins have taken full advantage of the nation's outrage over 9/11 to advance their already fully formed drive for empire. They have helped rekindle America's long-standing propensity for global involvement. Knowingly or unknowingly, President Bush has become the new Jacobins' leading spokesman, and he is receiving their very strong support. Reflexes developed by American politicians and commentators during the Cold War have boosted the imperialistic impulse. Many cold warriors, now lacking the old enemy of communism, see in the goal of a better world for mankind another justification for continued extensive use of American power. President Bush's moralistic interventionism gains additional support and credibility from a number of antecedents in modern American politics. Woodrow Wilson comes immediately to mind. But the current ideology of empire goes well beyond an earlier, more tentative and hesitant pursuit of world hegemony, and it has acquired great power at a new, formative juncture in history.

The most conspicuous and salient feature of the neo-Jacobin approach to international affairs is its universalistic and monopolistic claims. The University of Chicago's Allan Bloom (1930–92) argued in his best-selling *The Closing of the American Mind* that what he called "the American project" was not just for Americans. "When we Americans speak seriously about politics, we mean that our principles of freedom and equality and the rights based on them are rational and everywhere applicable." World War II was for Bloom not simply a struggle to defeat a dangerous enemy. It was "really an educational project undertaken to force those who did not accept these principles to do so."[4] If America is the instrument of universal right, the cause of all humanity, it is only proper that it should be diligent and insistent in imposing its will.

The new Jacobins typically use "democracy" as an umbrella term for the kind of political regime that they would like to see installed all over the world. In their view, only democracy, as they define it, answers to a universal moral imperative and is legitimate. Bringing democracy to countries that do not yet have it ought to be the defining purpose of US foreign policy. One may call this part of neo-Jacobin ideology "democratism." It has been espoused by many academics, Duke University political scientist James David Barber prominent among them. "The United States should stand up and lead the world democracy movement," he wrote in 1990. "We have made democracy work here; now we ought to make it work everywhere we can, with whatever tough and expensive action that takes."[5]

Numerous American intellectual activists, journalists, and columnists, many of them taught by professors like Bloom and Barber, sound the same theme. It has become so common in the major media, newspapers, and intellectual magazines and has been so often echoed by politicians that, to some, it seems to express a self-evident truth.

Not all who speak about an American global mission to spread democracy are neo-Jacobins in the strict sense of the term. Some use neo-Jacobin rhetoric not out of ideological conviction but because such language is in the air and appears somehow expected or because war is thought to require it. Many combine Jacobin ideas with other elements of thought and imagination: rarely, if ever, is an individual all of a piece. Contradictory ideas often compete within one and the same person. The purpose here is not to classify particular persons but to elucidate an ideological pattern, showing how certain ideas form a coherent, if ethically and philosophically questionable, ideology.

NEW NATIONALISM

Two writers with considerable media visibility, William Kristol and David Brooks, who label themselves conservatives, have led complaints that the long-standing prejudice among American conservatives against a larger federal government is paranoid and foolish. Big government is needed, Kristol and Brooks contend, because the United States is based on "universal principles." Its special moral status gives it a great mission in the world. In order to pursue its global task, the American government must be muscular and "energetic," especially with regard to military power. Kristol and Brooks call for a " national-greatness conservatism," which would include " a neo-Reaganite foreign policy of national strength and moral assertiveness abroad."[6]

Similarly, foreign policy expert Robert Kagan writes of his fellow Americans: " As good children of the Enlightenment, Americans believe in human perfectibility. But Americans . . . also believe . . . that global security and a liberal order depend on the United States—that 'indispensable nation'—wielding its power."[7]

International adventurism has often served to distract nations from pressing domestic difficulties, but in America today, expansionism is often fueled also by intense moral-ideological passion. Since the principles for which America stands are portrayed as ultimately supranational (for Bloom they are actually opposed to traditional national identity), "nationalism" may not be quite the right term for this new missionary zeal. The new Jacobins believe that as America spearheads the cause of universal principles, it should progressively shed its own historical distinctiveness except insofar as that distinctiveness is directly related to those principles. Though countries confronted by this power are likely to see it as little more than a manifestation of nationalistic ambition and arrogance, it is nationalistic only in a special sense. Like revolutionary France, neo-Jacobin America casts itself as a savior nation. Ideological and national zeal become indistinguishable. "Our nationalism," write Kristol and Brooks about America's world mission, "is that of an exceptional nation founded on a universal principle, on what Lincoln called 'an abstract truth, applicable to all men and all times.'"[8]

This view of America's role can hardly be called patriotic in the old sense of that word. Neo-Jacobinism is not characterized by devotion to America's concrete historical identity with its origins in Greek, Roman, Christian, European, and English civilization. Neo-Jacobins are attached in the end to ahistorical, supranational principles that they believe should supplant the traditions of particular societies. The new Jacobins see themselves as on the side of right and fighting evil and are not prone to respecting or looking for common ground with countries that do not share their democratic preferences.

Traditionally, the patriot's pride of country has been understood to encompass moral self-restraint and a sense of his own country's flaws. By contrast, neo-Jacobinism is perhaps best described as a kind of ideological nationalism. Its proponents are not precisely uncritical of today's American democracy; Bloom complained that American democracy was too relativistic and insufficiently faithful to the principles of its own founding. But it should be noted that he regarded those principles as "rational and everywhere applicable" and thus as monopolistic. Greater dedication to "American principles" would by definition increase, not reduce, the wish to dictate terms to others.

NEW UNIVERSALISM

Having been nurtured for many years in pockets of the academy, American neo-Jacobinism started to acquire journalistic and political critical mass in the 1980s. It was well-represented in the national security and foreign policy councils of the Reagan and Bush Sr. administrations. As Soviet communism was crumbling, it seemed to people of this orientation increasingly realistic to expect an era in which the United States would be able to dominate the world on behalf of universal principles. Missionary zeal and the desire to use American power began to flood the media, the government, and the public policy debate. Columnist and TV commentator Ben Wattenberg offered a particularly good example of this frame of mind when he wrote in 1988 that the prospects for exporting American values were highly propitious. "Never has the culture of one nation been so far-flung and potent." Wattenberg pointed out that "there is, at last, a global language, American."[9]

After the Cold War, American culture could only spread, he continued, with global sales of American TV shows, movies, and music. "Important newsstands around the world now sell three American daily newspapers. There is now a near-global television news station: Cable News Network." Not mentioned by Wattenberg was that the content being transmitted to the world might be of dubious value and a poor reflection on America and democracy. What intrigued him was the potential to expand American influence by exporting America's culture.

Behind the argument that the United States and its values are models for all peoples lurked the will to power, which was sometimes barely able to keep up ideological appearances. Again by way of example, Wattenberg desired nothing less than world dominance: "It's pretty clear what the global community needs: probably a top cop, but surely a powerful global organizer. Somebody's got to do it. We're the only ones who can." He called "visionary" the idea of " spreading democratic and American values around the world." As if not to appear immodest, he wrote: "Our goal in the global game is not to conquer the world, only to influence it so that it is hospitable to our values."[10] Later he urged, "Remember this about American Purpose: A unipolar world is fine, if America is the uni."[11]

In the major media, one of the early and most persistent advocates of an assertive American foreign policy was the columnist and TV commentator Charles Krauthammer. In 1991, for example, he urged "a robust interventionism." "We are living in a unipolar world," he wrote. "We Americans should like it—and exploit it." "Where our cause is just and interests are threatened, we should act—even if . . . we must act unilaterally."[12] This point of view would eventually become a commonplace.

The idea of spreading democracy sometimes took on a religious ardor. In a Christmas column published in 1988, Michael Novak said about the Judeo-Christian tradition that it "instructs the human race to make constant progress. . . . It insists that societies must continually be reshaped, until each meets the measure the Creator has in mind for a just, truthful, free, and creative civilization." All over the world people were "crying out against abuses of their God-given rights to self-determination." The spread of democracy was for Novak a great religious development that he compared to God's Incarnation. The " citizens of the world . . . demand the birth of democracy in history, in physical institutions: as physical as the birth at Bethlehem."[13] The enthusiasm of the Christmas season may have inclined Novak to overstatement, but he was clearly eager to have his readers associate democracy with divine intent.

This mode of thinking is in marked contrast to the old Christian tradition. Christianity has always stressed the imperfect, sinful nature of man and warned against placing too much faith in manmade political institutions and measures. Augustine (354–430) is only one of the earliest and least sanguine of many Christian thinkers over the centuries who would have rejected out of hand the idea that mankind is destined for great progress and political perfection, to say nothing about the possibility of salvation through politics. Although Christianity has stressed that rulers must serve the common good and behave in a humane manner, it has been reluctant to endorse any particular form of government as suited to all peoples and all historical circumstances. Here Christianity agreed with the Aristotelian view.

THE NEW DEMOCRATISM

Democratism has long had more than a foothold in American government. A look back in modern history is appropriate. President Woodrow Wilson, with his belief in America's special role and his missionary zeal, gave it a strong push. Harvard professor Irving Babbitt (1865–1933), perhaps America's most incisive and prescient student of modern Western and American culture, commented in the early years of the twentieth century on the imperialistic trend in US foreign policy. Babbitt, the founder of what has been called the New Humanism or American Humanism, was formally a professor of French and comparative literature, but he was also a highly perceptive as well as prophetic observer of social and political developments. He noted that the United States was setting itself up as the great guardian and beneficiary of mankind. "We are rapidly becoming a nation of humanitarian crusaders," Babbitt wrote in 1924. Leaders like Wilson viewed America as abjuring selfish motives and as being, therefore, above all other nations. Babbitt commented:

> We are willing to admit that all other nations are self-seeking, but as for ourselves, we hold that we act only on the most disinterested motives. We have not as yet set up, like revolutionary France, as the Christ of Nations, but during the late war we liked to look on ourselves as at least the Sir Galahad of Nations. If the American thus regards himself as an idealist at the same time that the foreigner looks on him as a dollar-chaser, the explanation may be due partly to the fact that the American judges himself by the way he feels, whereas the foreigner judges him by what he does.[14]

By the time of President Wilson the idea had long been common in America that in old Europe conceited and callous elites oppressed the common man. There and elsewhere things needed to be set right. Thomas Jefferson had been a pioneer for this outlook. But from the time of George Washington's warning of the danger of entangling alliances, a desire for heavy American involvement abroad had for the

> most part been held in check. By the time of Theodore Roosevelt's presidency, it was clear that the wish for American prominence and activism in international affairs had thrown off earlier restraints. Woodrow Wilson reinforced the interventionist impulse, not, of course, to advance selfish American national motives but, as he said, to "serve mankind." Because America has a special moral status, Wilson proclaimed, it is called to do good in the world. In 1914, even before the outbreak of the European war, Wilson stated in a Fourth of July address that America's role was to serve "the rights of humanity." The flag of the United States, he declared, is "the flag, not only of America, but of humanity."[15]
>
> Babbitt pointed out that those who would not go along with Wilson's "humanitarian crusading" were warned that they would "break the heart of the world." Babbitt retorted: "If the tough old world had ever had a heart in the Wilsonian sense, it would have been broken long ago." He added that Wilson's rhetoric, which was at the same time abstract and sentimental, revealed "a temper at the opposite pole from that of the genuine statesman." Wilson's humanitarian idealism made him "inflexible and uncompromising."[16]

THE POST-COLD WAR IMPERATIVE

The notion that America had a mandate to help rid the world, not least Europe, of the bad old ways of traditional societies with their undemocratic political arrangements has remained a strong influence on American foreign policy. In World War II, FDR's sense of American mission may have been as strong as Wilson's.

For a long time during the Cold War, most policy makers and commentators saw that war as a defensive struggle to protect freedom or liberty against totalitarian tyranny. But some of the most dedicated cold warriors were also democratists. They had a vision for remaking the world that differed in substance from that of the Soviet Union and other communist regimes but that was equally universalistic. With the disintegration and collapse of the Soviet Union, these cold warriors did not argue for substantially reducing the American military or the United States' involvement in international affairs. On the contrary, they believed that America should continue to play a large and, in some respects, expanded role in the world—that, as the only remaining superpower, America had a historic opportunity to advance the cause of democracy and human rights. This language had long been gaining currency in the centers of public debate and political power, and soon government officials and politicians in both of the major parties spoke routinely of the need to promote democracy. Many did so in just the manner here associated with neo-Jacobinism. It seemed to them that the American ideology had not only survived the challenge from the other universalist ideology, but had prevailed in a contest that validated the American ideal as applicable in all societies.

The first President Bush thought of himself as a competent pragmatist, but, as is often the case with persons who lack philosophically grounded convictions of their own, he was susceptible to adopting the language and ideas of intellectually more focused and ideological individuals. The rhetoric in his administration about a New World Order often had a distinctly democratist ring, in considerable part probably because of the ideological leanings of speechwriters. In 1991 James Baker, President Bush's secretary of state, echoed a neo-Jacobin refrain when he declared that US foreign policy should serve not specifically American interests but "enlightenment ideals of universal applicability." Whether such formulations originated with Mr. Baker or his speechwriters, the Secretary clearly liked the sound of them. He advocated a "Euro-Atlantic community that extends east from Vancouver to Vladivostok." This "community," he said, " can only be achieved on a democratic basis." The enormous size and political and cultural diversity of the region he described did not give him pause or make him question the United States' willingness or ability to take charge of such a daunting cause. No, the United States should promote "common . . . universal values" in those parts of the world, he said, and " indeed, elsewhere on the globe."[17] American power was there to be used. It seemed appropriate in cases such as these to talk of virtually unlimited political ambition.

The surge of globalist political-ideological aspirations was even more blatantly and pointedly expressed by the Bush Sr. administration in a draft Pentagon planning document that was leaked to the *New York Times*. It had been produced under the supervision of then Undersecretary of Defense Paul Wolfowitz. The draft plan dealt with the United States' military needs in the post–Cold War era, setting forth the goal of a world in which the United States would be the sole and uncontested superpower. The draft plan assigned to the United States "the pre-eminent responsibility" for dealing with "those wrongs which threaten not only our interests, but those of our allies or friends, or which could seriously unsettle international relations." The goal of American world dominance was presented as serving the spread of democracy and open economic systems. American military power was to be so overwhelming that it would not even occur to the United States' competitors to challenge its will.[18] This vision of the future might have seemed the expression of an inordinate, open-ended desire for power and control, uninhibited by the fact that the world is, after all, rather large. But significantly, many commentators considered the vision entirely plausible. The *Wall Street Journal* praised the draft plan in a lead editorial favoring "Pax Americana."[19]

Bill Clinton made clear in his 1992 presidential campaign that he would pursue a foreign policy similar to, if not more expansive than, the Bush administration's. In 1993 his Secretary of State–designate Warren Christopher addressed a group of neoconservative Democrats, including Penn Kimball, Joshua Muravchik, Peter Rosenblatt, Albert Shanker, and Max Kampelman, to assure them that he would fully back the president's commitments to making promotion of democracy a central tenet of US foreign policy.[20] Christopher's successor, Madeleine Albright, was even more comfortable with this stance. Democratist ideology was by now clearly dominant in top policy-making circles in Washington and elsewhere. It both generated and sanctioned an assertive, expansive use of American power.

When running for president, George W. Bush appeared to have substantial qualms about this broad use of American might. He questioned the desire to impose solutions to problems in all regional and local trouble spots around the world, seeming to recognize that such efforts betrayed arrogance and an undue will to power that other countries might resent. His adoption of a wholly different, far more assertive tone after the 9/11 attacks was surely induced in large part by war-like conditions. Although the change was probably motivated more by pragmatic than by ideological considerations, President Bush's rhetoric began to take on a neo-Jacobin coloring, as when he spoke of the "axis of evil," a phrase coined by neoconservative speechwriter David Frum.

In subsequent speeches, the president has often come to resemble Woodrow Wilson in assigning to the United States, the exceptional country, an exceptional mission in the world. He has asserted that an attack upon the United States was an attack upon freedom: "A lot of young people say, well, why America? Why would anybody want to come after us? Why would anybody want to fight a war with this nation? And the answer is because we love freedom. That's why. And they hate freedom."[21] Identifying America with the universal cause of freedom, Bush has even adopted Wilsonian imagery. Echoing Wilson in 1917, he said that the American flag stands "not only for our power, but for freedom."[22] Although the president used the term "freedom" rather than "democracy," which is the one favored by the new Jacobins, he seemed to agree with the notion that any enemy or critic of the United States is an opponent of universal principle. "They have attacked America," he said three days after 9/11, "because we are freedom's home and defender."[23]

Proponents of American empire had moved with great speed to head off any reluctance on the part of a devastated and disoriented American public to deal quickly and comprehensively with terrorism around the globe. Already on the morning after the attacks, when it was still not clear who was responsible, the *Washington Post* carried an article by Robert Kagan calling for sweeping countermeasures. The US Congress should, Kagan insisted, declare war immediately on the terrorists and any nation that might have assisted them. The situation required that America act with moral clarity and courage as our grandfathers did [responding to the attack on Pearl Harbor]. Not by asking what we have done to bring on the wrath of inhuman murderers. Not by figuring out ways to reason with, or try to appease those who have spilled our blood."[24] On the same day, William Bennett, Jack Kemp and Jeane Kirkpatrick issued a statement calling for war against the " entire" Islamic terrorist network.[25]

If the president thought that American actions might have contributed to the hostility to the United States in the world, he did not, and in the circumstances perhaps could not, say so publicly. What he did say and has said repeatedly is that the United States must be diligent, active, and forceful—preemptive even—in dealing with present or potential threats of terrorism. Paradoxically, given his earlier calls for American humility, he has presided over a massive push for greater American involvement in the world and for a vastly more intrusive role for government in the daily lives of US citizens. In fairness to a politician who is not also an intellectual and a historian, war has its own logic, and it may be premature to draw definitive conclusions about the president's statements and actions in the wake of 9/11, which was an act of war. But the fact is that President Bush's assertive approach and universalistic rhetoric has been seized on by American democratists who have been preparing the ground for a war and for a wider pursuit of empire. Charles Krauthammer praised the president for applying "the fundamental principle of American foreign policy—the promotion of democracy."[26] Political activist and writer Midge Decter pointed out that after 9/11 America could do something to clean up the world. She urged her countrymen "to hang onto what is most important to remember: that our country, the strongest on earth, has been pressed by circumstance—I would say, has been granted the opportunity—to rid the world of some goodly measure of its cruelty and pestilence."[27]

In mid-September 2002, President Bush sent to the US Congress the president's annual statement on strategy, the *National Security Strategy*, which gave clear evidence that he was abandoning his earlier calls for a more "humble" US foreign policy. Though the report was framed as a strategy for combating terrorism, the stated objectives supererogated any need to respond to acute external or internal threats. The report defined what amounted to a new and highly ambitious role for America in the world. Released the day after the president asked the Congress to authorize the use of preemptive military force against Iraq, it provided justifications for American intervention against potential security threats, while also formulating a new and much broader international agenda. The report in effect set forth a doctrine of American armed hegemony. The president justified this ascendancy as serving both America's security needs and its efforts to promote freedom, democracy, and free trade. The *Washington Post* said that the Strategy gave the United States "a nearly messianic role." It meant not only acceptance but also extension of the old Wolfowitz draft plan. Indeed, Wolfowitz is now Deputy Secretary of Defense and a highly vocal and assertive proponent of American activism around the world. According to the report, America's strength and influence in the world is "unprecedented" and "unequaled." The United States, "sustained by faith in the principles of liberty and the value of a free society," also has "unparalleled responsibilities, obligations, and opportunities" beyond its borders. The report calls for possessing such overwhelming military power as to discourage any other power from challenging American hegemony or developing weapons of mass destruction. It overturns the old doctrines of deterrence and containment. Committing the United States to a much expanded understanding of security, it argues that the United States must reserve the right to act preemptively and unilaterally against potentially threatening states or organizations. But the president approved an even wider goal. The *Strategy* commits the United States to making the world "not just safer but better." In explaining the report, a senior administration official said that besides leading the world in the war against terrorists and "aggressive regimes seeking weapons of mass destruction," the United States should preserve the peace, "extend the benefits of liberty and prosperity through the spread of American values," and promote "good governance." In familiar-sounding words, the report describes America's strategy as a "distinctly American internationalism that reflects the union of our values and our national interests."[28]

A NEW KIND OF WAR

The foreign policy of George W. Bush's immediate two predecessors, Bush Sr. and Bill Clinton, had a strong Wilsonian tilt. But neither president followed any sustained, consistent strategy. By contrast, the Bush Doctrine as set forth in the *National Security Strategy* and other places commits the United States to a bold, comprehensive, and elaborate foreign policy. The publicly and formally stated US goal, in sum, is to establish global supremacy. The United States would set itself up as the arbiter of good and evil in the world and, if necessary, enforce its judgments unilaterally.

Reservations expressed in Europe and elsewhere about American unilateralism and global aspirations have been scorned and dismissed by proponents of empire as a failure to recognize the need to combat evil in the world. Kenneth Adelman, a former deputy ambassador to the UN and a highly placed advisor on defense to the US government, couched his advocacy of imperial designs in terms of fighting terrorism. "I don't think Europeans should cooperate with the United States as a favor to the United States. They should be very grateful to the United States and cooperate because we have a common enemy—terrorism. In my mind, it's a decisive moment in the conflict between civilization and barbarism."[29]

Since America is at war it is, in a way, not surprising that some of its leaders should be portraying America as being on the side of good and those not eager to follow America's lead as aiding and abetting evil. Stark rhetoric has been used before to get Americans to support or sustain war, but the war aims spoken of today are derived from a consciously universalistic and imperialistic ideology. Therein lies an important difference, and a great danger.

The belief in American moral superiority knows no party lines. In an article critical of the George W. Bush administration's way of preparing for war against Iraq, Richard C. Holbrooke, ambassador to the UN under President Clinton, expressed a view ubiquitous in the American foreign policy establishment: "Over the past 60 years, the United States has consistently combined its military superiority with moral and political leadership."[30] The word "consistently" is telling. The notion that, unlike other nations, America is above moral suspicion provides the best possible justification for the desire to exercise American power.

It seems to the proponents of the ideology of American empire that, surely, America the virtuous is entitled to dominate the world. Some of them have worked long and hard to make this point of view dominant in American foreign policy. President Bush was merely echoing what others had been saying when he stated: "There is a value system that cannot be compromised, and that is the values we praise. And if the values are good enough for our people, they ought to be good enough for others."[31]

Many members of the so-called Christian right share the view that America has a special mission but give this notion a triumphalist religious cast beyond the moralism typical of neo-Jacobin ideology. They believe that the United States, as led by a man of God, has a virtually messianic role to play, especially in the Middle East, where God's chosen people, Israel, must be supported by the United States against their enemies. Breaking sharply with the mainstream of traditional Christianity, which has made a distinction between the things of God and the things of Caesar, this form of religion identifies a particular political power, America, with God's will. George W. Bush's rhetoric has sometimes suggested that he is drawn to such thinking. "Evangelical" Christianity of this kind may rest on rather simplistic theological, biblical, and historical assumptions and arguably have virtually no influence over America's dominant national culture, but it provides considerable political support for neo-Jacobinism, which does have such influence.

In its practical effects on US foreign policy, this religious triumphalism puts a religious gloss on neo-Jacobinism. It does not Christianize US foreign policy but makes it less humble and more belligerent.

Both in domestic and international affairs the new Jacobins are strongly prejudiced against the traditions of old, historically evolved nations and groups. These only retard the emergence of a new order based on what they consider universal principles. In their view, the distinctive traits of different societies and cultures should yield to the homogeneity of virtuous democracy.

The new Jacobins are trying to clear away obstacles to the triumph of their ideology and of their own will to power. They exhibit a revolutionary mindset that will inexorably lead to disaster. Alongside what President Bush called "history's unmarked graves of discarded lies"[32] lie the graves of the self-righteous, the people whose moralism concealed, even from themselves, their importunate will to power. As Ronald Reagan preached, the idealistic utopians and the well meaning are responsible for some of the world's worst evils. Self-righteousness blinds one to one's own sins.

Even if the opinions examined in this article are assessed in the most generous and charitable spirit, their element of political-ideological imperialism is hard to miss. A philosophically and historically inclined observer is reminded of the terrible and large-scale suffering that has been inflicted on mankind by power-seeking sanctioned or inspired by one or another kind of Jacobin moral and intellectual conceit. Communism, one of the most radical and pernicious manifestations of the Jacobin spirit, has disintegrated, at least as a major political force. But another panacea for the world is taking its place. The neo-Jacobin vision for how to redeem humanity may be less obviously utopian than that of communism. It may strike some as admirably idealistic, as did communism. But the spirit of the two movements is similar, and utopian thinking is utopian thinking, fairly innocuous perhaps if restricted to isolated dreamers and theoreticians but dangerous to the extent that it inspires action in the real world. The concern voiced here is that neo-Jacobinism has come to permeate American public debate and is finally within reach of controlling the military might of the United States.

Prudence, realism, compromise, and self-restraint are indispensable qualities in politics. They have been reflected in traditional American institutions, in great decisions made by American statesmen, and sometimes in American public opinion. They have constituted the first line of defense against all manner of foreign and domestic threats, including surges of passion and eruptions of extremism. Given the atrocities of 9/11 and the need for a firm American response, the prominence of crusaders in the Bush administration is perhaps not surprising. But it is also a sign that needed old American virtues are weakening or disappearing. The continued ascendancy of neo-Jacobinism would have disastrous consequences. By acting under its influence America's leaders may be setting in motion fateful developments that they and their successors will not be able to control.

JACOBIN CAPITALISM

(Excerpt from *America the Virtuous* [New Brunswick and London: Transaction Publishers, 2003].) "Capitalism" is one of the many general terms that are used as if they had some single agreed-upon definition. It does not. Karl Marx means one thing by it, Friedrich von Hayek another, and Wilhelm Röpke yet another. It is argued here that capitalism can assume many different forms and that the social setting, including moral and cultural circumstances, affect the nature of capitalism and free markets. They can serve the purposes of a civilized society, but, in another social setting, they can become effective destroyers of traditional culture. People of Jacobin inspiration can be pro-capitalist because they favor capitalism's capacity for destruction.

An important component of what the new Jacobins advocate is what they call "capitalism" or "free markets." These are considered closely akin to "democracy." Often the terms "democracy" and "capitalism" are used almost interchangeably. They are taken as names for different but closely linked dimensions of one and the same desirable society. Michael Novak popularized the term "democratic capitalism." Like democracy, capitalism should be introduced into all countries for the good of the inhabitants. Unfortunately, the term "capitalism" is as mired in philosophical confusion as is "democracy." The way in which advocacy of capitalism can be an outlet for the Jacobin spirit may be explained by demonstrating that there are major moral and theoretical connections between certain current notions of capitalism and the ideas of the French Revolution.

In their effort to bestow their allegedly noble insights on people far and wide, the French Jacobins combined adherence to abstract ideals with moralistic righteousness. Warnings from others, including Edmund Burke, that in the reform of society concrete circumstances and historical experience had to be taken into account and respected, seemed to the French revolutionaries morally perverse and reactionary. No guide was necessary other than their own universal principles. To liberate mankind from oppression and enact freedom, equality, and brotherhood, a clean break with the past was necessary. Jean-Jacques Rousseau had shown the need to abandon not only old beliefs but also all of the social and political structures from which they were indistinguishable. Western civilization could not be dismantled without destroying the concrete institutional and other arrangements through which it expressed itself.

The notion that all historically existing societies are full of exploitation and other evils and that a society of justice and well-being can be created only through sweeping and radical change has appeared in many versions since the time of the French Jacobins. The words "left" and "right" used to indicate the extent to which particular individuals and movements were drawn to that notion—the "left" finding it morally appealing and intellectually persuasive, the "right" finding it both morally repugnant and philosophically untenable. Today, sentiments of this kind are common across the political-intellectual spectrum. Indeed, some people called conservatives are in the forefront of those offering solutions for the world's ills. Conservatives used to be highly skeptical of sweeping proposals for changing society or the world; they reacted viscerally against panaceas and cant. They seemed to enthusiastic reformers to be spoilsports and killjoys. They drew attention to inconvenient facts and stated uncomfortable truths. The conservatives of the new kind are not so unpleasant and ornery. In fact, optimism and a belief in uninterrupted progress are their hallmarks. They propose political and economic programs that appear quite different from those advocated by the conventional left, and they usually speak a different language, but they share with the old left a belief in the salvific power and universal applicability of their programs. They envision ultimate goals for society that bear a much stronger resemblance to those of the old Jacobins than might first appear.

The Jacobin spirit found an uncompromising particular form in Marxism. Since Karl Marx looked forward to the destruction of capitalism and the triumph of socialism and communism, it might seem that a defender of capitalism could have little in common with the new Jacobinism. It is time again to insist on the need for distinctions and to point out that, like "free market," the term "capitalism" can have sharply different meanings. It should not be forgotten that a desire among the French middle classes to be rid of various old restrictions on commerce was among the major impulses behind the French Revolution. In today's Western society, the wish for economic freedom has been taken to an extreme by various radical "libertarians." It should be carefully noted that there is a sense in which a free market would become a reality only if the movement of goods and services were wholly unrestricted, unfettered not only by "external," legal, or institutional checks but by "inner" restraints, such as the inhibitions and tastes of civilized persons. A Rousseauistic, Jacobin desire to destroy traditional moral and cultural restraints and corresponding sociopolitical structures can thus be said to aid in the creation of a truly free market. It is not far-fetched but entirely consistent to be a moral, intellectual, and cultural radical and a strong proponent of the free market—by a certain definition of "free market."

Of those in the West today who are passionate advocates of capitalism and want it introduced all over the world, many are former

Marxists. The shift from being a Marxist to becoming a missionary for capitalism may be less drastic than is commonly assumed. Depending on the definition of capitalism, there can be considerable continuity between the first and the second position.

It should be recognized, first of all, that although Karl Marx predicted the replacement of capitalism by socialism and then by the stateless society of communism, he was a great admirer of capitalism. Like today's proponents of capitalism, he credited it with unleashing enormous productive power. In the words of *The Communist Manifesto* (1848), "The bourgeoisie, during its rule of scarce one hundred years, has created more massive and more colossal productive forces than have all preceding generations together." Far from opposing the spread of capitalism, Marx believed, again like today's enthusiastic champions of capitalism, that it must expand across the globe. It will lift mankind to a new level of development. For Marx, capitalism makes all peoples the beneficiaries of the historical progress that will finally end the suffering of mankind: "The bourgeoisie, by the rapid improvement of all instruments of production, by the immensely facilitated means of communication, draws all, even the most barbarian, nations into civilization." By "civilization" Marx here meant the productive potential of modern industrialized society.[1]

The parallels between Marx and some of today's missionaries for capitalism are thus evident. An obvious difference is that Marx sees capitalism as causing great travail. He regards the revolution of the proletariat and the overthrow of capitalism as necessary for mankind's final liberation. An important question to ask about particular proponents of capitalism today is whether they reject the doctrines of Karl Marx because of fundamental disagreements with his view of man, society, and history, or because they share much of his moral pathos but believe that the desirable society can be more efficiently achieved by avoiding revolution and socialism as he thought of them. A person may advocate capitalism not so much because he utterly rejects Marx's vision of a new society as because he regards the revolution of the proletariat and the socialist organization of production as blind alleys, quite unnecessary for realizing an essentially egalitarian society freed of the prejudices, injustices, and constraints of traditional civilization. A person may endorse capitalism because letting the market do its work is the best way of uprooting backward beliefs and related sociopolitical structures. Note carefully that, for Marx himself, one of the most important features of capitalism, as he understands it, is that it will completely destroy traditional civilization, not just in the Western world but wherever it takes hold.

A Jacobin in spirit could thus become an enthusiastic advocate of capitalism—provided capitalism is expected to function in a particular way. The destruction of old-fashioned civilized life that capitalism of this type brings with it is similar to that effected by plebiscitary democracy. In the end, the old decentralized and group-oriented society and the ethical, intellectual, and cultural beliefs that fostered it are left in ruins. It was the possibility of a capitalism of this kind that created unease about the free market not just in the old Roman Catholic Church and among Christians generally but among all who treasured the old heritage of humane civilization. Joseph Schumpeter, himself an admirer of the productive efficiency of capitalism, feared its capacity for destroying desirable features of traditional society. Capitalism pushes all but economic considerations aside. "Bourgeois society," he wrote, "has been cast in a purely economic mold: its foundations, beams and beacons are all made of economic material." In this society prizes and penalties are measured in pecuniary terms: "The promises of wealth and the threats of destitution that it holds out, it redeems with ruthless promptitude."[2] These observers of capitalism may be criticized for having had a one-sided and reductionist view of capitalism, but they did call attention to real potentialities of the economic system. Misgivings about such manifestations of capitalism continue to be strongly felt not just by socialists but also by friends of the free market who also believe that it ought to be integrated into and bounded by the higher purposes of civilization.

The Jacobin spirit can align itself with and try to boost those potentialities of capitalism that are most destructive of the ways of traditional society. It can do so in part by seizing upon and giving wider circulation to vague, nice-sounding, but sophistical notions like "equality of economic opportunity," "equality at the starting line," or "a level playing field." Because most people, especially in the United States, spontaneously oppose obstacles to opportunity that are unreasonable, irrelevant to tasks to be performed, or otherwise artificial, it is easily overlooked that, if taken quite seriously and literally, equality of economic opportunity requires a radical transformation of society. It requires the removal of all those considerations that, in traditional civilization, limit and structure economic activity so as to make it compatible with or supportive of humane values that lie beyond supply and demand. Equality of opportunity, taken literally, means treating all persons—moral and immoral, noble and ignoble, crude and refined—equally as long as they perform adequately by some narrowly economic, utilitarian standard. Other types of criteria should be set aside.

But civilization depends on not letting purely economic considerations dominate society. The logic of equality of opportunity is to drive out extra-economic standards, to remove premiums and penalties that nudge or force individuals to be of one kind rather than another. A couple of random examples may suggest the practical consequences of carrying equality of economic opportunity to its ultimate conclusion. The tax codes of all countries favor and disfavor some social arrangements. This is to slant economic opportunity, to make it unequal. Real equality would require, for instance, that families and homeowners be given no tax benefits not available to all others, including young singles and persons uninterested in the rootedness of home ownership. In business, equality of opportunity would mean that decisions to hire and promote should not favor the responsible, courteous, well-groomed individual over the slick, ill-mannered, sloppy person except insofar as the difference might affect productivity. In professional sports, the personally odious player should have the same chance to play and make money as the one who sets an example for others, as long as their professional skills are comparable. To bring about real equality it would be necessary to go down a very long list of changes until society has been drained of every civilized preference—which means that civilization will have ceased to exist.

The phrase "a level playing field" as a description of capitalism (or, for that matter, democracy) may seem rather innocuous. As used by some, it might mean simply that no one should have an unfair advantage over another. People of privilege should not be able to deny others the advancement and the rewards to which they are entitled by natural ability and hard work. Clearly, a soundly traditional society needs counterweights to social inbreeding, stagnation, and snobbery. All societies need the revivification of institutions and behavior that comes from challenges to old ways. Balancing the need for continuity and the need for change is a great task of civilization. But what is unfair advantage? Civilization attempts to enact its preferences precisely by giving advantages and encouragement to some, namely to those who come closest to embodying the values central to civilization, and placing obstacles in the way of others, namely those who deliberately and egregiously threaten those values. Except in a special, limited sense, civilization does not aim to treat people equally. Doing so would be unjust, for no two individuals are the same or have the same merit. Only a government based on great moral and intellectual conceit would consider it possible to ensure by central direction that all persons receive their just deserts, whatever the standard of fairness employed. Such a government would have to adopt totalitarian methods. Nevertheless, it is a general aim of civilization to structure life so that, to the greatest extent possible, those who enjoy or acquire advantages and influence are also, by the highest standards, deserving of them—which is far less a matter of political control than of decentralized, diversified, slow, protracted, piecemeal historical selection and adjustment. What is appealing to the Jacobin about the term "level playing field" is that it suggests the absence of traditional sociopolitical patterns that encourage some types of behavior and discourage others. As used by the modern Jacobin, the phrase indicates a society swept free of the discriminations between high and low through which civilization defines, manifests and preserves itself.

Ensuring real equality of economic opportunity as understood by the Jacobin would obviously require much interference with the economy as it exists in actual societies. Taken literally and seriously, the mentioned notions of equality of opportunity must, in practice, result in great expansion of the administrative state and in the eventual blending of capitalism and socialism. If capitalism means "equality at the starting line" and the latter is assumed actually to mean what it says, capitalism requires, among other things, the abolition of inheritance, which gives the children of the well-to-do an advantage over others. A certain kind of advocacy of capitalism turns out to have much in common with the Jacobin passion for an egalitarian, homogeneous society.

But it is possible to understand capitalism, or the free market, very differently. There is a need to distinguish between different forms of the free economy along lines similar to the distinction between constitutional and plebiscitary democracy. A free market of goods and services may exist in a decentralized, group-oriented society in which the outlook and behavior of individuals and firms are leavened by moral and other disciplines and in which both supply and demand are structured by corresponding civilized desires. In this economy, relations between competitors may be softened by mutual respect and consideration. A free market of this type would share in the ethos that is also characteristic of constitutional government. It would be an integral part of the civilized society with its institutionally expressed likes and dislikes.

The vital importance of the social setting of the market was stressed by the economist Wilhelm Röpke (1899–1966). "The market economy is one thing in a society where atomization, mass, proletarianization, and concentration rule," in which moral rootlessness robs competition of traditional ethical restraints, and in which producers cater indiscriminately to consumer demand. The market can be quite another thing, Röpke insisted, in the kind of decentralized, group-centered society that was described earlier in this book as fostering the character on which constitutionalism depends. "In such a society," Röpke wrote, "wealth would be widely dispersed; people's lives would have solid foundations; genuine communities, from the family upward, would form a background of moral support for the individual; there would be counterweights to competition and the mechanical operation of prices; people would have roots and would not be adrift in life without anchor."[3]

It must be understood that the distinction here developed between two forms of capitalism, or the market, is not between slightly different versions of one and the same economic system. It is a distinction between opposed potentialities that are no more compatible than are constitutional and plebiscitary democracy.

Critics of capitalism typically identify it with its worst possibilities: ruthless competition, exploitation, greed, crude commercialism, social atomism, and so on. These are said to be of the very essence of a free economy. That such phenomena are prominent in a particular economy is actually but a sign that capitalism is operating within a society in which people lack ethical, aesthetical, and other inhibitions and strong communal ties, a society in which institutional structures do not embody civilized purposes and in which neither supply nor demand recognizes any higher standards. Critics of democracy similarly identify democracy with its worst potentialities: unchecked majoritarianism, political irresponsibility, demagoguery, pandering to the lowest common denominator, and so on. Here, too, the phenomenon in question, democracy, is alleged to have its essence in how it performs in a society where civilized restraints are weak. Both points of view are unhistorical and reductionist. In reality, capitalism and democracy have no single definition or "essence." They exist only in particular historical manifestations. These can be sharply different depending on the ethical and cultural health of the particular society in which they operate. They can be compatible with the ends of a good society, in which case their institutions and practices are integral to the structures and practices of civilization. But they can also be destructive of higher values, in which case they manifest the structures and practices of a deteriorating society.

Röpke has described the social setting of a desirable free economy in a way that shows its connection with what was earlier explained as the moral and cultural context of constitutional popular government:

> Self-discipline, a sense of justice, honesty, fairness, chivalry, moderation, public spirit, respect for human dignity, firm ethical norms—all of these are things which people must possess before they go to market and compete with each other. These are the indispensable supports which preserve both market and competition from degeneration. Family church, genuine communities, and tradition are their sources. It is also necessary that people should grow up in conditions which favor such moral convictions, conditions of a natural order, conditions promoting co-operation, respecting tradition, and giving moral support to the individual. . . . It is the foundation upon which the ethics of the market economy must rest. It is an order which fosters individual independence and responsibility as much as the public spirit which connects the individual with the community and limits his greed.[4]

This book has argued that constitutional democracy has demanding ethical and cultural prerequisites and that it is not easily created and maintained. In a morally and culturally deteriorating society there is a great likelihood that democracy will be transformed into a plebiscitary regime, though one not answering to the Rousseauistic ideal of active, virtuous citizenship but relying on long-distance government. Among those with discriminating standards, popular passivity and abdication of power, together with the moral and cultural changes that lie behind them, will begin to give popular government a bad name. A similar argument can be made with regard to the free market. If the people who produce and consume cease to exhibit the discipline and responsibility characteristic of a civilized society, the free market, too, will, even if it continues to produce goods and services, begin to give itself a bad reputation among people who in trying to enrich civilization look beyond quantitative standards.

When observers inside and outside of the Roman Catholic Church expressed reservations about the free market, these were, in the final analysis, concerns about more general developments in Western civilization. Warnings about the possible dangers of the free economy could just as well have been directed against parallel dangers posed by other social freedoms and by popular government. The dangers did not inhere in the free market "as such," for no such market exists. They inhered in the free market in a particular part of the world and in a particular historical period, whose moral and other standards were becoming shaky.

As aligned with and shaped by a spirit of radicalism, capitalism can do much to obliterate traditional moral and cultural standards and uproot traditional communities. For some of today's proponents of capitalism one of its appeals is precisely that it can efficiently accomplish a task of destruction. Behind praise for capitalism one may find, among other things, resentment against traditional elites and a desire to sweep from positions of influence people who are seen as upholding old-fashioned, more aristocratic standards. Simultaneous advocacy of capitalism and majoritarian democracy broadens and intensifies the attack upon the old society. The spirit of Rousseau and Marx, if not all of their specific ideas, has in this way been updated and adjusted to new historical circumstances, and it has here found plentiful new opportunities.

JACOBINISM IN CHARGE

("Neo-Jacobin-in-Chief," *The American Conservative*, April 11, 2005.) Since the 1980s I had been warning, with little apparent effect, of neo-Jacobinism and its likely practical consequences. By the time this article was written, thinking of this kind almost completely dominated writing on American foreign policy, reinforcing and giving a new ideological twist to the interventionist, imperial outlook of America's foreign policy establishment. The president of the United States, the untutored, foreign-policy novice George W. Bush, had become the political figurehead of this new type of "American exceptionalism."

The president of the United States has been urging the use of American power to spread the allegedly universal principles of "freedom and democracy" throughout the world. On his recent European tour President Bush solicited the support of Europe in this cause, saying, "Our ideals and our interests lead in the same direction."

What that direction is had been tellingly indicated just a few days earlier by Condoleezza Rice. Speaking in Paris, she said that the founders of the American and French republics were inspired by the same values, a statement that implied common origins in the same revolutionary spirit. Though historically wholly erroneous, this view was consistent with the ideology that the administration has enunciated. It should by now be obvious that, in his foreign policy views at minimum, the president of the United States is no conservative. He is a Jacobin nationalist.

Inspired, guided, and supported by the ubiquitous neoconservatives, President Bush has adopted and fostered an ideologically charged missionary spirit that bears a striking resemblance to that of the Jacobins who led the French Revolution. The principles of "freedom and democracy" are to be promoted around the world by virtuous American power. The French Jacobins, too, saw themselves as virtuous champions of universal principles, "freedom" and popular rule prominent among them.

After the president's inaugural address, his ensuing news conference, and his State of the Union address, no doubt can remain about how he views America's role in the world. To advance freedom and democracy is, he said, "the mission that created our nation." At the news conference he added, "I look forward to leading the world in that direction." In the State of the Union speech he pointed to "the road of Providence" and said, "We know where it leads: it leads to freedom."

The neoconservatives have transformed the old American exceptionalism, which counseled isolation from the world, into an assertive, ideologically intense nationalism whose smugness seems to know no bounds. The president has long asserted that America's values are for all people. "There is a value system that cannot be compromised, and that is the values we praise. And if the values are good enough for our people, they ought to be good enough for others." In the State of the Union address he claimed, "We live in the country where the biggest dreams are born." He and America are called to enact the will of Providence.

That a particular leader or country could be identified with God's purpose is a notion alien to the mainstream of the Christian tradition, which insists that humans are fallen beings. Their knowledge is, at best, imperfect. Though statesmen, like others, should try to make room for the spirit of God by trying to purge themselves of tainted motives, not even a person of pure motive could in the infinitely complex reality of politics claim to have discerned God's will for the world. None of this has deterred the president, who exhibits just the kind of pride against which the older Western tradition—both classical and Christian—warned.

"Freedom" and "democracy" can mean radically different things. The president, his secretary of state, and their neoconservative idea-men have connected them with the Jacobin faith. The French Jacobins were followers of Jean-Jacques Rousseau, who argued, "Man was born free, but he is everywhere in chains." For men to be liberated, inherited societies and beliefs had to be destroyed.

The French Revolution was an attempt to enact his ideas. The Jacobins dealt harshly with "evil," guillotining conspicuous representatives of the old order and employing a general ruthlessness that culminated in the Terror. To France was assigned the mission of liberation. Europe and other parts of the world were thrust into protracted war.

In 1980, James Billington, the Librarian of Congress, used the phrase "fire in the minds of men" as the title for a book about the revolutionary faith. This faith would unsettle the entire Western world and eventually spawn the Communist Revolution of 1917. In his second inaugural address, the president used the same phrase, "fire in the minds of men," not to reject this impulse, which is what would be expected from a conservative, but to help define America's pursuit of freedom. He could not more clearly have aligned himself with Jacobinism. One wonders whether the president or his speechwriters understand that, rhetorically at least, he has adopted a faith that created some of history's most monstrous regimes.

Today communism has collapsed, but another universalist ideology, the new Jacobinism, has taken its place. A difference between the French and the new Jacobinism is that the latter has chosen not France but America as mankind's savior.

In a large number of speeches and statements since 9/11, the president has made clear that he considers armed world hegemony necessary to America's mission. At the inauguration, the massive security—involving some 30,000 secret service agents, police, and military personnel—and other telltale symbolism signaled the invincibility and willpower of the United States. Here was installed an American emperor, but one far more powerful and far more ambitious than any Roman counterpart. Neo-Jacobin ideology can be seen as the perfect justification for American imperial power.

Praising the president's inaugural address, neoconservative foreign-policy analyst Robert Kagan wrote in the *Washington Post* that America should pursue timeless "universal aspirations." Fighting terrorism was "too narrow, too limited" as a "paradigm for American foreign policy."

After the implosion of the Soviet Union, the neo-Jacobin neoconservatives argued that America should use its status as the lone superpower to spread its principles. They demanded "moral clarity" in US foreign policy. Good stood against evil. After 9/11, Bush became their chief spokesman. He committed the United States to what he calls "the global democratic revolution." The war against Iraq, he said, was "the first step" in that revolution. There has been not even a hint in the president's recent speeches that the Iraqi debacle and the tens of thousands of dead and maimed have made him question his own virtuous nationalism.

Rarely has an ideology been so strongly entrenched in a country's opinion-molding establishment. Especially with regard to foreign policy, the new Jacobinism is strongly represented in virtually all leading American media outlets. In the press, this is particularly true of the *Wall Street Journal*, but the *New York Times*, the *Washington Post*, *Newsweek*, *Time* and *U.S. News and World Report* all give it more than a hearing. Among the opinion magazines, the *Weekly Standard* is its main voice, but on foreign-policy issues at least, it also dominates formerly more conservative magazines like *National Review*.

In the commentariat, neo-Jacobin thinking is today challenging an older, more diffuse and less vigorous liberalism for pre-eminence. It is omnipresent in the think tanks, especially those emphasizing foreign policy and national security. Its brain-center is the American Enterprise Institute. On television, the Rupert Murdoch–owned Fox News Channel pushes the neoconservative foreign-policy line most conspicuously and reliably, but it flourishes on all the networks and major cable channels. By presenting itself on the radio waves and elsewhere as a form of kick-butt Americanism, neo-Jacobinism has also acquired millions of foot soldiers among flag-waving Americans.

What goes curiously unnoticed is that, despite their label, the neoconservatives think of themselves as representing a progressive, revolutionary force. The America they champion is not the America of history with its deep roots in a European and English past. In theory, they have constructed their own America, which represents a radical break with history.

"To celebrate America is . . . to celebrate revolution," writes Professor Harry Jaffa, a leading disciple of Leo Strauss, whose admirers are spread throughout the Bush administration. The American Revolution on behalf of freedom may appear mild "as compared with subsequent revolutions in France, Russia, China, Cuba, or elsewhere," Jaffa notes, but "it nonetheless embodied the greatest attempt at innovation that human history has recorded."

Another leading neoconservative, Michael Ledeen, who first came into view as an advisor on national security in the Reagan White House, openly portrays the America with which he identifies as a destroyer of existing societies. According to Ledeen, "Creative destruction is our middle name, both within our society and abroad. We tear down the old order every day. . . . Our enemies have always hated this whirlwind of energy and creativity, which menaces their traditions. . . . [We] must destroy them to advance our historic mission."

Some of the most prominent neoconservatives caught the revolutionary spirit when they were still Marxists, and despite their "second thoughts" they still harbor a deep desire for remaking the world according to a single model, their model. One of the reasons they are now fond of capitalism is that, like Marx, they conceive of it as an effective destroyer of traditional elites and societies.

According to Irving Kristol, the reputed godfather of neoconservatism, today's United States is "ideological, like the Soviet Union of yesteryear." His son William insists that for America vigorously to promote its universal principles abroad, it must have great military and other governmental might. The old conservative suspicion of strong, centralized federal government must be abandoned. According to the elder Kristol, it has been the role of neoconservatism "to convert the Republican party, and conservatism in general, against their wills" to this new conception of government.

To call people who are attracted to the new Jacobinism "neoconservatives" reveals profound confusion. Modern conservatism was born in opposition to Jacobin universalism. The father of conservatism, Edmund Burke, was an English liberal, a Whig, who was very friendly to the American colonists; he thought they had strong traditional grounds for challenging king and Parliament. What Burke argued passionately against, by contrast, was the French Revolution and Jacobin thinking, which he saw as expressing an unhistorical, tyrannical spirit and an importunate desire for power. Burke warned specifically against "liberty" in the abstract.

Like Burke, the Framers of the US Constitution associated liberty with particular inherited traditions; limited, decentralized government; checks on power; self-restraint; moderation; and a willingness to compromise. Jacobin "freedom," by contrast, justifies unchecked imperial power. That is the "freedom" for which George W. Bush has become the most prominent advocate.

DESCENT INTO BANKRUPTCY

("Debacle: The Conservative Movement in Chapter Eleven," *Humanitas*, Vol. XXI, Nos. 1 & 2, 2008.) In the years of the George W. Bush presidency and the Iraq war, American movement conservatism was inundated by imperial and interventionist thinking influenced by ahistorical theorizing. This mindset was incompatible with a historically grounded conservatism and with American constitutionalism, but the movement's lack of philosophical sophistication and historical knowledge made it possible for special interests and ideological activists to direct or confuse the movement.

As this article will discuss the state and future of the so-called "conservative movement," it is only fair to inform readers not familiar with the author's views that he has long been a critic of prominent features of that movement. He has complained about its obsession with politics and its disproportionate interest in public policy and economics. For a society really to change, its mind and imagination need to be transformed. The author has complained about the movement's propensity for formulaic thinking, its blithe acceptance of the anti-historical theorizing of Leo

Strauss and the Straussians, and about purported conservatives' thinking and acting like French Jacobins. He has criticized the movement for being less and less attentive to philosophy and the arts. Its trendsetters have been intellectual activists, journalists, and heads of foundations and think tanks rather than serious thinkers. Intellectual and moral confusion made it susceptible to manipulation by people with access to money and the media. The decline of the movement and of America was put into relief by absurd claims that conservatism had "triumphed."

These arguments will not be repeated here; they are in print in various places.[1] It should also be stated that, needless to say, the so-called conservative movement has had many admirable features. Some of its members *resisted* the trends that brought it to its present low point. Unfortunately, as it tries to recover, it may ignore those voices again and repeat its old mistakes.

To understand the predicament of the conservative movement, it is important to realize that it originated as a largely political alliance. It was cobbled together out of diverse intellectual currents. Some of these were philosophically remote from each other, but could agree on a limited range of political objectives, particularly opposing communism and defending limited government. But not even *those* objectives were understood in the same way by all. With the fall of communism the lack of intellectual coherence became more glaring than ever.

If self-described American intellectual conservatives were to be asked to give a summary definition of conservatism, most would probably say that it is a belief in freedom, minimal government and a strong defense. Advocating "principles" of this kind is what Rush Limbaugh means as he now stresses the need for more "philosophy." But this definition suggests an ideological rather than a philosophical frame of mind. It says nothing about what must surely be distinctive to conservatism—that it is *conservative of* something, a heritage that it wants creatively to preserve. Neither does the definition say anything about adapting a universal higher purpose to historical circumstance.

In addition, each component of the mentioned definition can be given vastly different interpretations. Here it is only possible to take up one, the belief in freedom—an issue that illustrates well the deep intellectual confusion within the movement. It was a simplistic, unhistorical understanding of freedom that made it possible for neo-Jacobins to invade the movement and cause disaster in US foreign policy.

All know the story of Benjamin Franklin being asked at the end of the Philadelphia Constitutional Convention what it had accomplished. He answered, "A republic, if you can keep it." Whatever his precise meaning, the Constitution could be sustained only if Americans would shoulder high responsibility. For liberty under law to be possible they had to keep their passions in check, exhibit the constitutional personality. The following words of Edmund Burke are relevant: "Men are qualified for civil liberty in exact proportion to their disposition to put moral chains upon their own appetites. . . . Society cannot exist unless a controlling power upon will and appetite be placed somewhere, and the less of it there is within, the more there must be without."[2] In other words, people wishing to be free have to exercise exceptional self-control. Human nature being torn between higher and lower potentialities, the latter have to be reined in. Without this self-restraint, no freedom. To the extent that order does not come from within, it has to be imposed externally. This was the moral-spiritual ethos of the American constitutional republic, which was deeply rooted in classical and Christian civilization as transmitted through British culture.

Most of today's defenders of the US Constitution proceed on the superficial assumption that it could be revived if only more people could be persuaded of its correct interpretation. But the original Constitution and the liberties from which it is undistinguishable presupposed Americans with certain historically formed character traits that could buttress them. Thus, for ordered liberty to be restored today, an older type of American, endowed with the constitutional personality, would first have to reemerge and begin to transform society.

But many so-called conservatives understand ordered liberty very differently, for example, as John Locke does. According to Locke, freedom is not the fruit of protracted moral and other struggle over time. It existed even prior to civil society, back in a purported state of nature in which freedom was simply bestowed on human beings. It is a free gift. "We are born free as we are born rational," Locke asserts.[3] Freedom does not result from individuals' taming their lower selves with the aid of civilization. No, nature fully equipped men to live to advantage. They left the state of nature only to remedy a few "inconveniences" relating to the safety of private property.

Unlike Burke, Locke has little or no awareness of what ordered liberty owes to history. He explains the existence of freedom in the state of nature by conveniently reading back into that state personality traits and ideas that could have evolved only in an advanced society. Seemingly an advocate of rationality and empiricism, Locke is first of all a liberal dreamer, an ideologue. He takes his bearings not from actual, historical experience but from purely hypothetical theorizing, rather naïve theorizing at that. His notion of the social contract could be given a more charitable interpretation, but a fondness for ahistorical Lockean speculation is not indicative of conservative leanings.

Locke has been a major source for the notion that freedom will flourish if only external impediments are removed. Just get rid of bad government! As combined with American nationalistic conceit, this kind of romantic dreaming helped form what this writer calls the new Jacobinism. The latter assigns to America the task of ushering in freedom and democracy everywhere. In the words of one conservative hero: "The American dream lives—not only in the hearts and minds of our own countrymen but in the hearts and minds of millions of the world's people in both free and oppressed societies who look to us for leadership." "America has always recognized our historic responsibility to lead the march of freedom."[4]

The ideology of freedom does not ask whether the preconditions for freedom are present in a particular society. It simply assumes that freedom will blossom once dictators have been kicked out. Utopianism used to be a monopoly of the left. In recent decades it has been the stock-in-trade of putative "conservatives."

The just-quoted conservative hero is Ronald Reagan. His speeches were filled with the romantic rhetoric of freedom. Like Locke, Reagan had little grasp of the moral and cultural preconditions of freedom. He proclaimed: "Liberty, just as life itself, is not earned but a gift from God."[5] Members of the conservative movement cheered Reagan's anti-communism and desperately wanted a political leader. Because of wishful thinking and lack of intellectual discernment they swallowed the sentimental dreaming. Operation global freedom was constrained in Reagan's case by the Cold War, but, with 9/11 as the pretext, George W. Bush could commit the United States to removing remaining obstacles to freedom in the world, starting in the Middle East. The ideological and political momentum for launching this grandiose project and for going to war against Iraq had been generated by the neoconservative network inside and outside of government, which, in concert with Big Oil, gave Bush its enthusiastic support.

To a Burkean or an American of similar outlook it is clear that the ideology of freedom misunderstands the origins of freedom. It is not surprising that such ideas should produce disastrous practical consequences.

Real freedom grows out of historically evolved character traits and institutions. It cannot strike roots in inhospitable soil. This is as true in the marketplace as in politics. You want maximum economic freedom? Then make sure that there is morality and culture that foster a maximum of individual responsibility. In an economy manned increasingly by gamblers and crooks and dominated by greed and short-sightedness the line between honesty and crime dissolves, and the misuse of economic freedom invites the imposition of external controls.

Has the conservative movement long protested the kind of economism that ignores the moral and cultural preconditions of a sound economy? Has it bemoaned the emergence of a crass, callous new economic elite? Has it called for the moral and cultural reinvigoration that might shore up economic and other freedom? Those setting the tone have not.

The new Jacobins and the worshippers of the free market in the abstract do not care about historical circumstances, only about adherence to their abstract "principles." With friends like them freedom does not need enemies. Even after the disasters in foreign and domestic policy in recent years the so-called conservative movement may not want to give up ideology and romantic dreaming, but chapter eleven reorganization demands it.

ANTI-HISTORICAL "CONSERVATISM"

("Allan Bloom and Straussian Alienation," *Humanitas*, Vol. XXV, Nos. 1 & 2, 2012.) The reception that movement conservatives gave a 1987 best seller about America and American education and culture, *The Closing of the American Mind*, confirmed a basic lack of philosophical discernment and raised questions about the ability of movement conservatives to address America's fundamental problems. This article was written on the occasion of the twenty-fifth anniversary of the publication of the book. The article explained that, contrary to superficial appearances, the book actually belonged to an old genre of writing whose effect was to sever Americans from their historically evolved culture, which was rooted in classical and Christian traditions as transmitted through British culture.

The reaction of putative conservatives to the publication of Allan Bloom's *The Closing of the American Mind* in 1987 was symptomatic of deep intellectual confusion. They treated the book as a defense of the American political tradition and the values of Western civilization—as a work of conservative thought. Some of these conservatives may have based their assessment only on excerpts from the book in which Bloom criticized spineless academic administrators and the drug and rock culture, but not even these sections were a clear indication of conservatism. Sentiments of this kind could have been expressed by people ranging from moderate liberals to communists and reactionaries. Although some on the left attacked the book, it was very different from its reputation among supposed conservatives. Curiously, it did not make them suspicious that a book by one of their own should receive an extraordinary amount of attention and be treated with high respect in places where conservative ideas were ordinarily disdained.

When *Modern Age* invited this writer to contribute to a symposium on *The Closing of the American Mind*, I tried to show that it was not a defense of the traditional American mind with its classical, Christian, and British lineage and resonances, but was largely a defense of the *Enlightenment* mind.[1] What Bloom bewailed was that the Enlightenment mind, which he rather loosely and arbitrarily equated with the American mind, was closing. That mind was being threatened, he argued, by the more extreme radicalism in American universities and elsewhere that had earlier manifested itself in the New Left and counterculture of the late 1960s and early '70s. According to Bloom, this extremism had roots in certain European, especially German, intellectual currents. In typical Straussian fashion, Bloom obfuscated by implying a connection between the Enlightenment he favored and the so-called "Ancients," *as he interpreted them.* For instance, he treated Socrates as a kind of pre-Enlightenment figure.

None of this should have surprised anyone. As a Straussian, Bloom had long sought to appropriate certain iconic historical figures, giving them new intellectual profiles that would support his intellectual agenda. His likes and dislikes were revealing. His fondness for Jean-Jacques Rousseau, if nothing else, should have tipped conservatives off to his philosophical leanings. Though a complex thinker not easily classified, Rousseau had long been seen as a major influence on leftist-revolutionary movements and as a theorist of so-called totalitarian democracy. He inspired the French Jacobins, including the notorious Robespierre.[2] But no—when *The Closing of the American Mind* enjoyed its great success, conservatives wanted to celebrate a supposed breakthrough for conservatism.

Bloom's book actually took its place within an old, large and familiar genre, that of turning America and its origins, especially the so-called Founding, into something different from what they actually were. Intellectuals uncomfortable with America's traditional culture had long tried to recast and replace it. Because Americans were, when these efforts first got underway, strongly attached to that culture and had a particular fondness for the Constitution as the political essence of the American tradition, attacking these head-on was not a very promising way of weaning Americans off traditional allegiances. Instead, these intellectuals adopted a strategy of deception and, in some cases, perhaps self-deception. Great energy went into persuading Americans that America's pedigree was not what it had seemed to be. America, they asserted, was not an outgrowth and continuation of Western classical and Christian civilization, as mediated by British culture, and affected also by more recent ideas. America represented a departure from or outright rejection of the bad old days of Europe. America was based not on a rich, complex, slowly evolved European heritage, but on abstract, ahistorical principles.

A prime example of this genre was Louis Hartz's 1955 book *The Liberal Tradition in America*, which declared that America is quintessentially liberal and that John Locke is pervasively paradigmatic for America. All the more thoroughly to sever America's connection to the old world, Hartz assumed an ahistorical, secularized, "enlightened," quasi-capitalist Locke. This Locke suited his intellectual purpose better than the actual Locke, whose ideas had a connection, however tenuous, with medieval thought. Bloom's book, like those of other Straussians, was yet another example of the effort to give America origins that would make it more appealing and favorable to people of enlightened views.

Whole ideologies and mythologies have grown up that draw

attention away from America's actual past and make Americans of an older type, the WASPs in particular, feel defensive and even out of place, certainly not entitled to any special status. The desire to have America be something different from its historical past and to make it perhaps also more palatable to an aspiring new elite is probably most evident and explicit in Bloom's fellow Straussian Harry Jaffa. Jaffa has made a career of asserting that America must not, repeat, not, be understood as owing anything of importance to an old historical heritage. It must be seen as born out of a radical break with the past and as based on abstract principles of an essentially Lockean cast—Lockeanism understood concomitantly as a departure from earlier thought. The American Founding, Jaffa asserts, "represented the most radical break with tradition . . . that the world had seen. . . . [T]he founders understood themselves to be revolutionaries, and to celebrate the American Founding is therefore to celebrate revolution." The American Revolution "embodied the greatest attempt at innovation that human history had recorded." This revolution was somewhat mild, Jaffa concedes, but belongs with "subsequent revolutions in France, Russia, China, Cuba or elsewhere."[3] There is in such statements not so much as a hint of the deep roots of the American rebellion in the old English tradition of constitutionalism and resistance to tyranny. That a particular heritage—classical, Christian, and British—decisively shaped American society and politics is for Jaffa evidently a distasteful notion. Far from being conservative of an ancient inheritance, Jaffa wants to be *rid* of America's actual past—a goal that he has pursued by arguing among the historically uneducated for his notion of an ahistorical, radical, revolutionary Founding. Bloom's view of America is similar. In *The Closing of the American Mind* he even asserts that the American Revolution was fought for the same principles as the French Revolution.[4] Putative American conservatives still sensed nothing particularly wrong with the book. They seemed to have been already affected by such a view of America and to have but a passing familiarity with the history of their country.[5]

Analogously, Bloom contends that Plato, whose iconic status and authority he would like to invoke on behalf of his own beliefs, is markedly different from how a long tradition of classicist scholarship has understood him. Contrary to all appearances, Plato is not scornful of democracy and democratic man. He is a democrat in disguise. Bloom writes about *The Republic*: "Socrates the philosopher desires democracy. He is actually engaged in a defense of democracy against its enemies."[6] Bloom similarly tries to claim the old normative idea of "nature," which appeared among the Greeks and eventually became central to the natural law tradition. To recast this idea and infuse it with content more pleasing to him, Bloom draws in part on Rousseau's primitivistic notion of "nature," which is at the core of Rousseau's wholesale attack on traditional Western civilization, especially its moral-spiritual heritage. Rousseau constructed the sharpest possible contrast between nature and tradition. Really to respect nature is to be *hostile* to tradition.

Leo Strauss, the teacher of Bloom and Jaffa, is not enamored of Rousseau or Locke, but his basic understanding of philosophy radiates distrust of tradition. He insists that real philosophizing is incompatible with according tradition respect, except in the limited sense that the philosophers, whose real thoughts are always a threat to tradition, may have to pay lip service to it to protect themselves against resentment. The philosopher is not concerned with history, Strauss contends, but with the universal, which is, in his estimation, by definition ahistorical, abstract. To philosophize, Strauss insists, is to disavow the traditional, the conventional, the ancestral. To philosophize is to consider "universal or abstract principles" and always has "a revolutionary, disturbing, unsettling effect." There is that idea again: What has evolved historically imperils goodness and truth. Strauss wants it understood that philosophy "tends to prevent men from wholeheartedly identifying themselves with, or accepting the social order that fate has allotted them. *It tends to alienate them from their place on the earth.*"[7] To philosophize is to become more or less alienated from the surrounding society. It seems for Strauss unacceptable that tradition at its best—as a kind of summing up of the findings of generations—might actually *help* intellectually and otherwise limited human beings to *find* universality and to achieve an intrinsically worthwhile existence. Joseph Cropsey, with whom Strauss co-edited a famous reader in political philosophy, echoes this prejudice against tradition. Expounding a Straussian conception of nature, Cropsey writes: "The conventional is *antithetical* to the natural." When conservatism respects convention and tradition, Cropsey adds, "it can be said to abjure nature and reason."[8]

Strauss and the Straussians thus go to great lengths denying any connection between philosophy and the universal, on the one hand, and tradition and the historical, on the other. To regard tradition as in any sense authoritative is to be guilty of the philosophical and moral offense of "historicism." Claiming yet again the support of an iconic figure for his thinking, Bloom writes in *The Closing of the American Mind* with specific reference to what Aristotle is supposed to have believed: "The essence of philosophy is the abandonment of all authority in favor of individual human reason."[9] Another ancient thinker is here found to have anticipated the modern notion of reason that Bloom favors. His Aristotle looks very different from the Aristotle who emphasized the social and political nature of man and philosophized about politics on the basis of a comparative historical study of regimes.

Whence this Straussian unwillingness to consider that philosophy and morality might have something to gain from weighing historical evidence, most generally the experience of the human race and, more particularly, the experience of classical and Christian civilization? Whence this assumption that tradition must contradict and threaten philosophy?

Christian civilization fostered a rather different attitude towards tradition. It negated any sharp dichotomy between philosophy/universality and history. A sense of preserving and transmitting a heritage is integral to Christianity. *Remembrance* of sacred events and how they inspired the Christian community is central to the Christian intellectual and moral sensibility. Particularly in its more Catholic and Orthodox strains, Christianity has regarded tradition as one of its pillars. For Thomas Aquinas, natural law, which he regards as accessible not only to Christians, tends to coincide with custom.[10] One of the obvious reasons for taking a sympathetic interest in history is that, according to Christianity, the Universal and the historical became one. The Word became flesh. In keeping with the notion that the divine was incarnated, Christians have been sensitive to history being more than an amorphous flux. They have looked for and tried to realize as much as possible of life's higher meaning not in the intellectual abstract, but in concrete, historical action. Though it has not been unencumbered by rationalistic leanings, Christianity greatly modified the over-intellectualization of the moral-spiritual life and the philosophical ahistoricism to which the ancient Greeks, especially Plato, were prone. "By their fruits ye shall know them" means to Christians that the spirit manifests itself first of all in things concretely done. In its encounter with more abstract, rationalistic modern thinking, Christian civilization generated a heightened awareness of the higher aspects and potentialities of man's historical existence, a more acute, self-consciously historical view of life and of how, despite the chronic perversities and limits of human life, the universal might find expression in the particular. Edmund Burke strongly defends tradition, not, as Strauss clumsily alleges, as a normative *alternative* to moral universality, but, on the contrary, as a source of guidance in the search for universality. Burke regards "the general bank and capital of nations and of ages," as enlivened by what he calls a "moral imagination," as an indispensable support for individually weak and imperfect human beings in trying to discern and realize true universality.[11] Christian thinkers have not been alone in concluding that, as Burke argues, a purely abstract universality is an artificial and potentially tyrannical construct.[12]

It is hardly implausible to think that humanity has something to learn from its own experience and that it might over time evolve an improved sense of what makes life worth living. Why, then, is it so important to the mentioned Straussians to portray any such philosophical leanings as the product of an inferior, less than philosophical mind-set? Why their strong desire to pit what they call philosophy against tradition? Why must philosophy be conceived as inseparable from alienation from society and even as inducing a revolutionary disposition? Why are the Straussians not content with something like Burke's admission that tradition is but a guide and nowhere the final word and with his recognition that in a stagnant society tradition may become stultifying or perverse? It would appear that the Straussian discomfort with tradition does not have merely philosophical origins. It suggests a psychological predisposition to view a society's culture as inevitably threatening or hostile. It is as if the mentioned Straussians thought that only by disparaging and otherwise undermining the ways of the society in which they find themselves could they hope to achieve the influence or status to which they feel entitled. One wonders if, for these Straussians, the "philosopher" with his allegedly noble alienation and disdain for tradition is in effect a representative and spearhead for a rising elite that is trying to replace another.

Members of the Frankfurt School are known for their attacks on traditional authority and the "authoritarian personality," just as Marx and Lenin before them exuded alienation and revolutionary sentiment. Because of the reputation of the Straussians, it might seem far-fetched to regard them as radicals in any sense, but, whatever the best way to describe them, they do in their disparagement of tradition resemble the open, unqualified left. Their ostensible defense of universality or "natural right" seems to connect them with more traditional views, but, as has been shown, they define universality or natural right abstractly and in *contradistinction* to historical particularity and individuality. That universality and history might be synthesized, as assumed, for example, in the Christian notion of incarnation, is for them unacceptable, even inconceivable. In the Straussian conception, the universal must be empty of specific, historical content. Having dismissed Burkean "historicism" in *Natural Right and History* and associated it with the pernicious "moderns," Strauss aligns himself with the "ancients," *as he understands them.* He writes: "The quarrel between the ancients and the moderns concerns eventually, and perhaps even from the beginning, the status of 'individuality.'"[13] To attribute to individuality or particularity any kind of higher significance or authority is to have succumbed to "historicism," than which there is no greater philosophical failing. It must here be conceded that the ancients, especially Plato, did have an undeveloped sense of the intimate connection between particularity and universality, but Strauss introduced his dichotomy long after philosophy had broached and extensively discussed the possibility of a synthesis of the two. His dichotomy is therefore more deliberate and radical than anything that the ancients could have advocated.

The criticism of "historicism" is one of Strauss's most well-known and celebrated philosophical themes. He goes to great lengths to discredit respect for tradition and historical particularity. Though this is not the place to explore the topic, one might ask if Strauss was able to reconcile these philosophical efforts with his strong identification with Jewish culture and Zionism. Philosophical consistency would require that his "anti-historicism" be directed also against the tradition with which he identifies and would mean that he is undermining his own heritage. If his anti-historicism is addressed only to general audiences and directed only against competing traditions, it would not be a philosophical stance but a merely rhetorical one, part of a political strategy. A posture of that sort might have seemed appropriate when in the Germany of his youth Strauss was a member of a Zionist alternative to the Hitler youth.

It is a much-debated question whether, for leading Straussians, a defense of "universality" or "natural right" is merely theoretical window-dressing, hiding a kind of Nietzschean nihilism and despair or at least a deep ambivalence regarding the existence of moral universality. Be that as it may, the Straussians, including Bloom, insist that universality or nature must be understood as purely abstract. Their fondness for ahistorical, anti-traditional "principles" becomes hard to tell apart from that of the French Jacobins. These philosophical inclinations are loaded with practical ramifications. It is relevant that abstractly conceived principles typically express an impatience with the complexities of historical existence and a desire to dominate by decree. People of such "principle" tend to ignore historical circumstances and see moral and other issues in black or white.

But if Bloom and the Straussians associate philosophy with alienation and abstraction, how to explain that so many American Christians, particularly Roman Catholics, have been so attracted to their thinking? One obvious and partial explanation is that Leo Strauss and the Straussians presented themselves as defenders of the ancients, which seemed to accord with long-standing Western intellectual tradition. There are strains of Straussian thought—including a form of elitism and an apparent concern for a higher, common good in preference to narrowly economic interest—that appear to overlap with that heritage. The elements of Straussianism that most clash with the classical and Christian traditions were also typically formulated in indirect, shrouded ways that kept philosophically unsophisticated traditionalist readers from recoiling. The Straussian method of turning respected historical figures into something different from what they were was sufficiently convoluted not to arouse suspicion among such Christians. From the point of view of attracting followers among Catholics, Straussian thinking had the advantage that its anti-historicism and abstractionism could appeal to and connect with the weakest aspect of the natural law tradition, its propensity for abstract rationalism. Catholics may in addition have detected that, almost from the beginning, leading Straussians had a special and growing influence that was unexpected in supposedly conservative intellectuals. The Straussians were attacked by leftists and rigid positivists, but they simultaneously had some kind of rapport with portions of the academic establishment, and they had access to growing financial resources. Even as Catholics sensed that pleasing the leaders of this school might bring a career advantage, the smarter and better-educated among them must have felt some considerable intellectual and moral-spiritual discomfort. But, to the extent that they sensed peril, they seem to have lacked the philosophical tools to articulate just what it was and to have been, in any case, able to suppress their unease.

It should be added that some Catholics may have been attracted to the Straussian disparagement of tradition because of similar developments within their church. As became evident in connection with the Second Vatican Council, many progressive Catholics sharply challenged Church authority and argued that the Church had relied overly on tradition and resisted modernity too strongly.

There is yet another possible explanation for the apparent paradox that Catholic intellectuals should have been attracted to Straussian alienation and anti-"historicism." Could it be that as outsiders of a sort—as the descendants of recent arrivals in Protestant America—some Catholics found the Straussian discomfort with tradition in general and with old America and its elites in particular subtly appealing? Even if they did not need to feel greatly alienated from an essentially Christian America, they might have carried with them from their families stories or echoes, however faded, of the slights and indignities suffered at the hands of WASP America or have harbored just a vague general sense of inferiority. Did some Irish-Americans prefer to ignore America's English origins?

The Straussians refer with apparent admiration to a few iconic American figures, whom they like to call the Founders. To give them that name is to imply that America was a new creation, that it did not really exist until the Declaration and the Constitution were written. The Founders, as presented by leading Straussians, have no deep, substantial cultural roots. They are not portrayed as having the thick historical identity of essentially British Christians living on the East Coast of America. The Straussians like to present them instead with reference to specific ideas that they supposedly held—sometimes just single phrases they used—which are typically taken out of historical context, that is, made as abstract as possible, or taken out of their context in a particular document. It seems that Straussian interpreters have been concerned to *empty* these figures of their cultural distinctiveness, specifically, of their WASPishness, and to turn them into mere embodiments of or stand-ins for abstract, formulaic notions. Their iconic status attaches, then, not to their substantive minds, characters, and imaginations, including their historically formed ideas, but to ahistorical, putatively universal "principles."

Is it frivolous to speculate that descendants of the late arrivals in

America, not least the Catholic so-called ethnics, found it somehow pleasing to think with Hartz, Strauss, Jaffa, Bloom, and many others that America did not really originate with quasi-aristocratic WASPs but with abstract principles espoused by culturally almost vacuous, non-descript Founders? If America is thought of as an ideological cause rather than as the creative development of a thickly constituted and ancient historical heritage, then whoever embraces the same principles is as entitled to feeling American as any WASP. To measure up, you do not have to conform to the snobbish expectations of a WASP elite but only need to repeat certain formulas. People with a social chip on their shoulder might, in other words, have felt a kinship with Straussian theorists who clothed alienation from the old Americans in a noble-sounding advocacy of universal principles.

To the extent that Catholic ethnics more or less consciously joined with the mentioned Straussians in an alliance to diminish and dislodge the WASPs, they seem not to have worried that, despite their vast superiority in numbers, they would be the distinctly junior partners or that Straussian alienation and anti-historicism would undermine their own beliefs and general culture.

Perhaps the prime example of a prominent Catholic who rather uncritically and unsuspectingly promoted Straussianism was William F. Buckley Jr., a central figure in the shaping of the American post–World War II conservative movement. As the founder and editor of *National Review* he could promote ideas and perspectives in a sustained manner. He could make reputations. As a gifted intellectual and polemicist he became a conservative celebrity. His well-advertised Catholicism helped pull aspiring young Catholic intellectuals in the direction that he recommended, and he did much to assist the Straussian cause. It is illustrative of Buckley's role in that regard that in 1988 he let Charles R. Kesler, a disciple of Harry Jaffa, co-edit with him a revised edition of his 1970 anthology *Modern American Conservative Thought in the Twentieth Century*. The new edition, called *Keeping the Tablets*, gave great prominence to Straussians, especially Leo Strauss and Harry Jaffa.

Much of that writing, including the ideas of Harry Jaffa cited above, could not be construed as conservative in any meaningful sense. Though intellectually agile, William F. Buckley, Jr., was not prone to philosophy in the stricter sense. He cared less about philosophical veracity, precision, and consistency than about creating a broad intellectual political alliance. Trying to decide whether a thinker belonged to the good guys or the bad guys, Buckley would go more by the person's stand on certain public policy issues than by the person's basic view of human nature and society. That Harry Jaffa supported Barry Goldwater for the presidency seemed under Buckley's loose, public-policy-oriented definition of conservatism sufficient proof that Jaffa was on the right side. Yet apparent similarities among thinkers on political issues may be quite superficial, indeed, conceal all-important differences. Supporters, for example, of "the free market," "limited government," or "liberty" may mean greatly different things by these terms and have sharply contrasting worldviews. Really to sort out questions of this type requires careful philosophical analysis, a need that becomes all the greater when trying to distinguish different meanings of such terms as "natural right," "reason," "universality," "history," and "tradition." For this kind of scrutiny and discernment Buckley was not well equipped. He was one of many supposedly conservative intellectuals who made do with a kind of near-philosophy or pretend-philosophy. He did not realize that failing to address seemingly "fine" philosophical points was a major obstacle to understanding what was what and that this deficiency was bound to produce vast intellectual confusion and have large practical consequences.

Historians will have to assess the extent to which non-philosophical factors, including social prejudice and ambition, accounted for some of the susceptibility of Catholic intellectuals to Straussian alienation and anti-"historicism." A basic lack of philosophical and historical education may have been more important. In the case of the leading Straussians, a psychology of alienation appears to have been a major factor. If we take seriously Leo Strauss's comments on the nature of philosophy, philosophizing that is not shot through by alienation is for him not really philosophy. Yet philosophers who do not approach ideas from within a psychology of social discomfort or ambition need not see any necessary connection between philosophy and alienation from the culture in which they live. They do of course recognize that the philosophical intellect is never the captive of tradition and must clash with stale and rigid convention and that the philosopher must often be critical of old or merely prevalent beliefs, but this is an elementary, virtually self-evident disposition. It does not produce an entire philosophical mindset, a preoccupation with undermining an existing culture and its elites and protecting yourself against the inevitable backlash. Conceiving of philosophy as having a conspiratorial dimension looks rather idiosyncratic and is out of place in thinkers who speak in the name of high principles, "nature," "universality," or "natural right."

Alienation from traditional American and Western society often surfaces in *The Closing of the American Mind.* It is palpable in Bloom's comments on the American South, a region that happens to have been especially respectful of tradition. He disdains its championing of the principle of aristocracy. Southern defenses of local community and protests against leveling and money-grubbing he dismisses as the special pleading of "snobs" and "malcontents." Yet among Southerners, too, the Straussians made recruits, though not of the more doctrinaire, enthusiastic sort.

Bloom's 1987 triumph was not due to his having written a profound analysis of the state of America. He had produced another barely veiled attack on traditional America while at the same time providing a defense of the new American establishment that is replacing the disoriented, decadent WASPs. Like Bloom, parts of the new establishment did not want to yield to even more radical forces, such as members of the New Left and the counterculture. Now that we are on the inside, they seemed to say, it is only necessary to make sure that extremists do not undermine our gains or that the WASPs will not stage a comeback.

One of today's leading literary scholars, the Harvard "new historicist" Stephen Greenblatt, feels no need to conceal his animus against what remains of the old Western world, specifically Christianity. It is not a part of his intellectual strategy to appeal to some of the conservative elements of the abdicating, essentially Christian order. He openly celebrates the destruction of traditional beliefs and structures. At first blush, Bloom might seem the antithesis of Greenblatt. After all, Bloom *criticizes* historicism, and Greenblatt approves it. But Greenblatt's historicism is very different from Burke's. The latter is indistinguishable from a *defense* of traditional Western civilization as well as of universality, though understood in a partly new way. Despite Bloom's disdain for tradition and traditional elites, self-described conservatives thought that he might be one of them. Bloom is indeed much less obvious in his attacks on old America and old Western civilization than Greenblatt, and he is not as radical as the latter in what he wants to jettison. He is also protective of aspects of the "modern," Enlightenment mind. Yet Bloom *shares* with Greenblatt a deep prejudice, evident to any attentive reader of *The Closing of the American Mind*, against traditional Western civilization. The obfuscation that he and other Straussians have employed—notably that of using iconic Western and American figures to give themselves a distinguished and to traditionalists reassuring pedigree—proved sufficient to disarm and deceive philosophically semiliterate readers. Straussianism in general is most certainly not without merit, but the failure of so-called conservatives to discern its element of cultural radicalism and intellectual intrigue revealed a great need for philosophical and historical education.

PART FOUR

THE GREAT NEGLECTED POWER

A MATTER OF PRIORITIES

("What is Left? What is Right?," from a symposium in *The American Conservative*, August 28, 2006.) Looking to politics as the way to change America for the better, American movement conservatives have greatly underestimated the role of "the culture" in shaping the evolution of society. They have shown very limited interest in the deeper sensibilities and assumptions that over time guide human conduct. Yet, for civilization to thrive, the mind and the imagination have to form a sound sense of direction and proportion. But while deep cultural trends transformed America and even changed the meaning of basic political terms, the priorities of many movement conservatives were reflected in the extraordinary amounts of money devoted to public policy research and political activism.

Modern American conservatism has been enthralled by politics. It should be obvious to all by now that this has been a debilitating preoccupation. Society's long-term direction is not set mainly by politicians. It is set by those who capture a people's mind and imagination. Conservative politicians and policy wonks have failed to reverse any of the main deleterious social trends of the last half-century not because they have lacked financial resources but because efforts like theirs have limited efficacy in the first place. While they have gobbled up millions and millions of donated dollars, the activities that shape the deeper sensibilities and desires of Americans have continued to be dominated by people trying to dismantle what remains of traditional American and Western civilization.

Fascination with politics pushed into the forefront of the conservative movement individuals of limited philosophical and historical discernment. More and more they came under the influence of the zeitgeist and manipulative donors, which has contributed to sometimes ludicrous terminological confusion. Today "conservative" often means leftist, as in wanting to reshape the world in the image of a single ahistorical model ("democracy"). Many so-called conservatives are better described as Jacobins. Most neoconservatives are ideologically intense universalistic liberals. Needless to say, what Americans call liberalism has long been difficult to tell apart from European social democracy.

To recover, American conservatism would have to reorder its priorities and most especially put politics in its place. America's crisis is at bottom moral-spiritual and cultural. Though a new alliance of homeless political groups is desirable, a realignment would be unavailing in the long run unless the old obsession with politics were also broken. The issues most needing attention will make the eyes of political junkies glaze over.

Modern American conservatism did not take to heart the insights of its most perceptive minds. Those who came to set the tone in the movement as a whole, William F. Buckley Jr. prominent among them, were political intellectuals. It seemed to them that dealing with the moral-spiritual and cultural foundations of civilization was not the most exciting and pressing need. The political intellectuals drew attention and respect away from efforts whose relevance to politics was not immediately obvious. That advanced philosophy and artistic imagination might over time do more than politics to change society did not even occur to most of them. Other than politics, what most interested them was economics.

Some paid lip service to philosophy and to what Russell Kirk, following Edmund Burke and Irving Babbitt, called "the moral imagination," but the humanities seemed worthy of little more than a polite nod.

The problem, simply put, was lack of sophistication—an inability to understand what most deeply shapes the outlook and conduct of human beings. Persons move according to their innermost beliefs, hopes, and fears. These are affected much less by politicians than by philosophers, novelists, religious visionaries, moviemakers, playwrights, composers, painters, and the like, though truly great works of this kind reach most minds and imaginations only in diminished, popular form.

Yet the conservative movement did not direct its main efforts toward a revitalization of the mind, imagination, and moral-spiritual life. There it relied on shortcuts. In the area of ethics, for example, it assumed that churches would handle the job. But the churches, too, had been deeply influenced by the general moral, intellectual, and aesthetic trends of society. The god worshiped by many was a figment of a polluted, sentimental imagination. The so-called evangelicals did little to break out of their accustomed intellectual poverty. Roman Catholics formed a core within post-World War II conservatism. Their church had more than superficially resisted major destructive trends in Western society. But as conservative intellectuals they, too, cut corners. For the most part avoiding an advanced engagement with philosophy and the arts, they were satisfied with upholding "orthodoxy," which they did with Protestant-like earnestness.

The kind of intellectual, aesthetic, and moral-spiritual renewal that might have transformed the universities, the arts, the media, publishing, entertainment, and the churches never quite came off. Without a major reorientation of American thought and sensibility, conservative politics was bound to fail.

The neoconservatives reinforced the preoccupation with politics and public policy. They claimed that before their coming to the rescue American conservatism had been intellectually feeble, but in reality, it had exhibited far greater scope and depth prior to their arrival. Mentioning just a few thinkers of the 1950s and '60s proves the point: Friedrich Hayek,

Russell Kirk, John Lukacs, Thomas Molnar, Robert Nisbet, Peter Stanlis, Wilhelm Röpke, Peter Viereck, Eliseo Vivas, Eric Voegelin, and Richard Weaver. Behind several of them stood the perhaps most powerful and prophetic American thinker of the 20th century, the Harvard Professor Irving Babbitt (1865–1933). Instead of fully exploring, developing, and applying the insights of such thinkers, the conservative movement wanted to get down to politics without delay, first by trying to elect Barry Goldwater president. Having a flawed sense of priorities, conservatism would before the end of the 20th century go almost completely off the rails, becoming a captive of party, money, and media celebrities.

To complain about today's terminological confusion is not to imply that the terms used here have single, settled definitions. Words like "conservative" and "liberal" can be meaningfully defined and be useful, but any definition of this type simplifies complex reality. The more philosophical the study of life, the more inadequate such definitions appear. It is partly for this reason that traditional conservatives have insisted that conservatism is not an ideology. Even the best of principles are transcended by the enduring higher purpose of civilization. The means chosen to advance that purpose must change as historical situations change. For example, a conservative would never say, as would some classical liberals (or libertarians), that the legitimate functions of government are always and everywhere the same.

The word "conservative" was always problematic. It seems to imply that conservatism is all about conserving something already achieved. But conservatism wants to conserve the best of the humane heritage because the latter is an indispensable guide to finding and promoting the good, the true, and the beautiful in the present. The spirit of civilization must forever adapt to new circumstances.

Today highly destructive social trends have themselves become traditions of a sort. Hence the spirit of civilization will have to assert itself in sometimes radical-looking ways, not least in politics. It must free itself of incapacitating habits. One such habit is the increasingly philistine obsession with politics.

HOW CONSERVATIVES FAILED "THE CULTURE"

("How Conservatives Failed the Culture," *Modern Age*, Vol. 38, No. 2, 1996.) Not understanding the power of "the culture" to shape society and politics has been a major and chronic weakness of American movement conservatism. By failing to absorb central insights of major figures in early postwar conservatism and by placing undue emphasis on politics, the movement undermined its ability to analyze and to address the fundamental problems of American and Western civilization. This article was published in *Modern Age*, the journal of the Intercollegiate Studies Institute, but because of unusual circumstances, it might not have appeared there. Many months after the editor had accepted the article in final form and just days before the relevant issue of the journal was to go to press, the publisher suddenly informed me by express mail that unless within a day or two I had approved the excision of two passages in the article, it would not be published. I was very reluctant to accept this abrupt, last-minute demand. I realized that the publisher did not want to offend neoconservatives and Straussians who could be helpful raising money. The contested passages were not indispensable to the article, but I resented the high-handedness of the ultimatum. The publisher's decree greatly upset the editor of the journal, a prominent professor. He let me know that if I was unable to accept the excisions, he would resign from the journal. Not wanting to be the cause of such a drastic development, I acceded to the publisher's ultimatum. Here, the passages cut from the published article have been restored within brackets.

Official professions to the contrary, many self-described American intellectual conservatives have a thinly veiled disdain for philosophy and the arts. Even among academics indifference to what lies beyond broad ideas and popular culture is common. The ruling assumption of the now dominant strains of intellectual conservatism seems to be that the crux of social well-being is politics: bad politicians ruin society, good politicians set it right. Nothing fascinates conservatives more than presidential politics. For social problems to be effectively remedied and for worthy objectives to be achieved, "our" candidate must win the next election, our people man the government.

Many supposedly intellectual conservatives seem to consider ideas and culture from afar, as it were, feeling no deep personal need for or intimate connection with them. Some are in a way attracted to the arts or even to philosophical speculation, but see no significant and immediate connection between these and the life of practice. Ideas and the arts are mainly pleasant diversions. Many others have only slight interest in philosophy and culture for their own sake. More or less consciously, they tend to assess either thought or imagination from the point of view of whether it advances or undermines the political cause that they assume to be incontestable. Does the book, lecture, play, movie, or song help or hinder the cause? Although such works may enlighten or entertain, they do not strike these individuals as having intrinsic and independent authority. Works of thought and imagination are for them not intriguing and potentially unsettling forces that might trigger painful self-examination and unpredictably reconstitute one's own accustomed views; making sense of them is not so much a matter of soul-searching as of locating them on the political spectrum.

One might explain these reactions as instances of the social decline now widely bemoaned. Schools, families, and other institutions have not conveyed the excitement of ideas and the higher arts, leaving the young largely "tone-deaf" and unaware of their deeper appeal and formative influence on civilization. For persons not strongly drawn to them in the first place, the element of sheer decadence in the dominant intellectual and cultural life of today has only reinforced existing prejudices.

A related explanation for truncated conservative approaches to thought and imagination is the spread of an ideological frame of mind. In this century leftist ideology has been the most influential. It has been often extreme and has caused great human suffering. But the left has no monopoly on ideology. Even the best of ideas can start to separate from the changeability and complexity of real life and harden into reflexive and reductionistic propositions.

There is a sense in which ideology—as well as party programs, slogans, etc.—is not only inevitable but legitimate: to advance practical objectives it is frequently necessary, especially in politics, to summarize and codify ideas in order to mobilize support and exhort to action. Ideology in that sense is not necessarily incompatible with humane purposes. Neither is there anything inherently objectionable about the popularization of difficult ideas. The full import of sound philosophy may be apparent only to relatively few, but those insights need to be communicated beyond the circle of learned experts. What is complex must be made simple. In the process of transmission there is a danger that thought will harden into ideology, but good popularizers will try, by means of well-chosen concrete illustrations, for example, not to turn ideas into abstract and sweeping generalizations that ignore the texture of real life.[1]

The health of society requires that elites be continuously reminded by genuine intellectuals and artists not to mistake ideology for eternal verities. If that indispensable task is not performed or if the reminders are not heeded, undue influence will fall to the more inventive and ambitious ideologues. Their politically charged formulations may start to acquire a life of their own. In the absence of a vital intellectual and aesthetical culture that challenges and breaks up the encrustations of ideology, such persons may gather unto themselves large new responsibilities unsuited to their preparation and temperament. They may start acting the role of arbiters of goodness, truth, and beauty, perhaps establish themselves as authorities in the universities. Trying to meet the expectations that traditionally surround such roles, ideologues may acquire greater subtlety, but the affected disciplines and institutions are damaged by the association.

Ideology is now rampant in the universities. Since virtually all of it is of the left, it might seem beneficial to have it balanced in some small measure by ideology of the right. Yet for political correctness of one kind to compete with political correctness of another kind may be a marginal intellectual advantage for the longer run. Together, the weeds in the garden suffocate and crowd out the flowers.

The ideological mindset, formed as it is at bottom by a desire to dominate rather than illuminate, is an intruder in philosophy and the arts. It is closed in upon itself and resentful of competition. Instead of cultivating the openness to new influences that marks real philosophy and art and letting itself be exposed to the possible intellectual turmoil of fresh insight, ideology shunts inconvenient thought and imagination aside. Ideologues produce propaganda, although sometimes propaganda of a sophisticated kind. When such individuals set the tone, the intellectual and artistic life suffers.

In all avenues of human action, achieving particular objectives requires that the will be asserted and available resources marshaled. It takes power. The power sought and exercised in politics is but an example of an ever-present need of human action in general. Without power, great or small, nothing gets done, be it for good or ill.[2] Yet a drive for power that is not substantially and integrally connected with the free and independent sphere of ideas and culture—to say nothing here of the all-important imperative of morality—becomes a merely self-advancing and self-gratifying manipulation of other human beings.

Who is today the paradigmatic conservative intellectual, the kind of individual to whom educated and reading conservatives look for authoritative judgments and to whom they ultimately defer? He seems to be a cross between an intellectual and a political activist, less a thinker concerned with the fundamental and enduring questions of life than a "policy wonk," less a learned scholar than a media pundit. Although possibly bright and articulate, this type cannot long be distracted from his absorbing interest: politics and politics-related questions and schemes. He seems untouched by philosophical depth or by any deeper aesthetical need or sensibility.

Individuals of this description can wield considerable influence over the kind of decisions that appear to them most important. But these persons are not so much independent agents as unwitting instruments of larger forces—a fate they cannot bemoan because it does not reach their consciousness. Because of a weak grasp of the dynamic of human existence, they have difficulty understanding the scope of social problems. Their limited awareness of what really shapes the long-term direction of a society or civilization—specifically, of the roles played by thought and imagination—leads to inadequate analyses of the existing political and social situation and of what might bring real and lasting improvement. These persons are frequently surprised by events and are prone to defeating their own stated objectives.

Unless ideas and art have some direct and obvious relationship to politics, many intellectual conservatives regard them as having negligible practical importance and to be provinces of the left in addition. Because philosophers and artists can be expected to favor the wrong causes, it is desirable to mobilize opposition to them from within their own ranks; yet, apart from this political problem, these conservatives see no large and compelling reason to worry about professors, writers, composers, and artists. After all, society is moved not by them but by individuals who pursue more "practical" pursuits, especially persons who affect public policy and, most prominently, leading politicians. To the bearer, this view of where the real power lies represents hard-nosed realism. In actuality, it exemplifies a narrow and shortsighted understanding of what shapes the future.

The decline of academia and the general culture has assumed such blatant forms and started to have such an obvious impact on society at large that nowadays the conservative political intellectuals are paying more attention. But the seriousness of those problems is not unrelated to the mentioned assessment of what sets society's long-term direction, an assessment that is in line with the more questionable aspects of American pragmatism. In the last two decades especially, the "realism" of conservatives who assume the centrality of politics has detracted from and undermined an earlier and rather different kind of American conservatism, which started to gain new momentum in the early 1950s. Its leaders saw ideas and imagination as being at the bottom not only of the troubles of civilization but also of any possibility of renewal. "Realism" competed with and drew attention away from efforts to bring about the kind of intellectual and cultural renaissance that eventually might have arrested or reversed ominous developments in academia and the arts and more deeply penetrated society.

Some brief comments on what really moves human beings and originates social change will help explain the seriousness of not recognizing the actual role and importance of thought and imagination. The power of even the ablest and most knowledgeable wielders of political influence is sharply circumscribed by another power. That power does not marshal and deploy resources in a utilitarian political fashion. It works in a more subtle and yet efficacious manner: it shapes the fundamental sensibilities, desires and views of a people.

Every society and individual has a vision, however inarticulate, of what life is like and might become. Deep within, we carry fears and hopes. What we ultimately live on, and live for, are our most cherished dreams about the future. Held and nurtured in the imagination, their vividness and concreteness stir us to action. We live by what we thrill to, says D. H. Lawrence. The imagination is more generally at the bottom of our sense of the whole, of how we see human existence, its opportunities, dangers, joys, and sorrows.

On the basis of that concrete feel for the texture of life, we also form ideas. They give conceptual expression to our intuitions. Some individuals undertake that intellectual articulation systematically and in depth. The result is philosophy.

Our dreams and ideas bear the distinctive imprint of our individual personalities, but every society has a dominant sense of its own identity and purpose that affects even the innermost beliefs and wishes of the person. Individuals are connected by ideas and intuitions that give them a similar outlook on life. By virtue of that commonality, certain works of thought or imagination—of philosophy, history, fiction, poetry, drama, music, or movies—can give voice to the groping needs and intuitions of their audience; they capture the mind or imagination of a people or its elites. Some of these works catch on in a special way that places them among the enduring treasures of civilization. By the same token, the pioneering, eye-opening works affect how particular people view themselves and human existence.

Great power for shaping society lies with those who make us see life through their eyes. Deep within our personalities are the marks left by the imaginative and intellectual masterminds—poets, religious visionaries, painters, composers, and philosophers—the individuals whose intuitions or ideas leave others changed. Directly or indirectly, those individuals create the tenor of an age, for good or ill. They may be long dead, but their visions move the living.

Great works of art or thought may discuss or depict politics, and they always present a point of view, but their primary inspiration is never merely political passion. They transcend the concerns of particular historical situations. They throw light on the human condition, sometimes on the reality of politics, but they do not preach and exhort. Art and didacticism are incompatible, as are philosophy and propaganda. Still, as illuminating, orienting statements, the great works of art or thought always carry implications or have consequences for practical politics, however indirect and unanticipated. They are typically a reaction against life going wrong and present a vision of new possibilities. By affecting how people imagine or think about the world, these works affect political attitudes.

It is objected perhaps that most people are rarely exposed to high culture—and do not even want to be. Only a small minority becomes familiar with the great works of art or thought and is substantially influenced by them. It may be said of some of these works, in fact, that in particular generations only a handful of persons, perhaps only one or two, can be said really to have absorbed them. How, then, could they have any impact on society in general?

The answer is that the elite culture—including works that are fully accessible to but a few—is transmitted to others by those who have felt its power. Individuals inspired by a great work apply and diversify its vision in their own artistic or intellectual efforts, spreading it to new audiences at different levels of refinement. The transformative power of the great work eventually affects the sensibilities, dreams, or thoughts of all, even if it does so very indirectly and in watered-down form. The perspectives of the seminal works eventually find their way into the general culture—schools, newspapers, movies, television soap operas, novels, and, not least, the imagery of advertising.

Those who enter our minds and imaginations are in a position to make particular ideas, attitudes, behaviors, and experiences seem inviting or repulsive. They can affect our notions of what to admire, what to fear, what to scorn, and what to laugh at, and they can incline us to action that corresponds to these responses.

Especially over time, the power of all the politicians in the nation's capital is dwarfed by the power of those who influence us through teaching, writing, preaching, art, and entertainment. Even if the latter group represents a variety of viewpoints, a particular cultural and intellectual ethos tends to predominate that can be traced back to groundbreaking works of art and thought. In our own time, egalitarian pressures and mass communication have produced a perhaps more thoroughgoing like-mindedness than seen before. Behind what counts as moral sensibility today, for example, who but the ignorant and dull-witted could fail to discern the deep and brilliant, if deleterious, influence of the thought and imagination of Jean-Jacques Rousseau?[3]

Whatever the dominant fundamental mind-set that artists and intellectuals have cultivated, it has planted in us certain expectations and desires. It has prepared the ground for or built obstacles to political action of a certain type. Politicians who run afoul of the prevailing sensibilities and ideas of their time risk their political lives. In other words, they are at the mercy of a power that is not of their own making. Only marginally can they change the "rules of the game" that are determined deep within the consciousness of a people.

Many conservatives believe that intellectuals and artists are naturally and almost inevitably on the left. If this were the case, all efforts to move society in a different direction would be condemned to failure. There simply is no overcoming those who can shape our sense of what makes life worth living.[4]

Conservatives whose culturally and intellectually "unmusical" natures make them indifferent to philosophy and the higher arts do nevertheless have minds and imaginations. They, too, live by what they thrill to. Their fascination with Washington, DC, and presidential politics has been nurtured by images of power and corresponding ideas in the popular culture. Imaginative and intellectual impulses subversive of general trends have also made them critical of the powers-that-be, but, to a far greater extent than they know, they live within the patterns of sensibility and thought that define the ethos of their troubled civilization.

A disparagement of thought and imagination is discernible also among intellectuals on the right who are critical of the now dominant strains of conservatism. Although sometimes perceptive in other respects, they tend to view ideas and culture "sociologically," as the expressions of group interest. The fundamental reality of politics is for them the conflict between "us" and "them." Ideas and art may be influential but do not rise above conflict; they are essentially instruments whereby people who seek power advance their cause (a perspective not unlike that of Karl Marx).

Writers of this persuasion consider themselves consummate realists. They see conservatives for whom literature, art, and philosophy are keys to social renewal as not quite attuned to the hard facts of life. This complaint is not wholly unjustified in that some conservatives are attracted to thought and imagination—and, for that matter, religion—more as avenues of comforting escape than as sustenance for living in the world as it is. What the "realists" do not recognize is that thought and imagination, far from being mere symptoms of power-realities, have everything to do with the very definition of "us" and "them" and that they can either mute or intensify hostilities. That thought and imagination are often vehicles for partisan interest has been here not only acknowledged but highlighted, but it is also the case that political passions and patterns of strife originate deep within the mind and the imagination. One may recognize and even underscore the element of truth in a Niccolò Machiavelli or a Thomas Hobbes and still insist that culture and philosophy—no less than morality—can transcend and therefore modify the boundaries of political conflict. Realism is highly desirable, but to be more than superficially such it must understand the scope and power of art and ideas.

In the decades just after World War II several leading American conservative intellectuals understood well the historical origins of civilization and the great influence of thought and imagination. Russell Kirk and Peter Viereck are good examples. The two differed politically, Viereck being less opposed than Kirk to the budding federal welfare state inherited from Franklin Roosevelt and now managed by the Eisenhower administration. Although sharply critical of the Eastern intellectual-cultural-political elites in important respects, Viereck also felt a stronger bond with them than Kirk. But the two men agreed on the primacy of the "pre-political" sphere of ethics, ideas, and culture. There could be no real recovery of Western civilization without a renewal of mind and imagination.[5]

Kirk and Viereck were inspired by a seminal American thinker, Irving Babbitt (1865–1933), the Harvard professor of French and comparative literature who founded the so-called New Humanism or American Humanism. Babbitt had diagnosed a deepening crisis of civilization. If there were to be any chance of overcoming it, the foundations must be laid for a reorientation of the ethical, aesthetical and intellectual life. Babbitt was particularly concerned to unmask certain moral-imaginative habits—the "sham spirituality" of Rousseauistic sentimental pity—which had become the hallmark of elites in the Western world, and to demonstrate their potentially disastrous social and political consequences. To get to the bottom of the powerful and insidious impulse of "sentimental humanitarianism," Babbitt wanted to expose its deepest roots in morally conceited and self-indulgent imagination. More generally, he sought a broad intellectual and cultural movement that might in time redirect the moral and political life of civilization.[6]

Babbitt strongly influenced the perhaps most fertile strain of conservative thought after the war. But on the whole, American intellectual conservatism has not carried through on its most promising potentialities. It has had difficulty accepting or understanding that real and lasting social change must begin deep within the mind and the imagination and work itself out over generations. Although paying lip-service to the need for ideas and imagination, many of the leaders of the movement wanted immediate results, by which they meant, first of all, political victories. Intellectual conservatism did not fully assimilate or go very far developing and supplementing the work of its leading minds, dead or living. It did not develop the wide-ranging and philosophically mature intellectual culture that might have held and expanded its ground in academia and thence more deeply penetrated society. The element of intellectual and imaginative vitality was diluted or made to seem secondary by the ever-present concern with practical politics and, of course, economics.

Early examples of a preoccupation with politics that prefigured later developments could be cited at length. The *National Review* magazine, which was founded in the mid-1950s, exhibited from the beginning a strong tendency to let political concerns overpower intellectual-philosophical considerations. In 1956 Peter Viereck published a concise but broadly informative historical and typological survey intended primarily for students, *Conservatism from Adams to Churchill.* The book conveyed the richness and variety of the subject while presenting the author's own view of conservatism. In *National Review* one of the editors, the ex-communist Frank S. Meyer, dismissed the book and excommunicated Viereck on grounds of deviation from conservative political orthodoxy, as defined by Meyer—as if issues of practical politics must always take precedence.[7]

The example is revealing in that Viereck, whatever the flaws of his practical politics, understood the sources of genuine civilization a good deal better than most leading American conservative intellectuals. It is no coincidence that, although Russell Kirk long wrote for *National Review,* he was always uncomfortable with its editorial regime and resisted efforts to have his name affixed to its masthead.

In 1951 the young William F. Buckley Jr. had published *God and Man at Yale.* The book denounced "collectivist" teaching at Yale University and argued that the financial backers of academic institutions should ignore disingenuous talk about academic freedom and use their influence to ensure teaching favorable to "individualism" and the market. In his book *Academic Freedom* (1955), Kirk offered a much different point of view, stressing the importance of free inquiry. He politely but firmly rejected what he called Buckley's "program of indoctrination."[8]

The politicizing trend within American intellectual conservatism was by no means all-encompassing, and the movement did make strides in many respects. It gained some ground in academia. Still, the early signs of ambivalence about the free and independent sphere of thought and imagination made it not entirely unexpected that the movement would eventually start losing its cultural-intellectual way. Feeling no deep and continuing need to refresh itself from regenerative philosophical, historical, and literary-artistic sources, it started to become more formulaic, predictable and repetitive, in short, ideological.

The importance of practical politics and public-policy studies is undeniable; the higher their quality, the better. But, in the last couple of decades especially, concentration on such matters has moved the center of gravity even within intellectual conservatism. The tendency was in full view already in the early 1960s with the effort to promote Barry Goldwater for the presidency. It was widely assumed, in *National Review*, for example, that winning the presidency was the ultimate goal, the real "pay-off," as it were, of intellectual work. With the ultimate political prize seemingly within reach, F. S. Meyer (who predicted Goldwater's victory) and many other intellectuals could think of little except the coming election. After the defeat of Goldwater, conservatives were fascinated by books and articles that chronicled the Goldwater campaign, analyzed what had gone wrong, and discussed how the campaign had set the stage for future political gains.

In the 1970s and 1980s the tendency among intellectual conservatives to look to politics as the heartbeat of society only grew stronger. Writers gained prominence who declared that heretofore conservatism had been intellectually feeble and impractical. These writers, based mainly in the New York–Washington corridor, actually knew little of earlier conservative thought, and philosophically their own interests and emphases meant a narrowing of the horizons: public policy and related questions took center stage. Their journalistic aptitude and ability to appeal to the existing media and publishing elites, together with their success in acquiring influence within the Reagan administration, gained them much attention. They tipped the balance within a movement that remained uncertain of its cultural and intellectual identity and always susceptible to the lure of practical politics.

Young conservative intellectuals had once to some appreciable extent looked to leading representatives of the mind and the imagination for direction. Now the kind of philosophical and scholarly work that over time might have brought real change in the universities and elsewhere somehow looked less appealing and important. It yielded increasingly to public-policy debate and high-level journalism, which bolstered already existing trends in the universities. Some of the new leaders were intelligent and articulate but did not read very deeply, scanning books for their political cash value. The movement as a whole started to get its signals, literally as well as figuratively, from op-ed pieces in the *Wall Street Journal* and talking heads on television. Feeling the urge to be where the real action is and to be close to people of real power, many left academia for government and the public policy networks, a trend that both exacerbated and was exacerbated by the continuing advances of the academic left.

Because the conservative discussions of public policy and adjoining issues have not been inspired or informed by the kind of advanced intellectual and artistic culture that once seemed in the making, those discussions have been more prone to ideological reductionism and lack of imagination than need have been the case. It is instructive to compare the emphasis that now prominent intellectual conservatives place on policy analysis and journalism with the assessments of Kirk, Viereck, and others of where to look for sources of renewal. The latter group did not look for the most needed knowledge in "that up-to-date journalism of the academic world, the courses in current politics, economics, and other uselessly 'useful' techniques"[9]—to say nothing of day-to-day political discussion. Vastly more important to understanding the prerequisites of a humane society were literature, the arts, history, philosophy, and ethics.

American conservatism with academic pretensions has also undergone a philosophical transformation, although ideas of an earlier type are still in evidence. Many of the academics identified in the opinion magazines and newspapers as the main intellectual alternative to campus radicalism differ markedly from earlier intellectual conservatism. A well-known representative of the new outlook was Allan Bloom at the University of Chicago. Like him, many so-called conservative academics take an anti-historical approach to ideas—a paradox, to say the least, since intellectual conservatism long had the reputation of distrusting abstract rationalism and of stressing the need for joining thought to the historical sense. Many academics called conservatives today espouse abstract principles, or "values," according to which they would like to see the world remade. Paradoxically, one of their cherished principles is "equality." In fact, some of these intellectuals bear a striking resemblance to the eighteenth-century French Jacobins—yet another paradox, since the acknowledged father of modern conservatism, Edmund Burke, focused his ire on precisely those ideologues.[10]

Academics of this type may have doctorates from and even teach in "name" universities, but most of them seem rather thinly educated and typically focus on political ideas narrowly understood. They even study works of literature from the point of view of their political "teaching," implying that the highest import of art is its political message. These academics usually argue toward preconceived ideological conclusions, finding prestigious classical authors to be supportive of their own modern political prejudices. Academics of this kind are numerous, and many are well-connected in the public policy networks, foundations, and media. They can expect favorable publicity and other attention, which is a source of influence especially in a society in which celebrity status confers intellectual authority.

[A few years ago extraordinary attention was given to Bloom's *The Closing of the American Mind*, which acquired the reputation of being a work of conservative educational philosophy. Having become a much-discussed best-selling writer, Bloom also became widely viewed as one of the great intellects of the West.[11]]

In recent years individuals known as conservatives have taken a greater interest in the state of "the culture." In part this development may be a sign of an awakening to the importance of thought and imagination. At the same time it confirms and gives new impetus to the ideologization of American conservatism in that interest in "the culture" is often heavily slanted by the old fascination with political power. Issues of cultural decline are discussed as if the key to reversing the trend lay in the hands of politicians and their intellectual allies.

[One celebrity, who is widely viewed as an intellectual conservative spokesman, has published a best-selling book of readings on "virtue." He has also attracted much attention for formulating "cultural indicators" and tracking America's cultural decline (efforts that may have alerted the deaf and blind to trouble). Regarded as an authority on culture, morality and philosophy, the same person has been for many years immersed in politics, embodying the conservative tendency to connect ideas and art with activism. It seems equally anomalous that an individual serving as arbiter of culture should be, according to his own repeated public declarations, a devotee and collector of "rock 'n' roll."]

Much of the present conservative interest in "the culture" is due to a growing awareness of the political impact and propaganda potential of the mind and the imagination. It has also become politically opportune to bemoan cultural sleaze. Although it can certainly be salutary for well-educated and aesthetically discerning politicians and other public figures to comment on a harmful cultural and academic situation, the fact that such a task has fallen to, or been seized by, politicians and political intellectuals is a sign of the failure of intellectuals and artists. Criticisms of cultural, intellectual and moral decadence that politicians address to large audiences are likely to be simplistic and heavy-handed. They may also feed the spurious and dangerous notion that the key to social health is political action.

The Speaker of the US House of Representatives, a person with some credentials as an intellectual, has complained, on good grounds, about a lack of shame in American society. Public discussion of the Speaker's concern showed wide support for promoting shame by having political and civic leaders set moral and other standards and start campaigns to elicit the desired reaction. It seemed out of place to point out that shame of the kind that formed part of an older Western morality is not so easily manufactured. It had origins deep within the personality of Western man, as shaped by the long moral, religious, aesthetical, and intellectual history of his society. Shame of that type could not be replaced through civic boosterism.

Does it need to be said that the views about culture, truth, and morality that are put forth by intellectuals who live and breathe political strategy and tactics are no real alternative to the thinking now dominant in academia and beyond?

An authentic revitalization of will, imagination and reason would deepen and enrich human existence as an end in itself, not serve a particular political agenda. A characteristic of a creative civilization is that you cannot fully predict where it might lead in thought, art, ethics, and politics. Many purported conservative intellectuals currently concerned about "the culture" seem to know exactly what will bc the political-ideological consequences of "improving" it: more "capitalism," "democracy," and "equality." Perhaps in some future Washington administration there will be appointed a "culture czar." A more appropriate title might be "commissar."

Rather than submit to a reign of conservative political correctness, a cultural and intellectual movement worthy of the name would take its chances with poets, artists, philosophers, and men and women of conscience.

PETER VIERECK AND CONSERVATISM

This study of Peter Viereck has its roots in a large article published in the *Political Science Reviewer* in 1977. It was written in part in reaction to American movement conservatism placing ever more emphasis on the importance of politics and neglecting the world of ideas, art, and other forms of culture. While I turned to other projects, I had the idea that I might at some point turn this article into a small monograph or include it in a larger study of politics and culture. I returned occasionally to the article to revise and expand it. One of the reasons I kept this vaguely-defined project at the back of my mind was that American conservatism was straying rather far from what had been a more promising direction, one showing a deeper, subtler understanding of what moves human beings. That American conservatism might follow this other emphasis, which assigned a less dominant role to politics, had seemed a distinct possibility in the 1950s. At that time Viereck's thinking and that of Russell Kirk, as well as that of kindred thinkers, had enjoyed considerable purchase. Their recognition of the importance of mind and imagination for shaping the future, including politics, suggested that American intellectual conservatism might develop a sound sense of priorities. Instead a preoccupation with politics narrowly conceived asserted itself and intensified. Then, in the 1980s, Ronald Reagan won the presidency twice. Movement conservatives started celebrating the "triumph" of conservatism. I shook my head at this theme. It showed such scant understanding of what most fundamentally moves a society that movement conservatism seemed highly unlikely really to reverse America's decline. I knew that discussing issues central to Viereck's conservatism would be a way of demonstrating the hollowness of the supposed "triumph." I worked on the manuscript from time to time but remained unsure of what to do with it. It was too long to be another article but too short to be a book.

In late 2004 or early 2005 something wholly unexpected happened. I learned from a publisher's announcement that Peter Viereck was about to publish a new edition of his book *Conservatism Revisited.* To my complete surprise, it would have an "introduction" written by me. I had never been consulted about such a possibility! I learned that Viereck wanted to use the old 1977 article as the "introduction." I disliked the idea for several reasons. The old article was simply not an introduction. It was a free-standing article about Viereck's prose works in general, it had been written in other historical circumstances, and I had extensively revised and expanded the old article. In the abstract, I would have preferred to tell Viereck and his publisher to leave me out of the new edition of *Conservatism Revisited*, but Viereck and I had become friends, and he really wanted my commentary in the book. He was now quite old and frail. (He died in 2006, the year after the publication of the book.) I finally let Peter use the emerging draft manuscript. We agreed that while my study would be printed together with *Conservatism Revisited*, it would not be presented as an introduction. The volume would, in effect, have two separate authors. I would retain the copyright for my portion. The publisher accepted this agreement, but readers probably still got the impression from the cover and layout of the book that my study of Viereck had been written as an introduction. (The edition made me uncomfortable also because of significant flaws of copy editing and typesetting.)

To include in the present collection of my writing a short monograph that concentrates on a single thinker might suggest that, in my opinion, this thinker merits more attention than any other post–World War II American conservative intellectual. This impression is not intended. But Viereck was an important figure in the early years of the new American conservatism, and he gave brilliant, evocative expression to indispensable ideas. His thought should, despite its flaws, have been much more widely considered than it was. Opposition to him in *National Review* sharply limited his influence in movement conservatism. This study of Viereck is included in this book also because it addresses in some depth questions that are central to any discussion of conservatism. More specifically, it advances the purpose of assessing American intellectual conservatism. As is evident from other parts of this volume, I believe that inadequate awareness of how politics relates to ethics, aesthetics, and epistemology has been a debilitating feature of movement conservatism. Viereck's work affords an excellent opportunity to demonstrate the importance of these relationships.

The general structure of the 1977 article is still discernible in what follows. The same is true of the much revised and expanded version that appeared in the Viereck-Ryn volume of 2005. Although what is published here has been revised and expanded yet again, its perspective remains that of the 2005 version.

CONSERVATIVE REVIVAL AND CONTROVERSY

In recent years many American political intellectuals and activists calling themselves conservatives have asserted a "triumph of conservatism." Conservative ideas are said finally to have overcome "liberalism" in American politics. One of the many problems with this assertion is that there is no seamless continuity between the revival of conservative ideas that started half a century ago and what is now called conservatism; there have been major shifts in emphasis and thinking. Especially in practical politics, so-called conservatism has moved closer and closer to what used to be called liberalism. Significantly, conservative intellectuals have become increasingly preoccupied with issues of public policy and the short term, while interest in the more fundamental, enduring, and philosophically demanding questions of human existence seems to be waning. A closely related problem with the "triumph of conservatism" thesis is that intellectual conservatism is still fighting for its life on American college and university faculties, which does not augur well for its influence on American culture and politics. One sign of a loss of intellectual vitality is that few conservatives are strongly drawn to the serious, systematic study of those issues—religious, moral, philosophical, aesthetic—that finally count the most in shaping society's basic long-term trends. More specifically, it is a symptom of weakness, as well as a paradox, that intellectuals thinking of themselves as conservatives should not be showing greater interest in revisiting and developing the ideas of major thinkers from the tradition to which they claim to belong. When they invoke legendary names, it is usually for rhetorical or ceremonial purposes.

One thinker who contributed substantially to the revival of American intellectual conservatism after World War II but who has been largely neglected, even dismissed, by so-called movement conservatism is Peter Viereck (1916–2006). Viereck wrote a number of books that challenge modern progressivism and define a modern conservatism that builds upon and develops central insights of the classical and Christian traditions. Born in New York City, Viereck studied at Harvard, where he completed his bachelor's degree in 1937. He also studied at Oxford. He completed a doctorate at Harvard. Having taught briefly at Harvard and Smith College, he was for decades until his retirement a professor of history at Mount Holyoke College. As much a poet as a historian, Viereck received Guggenheim Fellowships in both fields. He won a Pulitzer Prize for poetry in 1949 for *Terror and Decorum.*

A comprehensive study of Peter Viereck's work would obviously have to include a consideration of his poetry. Here the purpose is more limited: to examine Viereck's conservatism as set forth in his prose writing.[1] For various reasons, including those just mentioned, Viereck's central ideas have not, in spite of the mentioned honors and the considerable visibility he enjoyed in the decade and a half after World War II, received the kind of systematic attention that they deserve. In conservative movement circles, his sometime liberal-seeming leanings in practical politics and his run-ins with other conservative intellectuals created a strong prejudice against him. Among liberal intellectuals, on the other hand, he had to contend with the fact that his own outlook on life ran in a direction much different from that of the *Zeitgeist.* In spite of efforts to convince intellectuals to his left of his moderation, he could not become a part of the American intellectual establishment and receive the kind of notice and approval that it reserves for its reliably liberal or leftist representatives.

Viereck's work will be reconsidered here not just because it has been insufficiently understood and appreciated, but also because a study of Viereck's conservatism provides a context for assessing the evolution and present condition of American intellectual conservatism. Viereck is a brilliant thinker with a powerful intuition, whose central ideas merit close attention, but his temperament is not that of the systematic philosopher who feels compelled to organize his thoughts carefully and to give maximum clarity to his key terms. Though a penetrating thinker, he is more interested in conveying a general point of view than in expressing each important idea fully and precisely. He wants to get on as quickly as possible to the next point in his argument. Viereck is at times even prone to stylistic playfulness and imagery rather than tight reasoning, which critics may see as indicative of a lack of seriousness. This impression is wholly misleading. Viereck is no less rigorously philosophical than other thinkers who have influenced the basic views of modern American conservatism. To help demonstrate the meaning and importance of his insights, this study of him will supply explication and conceptual clarification that he does not himself provide but is supported by familiarity with his work as a whole. This philosophical elaboration and analysis will supplement or extend Viereck's thinking but will also bring out weaknesses in his thinking and suggest correctives to them.

A few preliminary words should be said about two general terms that will be ubiquitous in these pages—"conservative" and "liberal." Both have many possible meanings. The term "conservative" will be used here, at least initially, in a way that corresponds roughly to, or at least does not radically deviate from, current American usage, but the term will acquire a fuller and more nuanced meaning as the discussion of Viereck proceeds. To complicate matters, the meaning of the term has changed considerably in American public discussion since Viereck came to prominence. One of the purposes of this study is to help give greater stringency to the definition by lifting it out of journalistic and narrowly political discourse. As for "liberalism," what needs to be pointed out in the present context is that, for most of the twentieth century and into the twenty-first, in America "liberalism" has not meant what it originally meant, especially in Europe: a belief in small, constitutionally limited government, a free market, and a maximum of individual freedom. That kind of liberalism is today often called "classical" liberalism or "libertarianism." In America, "liberalism" has long meant a preference for large, benevolent government that serves the people through social and other programs and extensive regulation of business and social life. American liberalism has become more and more difficult to tell apart from European social democracy, that is to say, from moderate democratic socialism willing to tolerate the institution of private property and some market freedoms. "Liberalism" also means a willingness to tolerate and even to promote unorthodox views when those views challenge traditional Western beliefs. On moral and cultural issues especially, American liberalism has become increasingly radical. It is common in American journalism to say about people attracted to socialism and even Marxism that they are more "liberal" than people who criticize them.

When Peter Viereck published *Conservatism Revisited* in 1949, the ideas in vogue in American academic and intellectual circles were those of socialism and the liberal left. "Conservatism" meant primarily minimal government, free-market economics, fiscal discipline, and a bias favoring business. Viereck's advocacy of ethical, aesthetical, and political principles drawn from the classical Greek and Judaeo-Christian traditions was decidedly inopportune. He sharply criticized the secular religions of progress, which offer salvation through politics, and inveighed against "a morally illiterate culture of unhappy, and untragic pleasure-seekers" which "has failed to root its masses in the universals of civilization."[2] *Conservatism Revisited* was followed in the next few years by several prose works that continued Viereck's effort to define conservatism. They gave him a reputation as a spokesman for a theoretical position to be reckoned with. Some moderate representatives of the dominant liberal ideological currents accorded his books a not unsympathetic reading. The overlap between some of his ideas—such as concern about civil liberties and acceptance of elements of the welfare state—and more fashionable doctrines blunted the edge of liberal criticism and gave a certain respectability to his conservatism, but it could not conceal the tension between his own central inspiration and the moral and intellectual spirit of the times.

Seeing in the preference for laissez-faire economics a prejudice unduly favoring commercial and utilitarian values, Viereck thought of his own position as representing a "new" American conservatism, one closer to the great Western cultural traditions and supporting ethical and other restraints on the forces of the market. He was to find little or no concern about such restraints in William. F. Buckley Jr.'s *National Review,* which was started in 1955.

In spite of Viereck's early prominence, the multifaceted intellectual and political movement that eagerly adopted and became most widely associated with the conservative label did not come to regard him as one of its leading figures. The relative lack of interest in his ideas can be explained in no small measure by the opposition he encountered in the *National Review*, whose definition of conservatism deviated less from the then-dominant American use of the term. The amount of approval that Viereck received from the so-called "liberal establishment" and his partial deviation in practical politics from positions that Buckley and his circle regarded as essential to conservatism created uneasiness and even irritation. Viereck was not willing, for example, to categorically denounce the New Deal. He argued against rigid, aprioristic notions about the proper functions of government. Its role had to be adapted to particular historical circumstances. A vigorous anti-communist, he also objected strongly to Senator Joseph McCarthy, going considerably beyond the demurrers of some of the leading contributors to the *National Review*. Such stands on the issues of the day made him a suspect figure, a Trojan horse in the conservative camp according to some. These feelings were only intensified by Viereck's making some sharp attacks on his conservative detractors.

Because Viereck's leanings in practical politics were viewed as symptomatic of a fundamental deficiency in his thought as a whole, his philosophical principles received very limited attention on the right. In 1956 when Viereck published *Conservatism: From John Adams to Churchill*, a small survey of European and American ideas, *National Review* senior editor Frank S. Meyer summarily dismissed Viereck's attempt to define broadly the conservative view of human nature, society, and politics. His conservatism was "counterfeit." Meyer accused Viereck of "passing off his unexceptionably Liberal sentiments as conservatism."[3] This sweeping opinion was based not so much on the contents of the book, which were barely discussed, as on Meyer's general impression of Viereck as at heart a liberal in practical politics. Meyer's propensity for categorical, dogmatic judgments may have been a leftover from his intellectual past as well as a result of his being a convert to what he called conservatism. Meyer had been an ideologically intense communist and had even been a member of the Soviet-directed underground "cadre." Another example of conservative political dissatisfaction with Viereck is from 1960, when the leading conservative scholarly journal *Modern Age* published one of Viereck's articles, which was on poetry and religious fundamentalism. The editor felt compelled to insert an apologetic comment in which it was made clear that Viereck exhibited a deplorable "tendency toward splinter-conservatism."[4] These and similar politically inspired reactions drove a wedge between Viereck and potential young readers which has had an effect to this day.

The lasting contribution of postwar American intellectual conservatism has still to be assessed. It enjoyed obvious success in some respects.[5] Some liberal and socialistic ideas regarded as compelling in academic circles in the 1930s and 1940s could a few decades later be maintained only through intellectual inertia and dogmatism. By the 1980s the word "liberalism" had lost much of its luster in America and was increasingly shunned by political candidates, while the word "conservatism" was coming into vogue. Yet, with some exceptions, the burst of deep intellectual creativity that sustained the movement for several decades seems by the turn of the new century to have been nearly exhausted. The lack of dynamism at the contemplative-intellectual center would appear to be due in part to growing lack of interest in or impatience with ideas that seem to have no clear and direct application to practical politics or economics, a weakness to which the pragmatic and sometimes even anti-intellectual American temper is always prone. In recent decades this danger has been heightened by the rise of so-called "neoconservatism," a movement that is in important respects markedly different from the "new" conservatism of the postwar years. Neoconservatism, which will be discussed further below, has helped draw attention away from penetrating study of moral-spiritual and cultural issues to discussion of public policy. The potential for especially propitious conservative ideas spreading and for conservatism breaking new intellectual ground had already been hampered in the 1950s by a measure of ideological-political partisanship—a predilection that is acceptable and sometimes even necessary in practical politics but alien to the free spirit of philosophy. The attempt to judge the work of Peter Viereck by narrowly political standards was an early symptom of this weakness. It was hardly a sign of philosophical openness and sophistication that the polemical opinion of a writer like Frank S. Meyer should be regarded as authoritative and final.

The point of these preliminary observations is not that Viereck was right and his critics wrong about the contested issues of the day. The intention is to suggest that some considerable disagreement on matters of practical politics among thinkers of largely the same view of man and society is entirely to be expected. Life has a way of defying neatly formulated principles, to say nothing of political programs. The world of sharp political demarcations is the world of ideology. In a condescending but understandable retort to dismissive critics who had him pegged as a "liberal," Viereck admonished: "Children, don't oversimplify, don't pigeon-hole; allow for pluralistic overlappings that defy abstract blueprints and labels."[6]

Peter Viereck's main political writings appeared during World War II or in the two decades just thereafter. Although from time to time he has revised and supplemented these works, sometimes substantially, they contain the core of his contribution. The political and intellectual context of some of those original writings makes them in some ways dated today, but their central themes are separable from the particular historical situation in which they were developed, and they are easily adapted to new circumstances. Here the emphasis will be on those of Viereck's ideas that seem to be not only most distinctive but to have the most enduring value.

Over the years the writing of poetry, which always occupied much of Viereck's time, appears to have become increasingly important to him. His poetical gifts were evident even from the quasi-poetical style of passages in his prose writing. Undoubtedly, the primary reason that Viereck was drawn more and more to poetry was the promptings of his own creativity, which is indistinguishable from his recognition that poetry at its best reaches even more deeply into the mystery of existence than historical-philosophical prose. He understood very well the central role that the imagination plays in illuminating and affecting the human condition. As we shall see, his political thinking, too, was deeply affected by that insight. One may also speculate that, having produced a great burst of prose writings early in his life, he gravitated toward poetry because his prose works had had a mixed and, in some instances, seemingly uncomprehending reception. People calling themselves conservatives had treated his conservatism with indifference or disdain, and liberals would never embrace those of his ideas that mattered most to him. Why, then, persist in pushing an intellectual position that seemed destined to appeal to no more than a small minority?

THE PRIMACY OF UNIVERSAL VALUES

Although Viereck had much to say about practical politics and related issues of the day, the central inspiration of his conservatism was nonpolitical. Calling himself a "value-conserving classical humanist,"[7] he gave the paramount place in the articulation of man's higher purpose to the independent men of ideas and imagination. History is not shaped by impersonal material forces but by those who capture the mind.

In the early 1950s Viereck writes: "The proper start for a new American conservatism, aiming not at success but at truth, not at activism but at long-range education, is in the world of literature, the arts and sciences, intellectual history, the universities, the humanities." The way for Western society to recover its bearings is for intellectuals, poets, and artists to refresh themselves from the wellsprings of their civilization. Such a rediscovery of enduring values will indirectly transform politics and economics by integrating them into a more comprehensive understanding of man and society. A conservatism that begins by being directly political and economic, activistic rather than contemplative, "will at best fail and transform nothing at all."[8] Since human life is an organic whole, truly creative contemplative acts, far removed from issues of "public policy," are bound to have effects sooner or later in the realm of practice. "There is no intellectual gesture, no matter how intimate, which is not by implication a moral and political act." Viereck here agrees with the Italian philosopher Benedetto Croce (1866–1952), with whom he has much else in common.[9]

MAN'S MORAL NATURE AND PURPOSE

The central goal of a genuine conservatism, Viereck argues, is to rekindle in Western man, now threatened by the stereotypes of hedonistic and arid utilitarian mass culture, the sense of higher moral destiny that is at the core of the classical Greek and Judaeo-Christian traditions. As the "social and cultural cement, holding together what western man has built,"[10] conservatism must challenge the corrosive moral nihilism of modern positivistic education. Employing characteristic language and imagery, Viereck writes in 1953: "Now listen carefully, you logical positivists, you progressive educators: this is the Katyn-Belsen decade; it matters to us deeper than tears whether our civilization lives or dies; we need help, and it's no-go telling us again and again—waiting in that line at Katyn together, it's no-go your telling us with a superior, bored patience—that concepts like 'ethics,' 'absolutes,' 'values,' 'human dignity,' 'tragedy,' and 'death' are incorrect, amateurish semantics."[11]

Arguing passionately for the existence of universal moral values, Viereck also recognizes that the Western tradition in ethics is a "Christian-Hebraic-Roman-Hellenic amalgam, with inner contradictions, sometimes reconciled but sometimes not." Our heritage is "diversity within unity" and thus "allows for a generous dose of tolerant pluralism" in the effort to articulate man's spiritual destiny.[12] Viereck believes that the popular mind is correct in associating conservatism with religion, and he repeatedly returns to Western man's profound indebtedness to Christianity, but he also wants it understood that religion is "a house with many mansions, finding room not only for literal but for symbolic interpretations of church dogma."[13] The real alternative to modern moral relativism or nihilism is not a "religious absolutism" of the kind found in T. S. Eliot's *Idea of a Christian Society*. This type of "artificial clerical unity" is often found to be a refuge for the disillusioned liberal relativist who is not truly converted but is "attempting by pious intolerance to shout down that nagging inner voice of doubt."[14]

Conservatism must at the same time expose the pseudo-spiritual primitivism of those who, like Rousseau, would base morality on a sentimental belief in the natural goodness of man. The real essence of the human condition, Viereck is convinced, is an ineradicable tension in the person between a moral, universal self and inclinations that threaten a higher meaning and purpose. The true conservative senses deeply man's limitations and frailties and potential for evil. The values of civilization are being undermined by the superficial optimism of both the Rousseauistic humanitarian with his sentimental dreams and his frequent ally, the more rationalistic materialist. Far from being a roadblock to human happiness, the Western cultural heritage at its best is what makes real progress possible. It helps to liberate man's higher inclinations by restraining his lower. The function of education is not "to deify the child's 'glorious self-expression,'" for in his natural instincts man is still a primitive brute. "What prevents today's baby from remaining a cave man is the conservative force of law and tradition, that slow accumulation of civilized habits separating us from the cave."[15] Sound cultural tradition counteracts the tendency to indulge the primitive ego and inspires the moral and other self-discipline that introduces man to the universal values of humanity.

The norms of tradition are only an inducement to action. The ethical life is finally a matter of individual responsibility. Since the moral conflict of existence is centered in the soul of the person, only the individual himself can overcome the inclination to arbitrariness and evil. Sound tradition can encourage and support the necessary moral effort but never take its place. This insight is itself at the very core of the Western heritage. Viereck's deep belief in moral self-development as the key to genuine social progress makes him reject as dangerously shallow the modern progressive or revolutionary view that men will be made better and happier by remaking the socio-economic exterior. Reform can aid the higher purposes of society only if it is based on an adequate understanding of man's moral predicament.

The way to recover a sense of moral direction is for Western man to take possession again of his cultural heritage through education. Here, narrow specialization will not do. The aim, in the tradition inspired by ancient Greece, must be to "train the complete man rather than the fragmentary man." What is needed to educate decent human beings is "a curriculum in the broad humanities."[16] More specifically, Viereck believes strongly in the need for training the imagination, partly by dispelling enticing but destructive illusions. Here as in other respects, he is deeply influenced by one of the greatest American thinkers of the twentieth century, Irving Babbitt (1865–1933), author of such books as *Rousseau and Romanticism* and *Democracy and Leadership.* Babbitt taught French and comparative literature at Harvard. His ideas were still widely discussed, especially among scholars with literary interests, when Viereck's central ideas were taking shape. Viereck started his doctoral dissertation at Harvard just a few years after Babbitt's death. This dissertation, which deals with the artistic-cultural origins of German National Socialism, reflects Babbitt's stress on the decisive power of the imagination, for good or ill, as well as Babbitt's extensive critique of romanticism and its more rationalistic cousin, scientific naturalism. Babbitt's view of the centrality of the imagination in shaping human life and of the imagination's morally opposed potentialities had a decisive and profound effect on Viereck.

In the final analysis, human action is governed neither by precepts of reason nor by inarticulate desire. The direction of our lives is determined first and foremost by the imagination, which gives concreteness, color, and inspirational force to desires and goals for the future. Whether the imagination will pull us towards a meaningful existence or away from it will depend largely on the *quality* of our imagination. Modern utilitarian and sentimental civilization is what it is because it has directed the imagination to the lower reaches of human potential. The effect of redirecting the imagination with reference to the deeper and more comprehensive classical and Judaeo-Christian view of life would be to lift human effort toward man's true destiny. For Viereck, the most important bridge to universal values is great literature: "The distinctive value of literature is that it enables one to share intensely and imaginatively the rich, varied experience of men of all ages."[17] It probes both the depths and the heights of humanity. The best of literature assists self-discovery and self-realization. Sound imagination inspires the individual to try to realize in his own life the equivalent of elevated experience encountered in art.

A recovery of man's sense of moral purpose will not come about through some merely conventional application of principles of the past to the present: "The conservative conserves discriminately, the reactionary indiscriminately."[18] A crucial role will be played by the creative free spirit who manages to join the past and present in a new synthesis guided by intuition transcendent of both. Sound traditionalism leads to what Viereck calls "inner liberty," which is a special type of autonomy born of reverence for universal values. One detects in Viereck's emphasis on the role of the responsibly creative individual the influence of Babbitt, but also of Friedrich Nietzsche. Most traditionalists reject what they consider the moral nihilism of Nietzsche's rebellion against tradition and supposedly universal values, but Viereck reads him as opposing timid, paralyzing acceptance of stale, dogmatic authority. God is dead, yes, but only the god of the unoriginal, faint-hearted, and pseudo-humble dogmatists. To make possible the genuine morality of inner liberty, "idols" do need to be smashed.

THE CREATIVE IMAGINATION

Viereck's sensitivity to the simultaneous importance and precariousness of the private sphere reflects his extensive work as a poet. Although it is not possible here to examine his poetry, his literary credo is central to understanding his conservatism. Examining Viereck's aesthetical ideas with some care is especially appropriate as he regards the imagination as playing a decisive role in human conduct and not least politics. His view of the creative synthesis in art is analogous to his conception of synthesis in the moral life. His literary credo is touched upon in many places, but is most fully developed in *Dream and Responsibility* and *The Unadjusted Man*.

Like Croce and Babbitt, Viereck sees art as joining two elements that need each other, individuality and universality. The artist brings to his work the uniqueness of his own talent and experience, but insofar as he creates aesthetic value his intuitions are guided by the supra-individual value of beauty. The universal acquires concrete life in the particular work of imagination, which is to say that the individual artist is the creator of a synthesis of transcendent and immanent. Although art is always to some extent dependent on tradition, genuine artists are never slaves to convention. Viereck devotes much space in different contexts to warning against a sterile, unimaginative conformity to the standards of conventional society, what he calls "over-adjustment." Because French neoclassicism was not sufficiently sensitive to the fact that art must find its material in infinitely diverse and constantly changing circumstances, it tended, also because of its rationalistic bias, toward a static conception of beauty. It stifled creativity by imprisoning it in formalistic rules believed to capture once and for all the essence of artistic unity.

Viereck's emphasis on originality and free creativity might seem to suggest an element of romanticism in his outlook, but the term "romanticism" can mean many and even contradictory things. To avoid misunderstanding of Viereck's theory, a crucial distinction needs to be made. The romantic revolt against the restrictive and rigid neoclassical formulas was mixed in orientation. The new program of individual self-expression tended in two different directions, the one incompatible with and the other at least potentially compatible with the classical notion of human normality. The first was toward a cult of formlessness and individuality for their own sake, a self-intoxicated exaltation of Original Genius. The second was toward the discovery that while art serves a universal standard it has its own intrinsic freedom; the aesthetical imperative of beauty cannot be captured for all times in specific rules but must be discovered by each artist for himself. This tenet of modern aesthetics, which is romantic in a special sense, was identical to the discovery that the imagination is not, as long believed, merely passive and imitative. It captures potentialities of existence not brought to conscious awareness before. Out of previously inchoate and unrelated fragments of life the imagination forges an intuitive whole that makes us see life with new eyes. This general theory of aesthetic creation has been developed and reconciled with central elements of classical aesthetics by a chain of important thinkers from Coleridge to Babbitt and the mature Croce. Aesthetics here took a major step forward. There is considerably more of an appreciation of the need for fresh creativity in Babbitt than appears on the surface. Babbitt is known as a critic of romanticism, especially of its Rousseauistic variety, but his aesthetical theory is, despite its seemingly heavy classical emphasis, more indebted than he realizes to romanticism, only to a very different kind—for example, that of Edmund Burke. Viereck's thinking is very similar, but in his simultaneously classical and modern aesthetics the romantic stress on creativity comes through more clearly.

An important feature of romanticism is the discovery and appreciation of the uniqueness of personal individuality and of the originality of true creativity. Indeed, as Babbitt and Viereck point out, romanticism often takes this emphasis in the direction of a cult of original genius and untrammeled expression of personality. Both thinkers warn of this lack of moral and other discipline, Babbitt especially so. Viereck is different from Babbitt in that he places more emphasis on the uniqueness of individuality as a conduit of higher values. Viereck's notion of a proper unadjustedness, which illustrates this emphasis, will be discussed further below.

Viereck's term for the free imagination in literature and especially poetry is "lyricism." He refers to it as an "unleashing function" in man's inner life,[19] meaning thereby that it expands the horizon and invites the individual to enter imaginatively into new possibilities of experience. The classical notion of human normality is retained in Viereck's aesthetic theory, but he expands and deepens it by recognizing that in synthesizing the changing and the unchanging the truly creative artist is true not to models but to fresh vision. He gives new life to normality by not letting himself be bound by conventional expectations. "Fusing the universal and the particular into the single creative act, the unadjusted imagination concretizes the spiritual, spiritualizes the concrete."[20]

For Viereck, genuine freedom of expression is not formless. Art has its own standard of order, namely the imaginative coherence that renders the intuitive whole compelling, or, to use another possible word for the aesthetic universal—beautiful. His resistance to formalism and defense of spontaneity should not, as he himself warns, "be confused with neo-romantic appeals for a bohemianism of would-be 'geniuses' or for a romantic revolt of song and emotion *against* restraint and form. No, only *within* strict restraint and classic form can song and emotion be compressed into lyric intensity, instead of sprawling forth sloppy, formless, diffuse."[21] The imagination thrives in a climate of aesthetic form, that is, when it is obedient to the special order which inheres in all real artistic creation. Form but not formalism, tradition but not conventionalism are the context of aesthetic liberty. "The net of strict form, the more traditional the better, is the challenge that best evokes, provokes, irritates forth the response of beauty. On the need for rigor of form, there is no quarrel here with New Critic formalists. The quarrel begins only at the point where the rigor becomes mortis."[22]

As imagination true to the imperative of beauty, aesthetic expression has a special integrity and independence, as in relation to morality. It constitutes an intuitive whole that must be understood, enjoyed, and appreciated on its own terms. Still, Viereck rejects the principle of "*l'art pour l'art,*" *as ordinarily understood.* No good artist can be oblivious of the non-aesthetic values of life. On the contrary, the great work of imagination incorporates, on its own terms, the discipline of ethical striving. Having learned much from Babbitt, Viereck is aware that, although art has its own artistic needs, *what* is expressed—the quality of experience depicted—may differ greatly in dignity and importance from artist to artist. The mark of great art is that it expresses in an aesthetically compelling manner, not fragments or distortions of human experience, but life in its totality, including its moral dimension. Only great art manages to convey life in relation to its higher meaning and purpose. It can do so indirectly by revealing the deficiency of life unfulfilled or directly by conveying the glory of fulfillment. Such artistic creation does not offer the vantage point of the thwarted, warped personality, but that of the complete personality, liberated first and foremost through ethics. To be able to render life in its wholeness and in the right proportions, the artist must himself have some acquaintance with life ordered by its highest values, though he will in his personal life display the typical flaws of a human being, perhaps even have some of them to a disconcerting extent. The imagination of a person who lives in restless, self-indulgent pursuit of pleasure is bound to be vastly different from that of a person who has attained, partly through the assimilation of a moral and cultural heritage, some of life's highest potential. Both persons may produce works of aesthetic quality, but only the latter person could create art that is comprehensive, proportionate, and elevating—art that apprehends life in relation to what finally makes it worth living.

Superior aesthetic sensibility should thus be joined to moral substance, so that art can express our highest humanity. Viereck rejects the type of literary criticism that would separate the two elements. Some of the poetry of an Ezra Pound may be criticized on merely aesthetic grounds as bad writing, but it is also vitiated in certain places, such as the *Pisan Cantos,* by an antihuman message. "What if you seek only the beautiful? Suppose, like so much 'new' criticism, you passively ignore the good and the true? Or suppose, like the fascist diabolism of some of Pound's *Cantos*, you actively attack the good and the true? In such cases, you usually find yourself losing the beautiful also." Irving Babbitt, adopting a phrase from Edmund Burke, defined the highest form of aesthetic expression, which is understood and appreciated by the highest form of criticism, as "the moral imagination." Without ever becoming didactic, this quality of imagination renders life in relation to the moral essence of existence, which gives the work of art a special fullness and depth. Viereck writes, "You will find the beautiful only when you seek more than the beautiful."[23]

Summing up the relationship between moral and aesthetic value, Viereck writes: "Every abstract, explicit, formulated code becomes stultifying and sterile unless refreshed by the concrete, the implicit, the unformulated, the passionate, the lyrical. Conversely, the lyric impulse degenerates into the vaguely exalted hogwash of romanticism unless refreshed by the discipline of ethics."[24]

Many American conservatives have over the years affirmed the importance of literature and art for a genuine revitalization of the West, but they have done so mostly with their lips. Few of them have really appreciated the large significance of the imagination and the life of culture in shaping society. Their actual sense of priorities has been reflected in their being strongly drawn to the theory and practice of politics. For this and other reasons, Viereck's aesthetic and literary ideas never attracted much interest among them. Yet man is an organic whole of will, imagination, and reason, and these dimensions of our humanity are forever interacting. If the imagination plays any role at all in shaping human behavior, which can hardly be denied, political thought itself should, if it is to have any of the comprehensiveness and depth of philosophy, have a prominent aesthetic component. More attention should be paid to the fact that the founder of modern conservatism, Edmund Burke, gave a central place to the creative, synthetic power that he called the "moral imagination." This idea has been considerably clarified and deepened since his time. Babbitt's pioneering work opened up a new perspective on Burke's understanding of the imagination in particular and his conservatism in general.[25] This important and original interpretation and elaboration of a central idea has been adequately absorbed by only a small number of scholars, Viereck being one of the most perceptive. A number of thinkers have been influenced more indirectly and lightly by this achievement. Far too many conservatives remain unaware of its profound and far-reaching implications, not least for political philosophy.[26]

Another thinker who was deeply influenced by Babbitt in this and other ways and who made no secret of his indebtedness was the late Russell Kirk (1918–1994). Viereck and Kirk, having studied both Burke and Babbitt with high understanding, ought to have been close allies. As will be discussed later, the close proximity of many of their ideas about literature and other subjects was clouded by disagreements regarding practical politics and other more personal factors.

The notion of a creative synthesis of individuality and universality also pervades Viereck's ethics. The transcendent moral good that man must always try to approximate more closely should not be viewed as an abstract static principle from which prescriptions for different situations can be deduced in a casuistic manner. The good transcends concrete moral actions in the sense that they are adjusted to particular circumstances, but it also lives through them. It is an inspirational force that acquires more definite content as men mediate through moral self-discipline between individual situations and universal value. What they achieve is a synthesis between their unique moment in history and the eternal. The ethical norms that emerge from the accumulated experience of the past are attempts to capture the essence of morality and are indispensable guides to conduct, but in the end they are only tentative, pragmatic codifications of the free spirit of love. Sound traditionalism in the field of morality is a creative, discriminating absorption of the moral insights of the past into the living present.

CONSERVATIVE INDIVIDUALISM

Viereck's emphasis on freedom in the aesthetic and moral life is translated in the area of politics into a deep concern for individual liberty as a protection for and means to "inner liberty." This may perhaps be regarded as a liberal trait in his thought, but again properly understanding Viereck requires that a distinction be made.

In literature and other art self-expression can, as Viereck knows well, be perverted into unsound romanticism by rejecting all types of restraint. Similarly, in the political realm, self-expression can by scorning the common good degenerate into a self-indulgent, arrogant individualism that makes use of political freedom for destructive ends. Viereck is a liberal and individualist in that he believes that human beings need freedom to develop their own distinctiveness, but he also believes that true freedom and individuality can be realized only within the community of civilization. The uniqueness of persons is then ennobled by mankind's best traditions and can enrich those traditions. Private and public life are elevated together. The purpose of education must be "to create a community of persons, not a mere aggregation of people."[27] Viereck's cultural hero, the Unadjusted Man, is not a romantic misfit or malcontent or some pseudo-Nietzschean Superman above norms of every kind. As Viereck writes: "A mere anarchic individualism, a mere bohemian nonconformity, means isolation from society; the conservative individualism of the Unadjusted Man means more elbow-room *within* a more organic belongingness."[28] The spirit of the Unadjusted Man is the very opposite of chronic rebelliousness. This person is trying to adjust to the universal human society that extends across the generations, becoming a member of it by absorbing humanity's highest moral, artistic, and intellectual traditions. This may require considerable independence in relation to currently fashionable norms, in some societies even drastic separation from the present mainstream of opinion. "The meaningful moral choice is not between conforming and nonconforming but between conforming to the ephemeral, stereotyped values of the moment and conforming to the ancient, lasting archetypal values shared by all creative cultures."[29]

If this be liberalism, it is obviously very different from what is normally so labeled today, and one has to wonder if any genuine conservatism could do without it. Without recognizing the need for what Viereck calls "inner liberty," that is, for a creative adjustment of universal values to new circumstances, how could anything be conserved? If by "conservatism" is meant, routinized, mechanical imitation of inherited habits and principles, it is not even reactionary, for it lacks all vitality. If the goal of civilization, including politics, is human fulfillment at the deepest level, then the type of individualism that Viereck espouses, which he shares with such predecessors as Babbitt and Croce, would appear to be not a mere supplement to modern conservatism but integral to its understanding of tradition and community. Edmund Burke, the father of modern conservatism, was in a similar special sense a liberal, one who recognized that, to survive, tradition must be forever revitalized through human creativity.

Viereck's notion of proper unadjustedness thus involves a kind of balancing or synthesizing of forces, but his way of expressing it is sometimes awkward, as when he writes: "Within the complete personality, the universal and the particular meet without sacrificing either: without chaotic romantic subjectivism on the one hand, without mechanical rationalist abstractions on the other."[30] The point Viereck is here trying to make is obscured by his seeming to associate particularity or individuality with romantic emotional flux and universality with abstract rationality.

First of all, it should be noted that he is pairing forces that do not really interact as he here seems to believe. Strictly speaking, the counter or balance to "chaotic" romantic feeling is not reason, especially not abstract rationality, which is a mode of consciousness ill-equipped to contain unruly emotion. The counter is a different kind of imagination, one that pulls away from romantic chaos toward the concretized universality of the higher imagination. Secondly, as will be discussed later, abstract reason is not the only kind of rationality. Thirdly, and most importantly, one can challenge what Viereck here seems to imply and that has long been assumed in influential strains of Western philosophy, that what is ultimately normative is a form of abstract rationality. It would appear that he regards the universal as an intellectual, conceptual quality. As becomes clear from his work as a whole, this is not really what he believes. His terminology reflects a lingering convention of philosophical language. This author has argued at length that it is not intellectual universality that ultimately matters most to human well-being, and that *abstract* reason in particular is alien to the highest standard of conduct. Viereck's thought as a whole points in the same general direction, but misleading terminology obscures his meaning. A strong case can be made that synthesis between universality and particularity actually takes place within four distinct categories of human life—the moral, the aesthetic, the philosophical, and the pragmatic—each of which contains a tension all its own between universality and particularity and each of which has its own intrinsic value: goodness, beauty, truth, and practicality, respectively. Synthesis is the joining and balancing of the universal value and the concrete *within* the particular category. Viereck's just-quoted sentence is misleading in that it gives the impression that the synthesis conducive to the higher unadjustedness is some sort of blending or balancing of abstract thought and unruly romantic intuition of the concrete. But these two categories of human activity are distinct, one being rational-conceptual and the other intuitive-imaginative. Abstract ideas have little or no power over unchecked imagination. Also, none of the values that concern Viereck the most—the good, the true, and the beautiful—are forms of abstract rationality, not even the true. It can be argued that what ultimately integrates and balances the personality is the value of goodness, which is a special quality not of reason but of will. [31]

If Viereck's notion of the Unadjusted Man, which is as important to his ethics as to his aesthetics, should be criticized for something other than detail and philosophically imprecise formulations, the criticism might be directed against a possible pedagogical weakness, against form more than substance. Granted that unadjustedness, spontaneity, impulse, and freedom, *as Viereck understands them*, are essential to a thriving culture, were they the aspects of creativity that most needed to be emphasized when Viereck started to give prominence to his theme of unadjustedness? Was the cultural life of America and the Western world most threatened by stale convention and orthodoxy? In the 1960s and 70s intellectual trends that had simmered at the universities burst into the open in the New Left and the counterculture, which stood for rebellion against all inherited cultural, social, and political structures. They gave a radically leftist twist to the civil rights movement and protests against the war in Vietnam. Viereck believes that human values are gravely threatened in modern Western society by a deep and pervasive mechanization and standardization that needs to be challenged, but what about the contemporary strong currents of sensual self-indulgence and excess, including erotic profligacy, and the general romantic revolt against order and authority? Because of these trends, Viereck's advocating creative independence and spontaneity and naming a book about the needs of our time *The Unadjusted Man* was bound to be confusing, perhaps even counterproductive.

But another consideration probably affected Viereck's phraseology. He may have adopted it in part because he empathized with the predicament of bright, sensitive young people who were finding little of obvious value to cleave to in the society in which they had grown up. Their parents and grandparents had pointed them toward conventional career paths and life plans but had left them largely adrift with regard to sources of a deeper well-being. Their being irritable and oppositional was understandable. Viereck may have wanted to tell these young people that there existed an alternative to indiscriminate leftist unadjustedness. A form of dissent was possible that was deeper and more rooted in the experience of mankind. In view of the progressive and radical trends in America's universities and general culture at the time, such an attempt to reach young people may have been unrealistic, but Viereck's purpose was clearly to subvert, not assist, those sentiments. Only inattentive or biased readers could mistake his opposition to the routinization of life and to mindless stereotypes for an attack on all order and structure. As has been shown, there is a world of difference between the disciplined spontaneity of Viereck's cultural aristocrats and the primitivistic cultural rebelliousness of the heroes of radicalism in the decades following the publication of his main works of prose.[32]

The serious reader of Viereck discovers in his notion of unadjustedness a subtle and balanced supplement to the thought of Babbitt, who in his opposition to the dubious but hugely influential cult of spontaneity and general liberation in Rousseau tends to emphasize the need for the disciplining element in art and life. Viereck's understanding of how inner freedom and creativity invigorates the normality and wisdom of the ages is more generally an important contribution to understanding the relationship between individual and society. Indeed, as old Western traditions erode and disappear and disorientation deepens, the need for the kind of creative adjustedness to the wisdom of the ages that Viereck advocates may be greater than ever.

Viereck's emphasis on the need for detachment from current practical concerns is also a needed counterweight to the American pragmatic temper. The latter can be a great strength to the extent that it acts as a check on unrealistic and utopian schemes, but it can also, especially at a time of cultural decline, be a major weakness in that it tends to produce immersion in the practical needs of the present moment. It can make the life of the mind and the imagination, especially the more difficult types of philosophical inquiry, look unimportant in comparison with putatively pressing practical needs. A pragmatic outlook gone awry can cause people to disdain nonutilitarian values and disincline even the intellectuals to pursue ideas whose applicability to the problems of the day is not yet obvious. To the extent that such pragmatism tolerates philosophy at all, it threatens to leave it at the level of broad generalities. Viereck's Unadjusted Man is an urgently needed reminder of the timeless importance, independence, and relevance of the intellectual-artistic life. It could have had a salutary influence not least on American intellectual conservatism.

THE NOTION OF NONTHEORETICAL CONSERVATISM

Viereck has much of importance and general interest to say about how the universal values of goodness and beauty are realized. He is more limited in his understanding of the subject of epistemology, how we obtain knowledge. In what he says about this subject, he evinces a contradiction that is not untypical of modern American intellectual conservatism and that reflects a disinclination to explore the more difficult problems of philosophy. Viereck freely admits that he lacks the "training" in "technical philosophy" required to address authoritatively some philosophical issues. Here he resembles figures greatly admired by conservative intellectuals, including Russell Kirk and Eric Voegelin. Specifically, American conservative thought tends to dodge issues of epistemology. Many of the conservatives, especially those who think of themselves as generally Burkean, like to assert that conservatism is "anti-ideological." What they mean is that conservatism does not claim to possess definitive truths and principles. It is nondogmatic and intellectually humble. But when it comes to explaining how it is that conservatism can nevertheless be persuasive, they have difficulty explaining by what method it persuades. What role does reason play?

Viereck addresses this general issue, and his way of doing so illustrates well the epistemological impasse in question.

On the one hand, Viereck's books are filled with spirited arguments for a definite view of man, society, and art and for the adoption of a certain hierarchy of values. On the other hand, he paradoxically professes not to believe that his conservatism can be defended *as a theory.* "The conservative mind does not like to generalize. Conservative theory is anti-theoretical."[33] Its values find their only compelling confirmation in intuition. That all men have a moral nature subjecting them to moral imperatives "becomes obvious through experience, but can never be 'proved.'"[34] Viereck repeatedly attacks what he calls the abstract, blueprint mentality of modern rationalism, because it bypasses or distorts actual human experience. Conservatism rejects this fondness for bloodless "general formulations." Since conservatism "embodies rather than argues, its most valuable insights are not sustained theoretical works nor well-organized, clearly presented, and geometrically consistent treatises, as in the case of liberal rationalism."[35]

> In ideological debates, the immediate winner will be the progressive, the man with *a priori* formulas for bettering society. The loser will be the conservative, the man who flounders confusedly, like some village idiot, amid concrete history-evolved *conditions* which he is unable to verbalize. . . . Indeed, the definition of a good conservative is that he always loses the theoretical debates with liberals and radicals. When he begins winning debates, it is a symptom of senility or ill health. . . . If he argues the conservative case too well, he has become a mere liberal of conservatism.[36]

This charmingly forthright but also untenable statement is an example of a fundamental weakness in the philosophy of knowledge that is common in modern conservative thought. The statement represents an unjustified abandonment of reason to the opponents. It has not occurred to Viereck that "reason" can be understood in a much different way.

When he rejects "theory," "abstract generalizations," etc. as incapable of capturing the essence of life, he is in one sense correct, for what he understands by these terms is the kind of rationality that is employed by the natural sciences and mathematics and, in a bastardized form, by such scientistic approaches to the study of man and society as positivism and behaviorism. This kind of rationality proceeds by means of empirical classifications that may be useful for particular practical purposes but that are in the final analysis arbitrary. Abstract reason of this kind does not attempt to capture life as it really is, a dynamic, living whole of continuously and organically interacting parts. Life as experienced by human beings is not, as rationalism asserts, a collection of "mechanically," "causally" related objects. Natural science and rationalism violate the context and texture of what it studies, reducing phenomena under study according to a preconceived pattern of explanation. In the natural sciences this method is appropriate; there is no alternative there to external observation of phenomena. Taking this kind of liberty with the experiential facts has produced a wide range of practically useful results. Nevertheless, the concepts and classifications of scientific reason cut pieces out of a living whole and attribute to them a distinct, definite, spatial existence that they do not really have in direct experience. In the humanities there is no excuse for setting such methodology up as the model, although there, too, an element of pragmatism is needed in the classification of phenomena. In the humanities it is possible to study man and society from "within," to try to articulate life as actually experienced. Positivism inappropriately imports formalistic, reifying logic, which has its usefulness in the study of external phenomena, into the humanities, which ought to study life as concretely lived and apprehended by human beings. Positivistic concepts and theories kill or distort what they touch. Viereck is therefore on solid ground when rejecting "reason" in the humanities. The pragmatic rationality of natural science or pseudo-experimental sciences like psychology in its most common form is not capable of speaking about the enduring "internal" structure of human existence. Recognizing that, Viereck concludes that reason has little to tell us about that which finally matters and resigns any claim to being able to "prove" the validity of his position. He writes about modern rationalistic philosophy that its formulations are "perhaps irrefutable but certainly irrelevant."[37] This is to overestimate hugely the doctrine of logical positivism and related forms of rationalism and to underestimate vastly the range and veracity of reason.

What Viereck does not recognize, just as, with few exceptions, modern philosophers do not recognize, is that formalistic, abstract reason has a rival and superior. There exists a more genuinely philosophical rationality that does not have to violate concrete human reality in order to speak about it. Ironically, it is precisely this kind of reason that allows Viereck to identify empirical rationality as blind to the most important facts of life. The following question should be asked of Viereck: How does he know that logical positivism can say nothing about the central questions of human existence? He does not know it just through intuition, for he *argues* against the rationalistic formulas; he can give *reasons* for his view. He knows about the distortions or blindness of positivism through a more truly philosophical, more truthful observation of experience. One kind of rationality, the philosophical, discovers the limitations of another, abstract kind of rationality. When Viereck asserts that the essence of the human condition can be grasped only through intuition, his view does contain an element of truth: before we can have a rational, conceptual grasp of life, we must know it in concrete experience. What Viereck has not discovered is that there is a type of philosophy that actually deserves its name because its office is faithfully to articulate the truth of lived experience. This philosophical rationality gives *conceptual expression* to immediate, prerational intuition. That means that instead of imposing abstract concepts and classifications on experience after the fashion of formalistic, positivistic rationality, philosophy tries to capture the actual texture and structure of experience, including the tension between opposites that permeates it. Real philosophy can express this dynamic reality—life—because its logic is not formalistic and reifying but dialectical.

This is not the place to explicate this notion of philosophical reason.[38]

These comments are only intended to show that Viereck need not have despaired of reason as an ally and thrown his lot with pure intuitionism. Although not a professional philosopher and not always aiming for the conceptual precision that is the special responsibility of philosophy, he does in fact argue for his positions. He does have a *theory* of life, which appeals to reason as well as intuition. Edmund Burke, too, rejected what he called "abstract" or "metaphysical" reason, but in his critique of that kind of rationality and in setting forth his own view of life and politics he employed a historically, experientially grounded reason. This is the reason of philosophy. If Viereck's *stated* view of knowledge opens him up to the charge of anti-intellectualism, his actual reasoning against rationalism offers little support for this charge. His critique of logical positivism and moral nihilism is by no means arational or irrational; it is not "a symptom of senility or ill health." Unbeknownst to himself, Viereck is being eminently theoretical, though by the standards of philosophical reason—if not philosophical reason in the more precise, systematic "technical" sense.

Postmodernists and other anti-positivists in the last quarter century are latecomers to the criticism of rationalism. They were preceded by conservative thinkers from Burke to Viereck, who, despite some superficial appearances, did not succumb to romantic irrationalism and especially not to denial and rejection of all order, weaknesses to which postmodernism has been strongly prone.

One of the reasons for the present apparent stagnation of conservative thought is that its intellectuals fall back much too quickly on moral or religious intuition as the ultimate source and support for their views. This propensity Viereck shares with a thinker like Eric Voegelin, whose hostility to "systematic" thought regarding the ultimate questions betrays unfamiliarity, in epistemological theory if not in philosophical practice, with the nonabstract rationality of philosophy. This prejudice has contributed to the common indifference toward the careful, sustained conceptual elaboration of experience. Intuition is most certainly fundamental to human knowing, but a theory of existence that rests in the end on little else will be rejected by those looking for philosophical argument in support of their beliefs. What needs to be much more widely understood is that genuine philosophy, while eschewing all claims to final knowledge, is fully attuned to the concrete historical texture of life and can speak in a compelling, truthful manner about human existence, including man's moral-spiritual nature. Pious and moralistic general affirmations are no substitute for the rigorous philosophical examination of experiential evidence.

HUMANE POLITICS AND ITS ENEMIES

Now that Viereck's fundamental ideas in the fields of ethics, aesthetics, and epistemology have been examined, it is time to review the way in which he has applied his central outlook on life to particular issues such as practical politics. He has dealt with a broad range of important topics, and his writings abound with ideas. His books are not always systematically organized in the sense of developing a single idea step by step. Almost all of them contain material published previously as articles and reviews, and a lack of connective tissue occasionally gives an unexpected turn to his argument. For these and other reasons, some commentators have come away with the impression that Viereck represents a "whimsical" conservatism.[39] This assessment shows a failure to grasp the connections between his various positions and illustrations. All his writings apply and develop his basic principles and form a coherent whole, although one may question whether all of Viereck's practical stands are successful or consistent applications of his basic ideas.

Only brief summaries can be given of some of Viereck's key beliefs. They may be organized around what can be described as a central objective of his work, to define the role of aristocratic man in different areas of life. By "aristocratic" he does not mean membership in a titled nobility, although a nobleman might have the qualities in question. The aristocratic person embodies and sustains the highest values of civilization. Viereck's use of the adjective echoes with the ancient Greek notions of wisdom and virtue, the traits of the "best" in society. He often deals with this topic by exposing perversions of the aristocratic idea.

Because the bulk of Viereck's prose writing was published over half a century ago and because he so often chooses to expound on his principles by analyzing political and other phenomena of the day, some of his illustrations and allusions may puzzle readers not familiar with them, but with the aid of some imagination it is usually not difficult to see the relevance of his observations for the present time.

The decadent political imagination

Most of Viereck's central ideas are present, at least in preliminary or undeveloped form, in his first book, *Metapolitics* (1941), which had been his Harvard doctoral dissertation. Some of it had actually taken shape while Viereck was still an undergraduate. His notion of true aristocracy is here thrown into stark relief against the characteristics of a thoroughly decadent and even diabolical "elite." He explains Nazism as the culmination of a romantic, nihilistic revolt against the Western traditions of civilization. The *Volk* (German for "people"), which is a word for the Nazis' arrogant and chaotic self-aggrandizement, becomes the source of political authority. *Metapolitics* breaks new ground in that it explores the *cultural, imaginative* roots of Nazism, which it does in a very perceptive if overly sweeping, manner. Viereck's powerful and penetrating intuition, which makes him able to discern what others missed and to see the connection between seemingly disparate phenomena, sometimes overpowers the need for distinctions and qualifications.

According to Viereck, Germany has embodied two divergent cultural tendencies, the one the origin of some of Western man's finest cultural achievements, the other exhibiting elements that, when isolated and taken to extremes, coalesce in a morbid revolt against moral and intellectual order. "Through the centre of German hearts runs the great Roman wall. Speaking metaphorically, on one side of the wall are the classical, rational, legalist, and Christian traditions (often mutually conflicting) of the Romanized German; on the other side (often mutually conflicting) are the paganism of the old Saxons, the barbaric tribal cults of war and blood, and the anti-rationalism and anti-legalism of the romantics."[40]

For the Nazis and their forerunners, there is a kind of instinctive wisdom which expresses more truly the spirit of the German people than any traditions of moral and intellectual discipline. *Kultur,* which is elevated above mere "civilization," puts the Germans in touch with their Aryan origins and instills in them a new patriotism. *Kultur,* Viereck argues, is a magic term refusing to be pinned down. It cannot be understood by any other races. "It is understood only by blood, by the subconscious. It is inexpressible in words. It is expressible only in feeling, the heroic feeling of German blood."[41] Viereck quotes from Hitler's *Mein Kampf:* "Civilization means the application of reason to life. Goethe, Schiller, Kant are reflections of the western mind. The patriot prefers to seek the 'life forces,' the irrational impulses, which seem to him more characteristic of the German mind."[42]

This Hitlerian revolt against the restraint and critical detachment of "over-civilization" had been prepared by several generations of increasingly decadent romanticism. Not primarily interested in the political or economic circumstances of the emergence of Nazism, Viereck describes the formation of the Nazi mind as the progressive perversion and pollution of the imagination. Hitler thought of himself as a great artist, and this attitude was rooted in the "romantic philosophy of ceaseless lawless expansion and, of self-justified self-worship."[43] "One hundred years of romantic literature and philosophy made Germany more susceptible to Nazi concepts than any other country in the world, already long before Versailles."[44] A gradual relaxation of inner discipline in the individual eventually acquired a collective counterpart in "limitless authoritarianism." Individual self-glorification became nationalistic and imperialistic tyranny. Viereck convincingly demonstrates the significance of various individuals and movements in the nineteenth century for the development of the Nazi mentality. The unabashedly primitivistic Friedrich Ludwig Jahn, spreading his message in the early part of the 1800s, preached relentless hostility to foreigners and especially Jews and sought the restoration of German "folkdom" *(Volkstum)* through a cult of Teutonic rough manners and gymnastics. Viereck calls him "the first storm trooper." Anti-Western influences were also contributed by men like Nietzsche and Spengler. Fichte, Treitschke, and others gave appeal to *Realpolitik.* Gobineau and Chamberlain were among those who gave pseudoscientific support to a belief in German racial superiority. But the best example of Nazi metapolitics is found in the person who pulls together these strands of cultural decadence into an imaginative whole—Richard Wagner. He and his many disciples "exalt Life (*élan vital*) against law, content against form, instinct against reason, synthesis against analysis, the organic against the atomistic, Volk legend against scientific truth; above all, the dynamic against the static."[45] The intensely anti-Jewish Wagner created a morbid "synthesis of communism and racial chauvinism" which profoundly influenced Hitler himself.[46] "Wagnerian metapolitics is Janus-faced. Simultaneously it looks back to romanticism and ahead to a machine age of wage slaves and unemployed. The result is a streamlined romanticism. As such, it is marvelously suited, economically and psychologically, for the prosaic monotony of industrialism and for bored shopkeepers with too many usurious debts and too little excitement." Wagner's music, too, has similar roots. One of the appeals of his operas is to "starved individual emotion (the love-duets of *Tristan*), and, in Germany's case, to frustrated national egotism (the Siegfried cycle)."[47]

The essence of the Nazi movement, then, is the revolt of a morally and intellectually perverted imagination against the demands of genuine civilization. Its corresponding "elite" offers diabolical leadership. It is a denial of "that training which is the best spirit of aristocracy—that is to say, the training in sane sense of proportion, in unbreakable universal standards, in emotional self-control, in the necessity of imposing classical form upon even the most inspired and daemonic content. Universal standards—that is what romantic anti-legalists consciously reject when they exalt Kultur against civilization."[48]

Viereck's insights into the Nazi mind are all the more impressive in that he arrived at them long before the full scope of the Nazi horrors had become known and removed all doubt about the nihilistic roots of the movement. His account in *Metapolitics* of the cultural decline that prepared the way for Hitler also has its weaknesses. It would have benefited from more distinctions and nuances. Viereck comes across as more rationalistic and unqualifiedly anti-romantic than he really is. He does not make sufficient allowance for the fact that romantic imagination can assume radically different forms. It does not have to be put to harmful uses and certainly does not have to take the disastrous turn that is analyzed in *Metapolitics*. The very conception of this book owes greatly to Babbitt's thinking regarding the effects of perverted imagination, and Viereck here actually exaggerates Babbitt's unfortunate habit of seeming to reject romanticism in every sense, as in *Rousseau and Romanticism*. What Babbitt and the young Viereck do not dwell upon, though in a way they do recognize it, is that romanticism, for all of its many frivolous and often destructive manifestations, also brought a much deepened awareness of the power and creative nature of the imagination. This important advance in aesthetics and epistemology is separable from the dubious forms of romantic art and thinking that have typically been associated with the term. A very different, higher kind of romanticism was exhibited, for example, by Edmund Burke, whose stress on the central role of the imagination, in politics as well as life more generally, was integrally combined with a deep sense of the need for moral and aesthetic discipline, order and classical balance. In *Democracy and Leadership* Babbitt presents the imagination of Burke as a counter to the dangerous romanticism of Rousseau, but, as if he wanted to reserve the word "romantic" for aesthetic and moral frivolity and irresponsibility, he does not take note of the romantic element in Burke. Viereck himself exemplifies the higher romanticism, not just in his understanding and practice of artistic creativity but in his political thought. One may wonder if at times he does not even flirt with a *lower* kind of romanticism, as when, in his poetry, he is tempted by Dionysian intoxication and wildness, and as when, in his political thought, he idealizes the American East Coast WASP establishment of the 1950s (see below).[49]

Viereck himself has criticized aspects of *Metapolitics*. He has apologized for the "youthful-emotional immaturity of some of the book's style."[50] His regrets may have extended to the kind of flaw that was just discussed. Yet what stands out about this book, especially when one considers the youth of its author and how early it was written, are its several strengths. It reaches deeply not just into the Nazi mentality but into a malady of modern Western culture by no means confined to its Hitlerian extremes. Viereck analyzes an anti-civilized, anti-aristocratic state of the imagination that found other equally dangerous manifestations. It is one of the serious failings of American postwar intellectual conservatism that in its analysis of the root causes of the floundering of Western society it did not, despite the partially parallel efforts of Russell Kirk, follow in Viereck's (and Babbitt's) footsteps.

Direct and indirect democracy

Viereck's attempt to define aristocratic values in modern circumstances is reflected in his view of democracy. A proponent of popular government in countries like the United States, he also insists on an important distinction, between what he calls direct and indirect democracy. The former serves the popular wish of the moment; the latter articulates a more lasting will of the people.

> Direct democracy is government by direct, unfiltered mass pressure, government by referendum, mass petition, and popular recall of judges, government by Gallup poll and by the intimidating conformity of the lowest common denominator of public opinion. Indirect democracy likewise fulfills the will of the people but by first filtering it through the people's representatives, through the parliamentary, judicial, and constitutional sieve, and through the ethical restraints of religion and tradition. Direct democracy is immediate and hot-headed, indirect democracy calmed and canalized.[51]

Direct democracy becomes government by demagoguery and majoritarian tyranny. Indirect democracy encourages self-restrained aristocratic leadership and the protection of civil liberties. Viereck points out that all types of government will have elites. But while the popular representative most in tune with indirect democracy is a person with deep respect for law and tradition, direct democracy replaces such individuals with opportunists pandering to the popular whim of the moment. The latter type of government also easily empowers and sanctions various types of despotic leadership. "The true opposite of despotism is not democracy (which often elects fascists) but restraint on power. No fascist or communist ever defined his ism as 'restraint on power'; many defined it as 'democratic.' The communists call their dictatorships 'people's democracies.' Hitler called himself an 'arch-democrat.'"[52]

Viereck rejects the kind of democratic thinking that makes majority rule a formula to be adopted without delay in every part of the world. Rhetorically he asks, "What stand will western liberal democrats take on the right of a voting majority, perhaps 51%, to enslave, torture, jail a minority, perhaps 49%?"[53]

Direct democracy is not only a threat to liberty but to all higher human values. "Most triumphs of humaneness were achieved by unpopular, highhanded, aristocratic actions, carried out against the democratic will of mass majorities."[54] Numerous advances in Western society in such areas as penal reform and removal of restrictions on religious and racial groups have been spearheaded by minorities against the majority. Civil liberties are much safer in the hands of constitutionally protected popular representatives than in the hands of the current majority. "Guarding the Bill of Rights even against majorities and even *against the people's will*, the American Constitution performs an aristocratic function."[55] As examples, Viereck takes "two magnificent defeats of 'the people'" in 1954. That year saw the censure of Joseph McCarthy by the US Senate and the Supreme Court's ban on racial discrimination in the schools. "Neither triumph of liberty would have been won in a direct democracy, a government settling issues only by majority vote."[56]

According to Viereck, there is a more truly popular will than the one manifesting itself at a particular moment. It emerges over time through the interplay of electoral majorities and responsible, independent representatives. Constitutional checks on the momentary popular passions help to articulate a lasting, higher will, recognized by the people themselves in their better moments as most truly their own.

The best friend of the people in the United States' founding period was John Adams rather than such self-proclaimed champions of the people as Thomas Jefferson and Thomas Paine. The latter two, and especially Paine, were far too close to the dangerous Jacobin illusions about the soundness of the unchecked popular will. Adams was "America's truest Burkean conservative, our most balanced apostle of indirect democracy. Balanced: because half aristocratic, half democrat, distrusting power concentrations in either half."[57]

Viereck's distinction between direct and indirect democracy is worthy of close attention. His related perceptive reading of certain American leading figures is in refreshing contrast to assessments of the same individuals that have long been dominant in American academia. The kind of distinction that Viereck makes between different forms of democracy, which is traceable in essential respects to Irving Babbitt, has yet to impact democratic theory in a decisive way. Viereck's ideas about popular rule are badly needed as a corrective to the type of uncritical majoritarian and egalitarian theorizing that passes as most democratic in today's universities.[58]

The Shame of the Intellectuals

The aristocrat for all times, Viereck believes, is the Unadjusted Man. He stands for the conservative principles *par excellence,* "proportion and measure; self-expression through self-restraint; preservation through reform; humanism and classical balance; a fruitful nostalgia for the permanent beneath the flux; and a fruitful obsession for unbroken historic continuity."[59] In times past hereditary nobility may have embodied many of these qualities, but in a modern Western context, and especially in the United States, they must be looked for in a natural aristocracy of will and talent. "Today what is precious is not the aristocratic class, increasingly anachronistic and functionless, but the aristocratic spirit."[60] The goal is to draw as many as possible into the sharing of enduring values by conserving and developing man's finest traditions. In that sense a friend and a servant of his people, the aristocrat abhors the one-dimensional, utilitarian mass-man. The latter knows nothing of a higher discipline. "To the plebeian, be he a millionaire or pauper, life is not a challenge to transcend himself and to carry a great heritage forward. It is a vast garbage pile in which he is ceaselessly rooting—like a wart-hog—for more swill."[61]

Looking for the kind of person most suited to fill the role of the aristocrat today, Viereck considers the professor and the intellectual, understanding the second term broadly to include also the artist and man of letters. Since the things of the mind are what finally decide man's destiny, the importance of intellectuals cannot be exaggerated. They should "stand up and assert and reassert, without apology, the glory of their function."[62] As men of truth and conscience they can offer society the kind of detachment from the passions and illusions of the present that is basic to civilization. Viereck is critical of turning universities into institutions of mass education. Instead, academic life should adopt far higher standards and be limited to a far smaller elite than today, an elite of intellectual ability and effort and not of money.

When intellectuals perform their task as intended, they are actually worthy of "awe and veneration."[63] Not only is Intellect then not an instrument of some special interest, such as Business and Labor, but the latter are properly the servants of Intellect. "If anything (let's be arrogant about it) the job of business and the job of labor in America is to serve intellect on the condition that intellect serves and ennobles the nation—as a whole. Intellect serves and ennobles whenever it searches for more truth and more beauty, in an unpretentious, impractical, haloed kind of way."[64]

If men of ideas have a special status and responsibility, their moral culpability for foisting destructive illusions on their fellow men is enormous. *They* at least should know better. Much of Viereck's writing is devoted to criticism of the betrayal inflicted on modern Western society by its intellectuals, a criticism that would have had to be intensified and expanded if it had been made a few decades later. The failings of the intellectuals are discussed in Viereck's *Shame and Glory of the Intellectuals*. Their most basic and pervasive shame is that they have turned their back on the great traditions. While enjoying the fruits of civilization in the form of tolerance and civil liberties, the intellectuals ignorantly and arrogantly undermine those traditions.

Still, in the 1950s Viereck entertained the possibility that in the modern world the professoriate and other intellectuals might be the prime candidates for serving as the aristocracy. Considered in the abstract, this idea was not implausible; members of this group might have assumed this kind of role—had the intellectual and cultural trends in the West been *different* from what they were at the time and have been in the last half century. Viereck himself bemoaned how the intellectuals were betraying the best of Western civilization. Was, then, the idea of the intellectuals as potentially the new aristocrats not more the product of wishful, romantic thinking even when he first advanced it? Actual developments since then have made the professoriate into the social group that is most hostile of all to the kind of higher continuity of civilization that Viereck deems essential. He clearly underestimated the potential for further "treason of the intellectuals," apparently because of a reluctance to recognize how deep and far advanced was the crisis of Western civilization already in the 1950s. Wanting to indicate a way out of present troubles, he seems to have looked away from Babbitt's sobering assessments a generation earlier.

To describe the specifically American breed of leftist liberal-progressive who set the tone during the period before, during, and after World War II, Viereck wittily and playfully but also sorrowfully creates two American cultural prototypes, both superficial philistines in their own way. Borrowing from Sinclair Lewis's *Babbitt* he calls them

Babbitt Senior and Babbitt Junior, both of them examples of what Irving Babbitt, too, bemoaned. The first, named George, is a boosterish Republican businessman and service club member. He waves the flag, hates political progressives, and is decidedly lowbrow in his literary and other tastes. His son, Gaylord, is the exponent of every progressive and quasi-sophisticated fad. One of these fads is to be the professed enemy of every kind of philistinism. In literature and poetry Gaylord is a thoroughgoing modernist. "The old Babbitt derides good poetry, good music, good painting for being modern and difficult. The new Babbitt praises bad poetry, bad music, bad painting for being modernist and obscure."[65] Both men have stereotypical minds. "While Babbitt *père* smugly denounces this obscurity as Long-hair Stuff, Babbitt *fils* with an exactly equal smugness applauds it as à-la-mode."[66] Gaylord Babbitt pictures himself as in all areas a member of the avant-garde. In politics he is friendly and understanding toward the extreme left and is constantly on his guard against the dangerous threat of right-wing tyranny. Gaylord stops short of communism but recognizes its followers as mistaken fellow-progressives. He is not exactly pro-communist but anti-anticommunist.

In Viereck's view, the corruption and decadence of the "progressive" intellectual in the mid-twentieth century is nowhere more clearly evident than in his evasive stand on communism. Many professors, artists, and writers have "an innate soft spot for some kind of almost unconscious fellow-traveling with communism."[67] Just as forthright and uncompromising opposition to Nazism was an instance of the glory of the intellectuals, so is their equivocation on the issue of communism, and especially Stalinism, their shame. Writing in the early fifties, Viereck observes, "Soviet imperialism has a far larger fifth column in the West than did German imperialism."[68]

A sharp critic of Joseph McCarthy, Viereck also deplores "the witch-hunt against 'witch-hunts'" as the "'liberal' version of McCarthyism."[69] Communist infiltration in the United States has been thoroughly documented, he believes, and must be taken seriously. "The evidence is overwhelming—and appalling."[70] Viereck has no patience with "liberals" who refuse to accept the guilt of such people as Alger Hiss. "To whitewash Hiss has become a compulsive defense-mechanism for those fellow-travelers who (unlike many candid men of integrity) don't admit they ever fellow-traveled for Communism. During 1930–47, they befriended its fronts, parroted its poppycock, but lacked Hiss's guts for logically translating a criminal ideology into criminal action. . . . Where they merely strip-teased with revolution for the thrill of feeling progressive and unbourgeois, Hiss is the intellectual who really meant business and eloped."[71] Writing in 1953, Viereck prophetically observes that "in future decades, Hiss may become an 'epic figure,' the mythic national symbol of the whole guilty 1930's." As for Hiss's accuser, Whittaker Chambers, Viereck believes that he performed an "act of public service and moral atonement."[72]

For the intellectuals to live up to their aristocratic mission during the Cold War, they had to become the leaders in a defense of civilized values against the totalitarian threat. Having been "moral saboteurs" and partly to blame for the anti-intellectualism of McCarthyism, they should take the lead in "uniting the West behind an anti-communism more fervent than before, yet more fairminded. This can still become their glory."[73]

In the early fifties, Viereck argues that "armed communism is obviously the greatest single threat to the world today."[74] Addressing himself to the issue of how to deal with it, he recommends a political course which would avoid both Scylla and Charybdis: "Scylla would be: an insane preventive war against Russia. . . . Charybdis would be: to buy 'peaceful coexistence' from the Politburo by callously ignoring the suffering Soviet peoples and by paying the ever increasing blackmail of surrendering our last defenses in Europe, Asia, and South America."[75] In 1965 Viereck qualifies these statements to make allowance for "polycentrist communism" and the new "atomic context."[76] He puts emphasis on exploiting splits among the communist powers and on closer contacts with the East.

But even those liberals who are really anti-communists often exhibit another illusion, the idea that freedom is best served by the United States in the world by always backing the revolutionary side, whatever the local circumstances. This is supposed to win the United States new friends. Often parroting communist propaganda, this type of progressive condemns as "fascist" every effort to head off even totalitarian insurrectionary movements. Every traditional status quo is assumed to be inferior. According to Viereck, this belief in the salutary effect of revolution is a dangerous ideological and romantic myth. Intellectuals repeating this cliché he regards as "the disruptive Katzenjammer Kids of world politics." In another world situation their talk would perhaps be harmless ideological play, but it is "a game of Russian roulette in the present context."[77]

Conservatism as Practical Politics

Because they are rooted in a notion of spiritual community, the great Western traditions have sought to harmonize the various groups of society. Just as for Viereck the Marxist idea of class war is symptomatic of the abandonment of the aristocratic mission of the intellectual, so does its spread into politics signify a sharp decline in the notion of statesmanship. A common trait of politicians who have Viereck's admiration is their concern for integrating all groups into society. The aristocrats among the politicians feel that they have a special bond with the unprivileged. In his controversial reappraisal of Prince Metternich in *Conservatism Revisited*, Viereck argues that Metternich saw the grab for power by the rising middle class as a threat to social harmony. The liberty for which the capitalists were fighting was too often just a means for substituting a narrow economic oligarchy for the more responsible political aristocracy in power. The self-interested pursuit of economic advantage would alienate the masses and polarize society. For all of his many considerable faults, including his inexcusable interference with academic freedom, Metternich was in some respects a protector and sponsor of the lower classes. He thought of himself as a "*socialiste conservateur*." By this he did not mean opposition to private property but to economic exploitation and the miseries of the industrial revolution. These he wanted to moderate through legislation. In the post-1789 era of tension between impatient liberal calls for restructuring society and often static traditional authority, Metternich on the whole represented "a patient conservative spirit of mediation."[78] Stability, he felt, was not the same as immobility. The way to reconcile various social groups was prudent reform.

Viereck applauds a similar concern for the common good in such English statesmen as Benjamin Disraeli and Winston Churchill. Disraeli's "Tory democracy" or "Tory socialism" sought restraints on the emerging liberal oligarchy and "reconciled 'the two nations' [the rich and poor] by making the party of aristocracy and conservatism take the lead in improving the working conditions of the poor."[79] This effort to avert class conflict, Viereck argues, was in the best tradition of Burke. Ignoring the question of whether social reforms instituted by conservatives like Disraeli and Churchill may have unnecessarily contributed to modern statism, Viereck suggests that their measures "were assimilating industrialism into traditionalism."[80]

The same theme runs through Viereck's assessment of Franklin Roosevelt. Viereck is in some respects sharply critical of the New Deal and Roosevelt as a person, but he also argues that the profound social problems created by the Great Depression called for unorthodox methods. There was a real danger that American workers and others would be radicalized and become receptive to the appeals of communism. In this potential prelude to class war, Roosevelt's New Deal may have saved American capitalists who were insisting on laissez-faire policies from themselves. Whatever the long-range economic wisdom or actual benefit to the poor of specific reforms, Roosevelt's obvious willingness to do something for those in need made workers feel that America was their country too. His reforms accomplished this important goal while leaving the capitalist system basically intact. In that sense, the year 1933 proved to be a triumph for conservatism. It gave assurances to the American masses, increasingly resentful of the unfeeling rich, that "their aspiration for economic liberty could be met—via the Squire of

Hyde Park—*within* the traditional constitutional, semi-squirearchical framework; hence, no need for Communist or even socialist alternatives to the plutocrats."[81] Roosevelt's willingness in the face of extraordinary circumstances to take on special interests and depart from economic and political orthodoxy was a crypto-conservative adjustment to the need of the times.

That the Roosevelt presidency also exhibited very dubious tendencies seems to Viereck equally clear. In his view, the New Deal had no consistent program, emerged from no coherent vision, but engaged in an "orgy of hit-or-miss." "Sometimes it was trust-breaking, sometimes it was trust-making; it prided itself on its antifascism, yet its NRA—its most unworkable blunder and its furthest venture in statism—resembled nothing so much as the corporate state of Mussolini." "The New Deal, at one and the same time, did most to smash communism in America—by removing the grievances it feeds on—and yet was partly infiltrated by it."[82] Although some of its reforms helped to stabilize society, its manner of enacting them at times had the flavor of populist despotism. "Its procedural aspect—direct democracy, trying to pack the Court, by-pass the Constitution—was sometimes just as radical as the business world believed it to be."[83] In foreign policy, Roosevelt naively and sometimes disastrously misjudged Stalin and communism.

In his preference for undogmatic, moderate politicians with a traditionally inspired sense of the common good, Viereck has a special fondness for Adlai Stevenson. Viereck goes as far as to say that "the finest conservative episode in American history, since the miracle of the *Federalist* papers, is the 1952 presidential campaign of Adlai Stevenson. No figure in our time has better expressed the good-humored, pluralist harmonizing of isms and interests that compose the American reality."[84] Stevenson joins political liberals "in defending civil liberties and humane reforms" but remains "a philosophical conservative in evaluating tradition and human nature."[85] The conservative half of Stevenson's outlook, which is played down or ignored both by his liberal friends and his critics on the right, is exemplified by his "extremely important insistence on reversing America's centralizing trend, on nurturing local patterns, traditional diversities." In foreign policy, he never shared "the former illusions of many New Dealers about Yalta, Red China."[86]

In Viereck's opinion, the United States does not have a genuinely conservative political party. The Old-Guard Republicans, to use one of his favorite phrases, are largely Manchester liberals with a predominantly commercial mentality. Of such thinking the true conservative must be suspicious. "A conservative sympathizes with aristocracy, never plutocracy. . . . Aristocracy serves; plutocracy grasps." What is needed to sustain American democracy is "whatever conserves not real-estate values but real values, not gold standards but cultural standards."[87] The Republican Old Guard has "more nouveau-riche cash than *noblesse oblige*."[88] As for the Democrats, the descendants of the New Deal are really Social Democrats. The United States needs a real political aristocracy with "patrician virtues." Here both parties have some potential. Adlai Stevenson is a civilized, unplutocratic intellectual-politician. Among the Republicans, Viereck points in the early fifties to Eastern internationalists like the Lodges and the Saltonstalls. Stevenson, he suggests, "has more in common with that special kind of Republican than he or they have with either of the two unaristocratic, west-of-center rivals: the folksy Truman Democrats and the commercial Taft Republicans."[89]

Viereck's judgments of American politicians are always interesting and sometimes quite perceptive, but a pronounced bias, other than what would have to follow from his own principles, is discernible. When it comes to assessing the conservative credentials of various politicians, those tending in the general direction of Viereck's own preferences in practical politics can usually count on receiving the benefit of any doubt. Others, such as the Republican Robert Taft, whom Viereck credits with some admirable personal characteristics, are allowed little leeway. Apparently, Viereck chooses not to take seriously Taft's conservative instincts and distrust of businessmen as politicians. Taft's political preferences are in themselves assumed to call his conservative credentials into question.

Though Viereck fairly castigates the ignorance, anti-intellectualism, and moral insensitivity of some of Joseph McCarthy's supporters and defenders, he is surprisingly reticent about the American political elite that, through its insufficient attention to a serious problem, made it possible for a second-rate small-town politician to emerge as the leading American spokesman for anti-communism. If Viereck is correct in his insistence that lack of concern about the domestic threat of communism was a serious failing, then it would seem to accord with his own principles to raise the issue of decadent aristocracy with reference to America's political leaders. Why the barrages of criticism against what Viereck regards as McCarthyite "plebeians," from whom presumably little better is to be expected, and the muted criticism of the supposedly aristocratic Eastern political elite, from whom the very best should have been expected? Theirs was the primary responsibility for alerting Americans to serious danger and for protecting them against it. Viereck's disinclination to look in these circles for the counterpart of the shame of the intellectuals opens him up to the charge of playing favorites.

Viereck defines the proper direction for a new American conservatism in the field of practical politics in a loose pragmatic way. Having decided that the New Deal neither could nor should be dismantled, he writes in 1956: "America needs a government both accepting the New Deal and pruning, purifying it. This dual need would be fulfilled by Stevenson-style Democrats certainly; by Eisenhower-style Republicans very likely; by Old Guard Republicans not at all (they would not accept the New Deal); by doctrinaire ADA-style New Dealers hardly (they would not prune it)."[90] Cautiously favorable to some social welfare reforms, Viereck recognizes that government action can pass beyond what he calls "the Statist Line."

> If humane social reforms seem "socialistic" or are against the fetish of laissez faire economics, that is not a substantial moral objection. When did we ever have laissez faire, and why is any merely material and economic system more sacred than the moral duty of compassion

> for want? A more substantial objection does arise when the proposed reforms cross a line beyond which welfare laws are inflated into the welfare superstate. Let us name this line the Statist Line. It *is* the line of diminishing returns for humanitarianism. Beyond it, the increase in security is less than the loss in liberty.[91]

It is understandable that Viereck's conservative critics have found some of his preferences in domestic practical politics frustrating. His positions are drawn from broad and sometimes ambiguously formulated general assumptions, and the connection between these assumptions and his particular practical stands can be tenuous. Viereck seems slightly uncomfortable and not a little impatient with economics. His attitude towards such questions occasionally even borders on the cavalier. Although on solid grounds when rejecting the type of rigid ideological definition of the proper role of government that is espoused by some so-called "libertarians," he is also prone to let a vague political prejudice take the place of weighing arguments on particular practical issues.

Viereck's reasoning has a way of filtering out aspects of complicated reality that will not support some contention or hope on his part. He argues persuasively, much like Wilhelm Röpke, that capitalism, if it is to remain a force for good, needs a social environment that integrates the individual into contexts of community and belonging.[92] He points to the effect of labor unions on the American worker: "They give him a human, cultural, social, and recreational unity with his neighbors, not merely an economic one. They give him an organic sense of community, more medieval (guild-style) than modern, . . . America's anticommunist trade-unions . . . are our most conservative, revolution-preventing force. Their *voluntary* sense of community is the best guaranty against communist or fascist collectivism."[93] Granted that unions that do provide such a sense of belonging could indeed be a conservative force and that Viereck's comments about American unions are not without truth, is he not also engaging in wishful thinking? Does he not have to look rather selectively and uncritically at the huge, centralized, bureaucratic, and progressively crass American labor unions to regard them as a bulwark for a sense of community?

What Kind of Conservatism?

In the late fifties and early sixties Viereck's ideas began to recede from center stage in the discussion of conservatism, partly because he published less prose writing, partly because he had more and more competition on the conservative side, such as the writing of Russell Kirk. The conservative label was snatched from him and his sympathizers by a broad and growing intellectual current tending to his right in practical politics. The definition of conservatism that was worked out in an eclectic and ecumenical manner among the contributors to William F. Buckley Jr.'s *National Review* became ascendant. The term came to mean a combination of traditionalism, often religious faith, especially Roman Catholic, devotion to the US Constitution, free market economics, and a preference for the right wing of the Republican party. Room was also made for unreconstructed classical liberals. Although most of these positions were at least partly or potentially compatible with Viereck's basic ideas, he seemed eager to distance himself from what he took to be the fruitful center of American opinion. As early as 1956 he had invented "Babbitt the Third," who was given the name Cabot. This is the faddish right-wing challenger to Gaylord, the faddish "progressive." One suspects that here Viereck had Buckley and his acolytes in mind. "Opportunistically riding the bandwagon of a periodic return to orthodoxy," Cabot engages Gaylord in debate. The object is "to out-snub the other's snobbery, out-avant the other's garde."[94] Both positions are superficial. "The same ear-to-the-ground literati who quoted Henry Wallace in the 1930's and 1940's, are now often sloganizing neo-conservatively about original sin, the need for a tragic sense, the need for roots."[95] There was thus in Viereck's attitude toward many of those who challenged his definition of conservatism no inclination to be generous.

In 1953 Viereck had criticized Buckley's *God and Man at Yale*

(1951). Writing in *Shame and Glory of the Intellectuals,* he gives Buckley credit for insisting on a return to certain principles. "These principles are that man has a moral nature, that statism threatens it, and that unmoral materialism results in a suicidal tolerance debunking all values as equally 'relative.'"[96] But Viereck also takes Buckley to task for giving the wrong answers to good questions. He is called "intelligent, sincere, and wrongheaded."[97] Showing an immature lack of sensitivity about academic freedom, "the Buckley school would subject intellect to money."[98] Viereck's reaction was here the same as that of Russell Kirk. Contrasting *God and Man at Yale* with Erik von Kuehnelt-Leddihn's *Liberty or Equality,* Viereck calls Buckley's book "neither aristocratic nor Catholic nor conservative. It is plutocratic, Calvinist, and Manchester-liberal."[99]

It is not surprising that Buckley's *National Review* would be unfriendly to Viereck. Intellectually more intriguing has been Viereck's complex relationship to Russell Kirk. In the early fifties Viereck praised his *Randolph of Roanoke* (1951) as "brilliant research in conservative Americana." He called one of Kirk's articles on Burke "extraordinarily perceptive."[100] As Kirk's prominence as a conservative thinker grew, especially with the publication of *The Conservative Mind in 1953*, Viereck's attitude began to change. In 1960 he quoted with apparent relish Clinton Rossiter's words, "Unfortunately for the case of conservatism, Kirk has now begun to sound like a man born one hundred and fifty years too late and in the wrong country."[101]

A part of the explanation for this dissatisfaction was that Kirk deviated in practical politics from the general direction mapped out by Viereck. While Viereck tended in his independent way toward the Democratic party in domestic politics, Kirk tended toward the Republican right, expressing himself in favor of Senator Goldwater. Allegedly of most concern to Viereck, however, was that Kirk had not taken a clear-cut stand on McCarthyism. Formulating what he called "the law of compensatory balance," Viereck wrote: "The law . . . makes the exposure of communist fellow-travelers the particular duty of liberals, the exposure of right-wing thought-controllers the particular duty of conservatives."[102] Kirk had "failed the acid test of the McCarthy temptation."[103] This, Viereck asserted, meant that "Kirk-as-thinker is bankrupt . . . for having been wrong—no, worse than wrong: morally evasive."[104] His conservatism had been discredited. And "what has been ethically corroded beyond repair is—beyond repair." These sweeping, uncompromising judgments were startling and difficult to explain. Viereck never did accuse Kirk of having been a McCarthyite. The closest he came to an allegation of that kind was to say, without offering any documentation, that "Kirk and most of his group" frequently adopted a "McCarthyism-minus-McCarthy."[105] Viereck did not explain how this supposedly pernicious attitude differed from his own recommendation in the early fifties to take the revelations about communist infiltration seriously and to expose communist fellow-traveling among the intellectuals. It was Viereck who then came out against the "liberal" "witch-hunt against 'witch-hunts.'"[106] Because it was left without support, Viereck's charge against Kirk had a curiously hollow ring.

Viereck's intellectual conservative rivals, Russell Kirk in particular, were said to be "bankrupt" also for another reason. They were accused of representing a "rootless nostalgia for roots."[107] This deficiency was evident from their taking a very dim view of the New Deal, which, in Viereck's view, signified a refusal to build, as true Burkeans would, on "the concrete existing historical base."[108] A part of that base was "the increasingly conservatized New Deal liberalism." "A genuinely rooted, history-minded conservative conserves roots that are really *there*."[109] American conservatives should make the best of "the deep-rooted American tradition of liberal-conservative synthesis."[110]

In their lack of respect for the "concrete organic growth of institutions,"[111] some intellectual conservatives had become "rootless doctrinaires."[112] This would not have been an implausible argument if directed against the kind of laissez-faire liberalism that is often called conservatism in America. But Viereck also directs this charge against a Burkean thinker like Kirk, who is a sharp critic of dogmatic libertarianism and who argues against some of the New Deal reforms because *they* do not respect the concrete American traditions of limited, decentralized government and of state sovereignty. By making acceptance of the New Deal the criterion of genuine Burkean conservatism in the United States, Viereck rather arbitrarily and inflexibly insists on a particular criterion of American conservatism that could hardly be beyond dispute. Viereck himself frequently refers to the long-time, powerful preference for and practice of minimal federal government and free market economics in the United States. Is not then that preference, too, a part of "the concrete existing historical base" and something to which American conservatives should adjust and try to give the most beneficial direction? Here a "liberal-conservative synthesis" different from Viereck's suggests itself that he does not consider. Again, his general principles do not necessarily dictate the practical position that he prefers.

In the 1950s Viereck opposed dismantling the New Deal but favored "pruning" it. Why would largely the same stance as Viereck had adopted be impermissible for Kirk and others just a few years later? Viereck clearly does not believe that conservatism requires quick acceptance of every new trend in politics. His notion of "unadjustedness" suggests that departure from present trends is sometimes necessary to protect sound tradition and promote enduring higher values. Viereck's notion provides an opening for challenging the New Deal, as he himself did, and, even more, for challenging the later enormous growth of American national government. These can be seen as violating long-standing American constitutional tradition, specifically, the federal system that is basic to the Constitution. Especially in view of Viereck's high admiration for the framers, should not American conservatives lean heavily in the direction of reviving rather than undermining their vision for America and of finding ways creatively to apply that vision to new historical circumstances?

It is worth noting that, if Viereck's idea of "pruning" the New Deal was a more than transitory, opportunistic preference in American national politics, he would today stand far to the right of the Republican party with respect to the size and function of the federal government.

Most Republicans have by now not only accepted the New Deal but most of the vast further expansion of the federal government in the second half of the twentieth century and later. If, according to Viereck, some of the New Deal unhappily passed over "the Statist Line," the Republican party, too, passed over that line long ago, to say nothing of the Democratic party. For Viereck to retain his bias from the 1950s in favor of the Democratic party today would, considering its view of the role of government, suggest a philosophically disquieting incongruity. It would be unlike Viereck to let adherence to party trump basic principle. A more likely consequence of applying Viereck's thinking to the present would be deep disillusionment with American politics.

Viereck's charges of intellectual and moral bankruptcy, especially as directed against Russell Kirk, had a harsh, uncompromising tone difficult to explain on purely intellectual grounds. Even if it were accepted as true that some of Kirk's stands on practical politics were unacceptable, it would not automatically follow that he was intellectually bankrupt. Would Kirk's work as a scholar-thinker be somehow invalidated or contaminated by his practical preferences? Viereck himself suggests the opposite when, with doubtful consistency, he writes: "Fortunately Kirk's positive contribution sometimes almost balances [his] embarrassing ventures into practical national politics."[113] It would appear that Viereck was turning against Kirk the type of politically inspired criticism that was so unfairly turned against Viereck by people like Frank S. Meyer in the mid-1950s. Could one not direct against Viereck the words that he used against his detractors?: "Don't oversimplify, don't pigeon-hole; allow for pluralistic overlappings that defy abstract blueprints and labels."[114]

Viereck's criticisms of Kirk coexist in his work with expressions of genuine admiration. Kirk's best-known book, *The Conservative Mind*, is called "brilliant."[115] Viereck lauds Kirk's insightful treatment of many subjects and especially his "perceptive rediscovery of literary and philosophical figures like Irving Babbitt for a true humanistic conservatism today."[116] Viereck's attacks on the same man deviate so sharply from this detached mood of appreciation that the reader is inclined to discount them.

These observations are not intended to deny that there is room for criticism of Russell Kirk. He may be criticized, for example, for not having sufficiently explored the strengths of modernity and the possible compatibility of new and old ideas. His traditionalism occasionally became too romantic and nostalgic, a hankering for institutions and ways of life that had been irreparably damaged. Rather than explore the possible humane use and development of technology he questioned, Kirk sometimes wrote as if the world would be better off without it. But even here polite discussion should have been possible between thinkers who had so much in common. When sounding unrealistic and even escapist, Kirk was often trying not to return to a previous age but to stir the imagination with new possibilities for creative reconstruction of the present. Like Viereck, Kirk understood that man is moved far more by the imagination than by reason.

A recurring feature of Viereck's writings, and especially *The Unadjusted Man,* is his deep suspicion of populist mass movements. He traces McCarthyism back to the progressive era and interprets it as largely a movement of "status-resentment."[117] The charge of pro-communism directed against the American political and economic elite was really a masked plebeian challenge to the refined, elevated values of the American Eastern aristocracy. "McCarthyism is the revenge of the noses that for twenty years of fancy parties were pressed against the outside windowpane."[118] The British-looking Dean Acheson was an ideal target. He was "schooled successively in Groton, Yale, Harvard Law, Wall Street—a quadruple provocation to the out-group majority!"[119] What is of special interest in the present context is that Viereck seeks to forge a link between this status-resentment and the conservative intellectual current of which he disapproves and that found one outlet in *National Review*. His line of argument is that many of the ideas of what he calls the New Right—a term he never clearly defines and that others would use differently many years later—merely articulate plebeian class-interest. "It was only when an unrich Catholic South Boston became allied, via the new American right, with newly-rich Protestant Texans (excluded from the *chicté* of Wall Street) and with flag-waving Chicago isolationists that the old American seaboard aristocracy was seriously threatened in its domination of both governmental and intellectual opinion and its special old-school-tie preserve, the Foreign Service."[120]

Although there is much of interest in Viereck's analysis of American populism, at least two objections can be made. One, touched upon earlier, is that Viereck does not inquire into the possible element of justification for the populist challenges. Normally he would be the first to admit that deep resentment in the mass of a people against their own leaders is likely to stem from some failure on the part of those leaders. Viereck himself points to serious weaknesses among members of America's elites. Specifically, they were disinclined in the decade after World War II to accept and act on the evidence of communist infiltration of the US government. More generally, looking at broad cultural and social trends, Viereck is aware that the best and the brightest in the old Eastern establishment had long and increasingly gravitated in the direction of finance and business, placing an ever-growing emphasis on money-making. The contrast between the traits and tastes of the emerging plutocracy and the republican virtue and simplicity admired by America's founders was all the time becoming more pronounced. He complains of the ruling class adopting utilitarian and progressive attitudes and betraying old traditions. That Viereck is nevertheless willing to look away from or excuse failings in the American eastern seaboard aristocracy suggests a romantic streak in his thought, a reluctance to give up on the possibility that what was commendable in America's old elites might make a comeback.

The second objection to Viereck's treatment of populism has important philosophical implications. In his attempt to associate certain brands of intellectual conservatism with populism, Viereck contradicts his normal emphasis on the fact that ideas are not primarily reflections or instruments of other factors such as class interest, which is what Marxism asserts, but are a part of what defines and directs human conduct. In his analysis of the New Right, he suddenly lapses into the kind of determinism that one might expect from bad modern sociology. Ideas become expressions of class interest or other factors. Are then ideas inert and merely symptomatic of something else and not dynamic and formative? Viereck does not here consider that in the possible meeting of poorly articulated populist resentment and a conservatively oriented intellectual current, the latter may exert a healthy moderating and refining influence. To the extent that responsible intellectuals are able to influence a popular movement, they can affect its sentiments and goals and, as needed, make them less harsh and simplistic. Ideas can have an educative function. Attempting to turn the part of the conservative movement that he dislikes into a mouthpiece for class envy, Viereck attributes to it a narrowness of mind that does not square with the facts and, uncharacteristically, commits a basic philosophical error.

Viereck's admirable trait of looking for valid insight in thinkers with whom he generally disagrees has a clear and marked bias. He is inclined to show understanding and patience towards intellectuals and politicians to his own left. The ideas of men like John Kenneth Galbraith or Arthur Schlesinger, Jr., who share most of the premises of the "progressive," left-leaning Western intellectual mainstream that Viereck criticizes, are found to be not without redeeming value. Intellectuals to his own right, by contrast, can expect little generosity. The presumed exaggerations of individuals who attack the illusions of the age more sharply than he does incline him to think of them as being beyond redemption. He lumps intellectuals to his right with more extreme groups or individuals. The specter of the nationalist semi-fascist thought-controllers—Viereck's description of those who have excused or supported McCarthy—is never far from his mind. Here Viereck tends to blur distinctions, and the reader sometimes has difficulty recognizing individuals and tendencies of which he disapproves because of hyperbole or far-fetched associations. Whereas Viereck frequently judges thinkers to his left by what strikes him as most appealing, he is prone to judge American contemporaries to his right by what strikes him as most *un*appealing or as *potentially* unappealing. Viereck's withdrawal of his customary open-mindedness from the latter is all the more surprising in that, unlike the intellectuals to his left, they share many of his philosophical assumptions.

Considering Viereck's view of human nature, history, and society, his readiness to speak well of or believe the best about prominent intellectuals to his left, provided they are not pro-communist, presents an enigma. It is surprising that after World War II, as the Cold War was starting, Viereck even associated himself with such barely veiled attacks on traditional Western society as the campaigns against "the authoritarian personality" and "the radical right." Viereck contributed to a 1955 book edited by Daniel Bell titled *The New American Right* and to the 1963 edition that was named *The Radical Right.*[121] Virtually all of the contributors were left-leaning liberals or social democrats. As if concerned not to be too closely identified with such writers, Viereck added to the 1963 edition a chapter in which he pointed out that there exists a kind of conservatism that is very different from the radical right and that he represented. The first edition of the book was a response to McCarthyism and related phenomena. The expanded and updated edition was motivated also by a desire to counteract the movement to get Barry Goldwater nominated as the Republican candidate for president. Viereck not only criticized Goldwater as a "*laisser-faire* Manchester liberal" but condemned romantic nostalgia, right-wing authoritarianism, and other defects of the putatively radical right.

There is a pattern in Viereck's life and work that looks like an intellectual and personal anomaly and that comes out in his contributing to the just-mentioned collective volume: On the one hand, he sharply criticizes progressive, positivistic, utilitarian intellectuals who also cross his "statist line," but he appears at times also to want to align himself with people of just that kind and to be seeking their approval. It is as if by vigorously agreeing with an opinion of progressives that happens to coincide with his own, he is trying to make amends for violating their basic beliefs. The point here is not that his criticisms of a Barry Goldwater are obviously unjustified, but that he seems to go out of his way to be liked by influential people who can affect his reputation.

A large part of the reason for Viereck's equivocal relationship to the intellectual powers-that-be is undoubtedly his wanting emphatically to disassociate himself from his father, George Sylvester Viereck (1884–1962). His father was a visible defender of Germany before and during the Second World War. The Viereck family, whose European branch included individuals of some literary and political accomplishment, had been represented in America for three generations when Peter Viereck was born, but his father was a naturalized American born in Germany. In America, George Sylvester Viereck became a prominent, economically successful poet, author, publisher, and journalist. He was long perceived as generally liberal. He had unorthodox, anti-Puritan, sexually *risqué* sentiments and was a pagan attracted to biological determinism. He was also a great admirer of Germany. Having founded the magazine *The Fatherland* in the year of the outbreak of World War I, George Sylvester Viereck became a recognized leader of German-Americans during that war and later. He devoted himself to promoting German culture in America, hoping to effect a kind of German-American synthesis. This advocacy continued after the Nazis had taken control of Germany. Though not himself an anti-Semite or outright Nazi, Viereck defended Nazi Germany and opposed American entry into the Second World War. He discounted reports of Nazi atrocities as anti-German propaganda. He would later concede that he had been wholly unrealistic to hope for the best regarding Hitler and Nazi Germany. George Viereck's pro-German writings and other activities led in 1941 to his being indicted and tried, and he eventually served time in prison. He was paroled after the end of the war.

Peter Viereck was acutely aware that his identifying as a conservative and his criticizing progressive assumptions made him suspect in America's intellectual and journalistic establishment. The Germanophobia that had been common in these circles even before the rise of Nazism also made his obviously German last name a drawback. His understandable desire to remove from himself any taint of being his father's son helps explain his wanting to reassure the powers-that-be.

His first book, on the roots of national socialism, demonstrated his utter rejection of thinking that was even more distasteful to the intellectual establishment than his conservatism. But more generally and in years to come, Viereck seems to have wanted to ensure that the arbiters of enlightened opinion would not shun him but regard him as a dissenter worth listening to. Trying to make a favorable impression on influential intellectuals who were ultimately unfriendly or hostile to his basic ideas gave a paradoxical twist to his life and work that may have taken a psychological toll.

VIERECK'S ACHIEVEMENT AND AMERICAN CONSERVATISM

Although Viereck's writings range widely from basic ethical and aesthetical questions to issues of practical politics, they form an impressively coherent whole, though one containing tensions and paradoxes. Going through his work, one becomes aware that its variety of topics, emphases, arguments, and illustrations radiates from a simultaneously unifying and dynamic center. Here is a creative intellectual of broad range, an original and synthetic thinker who can elevate and enrich both mind and sensibility. Though Viereck has learned much from others, he does not merely imitate their ideas; he makes them his own, puts his own mark upon them, and incorporates them into his own view of life.

The method and style of Viereck's scholarship does not conform to the positivist model with its preference for "meticulous," if sometimes mindless and mind-numbing, fact-gathering. Though in much of his writing Viereck has the historian's concern about evidence and documentation, his main strength as a scholar is his ability to discern and to understand the deeper significance of major historical trends and events. He is able to do so because he apprehends them in relation to the large ultimate questions of human existence. Viereck is guided to the heart of a matter by a highly developed sense of what is most important in explaining human conduct. By temperament he prefers a way of presenting his findings and ideas that may look essayistic and even informal when compared to that of much modern academic writing, but it would be superficial indeed to discount his books as taking a light approach to serious topics. There is nothing shallow about Viereck's work. His central ideas are based on a broad, incisive, and subtle reading of man's nature and history. Even when addressing current issues. his aim is always to relate them to enduring questions. Not all of his writing is on the same high level, but rarely does it leave the reader indifferent. His writings put their imprint on the mind even when triggering disagreement. If it is a measure of intellectual capacity to be able to draw others, even against their will, into a certain perspective on life, Viereck must be regarded as an intellectual of the first order. He should not be called a philosopher in the full sense of the word, because he is not primarily interested in the slow, sustained, systematic reasoning of philosophy and because some of his concepts lack precision. Neither is he an historian in the conventional modern academic sense because of a certain lack of formal rigor and attention to nuance and detail. Yet the depth and scope of his insight make him an important man of ideas with much to contribute to both philosophical and historical scholarship.

Briefly to review Viereck's books of prose individually, his *Metapolitics*, which has been expanded and updated more than once, is a pioneering study of the relationship between artistic-cultural decadence and political tyranny. His documentation of the central role of the imagination as an inducement to action begins a highly significant theme in his work. The accuracy of Viereck's interpretation of Prince Metternich in *Conservatism Revisited* has been questioned, but, whatever the quality of Viereck's historical scholarship, his development of the notion of conservatism as a spirit of mediation between inherited traditional authority and calls for reform merits attention. *Shame and Glory of the Intellectuals* takes a stand on many issues and persons and is bound to irritate some readers, but on the whole the book is a balanced, stimulating, and in parts brilliant statement of the proper role of the intellectual. The short but important *Dream and Responsibility* deals sensitively with the relationship between poetic imagination and society and with issues of literary criticism. Viereck's arguments have implications for political thought. *The Unadjusted Man is* Viereck's most uneven book. Some sections, such as those on the free imagination and direct and indirect democracy, deserve a close reading. Others, such as the treatment of the New Right, are lacking in nuance, balance, and analytical precision. *Conservatism: From John Adams to Churchill* is intended chiefly as a primer for college students but is of considerable value also to their instructors. It is in some ways Viereck's most impressive book. In about one hundred pages of his own text and less than eighty pages of excerpts from representative authors, he manages through tight organization and a flair for compact but expressive formulations to summarize the main currents of conservative thought since the French Revolution. He surveys a large number of thinkers, from authoritarians like de Maistre to moderates like Burke, John Adams, and de Tocqueville. His inclusion of certain figures, such as Nietzsche, will be questioned by some, but his flexible, eclectic approach is a strength and not a weakness. He also offers his own broad definition of conservatism. The book is in pleasant contrast to more narrow, ideological attempts to lay down the conservative line. The reader gets a sense both of the complexity of the central issues and of the general direction of the conservative mind at its best.[122]

Later editions of *Shame and Glory* and *Conservatism Revisited* contain added material, some of it printed in both books. Much of it has been on the theme "The New Conservatism—What Went Wrong?," the title of Book II of the first revised edition of *Conservatism Revisited.* In these writings and some separately published articles, chapters, and reviews, Viereck makes many plausible, if overstated, observations, but he is here assessing a movement that drew attention away from his own work. It is not far-fetched to suspect a relationship between the polemical edge and element of dogmatism in some of his judgments and a perceived reduction of his own influence. No doubt, unintelligent, ideological, and condescending reading of Viereck by conservative rivals helps explain the tone of some of these writings.

Viereck's prose style has drawn some criticism, most of it formalistic and pedantic.[123] It is true that his sentences and constructions can be awkward, careless, or imprecise, but for the most part his free and lively, sometimes quirky, use of language—in some ways similar to Carlyle's or Nietzsche's—makes for an unusually crisp, colorful, and frequently brilliant expressiveness. Through an unexpected turn of phrase or combination of words, a witty epigrammatic formulation, a neologism or striking image, Viereck sometimes manages to convey ideas that would have taken others pages or chapters. They also have a way of sticking in the reader's mind. Moreover, this distinctive, very personal style is clearly not some forced attempt to achieve effect. This is Peter Viereck being himself. Through this imaginative prose speaks a highly imaginative thinker.

A weakness of most of Viereck's books is that they consist of articles or reviews previously published in academic journals, magazines, and newspapers that have been arranged for publication in book form. Though all of these pieces are connected by central recurring intellectual concerns and address different aspects of the same subject, a reader may have some difficulty discerning the full meaning of and the links between the parts until able to view them from the vantage point of the particular book as a whole or of Viereck's work more generally. A more systematic style of writing, reflecting a more systematic way of thinking, would have given clearer evidence of the author's powers of synthesis and integration. Viereck's predilection for writing and publishing shorter pieces rather than working in the sustained, systematic, step-by-step manner of the book-writer may be related to his ability to say much in a limited space and a wish to get his ideas into print as soon as possible, but his manner is very likely due also to his previously discussed belief that conservatism is not "theoretical." It is not best expressed in "well-organized, clearly presented" treatises; conservatism "embodies" rather than argues.[124] As if proceeding according to his stated epistemological premise, Viereck brings to all of his prose writing some of the poet's knack for the concrete image, letting quasi-poetical prose elaborate what he has already seen imaginatively. The result is often a lack of philosophical clarity and conscientiousness. Yet the scattering of articles and reviews is not a sign of a lack of intellectual coherence. That Viereck is not fully persuaded of his own epistemological reasoning—as he should not be—is apparent from his having written more traditionally conceived books, too, which are high in theoretical content.

In spite of Viereck's objections, American intellectual conservatism took its direction in the period from the early sixties forward from his intellectual rivals rather than from him. Though it acquired considerable academic strength, its forward momentum was not sufficient to reverse the growing leftist dominance of university faculties. It has been able to shore up and revitalize lingering conservative sentiments in the American people at large and to effect some intellectual invigoration of practical politics, but it has not quite generated the kind of wide-ranging, penetrating philosophical and cultural movement that might really transform the American mind and imagination and through them American society in general. Unfortunately, Viereck's sometimes harsh words about other conservatives and his apparent wish to placate liberal arbiters of acceptable opinion helped deprive him of an influence among intellectual conservatives that he would not only have richly deserved but that would have undermined the deep-seated but superficial belief among many of them that politics and economics hold the key to shaping the future. Viereck goes further than Kirk in explaining the power and central role of the imagination and the culture. The far-reaching agreements among Viereck and other leading thinkers and the potential for cross-fertilization among them disappeared behind a façade of conflict partly of Viereck's own making. It is to be hoped that younger intellectuals not emotionally involved in this feud will not be diverted by old polemical condemnations from seriously examining his work as a whole.

What is called conservatism in American politics has moved closer to some of Viereck's preferences in practical politics, partly under the influence of so-called "neoconservatism," a movement about which Viereck had to be deeply ambivalent. It started to gain prominence in the 1970s and 80s. Its leading intellectuals included Sidney Hook,

Irving Kristol, Michael Novak, and Norman Podhoretz. In spite of its name, which seems to have been adopted by Kristol and others to take advantage of the growing popularity of the conservative label at the time, neoconservatism has in its predominant intellectual trend been a special form of liberal progressivism, though one appearing increasingly conservative because of the continuing leftward drift of American liberalism. The neoconservatives also resemble more traditional American conservatives by having been strongly anti-communist during the Cold War. Yet the roots of neoconservatism are chiefly in the liberal wing of the Democratic party, as represented by politicians like Hubert Humphrey, Henry "Scoop" Jackson, and Daniel Patrick Moynihan, and, to a considerable extent, also in Trotskyite communism, whose revolutionary fervor neoconservatives have tamed and transferred to a more liberal agenda of replacing historically evolved societies with "democracy." Because of their hawkish predisposition, many neoconservatives have aligned themselves with the Republican party in foreign policy. This move was facilitated by the Republicans becoming more and more accepting of strong, activist federal government. Alliances left over from the Cold War have helped conceal disagreements between traditional American conservatism and neoconservatism. Since the end of the Cold War neoconservatives have been able to redirect the Republican party's hawkishness into an assertive, even imperialistic US foreign policy, designed, ostensibly, to spread democracy in the world, especially in the Middle East.

The neoconservatives appear conservative to some because they claim to represent universal principles and to offer an alternative to liberal moral relativism and nihilism. On closer inspection, their allegedly universal principles turn out to have less in common with a conservative, Burkean understanding of higher values than with the ideas of the French Jacobins. Like the latter, most neoconservatives want traditional societies that are insufficiently democratic and progressive to be remade in the image of their universal principles. They have little or no respect for old, slowly evolved historical patterns of life. These they view chiefly as obstacles to progress and equality of opportunity. Their allegiance is to modern Enlightenment-style civilization. Having assigned to America the role of spearheading "the global democratic revolution," a phrase adopted by President George W. Bush, the neoconservatives want the American federal government to be muscular and hawkish, particularly in foreign policy, and to have great military power.[125]

Because of Viereck's anti-communism, his partly liberal leanings in politics, and his general tendency to seek common ground with influential people to his left, one might have thought that he would seek the approval of the neoconservatives. But unlike most of them, he gives primacy to moral and cultural questions, admires old Western traditions, and is deeply uncomfortable with modern progressivism, as he is uncomfortable with business and finance setting the tone in society. While the neoconservatives are impatient with the traditional American suspicion of strong, centralized government, Viereck shares the older sentiment. There is another even more important reason why his agreement with them could never be more than limited and tenuous: their fondness for ideological abstractions and their belief that the entire world should be made to conform to a single model, defined by such abstract principles as "democracy," "freedom," and "capitalism." Irving Kristol, a self-identified exponent of neoconservatism who is often called the "godfather" of the movement, promotes its belief that America is an "idea" rather than a historically evolved country and that America is called to spread that admirable idea around the globe. Kristol writes, "Large nations, whose identity is ideological, like the Soviet Union of yesteryear and the United States of today, inevitably have ideological interests in addition to more material concerns."[126] The notion of an ideological nation intent on remaking the world in its image runs counter to Viereck's most basic beliefs. He knows that in politics ideological abstractions and a lack of a sense of history and of respect for the diversity and complexity of life breed intolerance and fanaticism.

That conservatism should today be widely equated with neoconservatism, even among self-described conservative intellectuals, shows a glaring lack of philosophical depth and discernment and a lack of historical perspective. The new nomenclature reflects a markedly changed order of priorities relative to that of the leading thinkers in the postwar conservative intellectual movement. Neoconservatives have advanced the claim that until they appeared on the scene, American intellectual conservatism was virtually nonexistent or intellectually feeble. The allegation betrays deep ignorance or is a cynical attempt to draw attention away from what might challenge the neoconservative ascendancy. The conservatism of an earlier period had greater depth and breadth than neoconservatism—as exemplified by Viereck, Kirk, Mel Bradford, Francis Canavan, Whittaker Chambers, Gottfried Dietze, John Hallowell, Jeffrey Hart, Will Herberg, Milton Hindus, Ross Hoffman, Erik von Kuehnelt-Leddihn, John Lucaks, Thomas Molnar, Gerhart Niemeyer, Robert Nisbet, Wilhelm Röpke, Peter Stanlis, Stephen Tonsor, Eric Voegelin, Eliseo Vivas, Richard M. Weaver, and Francis Wilson (to say nothing of a conservative-leaning classically liberal economist like Friedrich von Hayek).

Neoconservatism has enjoyed great political success—for example, it played a decisive role getting the United States to attack Iraq—but that success has *weakened* opposition to statism, including constitutional checks on the president, and has assisted cultural radicalism by reinforcing the inclination of American conservatives to become preoccupied with politics. In 2003 Irving Kristol stated openly what had long been obvious but partly concealed, that neoconservatism was transforming and replacing traditional conservatism. According to Kristol, the "historical task and political purpose of neoconservatism would seem to be this: to convert the Republican party, and conservatism in general, against their respective wills" into a posture "more suitable to governing a modern democracy."[127] Many years earlier another neoconservative commentator had written about his own movement that it identified with modern liberalism and "progressivism." "Neoconservatives belong to the tradition of liberal-democratic modernity."[128]

The preference for progressive enlightenment thinking over the old Western traditions makes neoconservatism in its predominant form conservative only in a very limited and paradoxical sense: it is conservative of modern anti-traditionalism—that is, conservative with regard to thinking from a relatively short and recent period of Western history. It is conservative in the sense that it defends modern progressive liberalism against extreme radicalism. With reference to what precedes enlightened modernity, neoconservatism is radical. Its weak interest in moral-spiritual and cultural issues that an older American conservatism deemed central undermines the kind of long-range moral, cultural, and intellectual efforts without which no broader and more genuine revitalization of Western civilization is possible. Neoconservatism's willingness to use American military might to enact its goals for the world brings to mind the term "armed ideology." Its defense of a strong presidency as an instrument of imperial ambitions represents an abandonment of traditional American constitutionalism.

***

Peter Viereck's insistence that a genuine cultural renaissance must be prepared in the free and independent sphere of philosophy, ethics, literature, and art is a much-needed antidote to an increasingly philistine conservative preoccupation with elections, political programs, and economics. To disregard him because some of his political leanings have bothered others with more influence over the definition of conservatism is to ignore that the most valuable elements in his work may be those that transcend politics in the narrow sense. It has also been suggested here that not all of Viereck's political observations are clearly dictated by his most basic and general beliefs.

All intellectual movements are threatened by routinization and sclerosis. It is an open question whether modern American intellectual conservatism will prove to have prepared the way for a lasting revival of Western civilization. For all of its impressive accomplishments, the movement has barely developed those of its potentialities that offered the most hope from the start. It has shown no strong inclination to assimilate, extend, and deepen the main insights of its leading figures in an intellectually systematic and stringent way. The failure to absorb and develop the moral-cultural approach of which Viereck is a leading representative discloses a disabling deficiency. The pronounced tendency to overemphasize practical politics is one of the consequences. Formulating stances on public policy is important in its own way, but without a well-developed understanding of what most shapes the future of society, not even this task can be performed well. When it comes to responding to the greatest long-term need of American and Western society, politics in the ordinary sense can play only a limited role.

Deep fissures run through American and Western society. Ancient habits and beliefs that used to give some unity and continuity to the lives of most people have faded or been pushed aside by modern currents incompatible with the old ways. Sharply conflicting claims compete for the attention of individuals and create psychologically taxing dissonances. In this atmosphere of disruption and chaos, conservatives do not have access to some special, essentially intact, healthy, vibrant tradition with reference to which they can escape the general confusion and steer society right. They face a massive task of reconstruction: not of restoring the old in its original form but of giving it new life in exceedingly difficult circumstances. Only thinkers and artists of wide historical scope, acute intuition and discernment, and an exceptional capacity for synthesis can be expected to recover a sense of the deeper continuity of the higher life. They need to be able to recognize fragments of the old that belong together and to collect and blend them in new compelling ways adapted to current circumstances. This task requires powerful, discriminating *imagination.* Peter Viereck's portrayal of the highest form of imagination—his insistence that it is free and independent and at the same time respectful of the heritage of mankind—seems addressed precisely to the need for creative reconstruction in an age of great disruption.

In general, Viereck reinforces and supplements Russell Kirk's wise and urgent theme that a moral-cultural conservatism is needed. More specifically, Viereck's thought runs parallel to Kirk's with regard to the importance of the moral imagination and the dangers of the opposite kind. But Viereck goes more deeply into the nature of the imagination, how it shapes individual and society, and how its special creativity can connect past and present. Behind Viereck and Kirk stands Irving Babbitt, one of the great and most original but also most unfairly neglected American thinkers of the twentieth century.

It should be emphasized that only a fundamental reorientation of mind and imagination, supported by a new education, can offer any real hope of a lasting renewal of the central insights of the old Western world. The essential values of civilization, Viereck writes, "are transmitted more through the humanities than through that up-to-date journalism of the academic world, the courses in current politics, economics, and other uselessly 'useful' techniques."[129] Viereck's argument for the critical detachment and free creativity of the Unadjusted Man is a counterweight to pragmatic dilution or ideological debasement of the mind. The timeless higher responsibility of the intellectual-artistic life, he writes, "moves beyond the propagandistic, the temporary, the overadjusted—beyond the corrupting successes of even the best of isms—and gropes toward the lasting aspect of things."[130]

But American intellectual conservatism has been prone instead to losing its historical perspective and critical distance to current trends. Its being attracted to intellectual and political fashion hard to reconcile with the conservative temperament suggests a chronic identity crisis.

PART FIVE

IN THE ELEVENTH HOUR

THE DECLINE OF AMERICAN INTELLECTUAL CONSERVATISM

("The Decline of American Intellectual Conservatism," *Modern Age*, Vol. 49, No. 4, 2007.) In observance of its fiftieth anniversary, the journal *Modern Age* devoted all four issues of the forty-ninth volume to a retrospective and assessment of American intellectual conservatism since the founding of the journal. I was invited to write the "Conclusion" to this volume. I had offered a similar general assessment twenty-five years earlier and now related my observations to the previous commentary. Had this article been written not in 2007 but for the present moment, it probably would not have looked very different, but I would have pointed out that the popular rebellion against the American ruling establishment of which Donald Trump became the champion was due in part to failures of the American conservative movement.

A quarter of a century ago *Modern Age* asked me to assess the state of American intellectual conservatism for its 25th anniversary issue.[1] I had been a student of the subject for twenty years. In 1971, five years before George Nash published *The Conservative Intellectual Movement in America,* I and a co-author brought out a similar but shorter book—in

Stockholm, Sweden, of all places. It covered the movement's historical background, central ideas, main figures, books, and publications, its economic and foreign policy thinking and organizational and political influence.[2] As a professor in the United States I have for many years taught a graduate course on conservatism, including its American varieties, and have written much on that and related subjects. From the beginning, this study of conservatism formed part of larger philosophical objectives, and I pursued it with an emphasis on ideas and history rather than day-to-day politics. Having now been invited to assess American intellectual conservatism on the occasion of the 50th anniversary of *Modern Age*, I mention these facts to indicate the nature and extent of my interest.

The article for the 25th anniversary issue noted that, although American intellectual conservatism could celebrate great successes and strengths, it had to address several problems if it were to avoid stagnation and decline and have a chance to realize its potential for changing America for the better. As a prelude to offering a critical appraisal twenty-five years later, I should like briefly to restate the points that I made the first time. In summary form these may look obscure and less closely related to each other than they are, but the rest of the article should help explain their meaning.

I

The points made in the 25th anniversary issue were as follows: (1) American conservatism lacked philosophical continuity and maturity. Its development had been choppy and fragmented, intellectuals of different orientations showing little interest in really learning from their predecessors and each other. The movement had not quite absorbed the ideas of those of its thinkers who were most original and insightful. A prejudice favoring certain German and other European thinkers over American ones compounded insufficient attention to a major figure like Irving Babbitt. In general, American intellectual conservatism needed more philosophical incisiveness and conceptual precision. It needed a better sense of priorities. It had to resist an exaggerated interest in the practical politics and "public policy" issues of the day. The future is decided more by society's fundamental moral, aesthetical, and intellectual trends than by politics in the narrow sense.

(2) The failure or success of American conservatism would ultimately depend on whether it was able to spread "a new spirit of ethical realism." It needed better to understand that genuine morality is first of all a matter of personal character, of acts of will, and that moral virtue shows itself most especially in admirable conduct towards people up close. American conservatism had to guard against the danger of morality being mistaken for the kind of merely sentimental benevolence for the world's unfortunate for which Jean-Jacques Rousseau set the pattern. This self-congratulatory, pseudo-moral "virtue" hides dubious motives—usually the will to power—behind compassionate-looking, ambitious schemes for remaking society and the world. Some of the most passionate "lovers of humanity" have done great damage in the name of helping their fellow human beings.

(3) In spite of its frequent statements about the importance of history and tradition, American conservatism had achieved no more than a fumbling philosophical grasp of the connection between history and the moral and other universality that it affirmed. Specifically, it had not seriously considered that there is a form of "historicism"—represented, for example, by Edmund Burke—that recognizes the inescapable historicity of human existence but is nevertheless compatible with the notion of transcendence. This historicism provides an alternative to a more static, ahistorical conception of universality of the kind propounded, for example, by Plato. The latter conception may have psychological and nostalgic appeal for some today but is philosophically retrograde. One of the consequences of not taking account of the possible union of universality and historical particularity was an inability to distinguish adequately between two very different forms of individualism and liberalism, one atomistic and the other integral to a Burkean conservatism.

(4) American conservatism had to understand better the great extent

to which the imagination—ranging from great works of art to mass culture and everyday intuitions about life—shapes our most fundamental sense of reality and our wishes for the future. The imagination, interacting with the will, does so for good or ill. Civilization stands or falls with the quality of will and imagination that predominates within it. Perverted imagination distorts even rationality, for it is from the imagination that reason receives its fundamental sense of reality and proportion. Without a fundamental reorientation of the imagination, which prepares the mind to consider even unpalatable and discouraging facts, presumed intellectual victories for conservatism will not transform society.

(5) Intellectual conservatism had not done much to effect "a sorely needed restoration of philosophical reason." For that situation to change it had to get beyond a one-sided view of rationality. Being properly concerned to resist the intrusion of abstract and positivistic rationality into humane studies, some of its leading thinkers, including Russell Kirk, Peter Viereck, and Eric Voegelin, were, unfortunately, suspicious of *all* systematic, conceptual intellection, trusting instead in a higher intuition to provide the most important insight. They did not consider that there exists a form of rationality that is very different from rationalistic reductionism and the type of reason that Voegelin calls "egophanic." There is a deeper rationality that has always been at work in human beings but that has been hiding, as it were, behind flawed notions of its own nature. Recognizing the existence and form of this reason reinforces opposition to abstract rationalism where it does not belong but also requires revision of older, ahistorical conceptions of philosophical reason. It is not to deny the crucial importance of "immediate experience" or "moral imagination" to point out that there is a type of philosophical reason that does not distort or kill what it touches but that tries faithfully to *articulate* actual, living human experience, including experience of the universal. A problem with even the most profound and sober intuition, from the point of view of knowledge, is that it cannot *argue*; it is mute in philosophical debates. But this sound, full-bodied intuition has an ally in a historically grounded rationality that takes conceptual account

of what has been experienced. It tries to sort out the contents of experience, distinguishing between what belongs to the world of practice and what is mere imagining or unrealized desire. It is this deeper but humble rationality that makes us recognize the crucial importance of history for understanding human life.

The 1982 article ended with a call for a kind of historicism—"value-centered historicism"—that would reconstitute the theory of knowledge and make possible a more general philosophical strengthening of American intellectual conservatism.

Looking back on these observations, I find nothing that I would change. What were problems with American intellectual conservatism twenty-five years ago are problems still and have in some ways gotten considerably worse. Some promising higher potentialities of the movement remain largely unrealized.

A non-philosophical reader might ask why a discussion of the state of American conservatism would center on issues like these and not on matters like the market economy, foreign policy, education, the Republican Party, and the size of the Federal government. The answer is that the above points relate directly to each of these more obviously political questions, most generally to how they should be approached. The points help explain the pervasive intellectual confusion of today's American conservatism, not least its getting mixed up with imperialistic ideology and related causes subversive of traditional America.

The following discussion of challenges facing American intellectual conservatism will return to but supplement the old list of weaknesses and opportunities. I shall argue that the movement has to revise considerably its predominant notion of what is important and unimportant. It must recognize that some of its oldest and most deep-seated inclinations have been misguided.

II

American intellectual conservatism has been much-affected by a dubious pragmatism. One of its manifestations has been the just-mentioned preoccupation with practical politics and a corresponding neglect of philosophy and the arts. This emphasis is connected to the assumption that capturing political power is the key to shaping the future. I am not such a fool as to deny the importance of politics—I am a professor of politics. Politics forms an essential part of the effort to build and protect civilization. But, in trying to effect a renewal of American and Western society, winning and exercising political power cannot take the place of the patient and demanding intellectual and artistic efforts that, in time, might change the mind and the imagination of a people. It is such efforts, together with the practical actions that they inspire, that set the basic direction of society. The *sine qua non* of social health may be the inner and outer striving of morality, but morality urgently needs the oxygen of sound thought and imagination. If a corrupt intellectual and artistic culture is spreading ever new infections, no amount of political activism can create social health. It should be granted, of course, that in some particular circumstances well-considered political action might have a catalytic, generally beneficial effect, and that in a desperate situation it might, at least for a time, avert disaster.

Needless to say, it is highly desirable that some intellectuals should take a strong interest in the study of politics. Indeed, as thinkers or as participants in politics, they can exert a salutary influence on political practice, but they can do so only if they understand the realities of politics, including its limits, and understand how it is shaped by ideas and imagination. Activism that is not informed by this kind of realism is ineffectual or self-destructive.

The "pragmatic" preoccupation with practical politics in American intellectual conservatism is closely related to a fondness for economics and business, which is often so pronounced that it amounts to regarding the aims of conservatism and business as the same. But civilization, including a civilized market place, depends, as Wilhelm Röpke has observed, on moral, imaginative, and intellectual preferences that do not arise spontaneously from the economy as such.[3] The priorities set by businessmen and financiers in their economic activities are not ordinarily prescribed by the good, the true, and the beautiful. Too many conservatives with libertarian leanings underestimate the extent to which purely economic considerations need to be subordinated to other motives and the extent to which habits, institutions, and gatekeepers must help foster moral restraints, good taste and respect for truth. If many businessmen in the Western world have exhibited admirable traits like honesty, good manners, and social responsibility, it is because, like others, they have been formed by an ancient civilization. They have been subject to the elevating pressures of priests, thinkers, aristocrats, teachers, and artists. Today, as our civilization deteriorates, the utilitarian one-sidedness and greed that business tends to generate when left to itself are being released from those traditional restraints.

As with politics, it is of course perfectly proper, nay, indispensable, for some intellectuals to study economic activities closely in order to understand them better. In its higher form, economics is a splendid discipline that blends into philosophy. But the economical must be understood as taking its place in a larger whole in which business and finance are means to higher ends.

There is a form of American pragmatism that is just what it should be: concerned to establish what can work in the real world of action. It properly refuses to engage in wishful thinking and in pointless, merely abstract speculation. More common, however, is a pragmatism that originates in a twisted, truncated view of human beings and their world. This pragmatism expresses a strong anti-intellectual and anti-aesthetical prejudice, as in the case of the obsession of so many self-described conservatives with politics and economics. In spite of America's great universities on the intellectual side and its great symphonies and museums on the aesthetical side, to mention just a couple of relevant institutions, American life has a powerful utilitarian bias. That predisposition is exemplified by an inordinate fascination with makers and doers and an inclination to look down on persons engaged in non-utilitarian, low-paying pursuits. The person most admired in America may be the self-made man with a great fortune. The best and the brightest are expected to gravitate in the direction of money-making and away from activities whose main rewards are non-economic. America and conservatism at their pseudo-pragmatic and anti-intellectual worst come through in that embarrassing old saw: "Those who can, do. Those who can't, teach."

Expressing and fostering a narrow, simplified notion of human beings and their needs, the prejudice against non-utilitarian pursuits has stunted intellectual and aesthetical life and thereby also the moral life. Its harmful effects have been compounded by spreading mass tastes.

American postwar intellectual conservatism at its best was in considerable part a protest against the contraction and perversion of the human range that are characteristic of this pseudo-pragmatism. Russell Kirk was prominent among those who criticized utilitarianism and sought to strengthen a sense of higher values.[4] Kirk and others stressed the moral-spiritual and aesthetical bases of the civilized society and our great dependence on, and indebtedness to, earlier generations for a proper sense of priorities. But from the very beginning such thinkers had to contend—within the conservative movement itself—with economistic and activistic thinking. Though Kirk was widely regarded as the central figure of post-war intellectual conservatism and received much praise, especially on ceremonial occasions, many reputed conservatives consciously or unconsciously regarded him and kindred thinkers as too literary, as too distant from what surely had to matter most—practical politics and free markets. The problems of "the real world" had to take precedence over disquisitions on the moral-spiritual sources of order, the moral imagination, and the renewal of education.

The old pseudo-pragmatism had an influence even where one might have least expected it—within the strain of conservatism that most *resisted* the utilitarian temper—although there it asserted itself more subtly and indirectly. Some of the anti-utilitarian thinkers were highly learned and saw deeply, but they expressed their ideas in a manner that was more essayistic, more conceptually tentative than philosophically rigorous, which left their ideas vulnerable to misunderstanding, misuse, and caricature. Kirk is a case in point, along with Voegelin and Viereck.

In fact, as has been mentioned, they were suspicious of the more stringent, systematic reasoning of philosophy; they mistakenly assumed it to be indistinguishable from rationalism.[5] One might have thought that others of philosophical disposition would have felt the need to clarify, complement, and revise important but ambiguously stated ideas, but the old anti-intellectual prejudice of pseudo-pragmatism, reinforced in this instance by opposition to rationalism, discouraged such efforts.

Whereas in France, for example, any self-respecting intellectual must at least feign interest in and admiration for the more advanced work of philosophy, among American intellectual conservatives the mention of such works, especially German ones, often elicits sighs, jokes and condescending smiles. How silly and tiresome that German obfuscation! If the most difficult, "technical" philosophy seems unappealing, the fault is assumed to lie with the philosophers, who are considered self-important and pretentious, and not with the reader's lack of preparation. Conservative intellectuals have felt all the more excused from the exacting and protracted labors of philosophy as its "abstruse" notions have appeared to have no relation to immediate practical needs. Is philosophy not also chiefly the province of weirdos and leftists? Though American intellectual conservatism has had major thinkers, its development has been retarded by disinterest in philosophy beyond the level of broad generalities. As the movement never quite understood the significance of the most demanding philosophical work, it never really respected it and therefore never developed a mature philosophical culture.

This criticism does not imply that philosophy proper is inherently wiser and more important than more essayistic writing. Some philosophy is wrongheaded, and frequently writing that is not philosophical in the stricter sense is more penetrating and illuminating than formally proficient philosophy. The best philosophers owe much of their perspicacity to poets and highly intuitive writers of prose who have steered their minds in the right direction. Yet without the work of philosophers that which sages have comprehended but have left compact and perhaps bewildering cannot be properly pinned down, elucidated, and transmitted. Neither can flawed or mistaken notions mixed in with wisdom be identified and weeded out.

It is in large part because of a lack of philosophical work and a disinclination to consult such work that important ideas of American conservatism have yet to be fully absorbed and appreciated and that major intellectual problems have gone largely unaddressed. Contrary to the expectations of pseudo-pragmatists, the consequences of this deficiency have not been negligible but far-reaching and partly devastating. They have extended from the universities to journalism and practical politics.

Most generally, a lack of philosophical rigor has permitted intellectual messiness and confusion. The conservative movement has had difficulty ranking intellectual contributions and distinguishing between profundity and superficiality, truth and ideology—a weakness that has festered and worsened with time. So-called neoconservatives have asserted that, before they provided fresh fire-power, American conservatism was intellectually weak and ineffectual. But a person really familiar with American intellectual conservatism in the decades just after World War II who compares it to neoconservatism is struck, on the contrary, not only by the marked shift in views but also by the intellectual *decline* among those reputed to be the leading thinkers. This is so especially in the area of humane, historically based study and reflection. Though not without its intellectual problems, the earlier movement exhibited considerably greater depth and range. To support this point one need only mention a few names from that period—for example, Mel Bradford, Francis Canavan, Whittaker Chambers, Gottfried Dietze, John Hallowell, Will Herberg, Milton Hindus, Friedrich von Hayek, Erik von Kuehnelt-Leddihn, Russell Kirk, John Lukacs, Thomas Molnar, Gerhart Niemeyer, Robert Nisbet, Wilhelm Röpke, Peter Stanlis, Stephen Tonsor, Peter Viereck, Eric Voegelin, Eliseo Vivas, Richard Weaver, and Francis Graham Wilson—a selective list that is merely suggestive of the intellectual resources of the earlier conservatism. The claim of neoconservatives to have raised the general intellectual level of American conservatism shows plain ignorance or is calculated to distract attention from thinkers not serviceable to neoconservative designs. But, if the original conservative thought was generally superior, why would the movement have been drawn to neoconservatism? Besides raising the issue of the power of money and connections, this question brings us back to the lack of philosophical discipline.

In the post-war period William F. Buckley Jr.'s *National Review* played a central role in constituting and setting the tone in the emerging conservative intellectual movement. The magazine gathered many intellectuals of real ability and was—though with such notable exceptions as the excommunication of Peter Viereck—admirably ecumenical. The openness to different points of view was, however, due in part to a lack of philosophical discernment and coherence. Though the magazine had an editorial line with regard to political issues, there was about its general intellectual demeanor a quality of hit or miss. It was indicative of the problem of philosophical integration that, despite his obvious intellectual gifts and stylistic talent, Buckley never tried publishing a book that systematically set forth his own conservative outlook. His forte was not binding ideas together into a larger whole. He attracted to his magazine leading intellectuals who, as individuals, did attempt something like an overarching point of view, but these individuals were, though in broad agreement on political issues, in important respects on different intellectual wavelengths.

The person at *National Review* who worked most diligently to define and enforce a specifically American conservative intellectual identity was senior editor Frank S. Meyer. His "fusionism" can be seen as an attempt to synthesize two major strains of thought in the magazine. Meyer was a libertarian and individualist in that he advocated a minimal state and maximum freedom for the individual, but he also tried reconciling that view with elements of a traditional understanding of moral virtue. Another editor concerned to formulate a genuinely American conservatism was Willmoore Kendall, who had been one of Buckley's professors at Yale. Kendall was an expert on the American political tradition. His notion of the special character of the American people and the US Constitution put its mark on the conservative movement. James Burnham, a professor at New York University, was already famous when he joined the magazine, partly as the author of *The Managerial Revolution.* A leading authority on communism, including communist infiltration of American institutions, and strategic foreign policy thinking, he was also a trenchant critic of modern liberalism and wrote an important book on American constitutionalism. Burnham was a synthesizing thinker of large scope. He became a pillar of *National Review*, was arguably its intellectually weightiest figure.

A comparison of these and other editors to their counterparts at today's *National Review* strikingly illustrates the intellectual weakening of American conservatism. Yet the reputations of Meyer, Kendall and Burnham as major conservative thinkers, acquired partly through the influence of *National Review* on conservative opinion, were exaggerated. These individuals, too—Burnham perhaps less so than the others—lacked something in philosophical subtlety and stringency and offered some less than felicitous combinations of ideas. Frank S. Meyer's fusionism may have made some sense as the theory for a possible political alliance—it can be said to have prefigured the Goldwater movement—but it was less philosophical than ideological in its attempt to define for all times and circumstances the legitimate functions of government and in drawing the line between governmental and other power. Meyer also underestimated the dependence of freedom and virtue on historically evolved human institutions and associations, including those of government. Willmoore Kendall was prone to incorporating intellectual influences without fully exploring their compatibility with his other ideas. He was simultaneously a defender of the Framers of the US Constitution and an admirer of Jean-Jacques Rousseau, not realizing that, in spite of superficial appearances, the latter advocated a view of human nature, society, and government radically different from that of the former. James Burnham did not advance conservatism by adopting a positivistic epistemology ill-suited to studying the spiritual nature of man and the higher values celebrated by the older Western tradition.

His purely naturalistic Machiavellian conception of politics, too, made for an incomplete view of human reality. Each of the three thinkers had a past on the extreme left. Meyer had been an ideologically intense member of the international communist underground. They were now strong anti-communists but had some difficulty shedding reductionistic habits of mind. That their respective basic assumptions were rather different, in part even incompatible, was not much noticed by a movement that was more interested in the advocacy of certain policy positions than in philosophical consistency and precision.

National Review was enamored of free market economics, and it could cite, promote, and publish many sophisticated economists. One of its favorites was Milton Friedman, who would become an icon for the conservative movement as a whole. Though Friedman made weighty arguments for a free market, his notion of capitalism did not dwell on what ordered liberty owes to historical development and non-economic considerations or on the need for the market to operate under civilizing pressures.

In sum, like *National Review*, the conservative intellectual movement as a whole was influenced by the ubiquitous pseudo-pragmatism and showed no strong inclination to get to the bottom of difficult philosophical issues. More concerned about seizing opportunities for anti-statist political coalition-building than about achieving intellectual coherence, the movement left some of its basic assumptions regarding human nature and society in provisional, poorly integrated form and got by with a partly jerry-built intellectual structure. Because of its shaky philosophical foundation, it was liable to adopting ideas that, though questionable, were endorsed by *National Review* or had other influential sponsors.

The last few decades have seen a confusion more glaring and egregious than any previously seen. The movement curiously and increasingly became associated, even identified, with ideologues whose central ideas had but a tenuous connection with conservatism as usually understood. In fact, these ideologues bore a closer resemblance to the eighteenth century French Jacobins. The Jacobins were the intellectual and political leaders of the French Revolution. Rejecting historically derived beliefs and practices, they wanted to remake society according to allegedly universal, ahistorical principles, which they summed up in the slogan "freedom, equality and brotherhood." They saw France as called to liberate mankind. The new Jacobins similarly have a disdain for historically formed societies and want to reconstruct them according to ahistorical and allegedly universal principles. These are summarized as "freedom" or "democracy." America, the new Jacobins assert, is unique in that it was founded on those principles rather than on tradition. America has the historical mission of spreading them around the world, giving other peoples the kind of fresh start that was provided by "the American Founding." It is paradoxical, to say the least, that a movement calling itself conservative would come under the influence of such beliefs and that people attracted to the new Jacobinism would be called neoconservatives. Even more surprising, advocates of neo-Jacobin ideology would eventually be allowed to decree who was and who was not a real conservative. They could do so by virtue of achieving strong position in the foundations, media, think tanks, and universities but mainly because of the intellectually frayed condition of the conservative movement. Had the latter been philosophically and historically better grounded, it would have recognized who the new Jacobins were and countered their attempt to divert and transform the movement. Conservatives would have known that modern Western conservatism originated as a reaction against the old Jacobinism.[6]

The upshot of these comments is obviously not that greater philosophical depth and stringency would have produced uniformity. Any intellectually vibrant movement will exhibit diversity and tension. The point is that philosophical maturity would have reduced the element of confusion, ideological simplification, and outright error and raised the general level of discussion.

III

There is a seemingly arcane but central philosophical issue whose inadequate treatment by American conservative intellectuals illustrates particularly well how a deficiency in thought can have far-reaching practical consequences. The issue concerns the very definition of conservatism. Oddly, the American intellectual movement that claimed the label never evolved more than a rather vague idea of the sense in which it was *conservative*. In response to the question "what is conservatism?," a typical representative of the movement would most likely recite a set of principles, such as belief in limited government, a free economy, and a strong defense. But if principles of this type define conservatism, why call it "conservatism"? All belief systems have principles of some kind. Jacobins of various types hold to principles with special tenacity, indeed, do so even in the face of reality that refuses to conform to their plans. The term "conservative" suggests something distinctive—a desire to conserve. But of what precisely is conservatism conservative? Of tradition, many say. Leo Strauss and his followers have rejected this view as "historicist," as endorsing whatever history has thrown up, which they regard as morally relativistic or nihilistic. Traditionalists have pleaded innocent to the charge, saying that while they believe in respecting tradition, they also believe in universal principles of some sort. But if there are principles to guide us, why pay any heed to history? Why be a conservative?

American conservatism has had difficulty understanding and articulating the meaning and significance of "the historical" and how it relates to universal values. Richard Weaver, a revered figure who did have a philosophical cast of mind, long held rather uncritically to a conventional classical and medieval assumption that historical individuality is ineffable and has nothing to do with what is knowable and normative. What, then, is distinctively conservative about conservatism? Going in a direction different from Weaver's on this issue, many traditionalists, especially Russell Kirk, appealed to Edmund Burke. But, on the whole, they did not really explain to themselves and others just how Burke's championing of "the general bank and capital of nations and of ages" is connected to his acute sense of universal right. Kirk had a strong intuition that the two could not be separated, and he was right. Charges by moral rationalists that Kirk was a historical "relativist" were unperceptive or were merely attempts to reduce his influence, and yet vagueness on a crucial matter exposed Kirk and the traditionalists to criticism. They might have advanced their understanding of the connection between universality and history by drawing, cautiously and selectively, from German and Italian philosophy from Kant and Hegel to Benedetto Croce, but they were disinclined to venture into the territory of professional philosophers.[7]

Value-centered historicism explains how the historical consciousness of a Burke is not only compatible with but also necessary for making sound moral, intellectual and aesthetical choices. As American intellectual conservatism has not, for the most part, gone beyond an approximation of philosophy, it has yet to grasp that real universality, as distinguished from abstract rationalistic conceptions or romantic dreams, is in this human world of ours indistinguishable from, and dependent on, historical particularity: The good, the true, and the beautiful come into being through discriminating incarnation in the concrete—through *synthesis* of the universal and the particular.[8]

Recognizing the importance of historical particularity and circumstance, most especially the possibility of union between universality and particularity, sharpens comprehension of the importance of individual personality and the need for creativity in the moral, aesthetical and intellectual life. Universality can be kept alive in changing situations through the creative synthesis of universality and particularity. This idea, so hard for many to grasp, could have enriched American conservatism in many ways. For example, it would have thrown new light on American constitutionalism, making it possible to transcend the artificial opposition between the school of interpretation called "originalism" and the one emphasizing that the Constitution is a "living document." One may affirm the need to adapt to new historical circumstances and yet retain the conception of an enduring constitutional purpose. The idea of synthesis of the universal and the particular could also have deepened the understanding of the American constitutional ethos as expressed in the phrase *e pluribus unum.* Do these words mean that unity must be obtained at the expense of diversity? Must the particular, such as a particular American state, give up its distinctiveness and independence in favor of some kind of ideological-political homogeneity, or can unity be achieved *through* diversity, by means of the harmonization of discrete but dynamically interacting parts? Having never developed a firm grasp of how universality relates to historical particularity, American intellectual conservatism has not been well equipped to deal with such questions, central though they are to explaining the genius of the American political tradition.

One of American conservatism's truly distinguished social thinkers is Robert Nisbet. His discerning explication and defense of the quest for community is an enduring achievement. Human beings sorely need the ties of intimate, close-up associations, starting with the family. Nisbet has demonstrated the devastating effects of social atomism, whether in the form of liberal individualism or Rousseauistic, socialistic collectivism.[9] Nisbet's acuity is due in part to his awareness of the role of history and tradition in constituting human groups and societies. Yet his discussion of associations would have benefited from more attention to the simultaneously individual and social nature of man and to the needs of individuality as a potential carrier of universality. Without some freedom for the individual to go his own way community may become stultifying and suffocate precious personal originality, thereby undermining community itself. Though not unaware of the issue, Nisbet does not, for all of his deepening and extension of Aristotle, go very far in the direction of giving human individuality its due. American conservative social thought would have much to gain from exploring further the need for balancing communal, traditional ways, on the one hand, with individual freedom and creativity, on the other. These two elements of social life should, as far as possible, be mutually supportive.

In the perspective of value-centered historicism, liberalism and conservatism, properly understood, are, in a sense, aspects of one and the same desirable approach to life. That Edmund Burke, the great traditionalist, should also be a Whig, a liberal of sorts, can be recognized as apposite. The crux of the philosophical matter is that in life at its best universality and individuality are mutually dependent on, and implicated in, each other. A firmer philosophical grasp of this relationship would have enriched American conservative thought on community and individuality, tradition and creativity.

American intellectual conservatism has been strongly affected over the years by concerted and persistent Straussian attacks on "historicism" and historical individuality. This campaign has created a presumption that abstract rational principles define higher values and that these must not be seen as in any way derived from history or tradition. For the anti-historicists, what is historical is merely accidental and conventional. The stated fondness of many so-called conservatives for ahistorical principles is incongruous, for modern conservatism was born out of the emerging historical consciousness—as in Burke—and was a reaction, specifically, against rationalism. Even if they did not express it clearly, Burke and others discerned an all-important and intimate connection between universality and history, which made them respectful, though far from uncritical, of tradition.

According to Strauss and the Straussians, that which is highest must not be associated with tradition or "the ancestral." To do so is to abandon philosophy and, with it, universality. The Straussians have taught Christians and others who have regarded tradition as one of the pillars of their beliefs to disdain the historical. They have, in effect, taught traditionalists self-contempt. Many traditionalists have naively and gullibly adopted the suicidal course urged upon them.[10]

What most Straussians call "natural right" bears only a faint resemblance to a traditional conception of natural law. Although many of them may not understand or concede it, their notion of universality has more in common with modern Jacobin thinking than with Thomism. Their advocacy of an anti-historical notion of what is ultimately normative is a prime example of how an error in a supposedly marginal and obscure area of philosophy can have consequences that are not only practical but also disastrous. In the last few decades an abstract, neo-Jacobin universalism blended with nationalistic conceit to form the notion of America as an exceptional, virtuous country called to export its "universal principles" to the rest of the world. Because of limited philosophical discernment even persons of some scholarly reputation became supporters of a political cause that has badly damaged America and the world. There could hardly be better proof of the crisis of American intellectual conservatism than that many of its self-designated representatives adopted or excused a reckless radicalism.[11]

One of the ways in which American conservatives have exempted themselves from philosophical effort is to suppose that, especially when it comes to questions of value, what really matters is religious commitment. A common conservative type is the earnest and ostentatious believer, Roman Catholic or Protestant, whose manner announces to the philosophically inclined person that having pious sentiments is much more important than making fine philosophical points. The proper religious commitment is assumed somehow to guarantee soundness of thought. The problem here is not that there is anything wrong with genuine religious devotion. It is that in the modern world religion has been so permeated by what Babbitt calls "sham spirituality" that it has become a major pollutant of the will, the mind, and the imagination. No one is immune from religious-moral confusion and smugness. There is an urgent need for scrutinizing spiritual claims. Secondly, religious faith is, especially in an intellectual movement, no substitute for intellectual labor. Insufficient philosophical effort and discipline clouds and distorts central questions of human existence and weakens religion itself. Letting pretentious religious sentiment take the place of thought has had just that kind of effect on American intellectual conservatism—a criticism that is not directed against religious faith but against a particular and common American form of anti-intellectualism.

IV

Space permitting, I would have liked to go deeply into an already mentioned weakness of American conservatism, the common neglect of the artistic. It is analogous to the belittling of philosophy and has similar origins. The role played by the imagination in shaping conduct, for good or ill, is central and decisive.[12] Nothing could be more important to a healthy society than exposing perverse, if superficially appealing, imagination and nurturing imagination of a different quality. These issues have been brilliantly, if incompletely, elucidated by Irving Babbitt, who has explained the moral-aesthetical dynamic of sound and unsound imagination. Unfortunately, although the phrase "moral imagination" is a part of the vocabulary of American intellectual conservatism, these ideas have been only partially assimilated and applied by a movement with a flawed set of priorities.

On the whole, American intellectual conservatives care not very deeply about the arts, especially not above the level of the popular. Conservatives tend to have what one might call unmusical personalities. They seem to feel no deep existential need for poetry, novels, paintings, symphonies, films, and such—though some swear by rock music. Any protest to the effect that a limited interest in the arts is hardly a significant flaw in a real man and a conservative simply confirms the debilitating weakness to which I am drawing attention. Some will predictably and smugly declare that religion offers all the nourishment for the soul that we really need. They indicate thereby a deformed and cramped conception of religion as well as of life in general. In fact, this kind of religiosity often goes together with a utilitarian-pragmatic attitude towards worldly matters.

I suggested earlier that the most basic need of civilization may be moral—"moral-spiritual" might better convey the intended meaning. But without a broad and penetrating imagination, one of whose benefits is to improve the incisiveness of the mind, the higher will in man has great difficulty finding its way.

V

This article has outlined major reasons why American intellectual conservatism is in crisis. The reasons discussed involve a deeply flawed pragmatism and an insufficient appreciation for the importance of philosophy and the arts.

Greater philosophical sophistication on crucial issues would have protected American conservatism against intellectual, aesthetical, and moral trends and their political manifestations that owed their momentum not to their intrinsic merit but to the Zeitgeist and the enormous resources wielded by their promoters. Most generally, conservative intellectuals of real philosophical education and temperament would not have been as prone to formulaic, ideological thinking. Specifically, conservatives more aware of the close connection between history and universality would not have been attracted to the anti-historical natural-right theorizing of a Leo Strauss or to such neoconservative "universal principles" as "freedom" and "democracy," which are hard to tell apart, both in ideological content and spirit, from Jacobinism. A stronger historical consciousness and a proportionally better immunity against moral-political utopianism would have made conservatives resistant to imperialistic dreaming and adventurism. Strengths of this kind as combined with more knowledge of the origins of American culture and constitutionalism in the classical, Christian, and English heritage would have made them understand that American ordered liberty did not result from implementing abstract principles but from the long gestation of a particular culture.[13] They would have been quick to realize that large and indiscriminate immigration and migration into the United States was bound to dilute and undermine traditional American culture in general and American constitutionalism in particular. Philosophically discerning intellectuals steeped in the spirit of traditional American constitutionalism would have opposed a "unitary," imperial presidency and a national security super-state of the kind propagated by neoconservatives.

It should be obvious, then, that the inadequate treatment of seemingly esoteric philosophical issues is no small matter. Weakness of this kind has badly damaged American intellectual conservatism across a broad range of practical affairs.

A better understanding of the central role of the imagination and the arts in shaping individual and society would have made conservatives more perceptive in diagnosing the problems of America and Western civilization and would have markedly changed their strategy for dealing with them. Their ability to identify and expose inhumane qualities of the imagination would have been much improved.

Historians of the future who trace the origins of the curious identity crisis of American intellectual conservatism will undoubtedly record the prominent role of careerism and greed. How easily the powers-that-be in foundations, think tanks, media and government were able to buy and instrumentalize purportedly conservative intellectuals! At the bottom of this development one finds, of course, a moral failing. But had it not been for the misguided pragmatism and the related problems of conservatism here described, the chronic weaknesses of human nature would not so easily have broken through the defenses of civilization. American conservatism would have been better prepared to resist intellectual shoddiness, corrupt imagination, and a false moral virtue. It would not have had to accept so much of the blame for damage inflicted upon America and the world by self-described conservatives.

AMERICA'S CRISIS

("Power Without Limits," *Humanitas*, Vol. XXVI, Nos. 1 & 2, 2013.) Defending the framers' Constitution was from the beginning a central feature of American intellectual conservatism. In as much as the Constitution had for so long formed an integral part of how Americans view themselves, this emphasis could not have been more apt. In the American context, what could be more important to conservatism than understanding, preserving, and developing the best of the country's constitutional heritage. But cultural and political developments have eroded this constitutionalism. One of the most destructive influences has been a brand of moral idealism that breaks with traditional Western notions of moral character and undermines decentralized and limited government. Considering the advanced decay of the Constitution, can it be protected and revived? This article questions superficial notions of constitutionalism. It argues that the state of the Constitution is a reflection of the state of the American people. The crisis of the Constitution is at bottom a moral-spiritual and cultural crisis. Assessing the prospects for American constitutionalism is the same as assessing the extent to which the American constitutional personality of old is surviving or can be revived. Some supposedly conservative theorists of the Constitution who have an ahistorical, abstract notion of its meaning are unable to analyze its actual predicament and understand what reviving it might entail.

For the framers of the US Constitution, no task seemed more important than to limit and tame power. The chief reason why they established a government of divided powers and checks and balances was their view of human nature, which was primarily Christian and classical. It seemed to them self-evident that human beings are morally cleft. They are potentially decent, even admirable, but also have darker inclinations that pose a great threat to themselves and others. Human beings cannot be trusted with unrestricted power. The constitutionalism of the framers assumed that the drive for power had to be contained first of all through the self-discipline of individuals, but corresponding external restraints, including constitutional checks, were necessary to protect the public.

Since the adoption of the Constitution American government and society have changed radically. The Constitution still enjoys a kind of ceremonial respect. It is cited as if it possessed an august authority. In actuality, political practice is today so different from the intent of the framers that, in substance, the original Constitution has been virtually suspended. Over the years sometimes tortuous and highly tendentious constitutional interpretation has combined with powerful political and intellectual trends to produce an enormous expansion and centralization of the federal government and a concomitant erosion of checks and balances. The claim that these developments have realized the hopes of Alexander Hamilton is blatantly anachronistic. The American federal National Security and Welfare State with its presidential system bears little resemblance to the scheme of the framers.

The reasons for the change are many and complex. They include the effects of wars, economic and scientific developments, and globalization. The change can also be traced to moral, cultural, and social developments that have had profound, transformative consequences. Briefly put, the way in which Americans today view themselves and the world is very different from what was the case at the time of the framing of the Constitution. That change is far-reaching and goes a long way towards explaining the mentioned political change. One major consequence is a muting of the old American fear of power and the creation of vast new opportunities for politicians who desire more power. Although these developments have distinctively American characteristics, they reflect trends throughout the Western world. Those trends have, in fact, been even more pronounced in Europe.

Although traditional religion and morality have long been in retreat, moralistic language seems more pervasive in American politics today than ever. Few public policy stands are advanced that are not said to be demanded by "justice" or "fairness." To oppose them is to be "greedy," "callous" or "intolerant"—to be morally inferior, even despicable. Moral indignation is, it seems, the favored posture of politicians and pressure groups.

But the moralism of today is very different from the notion of morality prevalent at the time of the writing of the Constitution. The purpose of this article is to identify a powerful strain within this new moralism and to elucidate its role in engendering the transformation of American society and politics. While sharply lessening the old American fear of power, the change has facilitated and even stimulated a desire for power. According to the new conception of morality, it is virtuous to want government, almost always the federal government, to expand its reach. In foreign policy, it is common for American leaders to claim, sometimes with great ideological fervor, that America is exceptional and has a moral mission in the world. American leadership is needed to remake insufficiently "free" and "democratic" countries. According to assertive nationalists, neoconservatives, and liberal interventionists in both parties, America should seek armed global hegemony—not, of course, to indulge a desire to dominate but to fulfill a morally noble destiny. The advocates of uncontested hegemony will deny that they desire, for its own sake, the enormous military power that would be necessary to achieving the stated goal; the need to wield enhanced American power is only incidental to the moral imperative of creating a better world. In domestic politics, many politicians similarly assume that their wish greatly to expand the scope and functions of government has solely moral motives. Here, too, the need to accumulate power at the political center is viewed as merely incidental to wanting a more just society. Yet one might wonder why the desire for moral public policy rarely, if ever, issues in calls for reducing the power of political leaders. So striking is this pattern that it raises the question whether the moralism in question and the wish to expand and centralize power might somehow be integrally connected. Whatever else this moralism might be, is it a subtle way of justifying a desire to rule others?

The purpose of this article is to analyze the "idealism" that has helped transform America and, in particular, to demonstrate that its moral-imaginative dynamic is quite different from its reputation. It would appear that indistinguishable from its ostensible caring for the welfare of others is a desire to direct their lives. Indeed, the deepest source of idealism's appeal may be that it is a sense of moral superiority that implies a right to dominate.

To argue this thesis it will be necessary to revisit points that this author has made in other contexts and to recast, combine, and supplement them for the present purpose.

THE OLD MORALITY AND ITS SOCIAL AND POLITICAL ENTAILMENTS

The traditional Western view of man's moral predicament carried with it a deep ambivalence about power. On the one hand, no political objectives could be achieved without the exercise of power. On the other hand, the prominent lower proclivities of human beings made power potentially dangerous, so that people in political authority had to be subjected to restraint. Both in personal and political life, it was important to foster moderation and a sense of limits. Even the political theory of Thomas Hobbes (1588–1679), which breaks with the

Western tradition with regard to both moral philosophy and the idea of restraints on power, offers a kind of confirmation of an older sense that governments must recognize limits. It never occurs to this advocate of supposedly absolute political rule to extend the sphere of sovereignty beyond matters touching law and order. He is in this respect a kind of forerunner of classical liberalism. In his view of human beings Hobbes rejects much of the older heritage, but in stressing man's wholly egocentrical nature he might be said to advocate a simplified and extreme Augustinianism. Representatives of the dominant modern notion of political morality do not much worry about possible egotism and ruthlessness in people who seem to them to have the right ideals. They tend to place any dark inclinations outside of the supposedly idealistic and hence benevolent politician, place it among those, especially, who oppose the supposedly moral cause. One of the reasons why virtuous politicians are thought to need great power is to be able to overcome the opposition of recalcitrants.

The framers of the US Constitution were acutely aware that the responsible exercise of power had moral preconditions. They feared original sin in themselves as well as others. They hoped that in personal life moral character would restrain the desire for self-aggrandizement, just as in national political life the checks and balances of the US Constitution would contain and domesticate the all-too-human desire for power as an end in itself. Personal self-control and constitutionalism were but different aspects of the need to subdue the voracious ego. Freedom and rule of law required republican virtue. They had to be achieved by the members of society over time through protracted inner and outer moral struggle. Freedom and rule of law could not be bestowed as a gift on a people that had not undertaken any of this work. Constitutionalism could be safeguarded in America only through the continuation of the kind of culture that fostered it.[1]

The Framers assumed that for the Constitution to work its institutions had to be manned by individuals who embodied its spirit of restraint. That spirit stemmed from America's *unwritten* constitution, that is, from the religious, moral, cultural, and social life that had inclined Americans to constitutionalism. To be capable of sustaining the constitutional order those working under its provisions had to be predisposed to virtues like moderation, respect for law, and readiness to compromise. They had to have what this author calls the constitutional personality. The main reason why the US Constitution has become a mere shadow of its old self is that it cannot function as intended without the aforementioned personality traits.[2]

It is important to understand that the moral character that the framers saw as the ultimate protection against arbitrary power and as the source of the constitutional temperament also generated a society of a certain type. Most Americans will vaguely remember that at the heart of Christian morality is the admonition to "love neighbor as thyself." What is commonly forgotten or is not very well understood are the far-reaching social implications of that moral vision. By "neighbor" is meant individuals within the person's own sphere of life, people of flesh and blood with names and faces. We are to treat them as we would like to have them treat us. Note carefully that traditional Christianity does not call upon us to love "mankind" or "humanity," which, by modern, idealistic standards, looks more generous and ambitious. What sounds so nice in modern ears—loving "humanity"—is very different from loving "neighbor" in that its object is not some particular person in the here and now. "Humanity" is highly amorphous and distant. Humanity is not here, in our way, where it might inconvenience us. By the standards of traditional morality, which are down to earth and rather crusty, loving mankind does not engage us where we live. It does not interfere with our ordinary lives and require acts of self-sacrifice. It takes place chiefly in the imagination. For that reason, it does not represent any moral challenge. All it requires is having supposedly noble sentiments, "feeling the pain" of a diffuse suffering collective somewhere far away. The proof to you and others that you are morally noble is that thinking about those who suffer puts a tear in your eye. Moral virtue is not, as for Christianity, charitable action toward particular people up close, but having warm feelings for nobody in particular. Those in trouble are not actually present, making uncomfortable demands. From the point of view of traditional Western morality, the sentimental notion of virtue has little to do with real morality, which is to shoulder responsibility for persons, for "neighbors." That older morality presupposes ability to overcome our native egotism and laziness. It requires strength of character. To be up to the task, the individual must have already learned to moderate his self-indulgence and callousness and to make the needs of others his own. It is because the problems of actual persons are concrete and nearby that loving neighbor can be very demanding. It may take up much of our time and energy. To compound the difficulty, neighbor may not even be likeable. Yet love him we should, not by emoting nobly and walking away, but by taking concrete, perhaps greatly inconvenient action. Without strength of will we may shrink from acting. Loving "mankind" does not require character. It takes place in the imagination and is to that extent morality made comfortable and easy.

People who believe that loving neighbor will give meaning to life will be prone to give their best in settings that are near and intimate—families, neighborhoods, schools, churches, and workplaces. There are many reasons why such groups and associations will be for most people the main sphere of life, but it is crucial to understand that it is here more than elsewhere that traditional morality has its center and primary outlet. Note that in small, intimate associations the person must repeatedly take others into account. There he cannot indulge his native self-indulgence and slothfulness without inviting immediate censure. In families and small groups where relations of mutual dependence are dense and numerous, the person is taught to behave with the well-being of others in mind. You cannot always have your own way. Each member must learn to perform little acts of self-denial. The person is habituated to doing his part, assisting others, and compromising. Character is bred and repeatedly tested. Where life is personal and up-close no one can get away with portraying himself as morally better than he is. Others will be quick to see through mere posturing. Never mind some conceited self-image of being a deeply caring friend of humanity; it is your actions toward real people that reveal who you really are, and they decide your reputation. To the extent that moral character is fostered through life in groups, the will is honed for the responsibilities of the larger society. The more people learn to restrain their lower natures and take others into account, the greater the likelihood that ties of community will be fostered and strengthened.

Traditional Western morality does not assume that people up close will be the only beneficiaries of moral responsibility. It assumes merely that genuine morality will originate in and be nurtured in intimate settings. Thus formed, moral character will have an effect wherever a person directs his attention. Some people will concern themselves with a world far beyond local associations and issues, but they will have learned from life in their groups and communities that what makes for a better society is not some nebulous warm sentiment, but a readiness to act responsibly in and to understand the world as it is, full not least of human weakness.

To be able to understand moral "idealism" and its various entailments it is important to recognize first the social and political ramifications of the rather different traditional ethic just described. The latter generates certain priorities. Love of neighbor is not for exceptional, grandiose circumstances but for the concrete life of the here and now. It shapes and enhances day-to-day relationships. Because it emphasizes that doing right by persons up close is essential to human well-being, it encourages people to give their best within their own groups, neighborhoods, businesses, associations, and local communities. From this understanding of man's higher calling is derived the old principle of subsidiarity, central not least to Roman Catholic social thought, which says that problems should be addressed, as far as possible, by those immediately concerned. Only if people cannot manage on their own should they seek assistance elsewhere, and then, again, as near to themselves as possible. This sense of moral responsibility will let them attain their full stature as human beings. It is not difficult to see that the traditional understanding of morality encouraged and built energetic, strong communities. What people felt that they should handle personally, privately, and locally minimized the need for government. This morality was a powerful decentralizing force.

It was in the 1830s that Alexis de Tocqueville commented at length on the vitality and proliferation of private and local associations in America. Americans had a strong inclination to collaborate and to address their needs within their own groups. De Tocqueville was particularly struck by the active role of members of churches. He noted the great reluctance of Americans to part with any authority over their own lives. Except perhaps for the *prominence* of these observations in *Democracy in America*, they should not be very surprising. Although there was no single reason for these social patterns, it should be easy to see the connection between a highly decentralized, group-oriented society and America's moral roots.

The same moral heritage that fostered cooperation, self-reliance, mutual assistance, self-restraint, modesty, respect for law, and a willingness to compromise helped shape the constitutional personality. These traits formed the mentioned unwritten constitution, which gave life and direction to the written one. Just as the traditional views and habits of Americans made them impose internal checks on themselves, so did they make them willing to accept and respect external legal constraints. Had these personality traits not been strong and widespread, nothing like the US Constitution could have been conceived or made to work.

That the American form of government today bears little resemblance to the constitutional design of 1787 reflects a change in America's unwritten constitution, in the basic self-understanding and priorities of Americans. There can be no question here of attempting a comprehensive summary of what brought about the present state of affairs. The emphasis will have to be on how the change in the understanding of morality and society helped produce a new attitude towards power and government. It is necessary to take account of an aspect of so-called "modernity" that has had profound and far-reaching effects but that is still poorly understood.

IDEALISM: MORALITY RECONCEIVED

Not all strains of modernity are incompatible with the older moral tradition, but special attention needs to be paid to the explicitly stated desire for liberation from earlier beliefs and ways of life that is most commonly called modernity. Two seemingly disparate but intimately connected currents have given that part of modernity its distinctive flavor and dynamic: one is a belief in rational enlightenment; the other is entertaining "idealistic" dreams of human existence transformed. Both currents assume the coming of a new, superior world, an era of liberty, harmony, and general well-being.

Modern idealism follows no single path, but one may discern a central, enduring pattern. The philosopher who gives the clearest and most thorough-going expression to the dream of a new world and who comes closest to being paradigmatic for this idealism is probably Jean-Jacques Rousseau (1712–1778). More than anybody else he inspired the kind of imagination that has, in more or less extreme form, exerted enormous influence in the Western world, first of all in literature, art, philosophy, and religion, but soon also in politics. "Idealism" as a term for the moral-political force that Rousseau helped create should not be confused with the nineteenth century school of German philosophy that is often given the same name.

Rousseau flatly rejects the ancient Western belief that human beings are morally torn between higher and lower potentialities and that they are their own worst enemies. Human beings have nothing to fear from themselves. They are naturally good, but traditional societies pervert and imprison their true nature. The way to a better life is to liberate man's natural goodness from inner and outer restraint. Rousseau dreams himself away from what he considers a dark and intolerable present. He starts the modern theme of estrangement from existing society—alienation, indeed, from all of life as it currently exists. He imagines a long lost idyllic past and a corresponding glorious future. Employing a new form of the imagination, he becomes the great pioneer in the West for envisioning a society wholly different from anything known in history.

The term "imagination" has been carefully defined by this author in other places. Here the context should provide sufficient definition.[3]

Human beings are dreamers. They often dream themselves far away. Capable of imagining something quite different from the present, they are free in a way that animals are not. But this power presents humanity with a big problem. They can use it to imagine and long for what simply cannot be, dream the impossible dream. The dream may become so captivating that they will try to enact it, which may bring disaster upon themselves and others.

A central feature of what used to be known as civilization is not letting human beings escape too far into dreamworld. They need to tether their visions of a better life to what humanity has found to lie in the realm of the possible. Civilization protects people against frivolous dreaming not least through its moral teachings and great works of art and literature, which seek to anchor the imagination in the world in which human beings have to act. More often than not experience in the world of action shows dreams to be mere wishful thinking. Civilization teaches that we cannot have the world just as we would like it. Children dream endlessly of what cannot be, but to mature as a human being means giving up childish things. Adults must face the facts of life, most importantly the limits imposed by man's moral predicament.

Yet in the last 250 years Western men and women became more and more reluctant to accept a world that limits their hopes. They did not want to remain imperfect creatures torn in the depths of their being between high and low, condemned to struggle against dark inclinations in themselves and others. Idealistic dreaming let them set aside the uncomfortable traditional claims about human nature. Leading idealistic artists, philosophers, and politicians nurtured their hope for a marvelous new world, free of the old restrictions.

Just where the imagination crosses over the line from contemplating real possibilities for improvement to dreaming the impossible dream we cannot say for certain ahead of time, but the mature person knows to adjust his aspirations to what historical experience has shown to be unavoidable facts of life. The dreamer of the impossible dream, by contrast, is not willing to let evidence from the world of human practice—the historical world—put a damper on his dreaming. For mature persons, daydreams are never more than momentary departures from life as it is, but for idealists dreams of a radically different, wonderful world are a permanent accompaniment of daily life, a vantage point from which the present can be seen to be all the more disappointing.

Rousseau represents the idealistic imagination in a particularly thoroughgoing form, but in one version or another this kind of dreaminess has continued to reverberate. It may indeed be the dominant moral sensibility of the contemporary Western world.

Rousseau declared that everything was the opposite of how it had seemed. Traditional civilization is not a support for making the best of life. It enslaves the goodness that belonged to man in a pre-civil state of nature. Evil is not in human beings but is due to wicked social norms and institutions. "Man is born free, and everywhere he is in chains." Even the works of culture helped enslave human beings. "The sciences, letters and the arts . . . spread garlands of flowers over the iron chains with which they are burdened."[4]

Returning to the primitive state of natural goodness is neither possible nor desirable, Rousseau averred, but the unimpeded spontaneity of the natural man can be restored in a radically reconstituted society. Doing away with inequality and dependence on others will create virtuous unity. Though Rousseau did not propose returning into the woods, the natural, uninhibited man was for him the standard for revolutionizing society. Rousseau gave a detailed account of the goodness of man in his original state. It is when most unaffected by civilization that men are at their best. To create a new society man must repair to the natural man, the child within, as it were, and make a fresh start.

Rousseau's dreams were greatly pleasing to many in that they seemed to free human beings from the hard, unending work of disciplining dark forces in themselves. He directed the blame for evil away from the individual onto the institutions of existing society. Human beings are the victims of perverse circumstance. But they can make a wonderful new existence for themselves by revolutionizing the social and political exterior. From the perspective of the classical and Christian view of man this is not a story for adults. It flies in the face of human experience. It is an elaborate fantasy. But it enthused Western readers. They *wanted* to believe this dream. How wonderful to be relieved of the never-ending struggle to improve self, to hear that man is already what he should be—that nature made him such! The vision promised a shortcut to fulfillment.

It should be carefully noted that the Rousseauistic dream of a transformed human existence involved from the very beginning an element of conscious or semi-conscious self-deception. It offered a striking example of an imagination of escape. Significantly, Rousseau was not wholly unaware of disregarding actual human experience. He *admitted* to wondering at times if there was not something frivolous and unreal about his own flights of fancy. It was, he said, as if his "heart," his dreamy imagination, did not belong to the same person as his "head," his moments of critical reflection. Yet he could not, *would* not, resist his dream. In the *Second Discourse* he introduced his elaborate survey of the state of nature and the origins of the corrupt civilized society by saying that his account should not be regarded as a historical narrative. He wrote: "Let us . . . begin by putting aside all the facts, for they have no bearing on the question." His "investigations" should not "be taken for historical truths, but only for hypothetical and conditional reasonings."[5] In other words, he asked his readers to follow him into an imaginary history and to find there the true nature of man and the inspiration for remaking society. Countless political activists have engaged in this kind of dreaming and pushed a political agenda of liberation.

It is important to realize that what Rousseau understands as natural and fulfilling is conceived as incompatible with trying to make the best of the historically known world. He does not employ his imagination to help us live to advantage in a world in which man is divided against himself and has to contend with various other impediments. He simply rejects what he considers an unacceptable human existence. He imagines life on wholly different terms. It is not possible here to explore why something that looks to the traditional Christian like a children's tale should have had such deep and enduring appeal. The time must have been ripe in the West for something like romantic escape and revolt. Rousseau offered happiness and enchantment without difficult moral striving. Fulfillment would be a free gift of nature.

It is relevant to the issue of morality and power that Rousseau found in human beings a natural inclination to sympathize with those who suffer. He pioneered a new notion of caring. Charity does not, as in Christianity, develop through character formation but is a spontaneous impulse. For Rousseau, the measure of being a good person is not to exhibit decency in practical conduct, but to have warm feelings, a supposedly benevolent "heart." The new caring takes place not in the world of action, but in the imagination of the caring person. Replacing the traditional understanding of love with teary-eyed sentiment became a powerful trend in Western morality. The new morality was appealing not only in that it did not require an effort of will, but in that it was inherently self-applauding, giving the sympathizing person a nice feeling of nobility.

Dreaming the impossible dream had dramatic social and political consequences. It inspired the French Jacobins and the French Revolution. Later it inspired socialism and communism. Even when modern idealism did not accept the Rousseauistic premise of man's natural goodness, it assumed a sharp contrast between a diseased present and a future of radiant health. Even National Socialism had its dream of a glorious time to come, the thousand-year Reich. In recent decades many have fantasized about global peace and democracy.

Rousseau himself did not much care for Enlightenment rationalism, but idealistic imagination formed in the West an anti-traditional alliance with rationalism. What the two currents had in common was that they rejected the old stress on moral character as the key to a satisfying life. All over the Western world this informal alliance exhibited a "head" that was narrowly technocratic and instrumentalist and a "heart" that was full of dreamy sensibility. The quintessentially modern Westerner combines with sophisticated technical ideas and equipment a sentimental imagination. Politicians of this type feel the pain of suffering collectives and dare to share that they care. They also have elaborate plans for reorganizing society. Their goals are idealistic; their method for enacting them is social engineering. Today the typical idealist espouses a special brand of ecologism and has very ambitious plans for cleaning up the planet. This idealism owes much to the Rousseauistic assumption that civilization has ruined a pure and wholesome nature.

Looking back on what has been said here about modern idealism, it might appear incongruous that, like Rousseau, persons can at the same time be intellectually brilliant and have imaginations that people of an earlier worldview would consider naïve and utopian. Yet nothing seems more common in the modern Western world. Many employ high intelligence to argue that their cherished dreams for remaking the world are wholly plausible. As already mentioned, there is something willful about Rousseauistic dreaming. It would appear that among those who seem most to need to be persuaded are the idealists themselves.

IDEALISM AND THE DESIRE FOR POWER

There is an aspect of idealism that may explain much of its appeal but that is poorly understood: its connection to the subject of power. Whatever else dreaming of this kind accomplishes for the dreamer, it seems to satisfy a desire to feel superior to others. The person who envisages a life far above the humdrum, routinized present is by this very act, in his own eyes, lifted far above those who are caught within that present and who, by definition, lack his fine, elevated sentiments. See how noble and superior I am, the idealist announces to self and others, words being unnecessary. The putatively benevolent dream is, among other things, a form of self-flattery. The one who thinks of self as committed to a better world for others also feels deserving of their praise. He feels entitled, moreover, to directing their lives. The greater the person's imagined caring for mankind, the greater the power to which the person feels entitled to do good for mankind.

This aspect of the idealistic dream is, it can be argued, no marginal component or hidden implication of the dream. The sense of moral superiority and the corresponding sense of entitlement are parts of what makes the dream what it is and recommends it to the dreamer. It is perhaps the most important source of its allure. To get pleasure from the idealistic dream the person does not have to receive the actual adulation of others or exercise power over them in practice. Short of engaging in politics, the person can experience them in the imagination. He can enjoy them viscerally by identifying with the idealistic political movement or with its virtuous leader whose rhetoric and actions confirm the idealist's moral authority and nobility.

To many admirers of modernity, the twentieth century was the most enlightened in human history. It was an era committed to noble ideals—"equality" and "democracy" prominent among them. Yet in that century far more people died at the hands of other human beings than in any previous century. Some of the biggest idealists, championing a vision of universal brotherhood—Lenin, Trotsky, Stalin, Mao—were also among the greatest killers and murderers. They caused enormous suffering. Yet the Western world seems to have learnt very little about idealism from this horrifying experience. Idealists *still* expect, and often receive, admiration for their allegedly noble visions. The *idealism* cannot be blamed for the homicidal mania, idealists tell others. There was nothing wrong with the *ideals*; they are as beautiful as ever. The ruthlessness was the result of practical means somehow getting away from noble ends.

But at this stage of the argument being presented it should be possible to see that there is a connection between the impossible dream and ruthlessness. The problem is not with poorly chosen means but with the impossible dream itself. The dream ignores basic facts of life, specifically the need for moral character. The typical idealistic goals fly in the face of reality. They more or less deliberately *hide* aspects of life that are crucial to any realistic assessment of whether change of a particular kind is desirable or even possible. In particular, the ideals conceal the darker side of human nature, letting it be acknowledged at most among opponents of the dream. To the idealist, issues of character seem trivial or beside the point in comparison with the need to end great social evils and realize great plans. As the champion of a noble cause, the idealistic leader does not need to be shackled. More power to him! The idealistic leader himself sees little need to worry about personal weaknesses of his own, such as an inclination to be ruthless in dealing with opposition. To oppose him is, after all, perverse.

How to explain that in many quarters the view that idealists have of themselves is still considered plausible? People who are not as heavily under the sway of idealism nevertheless sense that to attack its leading representatives is to attack a part of themselves. Idealistic assumptions come up against overwhelming philosophical and historical evidence, but so dependent is the self-worth of millions of people on the purported nobility of the dream that they cannot let it be challenged root and branch. Yet neglecting unwelcome but stubborn and salient facts of human life, as idealists do, is not admirable. Contrary to their reputation, the idealistic goals are not noble and beautiful. They are reprehensible and dangerous. The horrors of the twentieth century were not paradoxical or difficult to explain. In important respects, they emanated directly from a self-deluding, self-applauding moralism and a concomitant dearth of moral character. The brutality of the idealists simply brought the neglect of moral self-control into the open, just as it expressed a hatred of the existing world and a disdain for actual human beings that was contained in the ideal from the beginning. Edmund Burke fully expected violence to flow from the Rousseauistic dreams of the Jacobins.

Irving Babbitt calls Rousseau's imagination "idyllic," and so it is, in part. The term "idyllic" takes note of the fact that from Rousseau's imaginary "nature" all disturbing elements have been removed: life in the state of nature is simple, sunny and pleasant, a kind of vacation from life as known to history. But the term "idyllic" does not convey the potential for inhumanity that is a basic, if often unrecognized, part of this kind of imagination. Imagination of a reality-defying idealistic kind foreshadows and rather predictably calls forth certain dark practical consequences. These are consonant with the back side of the dream, its disgust with what exists. That disgust is part of what *defines* the dream. The apparent benevolence of the dream may to some extent hide its potential for ruthlessness, hide it even from the dreamer, but it surfaces as soon as the dream is brought into contact with the real world, the world of action, where it is bound to encounter opposition. The true believer's predictable response when others fail to yield unquestioningly is coercion. You are either for him or against him. The dreamer of the impossible dream sees no reason to tolerate opposition. In its assumption of moral superiority the dream is uncompromising. It demands monopoly. Those who do not acknowledge the moral authority of the idealist have to suffer his wrath. His reaction to opposition is not unlike that of the egotistical child: he throws a temper tantrum. Sooner or later idealism brings conflict, whether domestic or international. As the idealist tries to make uncooperative reality conform to the dream, the violence expands and intensifies. Through unbending zeal the dreamer tries to persuade even himself of the sacred nature of his vision. To show mercy for or to compromise with opponents would cast doubt on the moral nobility and necessity of the dream and would, in effect, denigrate self. To give up the dream is unthinkable, for it is the idealist's source of personal worth and pride. It alone legitimizes his power.

To capture idealism's potential for merciless brutality a term like "diabolical" is needed. The idyllic aspect of the ideals of the French Revolution was "freedom, equality and brotherhood." Their diabolical aspect, made evident by their practical entailments, was the guillotine.[6]

It should be possible to see that in its pure form the impossible dream expresses and serves, but also veils, unbridled moral conceit. It extends to the dreamer a right to unlimited power. It serves as a great *stimulant* and *justification* for self-aggrandizement. It is incompatible with traditional modesty, self-restraint, and limits on power. The gist of what has been argued so far about idealism is, then, not merely that "ideas have consequences," but that the dream is inherently, from the beginning, consonant with its practical expression.

To sum up on that point, imagining and advocating unattainable goals is from the point of view of traditional morality not admirable, but perverse and dangerous. It distracts human beings from attainable goals and from the need to deal realistically with the chief obstacles to moral well-being, which are in human beings themselves. Idealists who promise a different world are not sweet and well-intentioned. Their dreams reveal bad *motives*. Contrary to their reputation, their souls are not beautiful, but ugly and ignoble. The imagination through which they view the world is wicked and shoddy. Idealists have pulled entire societies into disaster, and they can do so again.

Many people regard the great suffering of the otherwise progressive and enlightened twentieth century as a terrible aberration, perhaps the birth-pangs associated with something glorious coming into being. Surely, mass killings and murder are now a thing of the past. But many people remain greatly susceptible to the lure of political idealism, if not always of the most extreme sort. For example, in the last several decades a powerful political and intellectual movement invested the United States of America with a worldwide mission to spearhead what George W. Bush called a "global democratic revolution." The French Jacobins of the eighteenth century appointed France as the liberator of mankind. The *new* Jacobins appointed America.

It was partly to wean Americans off the traditional fear of unlimited power and the view of life that it implies that the new Jacobins sought to transfer the allegiance of Americans to a *reinvented*, more uninhibited America. They propounded the myth of *America the Virtuous*—the myth of a morally noble America, according to which America should have free rein in transforming the world. The myth provided the moral justification for a great unleashing of power.

Political idealism is no less ravenous for power when applied to domestic politics. There, too, it assumes a monopoly of moral virtue. It feels entitled to mobilizing and directing great power to reshape society.

In America it does not care for a small federal government with checks and balances and does not like to share power with states, counties, and localities, to say nothing of citizens in their private capacities. Whether it considers itself "right" or "left," the imagination of political idealism thrills to the dream of maximum energy in the executive, of a virtuous president who overpowers opposition.

It might be objected that power seeking does not need some kind of idealism to give it energy. Most people are perfectly cynical in their pursuit of power. However true that may be, the will to power can hardly present itself as a desire to rule others for its own sake, especially not at a time when moral sounding motives are expected and there is a need to appeal to democratic majorities. Today that desire routinely wraps itself in idealistic rhetoric. For those in our era who desire expansion and concentration of power idealism is the great enabler. It discovers ever-new reasons for government to act benevolently. The greater the caring for others, the greater the need to place power in the hands of those who care.

If the argument of this article has any validity, it is no coincidence that idealistic benevolence always justifies giving more power to the benevolent—never less. So well does the will to dominate dress itself up in moralistic attire that it may at times deceive even the power-seekers themselves.

IDEALISM VS. CONSTITUTIONALISM

The old American idea of limited, decentralized government was conceived by people who believed that placing restrictions on self and on government and encouraging strong communities was essential to human well-being. Today, an increasingly common and influential human type espouses grandiose political objectives and correspondingly grandiose moral justifications for a desired expansion of power. The title of a book, *An End to Evil*, written several years ago by two enthusiastic advocates of American global supremacy during the glory days of the New Jacobinism, summed up the moral purpose of the desired reign.[7] America should get rid of dictators and other evil people. *An end to evil*—could any goal appeal more to the will to power? The task is surely the very essence of moral nobility, and because it is at once enormous and endless it requires power to match.

A wish to "end" evil would have been rejected out of hand by the old Americans. It betrays an unwillingness to face the human condition. Evil can be to some extent contained—that the Framers of the Constitution did believe—but evil is an inescapable part of human life, hence the great need for character and both internal and external limits on power.

The old Western notion of man's moral and intellectual shortcomings and the accompanying recognition of a need for self-control and humility can be traced back through Christianity to the ancient Greeks. This view of human nature and the political attitudes that it fosters tend to *forestall, censure,* and *defuse* an inordinate desire for power. For that reason, it is not pleasing to the ego that wants to dominate other human beings. Idealism has just the opposite effect. It is a potent *stimulant* for the desire for self-aggrandizement. Today idealism is letting a grasping, "imperialistic" ego throw off the old American constitutional personality and related constitutional restraints. It offers powerful support for the transformation of traditional limited, decentralized American government into a national Superstate.

It might be objected that the idealism described in this article is only an "ideal type" in the Weberian sense and that in real life we seldom encounter it in such pure form. In most people it is diluted or balanced by other factors. Also, this idealism is certainly not the only force to have contributed to the expansion and concentration of power. That many seek political power for the wrong reasons also does not mean that government cannot be a beneficial force. Each of these comments is well-grounded, and they are not contradicted by anything that has been argued in this article. It should perhaps be stated explicitly that, needless to say, there are reasons for wanting to expand the role of government that may have been argued here is not that political idealism, by itself, has caused the transformation of America, although it has exerted great influence. The main purpose has been to draw attention to a major, but poorly understood, factor in the transformation of America (as well as the rest of Western civilization) and to demonstrate the nature of its influence—to show how idealism changes morality and society and the view of power. In order to lay bare the moral-imaginative core of idealism, this article has examined this phenomenon in full flower, as it were, rather than in the practical politics of a particular society where it inevitably blends with or is balanced by other currents.

The effect of idealism in America as elsewhere has been to trivialize and weaken love of neighbor and thus to undermine the support for traditional decentralized political and social structures. At the same time it has helped inspire a vast accumulation and centralization of state power. In proportion as the moral sensibilities of Americans have become idealistic, Americans have come to expect more and more from government and less and less from themselves, their intimate groups, and communities. Not even the idea of the state as parent, which is far advanced in Europe, is without traction in America. To an extent that the Americans described by de Tocqueville would have found hard to fathom, Americans today are willing to rely on a distant central government for their well-being. Idealism has played a key role in undermining the old American distrust of a concentration of power. Wrapping itself in vaguely Christian-sounding rhetoric, idealism has been the Trojan horse for the forces wanting to dismantle traditional American constitutionalism. Most Christian churches, too, have been deeply affected by idealism. To that extent they have gradually abandoned the traditional concern about sin and the need for repentance and adopted a feel-good sentimentalism. As Americans lowered their moral guard, they became increasingly willing to abdicate old responsibilities and local and private autonomy. In practice, if not always in theory, they moved away from the principle of subsidiarity. This has been the case also with many Roman Catholics, whose notion of "social justice" has under the influence of idealism become indistinguishable from that of the centralized and secularized welfare state. Substituting idealism for traditional morality, people were able to persuade themselves that in abdicating personal responsibility they were actually behaving nobly. In fact, the greater their willingness to hand over power to virtuous-sounding leaders and presumed experts, the greater the evidence of having a superior moral sensibility. As government benevolence has replaced traditional morality, people have been freed from sometimes burdensome familial and communal ties and responsibilities and have been spared much inconvenience. Relieved of the need to show character and exercise up-close responsibilities, they can give more attention to their own personal interests and pleasures. Yet by the standard of an *earlier* understanding of man's humanity, their personhood has been greatly diminished.

Though idealism in one form or another has greatly affected all parts of American society, traditional morality is not extinct. It keeps buttressing some old social and political habits and structures. Americans are not of one mind. There is not yet any consensus in favor of the comprehensive, benevolent state. Opposition to it is stronger in America than in Europe. Still, the central power that idealism has done so much to boost is so far-reaching that it would have horrified an earlier type of American. So deeply attracted have Americans become to the idea that a distant central government can be their benign guardian that many of them barely notice or care that the sphere of private, local, and autonomous action is contracting precipitously. In recent decades the centralization and expansion of government has been greatly aided by benevolent-sounding arguments for protecting the American people against threats to its security, specifically terrorism. Already predisposed by idealism to regard federal power as a benign force, Americans have, more or less, invited the creation of an elaborate, massive national security apparatus that employs nothing less than totalitarian methods of surveillance.

Rousseau gave the West the image of the wonderfully natural child, uninfected by civilization. To be natural, men should be more like children. He did not want to consider the evidence that children are at least as prone to egotism and cruelty as adults. In partly unrecognized cooperation with rationalists, Rousseauistic idealists have had much success in overturning the ancient civilization of the West, but they have not rid society of egotism, greed, or the will to power. They have only managed greatly to weaken the old moral, intellectual, cultural, and political restraints placed upon them. They have produced, in abundance, immature, ill-behaved, ignorant, erratic egotists. Rationalist modernity has simultaneously placed sophisticated technology, including military and surveillance equipment, at their disposal.

Many defenders of the old American Constitution seem to think that all that would be needed in order to save the Constitution would be to persuade Americans of the correct interpretation of the framers' intent. These "constitutionalists" live in a world of abstractions, a dream-world of their own. The argument here advanced should have demonstrated that there is only one way to revive American constitutionalism, and that is for Americans, from leaders to people in general, to revive or freshly create something like the older type of morality and to start *living* very differently. Should that not be a likely development, the future of American constitutionalism is bleak.

CONSERVATIVES IN DENIAL

("Conservatives in Denial," *The American Conservative*, November/December 2016.) Genuine conservatism is aptly described as non-ideological. It does not let abstract ideas or romantic dreams stand in the way of realistically sizing up what is and is not possible in given historical circumstances. Although this kind of conservatism may have a strong sense of the general direction in which society ought to move, based on the experience and wisdom of humanity, serving that higher purpose requires an ability to adapt to and make use of actually available circumstances. Especially challenging historical situations call for creativity and even daring, not adherence to preconceived models. Despite the evidence that has accumulated in the last many decades that American society is precipitously declining, many movement conservatives have been markedly unwilling to consider that these new circumstances might require new departures. Their accustomed habits of mind seem to have militated against adjusting to the new uncomfortable challenges. Instead they have repeated their favorite ideas in protest, engaged in wishful thinking, or simply looked away from painful prospects. The fact that in the troubled circumstances of today much conservatism seems to be almost beside the point confirms the weaknesses that have been criticized in this book. For genuine conservatism the first responsibility is always to clear away illusions and abstractions and face up to reality.

When the going gets tough, most people take evasive action. We human beings resist accommodating a reality that might challenge our favorite assumptions and the supposed safety and predictability of our accustomed ways. That we might be poorly adapted to our historical circumstances is a profoundly unappealing possibility.

Most of us are not very flexible or creative to begin with. To take full account of a truly disturbing historical situation is to risk a potentially painful reassessment of basic motives and priorities. Nothing is more uncomfortable than having to question one's moral-spiritual health, to say nothing of having to change oneself.

Evasiveness being a part of life, it is an important task of civilization to counter this misuse of mind and imagination. Conservatives used to pride themselves on being anchored in historical reality and on thus being particularly resistant to illusion. But the reluctance to face facts has become epidemic in America and the Western world, and at present many putative "conservatives" are as prone as others to hiding from troubling historical circumstances.

Just what disturbing facts are being evaded? What human beings avoid the most is the truth about themselves, and it is in large part to keep that truth from surfacing that they look away from—or make light of—potentially disquieting historical circumstances.

The moral-spiritual and cultural roots of our accumulating difficulties have been much discussed. Here, to set the stage for discussing "conservative" forms of escape, a brief list of some of the more obvious symptoms of the crisis of American and Western civilization will illustrate the depth and range of our problems. The phenomena in question are in a way very familiar, but habits of escape keep them from being viewed together and truly registering.

Consider the trends promoted by America's most influential elites—what, using an Aristotelian term, might be called its "regime"—in the centers of finance and politics, the "name" universities, the media, the publishing houses, Hollywood and the entertainment industry, and, to a lesser extent, the churches. This regime—including leaders in many or most of the churches—is hostile to the old Western view of man and society. For example, the universities and "the culture" have virtually abandoned their traditional civilizing function and have become vehicles for self-indulgent desire and trendy, thought-controlling ideology.

In politics, patterns of profound irresponsibility are deeply ingrained. The United States is turning into an oligarchic banana republic pretending to be a democracy. Crony capitalism and unexampled greed are crowding out responsible business. The country is moving fast toward a $20 trillion national debt. States, counties, and municipalities are tottering on the brink of insolvency. The private debt of Americans is astounding. They and their government are routinely spending incredible amounts of money that they do not have. The Federal Reserve and the politicians routinely facilitate this indebtedness and assist in a huge transfer of wealth to those who make money on the indebtedness.

Income inequalities are stark. America's manufacturing base is eroding relative to those of other nations. Its infrastructure is crumbling. Unemployment is said to be back to "normal" levels, but in many places and in parts of the population those levels are staggering. Millions have dropped out of the labor force and are no longer counted among the unemployed. Many young people live with their parents and cannot afford to marry and raise families.

The country has lost control of its borders. In foreign policy the United States keeps intervening in the affairs of distant countries and provoking tensions with major powers. In the Middle East it has made a complete shambles, causing death and suffering of mind-boggling proportions. As for the enormous financial costs of these interventions, they are, like so many other public expenses, put on the nation's credit card.

Europe is in some respects even worse off. There, escapism is, if anything, more rampant. European leaders will not recognize that they and people like them have put their nations on a course of precipitous decline and chronic instability. And yet it should be obvious, for example, that the deeds of terror in places like Paris, Brussels, London, and Madrid are skirmishes or guerilla attacks in a simmering civil war in which sheer criminality, pseudo-religion, and ethnic-cultural tensions are prominent ingredients.

America's instability and conflict look a little different, but the trends of dissolution and fragmentation are the same. Yet simultaneously, the political center is trying to assert quasi-totalitarian control.

These developments are, in a manner of speaking, known to the public at large, and they do, subconsciously at least, bother large portions of the population. But their import for the present and the future does not quite sink in. A kind of somnambulism helps mask what the political, intellectual, and cultural regime has wrought. Even much of the opposition to what is happening evinces escapism and becomes dreamy or faint. To that extent it protects the regime by defusing, confusing, and distracting.

Two putatively conservative forms of opposition exemplify the general phenomenon of denial. Though quite different in appearance, the two are very similar in their practical effects. The one assumes the historical situation to be dark indeed; the other plays down the problems and tries to look on the bright side.

Many Christians are calling for a return to moral and religious basics and for a reinvigoration of family and community life. Nothing would seem to be more appropriate and encouraging or to be more conservative. Are not our problems at bottom moral-spiritual? But here as elsewhere habits of avoidance threaten to turn a sound impulse into self-deluding escape.

It is common for supposedly "traditionalist" Christians to say that the historical situation has become so bad that little can be done to reverse destructive trends. People of faith must resign themselves to retreating into their own separate spheres, to keep the flame alive in their corner of human existence. Has not Christianity always recognized an inevitable tension between faith and the world?

The great appeal of withdrawing from discouraging circumstances is familiar to history. Consider, for example, what Plato thinks of as the posture of philosophers in all but the most propitious circumstances. As the guardians of ideal possibilities, they will in ordinary and therefore dispiriting circumstances hide from the world and "keep themselves unspotted from wickedness and wrong in this life."

Christians of this kind might be referred to as "catacomb" Christians. The term does not describe members of terribly exposed minorities who are trying to escape ruthless persecution, as in Iraq or Syria today. These people are being realistic in their circumstances. The alternative would be martyrdom. For catacomb Christians, however, retreating from trouble is the default position. When does the world not represent a threat? Catacomb Christians flee the world even in anticipation of a dark age. They consider this withdrawal noble, true to the spirit of Christ. Should not a Christian to the greatest extent possible avoid entanglement with a fallen, perverse world?

Two objections immediately come to mind. It might be argued first of all that what is needed in threatening historical circumstances like ours is not a general disposition of retreat from challenges but a spirit of moral-spiritual toughness, a readiness and willingness to take on the world. In our era of flight from reality there is a danger that in practice a supposed return to moral-religious basics will turn into a combination of trepidation and dreaminess.

Secondly, the mainstream of historical Christianity does not regard a general withdrawal from the world as appropriate to the vast majority of humanity, except in the limited, obvious sense that human beings are to be acutely aware of and protect against sin, especially their own.

Almost from the beginning Christianity discerned two separate, though intimately connected and mutually supportive, paths to salvation. Both paths have the same ultimate purpose but involve different commitments with regard to life in this world. Other religions make a similar distinction. There is the special pursuit of holiness for which Jesus himself set the standard. This is the path for those few who feel personally called to take the most direct but also most demanding route to the Kingdom of God—now, before the end of time. To pursue otherworldliness and the peace that passeth all understanding in the most uncompromising manner, they leave to others the obligations and distractions of an ordinary, worldly life—parenting, enterprise, politics, military service—as the disciples did.

This attraction to an unqualified striving for holiness is what gave rise to monasticism and kindred forms of spirituality. For people on this path, certain words of Jesus are felt to be binding in a special, personal, and literal way: "Take no thought for the morrow," "walk the extra mile," "turn the other cheek," and so on. This path entails a moral and spiritual discipline and commitment far more demanding and focused than that of ordinary Christian devotion and responsibility.

The vision of otherworldliness is not irrelevant for parents, business owners, teachers, engineers, politicians, or soldiers, but they understand it from a distance, as it were, and for them it has a much different practical import. For parents, literally to take no thought for the morrow would be the height of irresponsibility. Their children would suffer the consequences of their lightheartedness. For the commander in chief of the US military or for a general to "turn the other cheek" in the face of attack would be to drag those in their charge with them into defeat and subjugation. It is different with the few individuals who have chosen the path of otherworldliness. They can pursue that path wherever it might lead without detriment to anybody else.

Conflating or blending "world-defying" otherworldliness with the proper way to live in this world breaks sharply with the mainstream of Christian thought. Especially in our era of escapism, turning rules that are intended for monks or other *religiosi* into a model for those who are to make the best of this world is to invite dreamy escape from large and acute problems.

But who would criticize a return to moral and spiritual basics, to churches, parenthood, neighborliness, community, localism, and charity—and to the front porch? For decades this author has argued for greater moral-spiritual realism, for a renewed emphasis on character as the center of morality, for shoring up families, local groups, and communities—for their own sake first of all but also because, without such reinvigoration, limited, decentralized government and constitutionalism would disappear.

But at a time of rampant moral-spiritual confusion, stressing the darkness of our age and encouraging believers to retreat into their own little corner of the world is likely to generate escapist idyllic dreaming. To associate a return to religious basics with the life of monks who have "renounced" the world risks creating the wholly misleading appearance that there might be but a small step between living appropriately in the world and pursuing the life of the *religiosi*. It is to suggest the possibility of a moral-spiritual shortcut to otherworldliness. However kindred the two paths may be in their ultimate purpose, they actually involve very different disciplines and roles. Blurring the distinction between them cheapens the notion of otherworldliness and undermines the type of moral-spiritual toughness that life in the mundane world requires.

A romantic, less-than-realistic approach to what needs to be done in the world may, for example, conceal from the believer that the powers that be, including the federal government, may not, or not for long, tolerate religious and communal autonomy. For this reason alone people concerned to return to religious basics must be disposed to engage hostile forces in a concerted and persistent way across a broad front. An idyllicizing notion of otherworldliness induces a shirking of responsibility for worldly matters that urgently need attention.

Realizing the limited reach and efficacy of politics must not become an excuse for a general retreat from the front line of life. Granted, different people must play different roles. Those who have chosen the special witnessing of otherworldliness do, by definition, leave ordinary worldly responsibilities to parents, entrepreneurs, doctors, teachers, politicians, soldiers, scientists, et al., although here and there their roles may overlap with those of people active in the world. Most who lead ordinary lives will, and should, give their best energy in family, church, and local community, but these efforts should be influenced as little as possible by sentimental spirituality. What seems most needed is the virtual opposite: a moral-spiritual toughness capable of taking on our historical predicament. We all have a responsibility—small or great depending on our personal gifts and circumstances—to do what might be done to reverse large, dangerous trends. A wish to stay away from potentially painful, daunting tasks, understandable though it is, aids and abets the destructive forces.

Another type of evasion that might be construed as "conservative" and religious is in appearance the opposite of the one just discussed. Rather than citing the radical perversity of the world as a reason not to engage its dark forces, this kind of escape justifies not confronting them by playing down their perversity. It is a form of whistling past the graveyard. The whistler tells himself that our historical situation is not so bad as it might appear. He knows the great power of the regime and dreads the sharp reaction that real resistance to it would elicit. Who wants to pay the price for openly and more than marginally criticizing the regime—getting a reputation as a troublemaker and extremist, being cut off from funding and preferment? Career considerations and greed combine with fear to produce a sometimes barely conscious pandering to the powers that be.

The whistler convinces himself and others that life is always full of problems and imperfections and that we should not exaggerate our difficulties. He persuades himself that a few minor adjustments or additions would make things pretty much what they ought to be. The edge can be taken off threatening phenomena by relabeling them. Traditional terms like "justice," "virtue," "love," "liberty," "compassion," "community," and "God" can be redefined to accommodate current trends. What could be more constructive and conservative?

So no need to pick an unseemly and personally costly fight with the regime. By politely asking it to make marginal corrections, there is a good chance that you will have bestowed upon you that most coveted of all titles, that of being a "moderate." This is the regime's reward to those who put up harmless opposition.

Hordes of nonthreatening critics surround the regime. They are ubiquitous in journalism, where *Washington Post* columnist Michael Gerson and *New York Times* columnist David Brooks might serve as particularly good examples.

From the point of view of the powers that be, minimizing our problems or looking away from them because they seem overwhelming come in practice to much the same thing. The regime is spared any serious challenge. Conservative opposition of this kind is positively useful to the status quo in that it helps disarm and divert potentially damaging criticism. Cautious, tentative critics can expect to be treated kindly, if condescendingly. Even those with little special ability can expect some scraps from the table. The more gifted among the loyal critics can achieve elevated status and become, for example, quasi-official spokesmen for "conservatism." They become, in all but superficial appearance, integral parts of the regime.

Really to assess and counteract the broad and precipitous decline of our society and civilization requires first of all resistance to sedatives. It demands realism, toughness, energy, and creativity. Such enormous damage has the regime done that even the normally placid and confused general populace is catching on. Despite the air of escapism emanating from the powers that be, popular demands for more than marginal and cosmetic change are growing and intensifying. In both major political parties there is open rebellion.

Members of the regime, including the permanent "Republicrat" government, are reacting to the nascent rebellion with incredulity and indignation. Imagine, questioning their right to rule! People whose careers are intertwined with the existing order lament the extremism and sheer vulgarity of the challenges to the regime. It is as if they did not know that American politics and general culture are already mired in vulgarity and that simplistic, demagogic forms of expression are already dominant in ostensibly respectable media and other public discussion.

But for dissent to adapt to the reality of a corrupt banana republic and democracy and to cleverly employ the methods of the regime against it—why, the temerity of it!

Yet another form of evasiveness that might have been discussed at length is ideology, whether of the right or left. Partly under the influence of the British statesman-thinker Edmund Burke, modern conservatism has taken pride in being anti-ideological: simplistic intellectual abstractions must not stand in the way of grasping and dealing with complex, concrete, historical reality. But in today's America, ideology is one of the most common forms of denial, even on the right. For example, representatives of Conservatism, Inc., rattle off their ready-made "principles," as if historical circumstances did not matter. For the ideologue, solutions to problems are always and everywhere the same—and here they are: 1, 2, 3, 4, and so on down the line. Nevermind the facts on the ground.

To repeat, reality can be hard to take in its unforgiving starkness. People who want to make the best of troubling historical circumstances must shake off tempting illusions and other escape mechanisms and employ all available levers and resources. They must avoid the twin forms of denial: retreat and surrender.

ENDNOTES

Introduction: The Larger Setting of Politics

1 See especially Claes G. Ryn, *Will, Imagination and Reason*, 2nd exp. ed. (New Brunswick: Transaction Publishers, 1997) and *A Common Human Ground,* 2nd. exp. ed. (Columbia: University of Missouri Press, 2019).

Part Two: American Constitutionalism vs. Majoritarian Democracy

1 See Chap. I, herein, pp. 25–26.

2 See Chap. I, herein, p. 22; Chap. III, p. 86; and Chap. VI, pp. 109–1I.

3 John C. Calhoun, *A Disquisition on Government and Selections from the Discourses,* ed. C. Gordon Post (New York: Bobbs-Merrill Co., 1953), 28.

4 Ibid., 38–39.

5 Walter Lippmann, *The Good Society* (New York: Grosset & Dunlap, 1943),346.

6 John Hallowell, *The Moral Foundation of Democracy* (Chicago: The University of Chicago Press, 1954), l08.

7 Edmund Burke, *Reflections on the Revolution in France* (London: Everyman's Library, 1964), 57–58 (emphasis in original).

8 Hallowell, *Moral Foundation of Democracy,* 64.

9 Lippmann, *Good Society,* 347.

10 Calhoun, *Disquisition,* 28 (emphasis in original).

11 According to Paine, wherever a constitution cannot be· produced in a visible form, there is none.... Can then Mr. Burke produce the English Constitution? If he cannot, we may fairly conclude, that though it has been so much talked about, no such thing as a constitution exists, or ever did exist, and consequently that the people have yet a constitution to form." Thomas Paine, *Rights of Man,* ed. Henry Collins (Harmondsworth: Penguin Books, 1971), 93–94. For some contrasting views of the nature of constitutionalism which are closer to my own see, for instance, Charles H. Mcllwain, *Constitutionalism Ancient and Modern* (Ithaca, NY: Cornell University Press, 1966), and Carl J. Friedrich, *Constitutional Government and Democracy* (Waltham, MA: Blaisdell Publishing Co., 1968).

Part Two: Constitutional and Plebiscitary Democracy Incompatible

1 Thomas Jefferson, *The Life and Selected Writings of Thomas Jefferson,* ed. Adrienne Koch and William Peden (New York: Modern Library, 1944), 492, 670, 324.

2 Ibid., 669, 670

3 Ibid., 671. I am relying in this paragraph primarily on Jefferson's illuminating letter to John Taylor of May 28, 1816.

4 Ibid., 413.

5 "On the basis of sensation, of matter in motion, we may erect the fabric of all the certainties we can have or need." Ibid., 700. Jefferson's thinking in this as in many other respects is influenced by John Locke.

6 Ibid., 638.

7 Ibid., 322.

8 James MacGregor Burns, *The Deadlock of Democracy* (Englewood Cliffs, NJ: Prentice-Hall, 1963), 323, 334–35, 341.

9 James MacGregor Burns, *Uncommon Sense* (New York: Harper & Row, 1972), 129,173.

10 Burns, *Deadlock of Democracy*, 338, 339–40.

11 Burns, *Uncommon Sense,* 175

12 Willmoore Kendall writes, for instance: "Since Burns and his friends *cannot* win under the existing rules, he asks us to change the rules so that he and his friends *can* win." *Contra Mundum,* ed. Nellie D. Kendall (New Rochelle, NY: Arlington House, 1971), 273 (emphasis in original).

13 Burns, *Uncommon Sense,* 173.

14 Cf. James Burnham, *Congress and the American Tradition* (Chicago: Henry Regnery Co., 1965), especially Chap. 25. See also Peter Viereck, *The Unadjusted Man* (Westport, CT: Greenwood Press, 1973), Chap. 15.

15 See, for example, Reinhold Niebuhr, *Moral Man and Immoral Society* (New York: Charles Scribner's Sons, 1960), Hans Morgenthau, *Politics Among Nations* (New York: Alfred A. Knopf, 1959), and Raymond Aron, *Peace and War* (New York: Praeger, 1967).

16 Nisbet's position is summarized in *Community and Power* (New York: OxfordUniversity Press, 1962).

17 Robert Dahl, *After the Revolution?* (New Haven, CT: Yale University Press, 1970), 102.

18 See Dahl, *After the Revolution?* and Peter Bachrach, *The Theory of Democratic Elitism* (Boston: Little, Brown and Company, 1967).

19 Dahl, *After the Revolution?*, 88–98.

20 Irving Babbitt, *Democracy and Leadership* (New York: Houghton Mifflin Co., 1924).

Part Two: The Written and Unwritten Constitution

1 Jean-Jacques Rousseau, *The Social Contract* (Harmondsworth, 1970), Bk. II, Ch. 3, 73. Rousseau's political philosophy is analyzed in depth with special attention to its ethical import and contrasted with American constitutionalism in Claes G. Ryn, *Democracy and the Ethical Life*, 2nd expanded ed. (Washington, DC, 1990).

2 The term "autonomous group" is used by Robert Nisbet. See, in particular, *The Quest for Community* (San Francisco, 1990), which explains the humane significance of life in small and independent associations.

3 See, for example, Alexis de Tocqueville, *Democracy in America* (New Rochelle, NY, undated), Vol. 1, 177.

4 The historical nature of philosophy is perhaps nowhere better demonstrated than in the work of the Italian philosopher Benedetto Croce (1866–1952). His most famous and central books, *Aesthetic* (1902), *Logic* (1908), and *The Philosophy of the Practical* (1908), present a mature and lucid, though not flawless, version of German idealism. Crocean ideas are revised and developed and incorporated into a reconstituted epistemology of the humanities and social sciences in Claes G. Ryn, *Will, Imagination and Reason* (Chicago and Washington, DC, 1986).

5 For an extensive discussion of the relationship of universality and particularity, see Ryn, *Will*. The sense in which philosophical abstractionism is "fundamentalistic" is explained in Ch. 7.

6 The relationship between moral abstractionism, as found, for example, among disciples of the late Leo Strauss, and currents of moralistic utopian ideology is explained in Claes G. Ryn, *The New Jacobinism: Can Democracy Survive?* (Washington, DC, 1991). Abstract universalism of the "Straussian" kind is no less questionable when its advocates think they are presenting it for "popular" consumption but hiding their real, putatively Nietzschean beliefs. Suggestions of "secret writing" simply claim credit for philosophical ambivalence and incoherence.

7 Hamilton, Madison, Jay, *The Federalist Papers*, ed. Clinton Rossiter (New York, 1961), No. 37 (Madison), 230.

Part Three: After a Quarter Century: Wither American Intellectual Conservatism

1 Letter from Burke to Earl Fitzwilliam, Nov. 29, 1793, quoted in Russell Kirk, *Edmund Burke: A Genius Reconsidered* (New Rochelle, NY: Arlington House, 1967), p. 128.

2 Babbitt develops aspects of this distinction in all of his several books. See, in particular, *Rousseau and Romanticism* (Austin: The University of Texas Press, 1978), and *Democracy and Leadership* (Indianapolis: Liberty Classics, 1979).

3 This argument is developed in my *Democracy and the Ethical Life* (Baton Rouge: Louisiana State University Press, 1978), esp. ch. XI.

4 See Lester J. Cappon, ed., *Adams-Jefferson Letters*, Vol. II (Chapel Hill: University of North Carolina Press, 1959).

5 Early examples of this theme are found in *The Conservative Mind* (Chicago: Henry Regnery, 1953) and *A Program for Conservatives* (Chicago: Henry Regnery, 1954) where Kirk assesses the doctrines of von Mises and Hayek.

6 Roepke's social and economic thought is well represented by his *A Humane Economy* (Indianapolis, IN: Liberty Fund, 1971).

7 This is also the title of one of Kirk's books, *Beyond the Dreams of Avarice* (Chicago: Henry Regnery, 1956).

8 See Robert Nisbet, *The Quest for Community* (New York: Oxford University Press, 1953).

9 The idea of a value-centered historicism is developed in my "History and the Moral Order," in Francis J. Canavan, ed., *The Ethical Dimension of Political Life* (Durham, NC: Duke University Press, 1982).

10 Leo Strauss's interpretation of Burke in *Natural Right and History* (Chicago: Chicago University Press, 1953), which portrays him as largely a precursor of historical relativism, is hardly on par with Strauss's best scholarly efforts. A partial corrective is Peter Stanlis's *Edmund Burke and the Natural Law* (Ann Arbor: The University of Michigan Press, 1958). However, Stanlis leaves mostly unexplored that important dimension of Burke which transcends the tradition of natural law.

11 The subject of the imagination is treated throughout the work of Kirk and Viereck. See, for example, Kirk's *Enemies of the Permanent Things* (New Rochelle, NY: Arlington House, 1969), Part Two, and Viereck's *The Unadjusted Man* (Westport, CT: Greenwood Press, 1973), Part Five.

12 Babbitt, *Democracy and Leadership*, pp. 127–28.

13 Of course, the poets also need and are influenced by the philosophers. Concepts are absorbed into but transfigured by intuition. See, John Dewey, *Essays in Experimental Logic* (Chicago: University of Chicago Press, 1916), p. 17; and *The Quest for Certainty* (New York: Minton, Balch and Co., 1929), p. 167 ff.

14 See Babbitt, *Rousseau and Romanticism*.

15 Kirk, *Edmund Burke*, p. 173. Perhaps it needs to be said: it is not implied in this illustration that President Nixon is blameless.

16 The problem of epistemology in its ethical, aesthetical, and logical dimensions is treated in depth in Claes G. Ryn, *Will, Imagination and Reason: Irving Babbitt and Benedetto Croce* (Chicago: Regnery Books, 1986).

17 Croce is still under the influence of Hegel's monism but he has valid logical and other insights which can be extracted from this questionable setting. See Croce, *Logic* (London: Macmillan, 1917). For a treatment of the problem of knowledge which is informed by elements of historicism but which is far removed from the doctrine of positivism, see my "Knowledge and History," *Journal of Politics*, May 1982.

Part Three: The Ideology of American Empire

1 Remarks, National Cathedral, Sept. 14, 2002, www.whitehouse.gov/news/releases/2001/09.

2 Statement to the US Congress, June 18, 2002, www.whitehouse.gov/news/releases/2002/06.

3 Jean-Jacques Rousseau, *The Basic Political Writings* (Indianapolis: Hackett, 1987), *Social Contract*, Bk. I, Ch. I, p. 141.

4 Allan Bloom, *The Closing of the American Mind* (New York: Simon and Schuster, 1987), p. 153.

5 James David Barber, " . . . And Democracy Needs Help," *Washington Post*, Jan. 25, 1990.

6 William Kristol and David Brooks, "What Ails Conservatism," *Wall Street Journal*, Sept. 15, 1997.

7 Robert Kagan, "The U.S.-Europe Divide," *Washington Post*, May 26, 2002.

8 Kristol and Brooks, "What Ails," Sept. 15, 1997.

9 Ben Wattenberg, "Chance to Champion Freedom," *Washington Times*, Dec. 1, 1988.

10 Ibid.; "Showdown Time . . . Wake-up Slap," Aug. 8, 1990; and "To Sow Seeds of Freedom," Aug. 1, 1990 (emphasis added).

11 Ben Wattenberg, "Peddling 'Son of Manifest Destiny,'" *Washington Times*, Mar. 21, 1990.

12 Charles Krauthammer, "Bless Our Pax Americana," *Washington Post*, Mar. 22, 1991.

13 Michael Novak, "Human Rights at Christmas," *Washington Times*, Dec. 23, 1988.

14 Irving Babbitt, *Democracy and Leadership* (Indianapolis: Liberty Fund, 1979 [1924]), pp. 337, 295. It is a national misfortune that Americans have paid less attention to one of their truly great thinkers than to a number of lesser European lights who impress by their denser, more technical, less essayistic philosophical style.

15 Woodrow Wilson, Thanksgiving Proclamation, Nov. 7, 1917, *The Papers of Woodrow Wilson*, Arthur S. Link, et al. (Princeton, NJ: Princeton University Press, 1966–93), pp. 44, 525; and Address at Independence Hall, Philadelphia, *Papers*, pp. 30, 254. For an in-depth study of Woodrow Wilson and his notion of America as servant of mankind, see Richard M. Gamble, "Savior Nation: Woodrow Wilson and the Gospel of Service," *Humanitas*, Vol. XIV, No. 1 (2001).

16 Babbitt, *Democracy*, p. 314.

17 Secretary of State James A. Baker, speech to the Aspen Institute in Berlin, Germany, June 18, 1991.
18 Patrick E. Tyler, " U.S. Strategy Plan Calls for Insuring No Rivals Develop," *New York Times*, Mar. 8, 1992.
19 *Wall Street Journal*, lead editorial, Mar. 16, 1992.
20 *Washington Post*, Jan. 9, 1993. The designation "neoconservative" for the mentioned individuals is taken from this article.
21 Remarks of President to United Brotherhood of Carpenters and Joiners of America 2002 Legislative Conference, June 19, 2002, www.whitehouse.gov/news/releases/2002/06; Peter Slevin, " The Word at the White House: Bush Formulates His Brand of Foreign Policy," *Washington Post*, June 23, 2002.
22 Remarks of President to West Point Commencement, June 1, 2002, www.whitehouse.gov/news/releases/2002/06. The same kind of imagery had been used by General George C. Marshall at the Commencement exercises in 1942, and the president began his speech by quoting Marshall, who had expressed the hope that "our flag will be recognized throughout the world as a symbol of freedom on the one hand, and of overwhelming power on the other."
23 Remarks, National Cathedral, Sept. 14, 2001.
24 Robert Kagan, "We Must Fight this War," *Washington Post*, Sept. 12, 2001.
25 Statement of three of the codirectors of Empower America, Sept. 12, 2001.
26 Charles Krauthammer, " Peace Through Democracy," *Washington Post*, June 28, 2002.
27 Midge Decter, "Unnecessary Wars," *Imprimis*, Sept. 2002, p. 5.
28 National Security Strategy of the United States of America, Sept. 17, 2002, http:// www.whitehouse.gov/nsc/nss.html, and Karen DeYoung and Mike Allen, "Bush Shifts Strategy From Deterrence to Dominance," *Washington Post*, Sept. 21, 2002.
29 "Six Degrees of Preemption," *Washington Post*, Outlook section, Sept. 29, 2002.
30 Richard C. Holbrooke, "It Did Not Have to Be This Way," *Washington Post*, Feb. 23, 2003.
31 Remarks by President George W. Bush, in taped interview with Bob Woodward, *Washington Post*, Nov. 19, 2002; excerpted from Woodward, *Bush at War* (New York: Simon and Schuster, 2002).
32 Address to Congress, Sept. 20, 2001.

Part Three: Jacobin Capitalism

1 Karl Marx and Friedrich Engels, *The Communist Manifesto* (Harmondsworth: Penguin Books, 1974), 84.
2 Joseph Schumpeter, *Capitalism, Socialism, and Democracy* (New York: Harper, 1950; first published in 1942), 73. The book exudes a melancholy pessimism about the future of capitalism. For examples of official Roman Catholic concern about the dangers of capitalism before the Church became heavily influenced by a socialist view of capitalism, see the papal encyclicals *Rerum Novarum* (1891) and *Quadragesimo Anno* (1931).
3 Wilhelm Röpke, *A Humane Economy* (Wilmington, DE: Intercollegiate Studies Institute, 1998), 35. See also, Röpke, *The Moral Foundations of Civil Society* (New Brunswick, NJ: Transaction Publishers, 1996).
4 Röpke, *Economy*, 125. For a brief but philosophically lucid and incisive discussion of the relationship between ethics and economics, see Joseph Baldacchino, *Economics and the Moral Order* (Washington, DC: National Humanities Institute, 1985).

Part Three: Decent Into Bankruptcy

1 For a sampling of the author's criticisms, see "American Intellectual Conservatism: Needs, Opportunities, Prospects," *Modern Age*, Vol. 26,Nos. 3-4 (1982); *The New Jacobinism* (Washington, DC: National Humanities Institute, 1991); "HowConservatives Failed 'The Culture,'" *Modern Age*, Vol. 38, No. 2 (1996); *America the Virtuous* (NewBrunswick and London: Transaction Publishers, 2003); and "The Decline of American IntellectualConservatism," presented as the "Conclusion" tothe fiftieth anniversary issue of *Modern Age*, Vol. 49, No. 4 (2007).

2 Edmund Burke, *A Letter from Mr. Burke, to a Member of the National Assembly in Answer to Some Objections to His Book on French Affairs*, 1791.

3 John Locke, *Second Treatise of Government*, paragraph 61 (Indianapolis and Cambridge: Hackett Publishing Company, 1980), 34.

4 President Ronald Reagan, Remarks at the Annual Washington Conference of the American Legion, February 22, 1983; Remarks at Flag DayCeremony, Baltimore, MD, June 14, 1985.

5 President Ronald Reagan, Remarks and a Question and Answer Session With the Studentsand Faculty at Moscow State University, May 31, 1988.

Part Three: Anti-Historical "Conservatism"

1 Claes G. Ryn, "Universality or Uniformity?," *Modern Age*, Vol. 32, No. 1 (1988).

2 On Rousseau's seminal contributions to totalitarianism, see, for example, J. L. Talmon, *The Origins of Totalitarian Democracy* (New York: Praeger, 1960). On the incompatibility of Rousseau's notion of democracy with American constitutional republicanism, see Claes G. Ryn, *Democracy and the Ethical Life*, 2nd rev. exp. ed. (Washington, DC: The Catholic University of America Press, 1990).

3 Harry V. Jaffa, "Equality as a Conservative Principle," in William F. Buckley, Jr., and Charles R. Kesler, eds. *Keeping the Tablets: Modern American Conservative Thought* (New York: Harper and Row, 1988), 86.

4 Allan Bloom, *The Closing of the American Mind* (New York: Simon and Schuster, 1987), 158.

5 For a historically based examination of the frame of mind that made the American colonists favor separation from England, see Joseph Baldacchino, "The Unraveling of American Constitutionalism: From Customary Law to Permanent Innovation," *Humanitas*, Vol. XVIII, Nos. 1 & 2 (2005), http://www.nhinet.org/baldacchino18-1&2.pdf.

6 Allan Bloom, " Interpretive Essay," in *The Republic of Plato*, Transl., with Notes and an Interpretive Essay, by Allan Bloom (New York: Basic Books, 1968), 421.

7 Leo Strauss, *Natural Right and History* (Chicago: University of Chicago Press, 1953), 13–14 (emphasis added).

8 Joseph Cropsey, *Political Philosophy and the Issues of Politics* (Chicago: University of Chicago Press, 1980), 117–18 (emphasis added in the first quotation).

9 Bloom, *Closing*, 253.

10 See Thomas Aquinas, *Treatise on Law*, esp. Qu. 97.

11 Edmund Burke, *Reflections on the Revolution in France* (Indianapolis: Hackett, 1987), 76.

12 For an in-depth philosophical discussion of the possible synthesis of universality and particularity, as conceived in a "value-centered historicism," and for a discussion of the weakness and danger of abstract conceptions of universality, see Claes G. Ryn, *A Common Human Ground: Universality and Particularity in a Multicultural World* (Columbia and London: The University of Missouri Press, 2003).

13 Strauss, *Natural Right*, 323.

Part Four: How Conservatives Failed "The Culture"

1 For a trenchant discussion of different meanings of the term "ideology" and of how to distinguish between acceptable and unacceptable forms, see Joseph Baldacchino, "Babbitt and the Question of Ideology," in George A. Panichas and Claes G. Ryn, eds., *Irving Babbitt in Our Time* (Washington, DC, 1986).

2 It is common, not least among professed religious believers, to view power as inherently subversive of morality, but one must question a form of moralism or spirituality that always casts aspersions on asserting the will in this world. A good, if not sufficient, antidote to dubious "otherworldliness" or "mysticism" is Benedetto Croce, *The Philosophy of the Practical* (New York, 1967). Unfortunately, the available English translation of this work is far from flawless.

3 The most penetrating analysis of Rousseau's imagination and the nature of its influence remains Irving Babbitt, *Rousseau and Romanticism* (New Brunswick, 1991). For an analysis of some of the political effects of Rousseauistic "virtue," see Claes G. Ryn, *The New Jacobinism: Can Democracy Survive?* (Washington, DC, 1991).

4 For a systematic and more technically philosophical discussion of the role of thought and imagination, and their relation to morality, see Claes G. Ryn, *Will, Imagination and Reason* (Chicago and Washington, 1986).

5 A dozen works from the early to the mid 1950s by the two authors set forth the view that sound ideas and culture must prepare the ground for healthy social and political change. These books include Russell Kirk's well-known *The Conservative Mind* (Chicago and Washington, DC, 7th. rev. ed. 1986; first published in 1953), the lesser known *Academic Freedom* (Chicago: Henry Regnery Company, 1955) and *Beyond the Dreams of Avarice* (Chicago, 1956), Peter Viereck's *Shame and Glory of the Intellectuals* (New York, 1965; first published in 1953), *Dream and Responsibility* (Washington, DC, 1953) and *The Unadjusted Man* (Westport, CN, 1973; first published in 1956).

6 Babbitt diagnoses the moral and cultural crisis of the West and suggests remedies in *Literature and the American College* (Washington, DC., 1986; first published in 1908). *Rousseau and Romanticism* explores the moral-imaginative dynamic that has tended to replace classical and Christian views of life in the Western world. *Democracy and Leadership* (Indianapolis, 1979; first published in 1924) examines the relationship between politics and ethical and aesthetical developments. For a collection of representative essays that spans Babbitt's wide range of interests, see *Character and Culture: Essays on East and West* (New Brunswick, NJ, 1995; first published posthumously in 1940).

7 Meyer's review of Viereck's book appeared in *National Review*, August 11, 1956. Called "Counterfeit at a Popular Price, it was reprinted in Frank S. Meyer, *The Conservative Mainstream* (New Rochelle, NY: [Arlington House], 1969), 67–70.

8 It would be wholly misguided, Kirk wrote of Buckley's proposals, to have trustees and alumni conduct "a rigid surveillance of all professors' work in the lecture room," which would create a climate of academic "servility." Kirk, *Academic Freedom*, 125–26.

9 Viereck, *Shame and Glory*, 248.

10 For a discussion of the Jacobin flavor of much contemporary political thought, see Ryn, *New Jacobinism.*

11 For a number of differing views of *The Closing of the American Mind*, including that of the present author, see the symposium on the book in *Modern Age*, Vol. 32, No. 1 (1988). *This article appears in modified form in the Winter 1996 issue of *Modern Age.* The passages within brackets were deleted by the publisher.

Part Four: Peter Viereck and Conservatism

1 For a discussion of Peter Viereck's poetry, see Marie Hénault, *Peter Viereck* (New Haven, CT: College & University Press, 1969) and Michael Weinstein, "Peter Viereck: Reconciliation and Beyond," *Humanitas*, Vol. X, No. 2 (1997). Weinstein's article accompanies a poem by Peter Viereck, "Gate Talk for Brodsky," in the same issue of *Humanitas,* which Viereck completed when he was eighty years old and predicted would be his last major poem. It deals with life and death and the ultimate things. It rounds out and extends themes from six decades as poet. For a philosophically ambitious and highly illuminating study of how Viereck's poetry relates to his prose writings and more generally of his view of the imaginative cultural origins of politics. See Jay Patrick Starliper *Aesthetic Origins: Peter Viereck and the Imaginative Sources of Politics* (New York: Routledge, 2014).

2 Peter Viereck, *Conservatism Revisited* (rev. and enlarged ed.; New York: The Free Press, 1962; first published in 1949), p. 49. (Hereinafter cited as *Revisited.*)

3 Frank S. Meyer in *National Review,* August 11, 1956. Reprinted in Meyer, *The Conservative Mainstream* (New Rochelle, NY: Arlington House, 1969), pp. 67–70.

4 Editorial note by "C.E.L." in *Modern Age*, Vol. 4, No. 3 (Summer 1960), p. 228. The article by Viereck in the same issue is "The Crack-Up of American Optimism: Vachel Lindsay, Dante of the Fundamentalists."

5 A huge and growing number of books analyze and evaluate various aspects of American intellectual conservatism. Among the earliest, written closer to the time of Viereck's greatest influence, are George Nash. *The Conservative Intellectual Movement in America* (New York: Basic Books, 1976), Noel O'Sullivan, *Conservatism* (New York: St. Martin's Press, 1976), Ronald Lora, *Conservative Minds in America* (Chicago: Rand McNally, 1971) and, in Swedish, Claes G. Ryn and Bertil Häggman, *Nykonservatismen i USA* (Stockholm: Almqvist & Wiksell, 1971), the first comprehensive study of American intellectual conservatism published anywhere.

6 *Revisited*, p. 136. Reprinted also in Peter Viereck, *The Shame and Glory of the Intellectuals* (rev. and enlarged ed.; New York: Capricorn Books, 1965; first published in 1953), p. 314. (Hereinafter cited as *Shame and Glory.*)

7 *Shame and Glory*, p. 12.

8 Ibid., p 248.

9 Peter Viereck, *Dream and Responsibility* (Washington, DC: The University Press of Washington, DC, 1953), p. 43. Cf. Benedetto Croce, *History as the Story of Liberty* (Indianapolis: Liberty Fund, 2000; first published in Italian in 1938).

10 *Revisited*, p. 32.

11 *Shame and Glory,* p. 45.

12 Ibid., p. 46.

13 *Revisited*, p. 45.

14 *Shame and Glory*, p. 46.

15 *Revisited*, p. 35.

16 Ibid., p. 33.

17 Quoted in *Revisited*, p. 34.

18 Ibid., p. 32.

19 Peter Viereck, *The Unadjusted Man* (Westport, CT: Greenwood Press, 1973; reprint of the 1956 original). p 279.

20 Ibid., p. 332.

21 Ibid., p. 282.

22 Ibid., p. 285.
23 *Dream and Responsibility*, p.22.
24 *Unadjusted Man*, p. 273.
25 For an in-depth analysis, critical assessment and development of Babbitt's aesthetics, see Claes G. Ryn, *Will, Imagination and Reason: Babbitt, Croce and the Problem of Reality*, with a Major New Introduction by the author (New Brunswick, NJ and London: Transaction Publishers, 1997; first published in 1986) (hereinafter cited as *Will*), which incorporates a synthesis of the work of Babbitt and Benedetto Croce into an epistemology for the humanities, including philosophy itself. For a perceptive and penetrating study of Edmund Burke's use and understanding of the imagination, see William F. Byrne, "Edmund Burke's 'Moral Imagination' and the Problem of Political Order," unpublished doctoral dissertation, The Catholic University of America, 2003
26 One example of a poor understanding of aesthetics and of unfamiliarity with the possibility of synthesis is the common but wholly inadequate interpretation of Burke according to which he is a historical relativist, an "historicist." A prime example of such misunderstanding is Leo Strauss, *Natural Right and History* (Chicago: The University of Chicago Press, 1953), whose treatment of Burke combines philosophical inadequacy with scholarly carelessness. See here Joseph Baldacchino, Jr., "The Value-Centered Historicism of Edmund Burke," *Modern Age*, Vol. 27, No. 2 (Spring 1983), which offers a compelling interpretation of Burke and lays bare Strauss's misunderstanding and scholarly lapses.
27 Quoted in *Revisited*, p. 34.
28 *Unadjusted Man*, p. 21.
29 Peter Viereck, "Inner Liberty," (Wallingford, PA: Pendle Hill Pamphlet, 1957), p. 21. Much of the text of this pamphlet appears also in *Unadjusted Man*.
30 *Unadjusted Man, p.* 332.
31 The notion that human life is constituted by four different categories of activity is developed in the extensive work of Benedetto Croce. For an explication and critical discussion of his philosophy, see Ryn, *Will*. See also Claes G. Ryn, *A Common Human Ground: Universality and Particularity in a Multicultural World* Columbia and (London: University of Missouri Press, 2003), which argues that the higher development of life involves synthesis between universality and particularity and that there is a special way of cultivating particularity that is not only compatible with but necessary for a deeper union among individuals, peoples and civilizations.
32 There is considerable continuity between the New Left and counterculture of the 1960s and 70s and more recent postmodernist attacks on order and structure. Much of the romanticism of these movements bears a strong resemblance to the romanticism of Jean-Jacques Rousseau. For an analysis of romantic leftism in the late 1960s and early 1970s, see Claes G. Ryn, "Youthful Dissent: Community and Counter-culture" *The Intercollegiate Review*, Vol. 9, No. 3 (Summer 1974).
33 *Unadjusted Man* p. 298.
34 *Shame and Glory*, p. 58.
35 *Unadjusted Man*, p. 299.
36 Ibid., p. 296.
37 *Shame and Glory*, p. 45.
38 The most impressive contribution to the development of a logic appropriate to the study of humanity is that of Benedetto Croce, who substantially revises Hegel. See, especially, Croce's *Logic as the Science of the Pure Concept* (London: Macmillan, 1917; first published in Italian in 1908). Croce's logic, as extracted from some of its questionable assumptions and combined with elements of ethics and aesthetics, is incorporated into a theory of knowledge and reality in Ryn, *Will*. For a clear and

succinct summary of Croce's logic, see Folke Leander's small study of Paul Elmer More's central philosophical concept, *The Inner Check* (London: Edward Wright, 1974), which, unfortunately, was never properly distributed.

39 See, for example, Clinton Rossiter, *Conservatism in America* (New York: Vintage Books, 1962), p. 223.

40 Peter Viereck. *Metapolitics: The Roots of the Nazi Mind* (Rev. and enlarged ed.; New York: Capricorn Books, 1965; first published in 1941), p. 5.

41 Ibid., p. 8.

42 Ibid., p. 9.

43 Ibid., p. 19.

44 Ibid., p. 142.

45 Ibid., p. 107.

46 Ibid., p. 122.

47 Ibid., p. 123.

48 Ibid., p. 309.

49 For an in-depth examination of the role of the imagination and its opposed potentialities, see Ryn, *Will*, which demonstrates the possibility of higher as well as lower forms of romanticism.

50 Ibid., p. iii.

51 *Unadjusted Man*, p. 131. Viereck here builds upon Babbitt, especially his *Democracy and Leadership* (Indianapolis: Liberty Classics, 1979; first published in 1924). (Hereinafter cited as *Democracy*).

52 Ibid., p. 136.

53 Ibid., p. 142.

54 Ibid., p. 145.

55 *Shame and Glory*, p. 220.

56 *Unadjusted Man*, p. 146.

57 Ibid., p. 148.

58 For a distinction similar to Viereck's, though developed in greater depth and with special attention to its ethical-philosophical implications, see Claes G. Ryn, *Democracy* and *the Ethical Life* (2nd ed., exp; Washington, DC: The Catholic University of America Press, 1990; first published in 1978). The book contrasts the ideas of Jean-Jacques Rousseau with those of the framers of the US Constitution.

59 *Revisited*, p. 32.

60 Ibid., p. 38.

61 *Shame and Glory*, p. 221.

62 Ibid., p. 14.

63 Ibid.

64 Ibid., p. 15.

65 Ibid., p. 68.

66 Ibid., p. 18.

67 Ibid., p. 109.

68 Ibid., p. 52.

69 Ibid., p. 58.

70 Ibid., p. 271.

71 Ibid., pp. 306–7.

72 Ibid., p. 307.

73 Ibid., p. 302.

74 Ibid., p. 132.
75 Ibid., p. 365.
76 Ibid., New Preface to the 1965 edition, xiv. See also the added section on foreign policy, pp. 326–30.
77 Ibid., p. 207.
78 *Revisited*, p. 87.
79 Peter Viereck, *Conservatism From John Adams to Churchill* (New York: D. Van Nostrand Co., 1956), p. 44.
80 Ibid., p. 47.
81 *Unadjusted Man*, p. 235.
82 *Shame and Glory*, p. 269.
83 *Unadjusted Man*, p. 236.
84 *Revisited*, p. 155.
85 *Unadjusted Man*, p.248.
86 Ibid., p. 247.
87 *Shame and Glory*, p. 252.
88 Ibid., p. 254.
89 Ibid., p. 253.
90 *Unadjusted Man*, pp. 236–7.
91 *Revisited*, p. 39.
92 Cf. Wilhelm Röpke. *A Humane Economy* (Indianapolis: Liberty Fund, 1971)
93 *Shame and Glory*, p. 122.
94 *Unadjusted Man*, p. 319.
95 Ibid., p. 321.
96 *Shame and Glory*, p. 61.
97 Ibid., p. 294.
98 Ibid., p. 295.
99 Ibid., p. 301.
100 Ibid., p. 203 n.
101 Quoted in *Revisited*, p. 140.
102 Ibid., p. 141
103 Ibid., p. 140.
104 Ibid., p. 150.
105 Ibid., p. 145.
106 *Shame and Glory*, p. 58.
107 *Revisited*, p. 124, p. 150.
108 Ibid., p. 126.
109 Ibid., p. 125.
110 Ibid., p. 126.
111 Ibid., p. 143.
112 Ibid., p. 144.
113 Ibid., p. 140.
114 Ibid., p. 136.
115 Ibid., p. 151.
116 Ibid., p. 140.
117 *Unadjusted Man*, p. 168.
118 *Shame and Glory*, p. 517.

119 *Unadjusted Man*, p. 168.

120 Ibid., p. 171.

121 Daniel Bell, ed., *The Radical Right* (Garden City, NY: Doubleday, 1963; first published in 1955 as *The New American Right*).

122 Viereck's view of conservatism was ably summarized in his article on the subject for the 1974 edition of the *Encyclopedia Britannica.* His treatment of contemporary American conservatism had a conspicuous omission, and polemics entered into the bibliographical references.

123 One commentator on Viereck's style of prose writing who seems overly bound by conventional standards is Marie Hénault. See her book *Peter Viereck.* Though the book deals with Viereck's prose writings, it is primarily about his poetry. Although many of the author's judgments are questionable and proceed from a formalistic and somewhat narrow approach to the subject, the book is insightful in part and useful as a source of biographical and bibliographical material.

124 *Unadjusted Man,* 299

125 For a discussion of the neoconservatives, with emphasis on their propensity for neo-Jacobin thinking, and for an in-depth exploration of how American neo-Jacobinism relates to a general decline of American and Western civilization, see Claes G. Ryn, *America the Virtuous: The Crisis of Democracy and the Quest for Empire* (New Brunswick: Transaction, 2003).

126 Irving Kristol, "The Neoconservative Persuasion. What it was and what it is," *Weekly Standard,* August 25, 2003.

127 Ibid.

128 Dan Himmelfarb, "Conservative Splits," *Commentary*, May, 1988.

129 *Shame and Glory,* p. 248.

130 *Unadjusted Man*, p. 332.

Part Five: The Decline of American Intellectual Conservatism

1 "American Intellectual Conservatism: Needs, Opportunities, Prospects," *Modern Age,* Vol. 26, Nos. 3-4 (Summer/ Fall, 1982).

2 *Nykonservatismen i USA* (Stockholm, 1971). My co-author, Bertil Häggman, wrote three of the nine chapters.

3 Röpke explains the moral and cultural preconditions of a sound market economy in *A Humane Economy: The Social Framework of the Free Market* (Wilmington, 1998; first published in German in 1948 under the title *Jenseits von Angebot and Nachfrage*). See also his *The Moral Foundations of Civil Society* (New Brunswick and London, 1996; first published in German in 1944 under the title *Civitas Humana.*)

4 Criticism of a utilitarian-materialistic view of life is a major feature of Russell Kirk's writing, starting with his early works, including *The Conservative Mind* (1953), which traces what he regards as a different and far superior American tradition. The title of another of Kirk's books from the 1950s, *Beyond the Dreams of Avarice* (1956) tellingly indicates the values that he deems central to a proper conservatism. For a pointed critique of and a proposed alternative to what Kirk calls "a national spirit of covetousness," see his chapter on "The Question of Wants" in *Prospects for Conservatives* (Washington, DC, 1989), which is a revised and abridged edition of his 1954 book *A Program for Conservatives.*

5 The general distrust of reason, rooted in rejection of rationalism, finds almost absurd expression in Viereck's statement that "the definition of a good conservative is that he always loses the theoretical debates with liberals and radicals." *The Unadjusted Man* (Westport, 1973; first published in 1956), 296. The fact that anti-rationalist conservatives have nevertheless argued strenuously against rationalism shows that they have unconsciously employed rationality of a different kind.

6 The nature and emergence of the new Jacobinism, how it is connected to neo-conservatism and how it relates to a general erosion of American and Western culture and the American political tradition are examined in my *America the Virtuous: The Crisis of Democracy and the Quest for Empire* (New Brunswick and London, 2003).

7 The philosophical core of Croce's work is contained in his early works *Aesthetic* (1902), *Logic* (1908) and *The Philosophy of the Practical* (1908). Croce criticizes, revises, and supplements Hegel but has his own distinctive and wide-ranging philosophy. To say that he is one of the truly great philosophers of the twentieth century is not to say that he is above criticism. Flawed English translations of Croce's works, especially *The Philosophy of the Practical*, have complicated absorption of his work in the anglophone world, which has had great difficulty, to begin with, breaking out of empiricist habits. Croce's book *History as the Story of Liberty* (Indianapolis, 2000; first published in Italian under a rather different title in 1938), is a powerful summary of his "historicist" philosophy, which should, however, be approached with caution by readers not yet familiar with his general outlook and use of terms. Croce prefigures what would later in the twentieth century be called post-modernism, poststructuralism and anti-foundationalism but avoids the indiscriminate rejection of structure and order that has rendered so much of the mentioned currents self-contradictory, undisciplined, extreme, frivolous, and even absurd.

8 Here it is only possible to hint at arguments regarding the synthesis of universality and particularity that I have set forth elsewhere. See, in particular, my books *A Common Human Ground: Universality and Particularity in a Multicultural World* (Columbia and London, 2003) and *Will, Imagination and Reason: Babbitt, Croce and the Problem of Reality*, 2nd exp. ed. (New Brunswick and London, 1997).

9 Nisbet's most famous book, *The Quest for Community* (London and New York, 1953), which in one later edition was called *Community and Power*, provided a strong and early antidote to atomistic, individualistic strains of thought within the postwar conservative movement. Russell Kirk was quick to draw attention to a scholar who would become one of America's most eminent social thinkers in the twentieth century.

10 Leo Strauss's most widely read attack on "historicism" in general and on Burke in particular is found in *Natural Right and History* (Chicago, 1953). Because Strauss appeared to be a defender of classical political thought, many philosophically uneducated young conservatives, not least Roman Catholics, looked to him for intellectual guidance. At a time when American conservatism needed to find its philosophical footing and evolve an adequate epistemology, especially with regard to questions of value, Strauss, unbeknownst to many of his followers, inserted into the movement an anti-conservative prejudice, making many suspicious of, or at least very ambivalent about, respecting history and tradition. For an extended analysis and critique of Strauss's attacks on historicism and of how his ahistorical conception of philosophy and universality undermines tradition, see my "Leo Strauss and History: The Philosopher as Conspirator," *Humanitas,* Vol. XVIII, Nos. 1 & 2 (2005).

11 For an in-depth discussion of the radicalism of neo-Jacobin "universal principles" see *America the Virtuous.*

12 This point is argued at length in *Will, Imagination and Reason.*

13 The deep roots of American constitutionalism in English political tradition and culture have been succinctly and persuasively demonstrated by Joseph Baldacchino in "The Unraveling of American Constitutionalism: From Customary Law to Permanent Innovation," *Humanitas*, Vol. XVIII, Nos. 1 & 2 (2005). The American colonists wanted independence not because they subscribed to ahistorical, abstract principles but because they saw King and Parliament as violating precedent and custom and introducing unacceptable *innovation.* The colonists protested a breach of continuity and sought to reclaim their historically evolved rights as Englishmen.

Part Five: In The Eleventh Hour

1 The points made in this paragraph are more fully argued and substantiated in Claes G. Ryn, *America the Virtuous: The Crisis of Democracy and the Quest for Empire* (New Brunswick: Transaction Publishers, 2003) and Claes G. Ryn, *Democracy and the Ethical Life,* 2nd exp. ed. (Washington, DC: The Catholic University of America Press, 1990; first published in 1978). Regarding the British origins of the American constitutional order, see Russell Kirk, *The Conservative Constitution* (Washington, DC: Regnery, 1990) and *The Roots of American Order* (Wilmington, DE: ISI Books, 2003; first published in 1974). See also, Willmoore Kendall and George W. Carey, *The Basic Symbols of the American Political Tradition* (Washington, DC: The Catholic University of America Press, 1995; first published in 1970).

2 On the relationship between the written Constitution and the unwritten one, including the constitutional personality, see Claes G. Ryn, "Political Philosophy and the Unwritten Constitution," *Modern Age,* Vol. 34, No. 4 (Summer 1992), available also at http://www.nhinet.org/unwrit.htm.

3 For a systematic analysis of the differences and intimate interconnections among will, imagination and reason, see Claes G. Ryn, *Will, Imagination and Reason: Babbitt, Croce and the Problem of Reality,* 2nd exp. ed. (New Brunswick: Transaction Publishers, 1997; 1986).

4 Jean-Jacques Rousseau, *First Discourse, Basic Political Writings* (Indianapolis, IN: Hackett, 1987), 3.

5 Ibid., 38.

6 For an in-depth study of the new Jacobinism and how it relates to more traditional American political thought and culture, see Ryn, *America the Virtuous.*

7 David Frum and Richard Perle, *An End to Evil* (New York: Random House, 2003). As a speechwriter for President George W. Bush, Frum coined thephrase "the axis of evil."

INDEX